Theodore Dreiser: Interviews

THE DREISER EDITION

Sponsored at

the University of Connecticut

by

the Thomas J. Dodd Research Center,
the College of Liberal Arts and Sciences, and
the University Research Foundation

and by

the University of Pennsylvania Library

THOMAS P. RIGGIO

General Editor

Theodore Dreiser:
Interviews

Edited by
FREDERIC E. RUSCH
and
DONALD PIZER

University of Illinois Press
Urbana and Chicago

Library of Congress Cataloging-in-Publication Data
Theodore Dreiser : interviews /
edited by Frederic E. Rusch and Donald Pizer.
p.   cm.
Includes bibliographical references and index.
ISBN 0-252-02943-7 (cloth : alk. paper)
1. Dreiser, Theodore, 1871–1945—Interviews.
2. Novelists, American—20th century—Interviews.
3. Journalists—United States—Interviews.
I. Rusch, Frederic E. II. Pizer, Donald.
PS3507.R55Z849   2004
813'.52—dc22   2003028183

CONTENTS

ILLUSTRATIONS

PREFACE

As a young journalist and freelance writer in the 1890s, Theodore Dreiser specialized in interviews. His newspaper and magazine credentials gave him access to personalities as various as Philip Armour, Emilia E. Barr, Andrew Carnegie, Thomas Edison, William Dean Howells, Lillian Nordica, Alfred Stieglitz, and Israel Zangwill. In the decades following the publication of his historic first novel, *Sister Carrie* (1900), when Dreiser had achieved his own celebrity, he became the subject of over 180 interviews. This edition is the first to collect the most significant of the newspaper and journal interviews of Dreiser conducted between 1902 and his death in 1945.

As a prominent public figure whose preoccupations were never purely literary, Dreiser was sought for his views on important social questions. The topics tended to be those most closely identified with his writing and special interests: literary censorship, leftist politics, the New Woman, the arts, Jews in America, communism, fascism, changing sexual mores, the world wars, Nazi Germany, Russia, and celebrated causes of the time such as the imprisonment of the labor leader Tom Mooney and the plight of the coal miners of Harlan, Kentucky. Consequently, the interviews constitute a significant primary source for information on many of the cultural and political concerns of the first half of the twentieth century.

The interviews are also valuable biographical documents. Because each article attempts to convey a sense of Dreiser's voice and presence, the cumulative effect is of a kind of oral memoir buried amid occasional pieces. The interview format lends itself to informality and spontaneity, leading to a portrait of Dreiser that is less guarded than the one he purposefully created in his autobiographies. Moreover, the interviewers were experienced journalists and at times persons of literary talent in their own rights. Writers such as Burton Rascoe, Esther McCoy, and Bruce Crawford give lively accounts of Dreiser within the framework of his daily routines, usually at home or in his office. They comment, often insightfully, on the writer's surroundings, idiosyncrasies, appearance, and temperament, giving a human dimension to even the more difficult aspects of his personality. Dreiser himself had something to do with this. Because he was familiar with the conventions of interview journalism, he made for good copy. He comes across mainly as an articulate subject who is well aware of his role as a kind of coauthor in producing vivid human-interest stories.

The editors have chosen a large selection of the more substantial interviews, relegating minor pieces to citations in a comprehensive bibliography. In keeping with the general editorial guidelines of the Dreiser Edition, they have edited the interviews as public documents and therefore have provided a clear text emended for typographical slips, misspellings, and demonstrable errors. They have cited the provenance of each selection, supplied explanatory notes to the text, and written a historical commentary that places the ideas expressed in the interviews within the context of Dreiser's literary, political, and philosophical beliefs.

* * *

Theodore Dreiser: Interviews continues the Dreiser Edition's tradition of publishing texts that are not easily accessible, even to the specialist. Such an undertaking would be unimaginable without the sponsorship of two institutions in particular: the University of Connecticut and the library of the University of Pennsylvania. Several individuals at the University of Connecticut deserve special mention for their initiatives and continuing support of this project: Ross D. MacKinnon, dean of the College of Liberal Arts and Sciences; Thomas P. Wilsted, director of the Thomas J. Dodd Research Center; and Janet Greger, vice provost and dean of the Graduate School. The goodwill and special training of the staff at the University of Pennsylvania's Annenberg Rare Book and Manuscript Library have been essential to the progress of the Dreiser Edition. Director Michael T. Ryan has generously devoted his own time and the resources of his staff to facilitating the work of the Dreiser Edition. Curator of Manuscripts Nancy M. Shawcross continues to contribute her expertise and special service to the project. John Pollack has consistently and untiringly assisted Dreiser Edition editors in their work. Finally, Dr. Willis Regier, director of the University of Illinois Press, has provided imaginative guidance and commitment to the Dreiser Edition at a pivotal point in its history.

Thomas P. Riggio
General Editor
The Dreiser Edition

ACKNOWLEDGMENTS

Several individuals have aided us in this enterprise. We both would like to thank Thomas Riggio for his strong support and wise counsel, Tammy South for her expertise in transferring interview texts to disk form, Paul Hightower for preparing the reproductions of the illustrations, and Jerome Loving for his careful review of the manuscript. We wish also to acknowledge the always cordial and expert aid of the staff (especially Nancy Shawcross and John Pollack) of the Annenberg Rare Book and Manuscript Library, Van Pelt–Dietrich Library, University of Pennsylvania. In addition, Donald Pizer thanks Carol Pizer for translating interviews in French, Professor Samuel Ramer for help in running down several references, and Patti Windham of the Tulane Interlibrary Loan Office for her patient and heroic efforts in locating newspaper microfilm files. Frederic Rusch thanks Indiana State University for a research grant and Professor Ronald Baker, chairperson of the Department of English at Indiana State, for his support throughout the project.

For permission to publish materials in the Dreiser Collection, we thank the trustees of the University of Pennsylvania. We also thank the following newspapers for permission to publish interviews still in copyright: the *New York Times* for "Dreiser Home, Sees Soviet Aims Gaining" and "Dreiser Says NRA Is Training Public"; the *San Francisco Chronicle* for "Dreiser Holds Mooney Bomb Sympathy Act"; and the *Salt Lake City Deseret News* for "Dreiser, Here to Talk, Asks U.S. to Awake."

Frederic E. Rusch
Donald Pizer

Theodore Dreiser: Interviews

Author of "Sister Carrie" Formerly Was a St. Louisan

*

St. Louis Post-Dispatch, 26 January 1902, p. 4.

The suppression of *Sister Carrie* is one of the most famous legends in American literary history. In this interview Dreiser gives his version of the events, which he would repeat often in succeeding years in letters, interviews, and articles, frequently adding to or revising some of the details.

Theodore Dreiser, a former St. Louisan, who has newly gained fame as a novelist, was in the city last week on his way to Montgomery City, Mo., to visit the relatives of his wife, whom he married in that city.[1]

Mr. Dreiser was employed in newspaper work in St. Louis from 1891 to 1894.[2] He went East and engaged in magazine work, publishing many short stories.

It is his first novel, "Sister Carrie," which has brought him into prominence. The British literary reviews, in particular, give it high praise, ranking it with "The Octopus," by Frank Norris, at the top of the list of novels for the last year.

It is interesting to note that Frank Norris, as senior reader for a publishing firm, first saw the merit of "Sister Carrie," and recommended its acceptance.

To the Post-Dispatch Mr. Dreiser told the history of his novel, which is extraordinary in some features.

The novel was written in six months, from October, 1899, to March 1900. It was rejected by one publishing firm because it was not considered an all-around interesting story.

He took the manuscript to Doubleday, Page & Co., April 1, 1900, where Frank Norris, author of "The Octopus," in his capacity as senior reader, read it. He sent for Mr. Dreiser and congratulated him.

1. Dreiser and Sara Osborne White (1869?–1942) were married in Washington, D.C., not Montgomery City.
2. Dreiser began working as a reporter in St. Louis in 1892, not 1891.

THEODORE, DREISER.
Sketched by a Post-Dispatch Artist From Life.

"Author of 'Sister Carrie'
Formerly Was a St. Louisan,"
St. Louis Post-Dispatch,
26 January 1902, p. 4

Mr. Norris passed it on to Mr. Lanier, one of the members of the firm, who read it and thought it was a good story. He, in turn, handed it to Mr. Page, and that gentleman said he considered it the best book brought into the house that year.

When Mr. Doubleday, the senior partner, returned from Europe, he heard so much about the manuscript that he took it home. Mrs. Doubleday read "Sister Carrie" and took a violent dislike to it. Mr. Doubleday read it and agreed with her. Before Mr. Doubleday had come home a contract had been drawn up and signed by which the work was to be published in the fall, and upon this Mr. Dreiser stood.[3]

3. Correspondence between Dreiser and Doubleday, Page and Company confirms Mr. Doubleday's desire to back out of his commitment to publish *Carrie*, but there is no evidence that he did so because his wife argued against its publication. Dreiser claimed he learned of her opposition from Frank Norris (1870–1902), although he more likely heard of it from his

A friendly member of the firm sent a number of copies to newspapers and critical journals.[4] They attracted much attention.

The newspapers, in fact, hailed Mr. Dreiser as the producer of a masterpiece of naturalism, and the critical journals, acquiesced. "Sister Carrie" became famous.

"A copy of the book," said Mr. Dreiser, "was sent to Mr. William Heinemann, a London publisher. That gentleman read it and entered into a contract with me and brought out the novel in England. It appeared in London in May, 1901."[5]

At this point Mr. Dreiser's triumph really began. There was a unanimous critical uprising in favor of "Sister Carrie." The Spectator called it "a work of utmost power, exact as life itself." The Academy passed upon it as the first important novel out of America.

The Atheneum, England's leading critical journal, used the phrase, "great, with all the greatness of the country which gave it birth," and declared that it introduced a new method of telling a story.

Other critical journals, such as the Times, the Literary World, the Chronicle and the Mail, devoted space to analyzing and declaring the power of this American novel.

This created a boom for the book in England, where it began to sell at once.

The American firm of J. F. Taylor & Co., hearing of its success abroad, sought the author and entered into a contract whereby the book was transferred to that firm, by which it is to be released the coming spring.[6]

"Sister Carrie" has been attacked, in America (not in England) upon the score of morality. Concerning these attacks Mr. Dreiser said:

"In 'Sister Carrie' all the phases of life touched upon are handled truthfully. I have not tried to gloss over any evil any more than I have stopped to dwell upon it. Life is too short; its phases are too numerous.

"What I desired to do was to show two little human beings, or more, playing in and out among the giant legs of circumstance.

---

friend Arthur Henry (1867–1934), who learned of it from Norris. The contract for the novel was drawn up and signed after Doubleday returned home and expressed his opposition, not before.

4. The "friendly member" was Frank Norris, who sent out over one hundred copies for review.

5. Heinemann (1863–1920) offered to publish *Sister Carrie* in May 1901 provided the first 200 pages of the novel were condensed to 80 pages. After Dreiser's friend Arthur Henry made the cuts, the abridged edition appeared in July 1901.

6. In the contract, signed in September 1901, Dreiser gave J. F. Taylor an option on his next novel. When Dreiser failed to make the changes to *Sister Carrie* suggested by Taylor and was unable to complete *Jennie Gerhardt,* the publisher did not reissue the novel.

"Personally I see nothing immoral in discussing with a clean purpose any phase of life. I have never been able to understand the objection to considering every phase of life from a philosophical standpoint.

"If life is to be made better or more interesting, its condition must be understood. No situation can be solved, no improvement can be effected, no evil remedied, unless the conditions which surround it are appreciated."

Mr. Dreiser is well remembered by St. Louis newspaper men and other citizens. He is still a young man.

Talks with Four Novelists: Mr. Dreiser

By Otis Notman

*

New York Times Saturday Review of Books, 15 June 1907, p. 393.

The occasion for this interview was the republication of *Sister Carrie* by B. W. Dodge and Company in May 1907. At the time Dreiser was a financially successful magazine editor, but just four years earlier he had been penniless and unable to write because of a nervous breakdown. Notman's question about Dreiser's intent in his fiction was probably suggested by a reviewer's comment, published in the *Times Saturday Review of Books* three weeks earlier, that the novel makes "no attempt to complicate facts as they are with notions of things as they should be morally."

"The mere living of your daily life," says Theodore Dreiser, "is drastic drama. To-day there may be some disease lurking in your veins that will end your life to-morrow. You may have a firm grasp on the opportunity that in a moment more will slip through your fingers. The banquet of to-night may crumble to the crust of the morning. Life is a tragedy."

"But isn't that a rather tragic view to take?" I asked. "Hasn't each man something in himself that makes life worth living? If, as you say, you want to write more than anything else, isn't that power or ability to write something that would make life worth while under all circumstances?"

"No, not under all circumstances, because you can't use ability except under certain favorable conditions. The very power of which you speak may, thwarted, only serve to make a man more miserable. I have had my share of the difficulties and discouragements that fall to the lot of most men. I know something of the handicap of ill health and the necessary diffusion of energy.[1] A man with something imperative to say and no time or strength for the saying of it is as unfortunate as he is unhappy. I look into my own

---

1. Dreiser wrote about this period in his life, from 1901 to 1904, in *An Amateur Laborer*. Drafted in 1904, the unfinished manuscript was published by the University of Pennsylvania Press in 1983.

life and I realize that each human life is a similar tragedy. The infinite suffering and deprivation of great masses of men and women upon whom existence has been thrust unasked appals me. My greatest desire is to devote every hour of my conscious existence to depicting phases of life as I see and understand them."

"What are you trying to show in what you write? Do you point out a moral?" I inquired.

"I simply want to tell about life as it is. Every human life is intensely interesting. If the human being has ideals, the struggle and the attempt to realize those ideals, the going back on his own trail, the failure, the success, the reason for the individual failure, the individual success—all these things are interesting; interesting even where there are no ideals, where there is only the personal desire to survive, the fight to win, the stretching out of the fingers to grasp—these are the things I want to write about—life as it is, the facts as they exist, the game as it is played! I said I was pointing out no moral. Well, I am not, unless this is a moral—that all humanity must stand together and war against and overcome the forces of nature. I think a time is coming when personal gain will rarely be sought at the expense of some one else."

"Where among people is there the greatest readiness to stand by one another, among the rich or the poor?" I asked.

"Among the poor. They are by far the most generous. They are never too crowded to take in another person, although there may be already three or four to share the same room. Their food they will always share, even though there is not enough to go around."

"Are you writing something else?" I inquired.

"I have another book partly finished, but I don't know when I shall get it done.[2] I have not the time to work on it, much as I want to."

"Have you been satisfied with the reception of 'Sister Carrie'?"

"Well, the critics have not really understood what I was trying to do. Here is a book that is close to life. It is intended not as a piece of literary craftsmanship, but as a picture of conditions done as simply and effectively as the English language will permit. To sit up and criticise me for saying 'vest,' instead of 'waistcoat'; to talk about my splitting the infinitive and using vulgar commonplaces here and there, when the tragedy of a man's life is being displayed, is silly. More, it is ridiculous. It makes me feel that American criticism is the joke which English literary authorities maintain it to be. But the circulation is beginning to boom. When it gets to the people they will understand, because it is a story of real life, of their lives."

---

2. The then-unfinished book was *Jennie Gerhardt*. Dreiser stopped working on the novel in late 1902 or early 1903 and did not return to it fully until October 1910.

"Sister Carrie" Theodore Dreiser

*

New York Herald, 7 July 1907, Literary and Art Section, p. 2.

The initial draft of *Sister Carrie* ended with the suicide of Hurstwood. But Dreiser grew dissatisfied with this ending and subsequently revised it, as he describes in this interview, to conclude the novel with an expanded passage on Carrie.

Speaking of this new novel, its author said to the present reviewer:—"There is one odd circumstance about the book. When I finished it I felt that it was not done. It was a continuous strip of life to me that seemed to be driven onward by those logical forces that had impelled the book to motion. The narrative, I felt, was finished, but not completed. The problem in my mind was not to round it out with literary grace, but to lead the story to a point, an elevation where it could be left and yet continue into the future. The story had to stop, and yet I wanted in the final picture to suggest the continuation of Carrie's fate along the lines of established truths.

"The note, the exact impression that I sought, evaded me. The drain of sustained imagination was beginning to tell. Finally, with note book and pencil I made a trip to the Palisades, hoping that the change of scene would bring out just what I was trying to express.

"Finding a broad, overhanging shelf, I stretched out flat on my back and allowed my thoughts to wander—gave them a sort of open air holiday.

"Two hours passed in a delicious mental drifting. Then suddenly came the inspiration of its own accord. I reached for my note book and pencil and wrote. And when I left the Palisades 'Sister Carrie' was completed."

Something of the effort which the book cost may be read between its lines. It suggests difficulties conquered. Mr. Dreiser has struggled to mould his words and ideas into artistic form and on the whole has succeeded. His book breathes the vitality of a man who feels his thoughts as well as thinks them. It is commendably frank. It faces life as it is—not as it ought to be. It reverses the canting code of the cheap moralist—the woman transgresses, but the man pays.

Caroline Meeber is the woman. Eighteen, crude, undeveloped, she leaves her home in Wisconsin to seek work in Chicago. She finds it, and with it a travelling salesman by the name of Drouet.

Already she is intently seeking in life the color and animation that it has not yet possessed, seeking, not with the reason of sophisticated womanhood, but with the blind, tendril like groping of girlish simplicity. Drouet maintains her in luxurious ease for two years. Then Drouet's friend, Hurstwood, comes upon the scene.

Hurstwood is the sleek, good natured and capable manager of a gorgeous barroom in Chicago. He has finer perception and greater facility of manner than the oxlike and amiable Drouet and a keener insight into the qualities that lie in Carrie still in the ore. Briefly, he determines to possess her. He deserts his family for her sake, turns his back upon his position, embezzles $10,000 and sinks down lower and lower until he reaches the bitter settlement of his score in a miserable Bowery lodging house.

The woman whom he has moulded and taught flutters away from the wreck on her butterfly wings to become a Casino favorite and win the ashes of a meretricious success. This sordid tragedy of everyday life is worked out to its legitimate climax with passion, energy and relentless truth.

Now Comes Author Theodore Dreiser
Who Tells of 100,000 Jennie Gerhardts
Writer, Whom Wm. J. Locke Declared England Regards
as Greatest American Novelist, in Successor to
"Sister Carrie," Deals with Outcast Woman,
and herewith Discusses That Theme

By Almer C. Sanborn[1]

*

Cleveland Leader, 12 November 1911, Cosmopolitan Section, p. 5.

In this interview, which appeared a few weeks after the publication of *Jennie Gerhardt*, Dreiser comments on the mechanistic world depicted in the novel and tells of the influences that led him to this philosophy of life. This syndicated interview also appeared in the *New York Morning Telegraph*, the *Buffalo Evening News*, and the *Pittsburg Leader* on the same date.

Jennie Gerhardt was the daughter of a poor glass blower in a Western city. She was reared in poverty and want. Her brothers picked up coal along the railroad track to provide fuel to cook the family's meals. Jennie did washing and scrubbing to furnish her share of the necessities of life. Dull, prosaic poverty was the keynote of the life the Gerhardt family led.

It was thus that Brander found Jennie. He was a United States Senator and was rich. He liked Jennie for a certain gentleness there was in her. She possessed a strange inward beauty which attracted him. He was interested in her poverty-stricken family, and out of the generosity of his heart he helped them to live more comfortably. He won Jennie's gratitude and love. He seduced her and then discovered that he really loved her. He promised to marry her, and really believed that he would, but chance willed otherwise. Brander died suddenly, before the formality could be gone through

---

1. Sanborn's name does not appear in the *Cleveland Leader*. The *New York Morning Telegraph* identified him as the author when it ran the interview.

with, and left Jennie alone and a mother, in a world which is governed by hard and fast conventions, which excuses nothing.

Then Lester Kane stepped into her life. He was a normal, well-balanced young American of a well-to-do family, eager for the comfort of feminine companionship, but unwilling to give up his personal liberty to obtain it. He was a masterful man and he and Jennie were drawn together. She had in mind all the time the idea of bettering the conditions of her family, and she seized upon the only way of doing it which presented itself. If she and Kane were not married, it was merely because he could not quite bring himself to do it, and kept putting the formality off from day to day.

The irregularity of their relationship was gradually forgotten, and they lived together peaceably, until one day Kane's father died and left him a fortune on condition that he would break with Jennie inside of two years. Kane weighed the situation carefully. If he stayed with Jennie he would be a poor man; he would be forced to work hard for their support. On the other hand, he would have not only wealth, but good society and the friendship of the decent women whom he had known in other days. There was one woman in particular whose comradeship he longed for. He hesitated for some time to leave Jennie, but he did.

Jennie took this new development in her life calmly. She had learned much about chance in the last few years, and there was little that could surprise her. Five years later Kane sent for her. She found him dying. She stayed with him until the last, and when it was over she returned to her home. "Before her was stretching a vista of lonely years, down which she was steadily gazing. Now what? She was not so old yet. There were those two orphan children to raise. They would marry and leave after a while, and then what? Days and days in endless reiteration, and then?"—

Such, according to Theodore Dreiser, is the story of the thousands, perhaps a hundred thousand, Jennie Gerhardts in this country. They are governed by chance. Life for them is meaningless; it is merely an accident. Their whole careers may be changed by one event, which simply happens, no one can tell why.

How many Jennie Gerhardts are here today who might have been among the most respected women in the world had not their Senator Brander died?

How many of them might have re-established themselves after their first mischance had not a fortune or another woman come in between them and their Lester Kane? Those who have fallen by the wayside have done so, not through any fault of their own, but because some fatal accident brought it about. And the same reason applies for those who have succeeded in making their way back into public esteem.

"There is no intelligent sequence of cause and effect in life," says

Theodore Dreiser, explaining his philosophy of life as brought out in the struggles of Jennie Gerhardt. "Life is not reasonable. All our actions are regulated by some previous happening. If Senator Brander had not died, he would have married Jennie Gerhardt, unless some other accident had happened to prevent it. And if he had married her, society would have been none the wiser, and she would not have been ostracized for her fault.

"But that one thing, for which no one was responsible, left her at the mercy of her friends and called down upon her their so-called righteous indignation. It shows how little influence reason has over us as compared with chance."

"Isn't that rather pessimistic?" I asked.

"It may sound so at first," returned Mr. Dreiser, "but it doesn't affect me that way. I don't feel any the less happy about life on account of it. Life interests me intensely for that very reason. It is dramatic. It is more thrilling than the most gorgeous spectacle that man ever planned. And these accidents merely serve to make it more entrancing. I consider the beggar sitting by the roadside one of the most dramatic things that could be imagined. He has a precarious existence and it depends entirely on chance. It is really thrilling to see the way in which he ekes out a living.

"Besides being dramatic, I consider life beautiful, and I believe that beauty is eternal. If I didn't, this feverish existence would be unendurable to me. As it is, I think the beggar I just mentioned is beautiful. His dirt and his rags, his bandaged feet and his sores are all beautiful to me. They are artistic. They complete the picture and make the whole perfect. It may not be pleasant, if you like, but it is artistic. Everything in life appears to me just that way. That would be the reason for life, if there were any reason. But I believe that life is merely an accident from the beginning."

"If there is no other force than chance, how do you account for the progress of humanity?" I asked.

"I do not believe that there is such a thing as progress, in the sense that we use the word. It is merely a change. Who can say that it is better to worship the home as we do today than it was in the old days to worship a bull? Our ideas have changed; that is all. We believe that it is better for us to worship the home, but that does not mean that it would have been better for the people of other times to worship the home instead of the bull or the spider. It may be wise in the present day to try to educate our sons in the teachings of Jesus Christ and keep our daughters virtuous, but we cannot say that it will always be our principle. I cannot believe that the teachings of Christ are eternal; that they have really held for two thousand years. It certainly isn't true in this day that one should turn the other cheek."

Mr. Dreiser's philosophy of life as he outlined it was very nearly just what

Hardy, Conrad, Zola, Tolstoi and Turgenieff have been preaching to us for the last fifty years. The French and Russian authors have been pervaded with the same principle for a great many years, but few writers in English have had the courage or the conviction to put these views before the public. Mr. Dreiser is one of those few. Ten years ago he published his first and only novel until the appearance of "Jennie Gerhardt." It was called "Sister Carrie," and made an even greater impression on the reading public in England than in this country.

The other day, when William J. Locke arrived in this country from England, one of the first questions that he asked was:

"And what is Dreiser doing these days?"

"Dreiser?" repeated his dinner host.

"The author of 'Sister Carrie,'" Locke added. Then as the guest on his right repeated "Sister Carrie?" Locke gazed about the table.

"And these Americans do not know," he mused aloud, "that England looks on 'Sister Carrie' as the finest American novel sent over in the last twenty years, and looks to Dreiser as the biggest American novelist who has sent us anything, and is waiting for 'Carrie's' successor."[2]

"Jennie Gerhardt" is a worthy successor to "Sister Carrie," and develops further the philosophy of chance as it was advanced in the earlier book. Mr. Dreiser has not had these views always. He admits that in his youth he was just as bound up in traditions and conventions as any one else. But his ideas changed as he grew older, and a wider experience gave him a broader view on life. He was born in Terre Haute, Ind., but went to Chicago early and started to work there.

"I cannot say just what I thought of things then. Life was a drift, a swirl. I read a great deal then. I was eagerly devouring Emerson, Hawthorne and Stevenson at that time. But better than these books were the tall smokestacks, the crowded streets, the boxes and bales and the river and lake of Chicago. I loved these and the knowledge that I was young and alive. The glory of life cannot be put into books. It cannot be even faintly suggested.

"Then I got into newspaper work and that gave me an insight into the brutalities of life—the police courts, the jails, the houses of ill-repute, trade failures and trickery. Curiously, it all seemed wonderful to me—not sad. It was like a grand magnificent spectacle. All at once I began reading Spencer, Darwin, Huxley and Tyndall, and life began to take on a new aspect. As they say in the slang of the day, I got a line on it. I shall never forget

2. Locke (1863–1930) was a popular British novelist whose best-known work was *The Beloved Vagabond* (1905). The occasion at which he made these statements has not been identified.

Spencer's chapter on the Unknowable in 'First Principles.' I was torn up root and branch by it. Life disappeared in a strange fog.[3]

"Just about then, in Pittsburg, where I was working as a newspaper man, I came across Balzac and then I saw what life was—a rich, gorgeous, showy spectacle. It was beautiful, dramatic, sad, delightful, and epic—all those things combined. I saw for the first time how a book should be written. I saw how, if I ever wrote one, I should write it. I did not expect to write like Balzac, but to use his method of giving a complete picture of life from beginning to end.[4]

"Balzac lasted me a year or two, then came Hardy, and after him, Tolstoi. From them I learned what, in my judgment, really great books are. In later years Daudet, Flaubert, Turgenieff and now only recently De Maupassant and George Moore have added to this knowledge. I have never read a line of Zola, unfortunately."

"Which do you consider the world's greatest books?" I asked.

Mr. Dreiser leaned forward and named them off on his fingers.

"I rank 'Anna Karenina,' 'Madame Bovary,' 'Evelyn Innes,' 'Fathers and Children,' 'Père Goriot,' 'The Woodlanders' and our own American 'Quicksand,' by Hervey White, as among the great books of the world."[5]

3. Dreiser is discussing his newspaper career in St. Louis and Pittsburg between 1892 and 1894; he later described this period fully in *A Book About Myself* (1922), which was later republished as *A History of Myself: Newspaper Days* (1931) and as *Newspaper Days* by the University of Pennsylvania Press (1991). His account of his introduction to Spencer appears in chapter LXIX of the 1922 and 1931 editions and chapter LXXXVI of the 1991 edition.

4. See chapter LXII in *A Book About Myself*.

5. Besides mentioning the novels of Tolstoy, Flaubert, Turgenev, Balzac, and White, Dreiser includes George Moore's *Evelyn Innes* (1898) and Thomas Hardy's *Woodlanders* (1887). Dreiser often cited *Quicksand* (1900), by White (1866–1944), as a major work of American realism.

Theodore Dreiser
The Author of "Jennie Gerhardt" Follows
in the Footsteps of Frank Norris—Woman the
Centre of Interest in Contemporary Fiction

*

New York Evening Post, 15 November 1911, pp. 6–7.

Sympathetic interviewers of this period often compared Dreiser's portraits of women with those by Thomas Hardy and (less frequently)
Arnold Bennett. In this instance the comparison led Dreiser into a
number of revealing statements about feminine nature, the fictional
portrayal of sexuality, and the moral and aesthetic character of experience. The interview was reprinted as "Realistic Novelists" in *New York
Daily People*, 20 November 1911, p. 3.

Even before Theodore Dreiser's "Jennie Gerhardt" left its publishers a week
or two ago, critics were hailing it as a masterly portrayal of a woman's soul.
About the same time, and quite by coincidence, Arnold Bennett was laud-
ing in his interviews the only other novel Mr. Dreiser had ever published,
"Sister Carrie," which came out about ten years ago.[1] Now, there are several
interesting things in common between the two novelists. Both are realists
in method, working on large canvases, which often cover the span of half a
lifetime, and both have had experience as editors of women's magazines. But
most interesting is the fact that both novelists have been absorbed chiefly
in woman as the theme for their novels. The very titles of their books—Mr.
Bennett's "Old Wives' Tale," "Anna of the Five Towns," "Helen with the
High Hand," "The Book of Carlotta," "Hilda Lessways," and Mr. Dreiser's
only books, "Sister Carrie" and "Jennie Gerhardt"—indicate how absorbing
that theme has been to both realists. There seemed to be some interesting
reason behind the fact, so the interviewer asked Mr. Dreiser about it.

"I don't think I can tell you off-hand why I chose woman as my princi-

---

1. Bennett's frequently noted comment occurred on his arrival in New York in October
1911; see the *New York Times*, 22 October 1911.

pal theme in both books," Mr. Dreiser said, as he lapsed into thought for a moment. He is tall and well proportioned. His face, with slightly parted lips and quiet blue-gray eyes behind gold-rimmed glasses, impresses you as being less mobile than habitually listening and observing.

"I think one reason I wrote chiefly about woman," he went on, "is that, as I look at it, she symbolizes the essentially artistic character of the universe more than man does. Everything in life is artistic in essence. But, of the two, man symbolizes power to me, while woman stands for beauty—which is art. She produces the same effect as music, poetry, or a Greek amphora.

"Another reason is that woman is at present what I would call the time idea—the thing in which the age is preëminently interested. This has been the century of the woman. The great feminist movement of the time is their struggle for a greater harmony of life—a yearning, a reaching out for beauty. And it is bound to have tremendous effects very soon. For one thing, I believe it will result in the great increase of beauty among women. The difference is already noticeable, and in our own time beautiful women will be as frequent as pennies. At present the struggle is to bring the material aspect of life into harmony. When we have reached the point when the physical and material elements for all of us, men and women, become harmonized, the time-interest will pass on to something else."

"Do you intend to keep woman as the dominant theme in all your writings?"

"Oh, no! My next books, 'The Financier' and 'The Genius,' will each have a man as the central figure. You see, when I first thought of 'Sister Carrie' and of 'Jennie Gerhardt,' in addition to the reasons I just gave you, I was interested in women, because I was nearest to the love period of my life.[2] But to preserve balance I expect to write chiefly of men, as I've done so already in the two forthcoming books."

"Do you find any fundamental difference between the psychology of men and of women?"

"Not fundamental. Mind is mind in both. The difference is that in each sex the mind works with the aid of somewhat different implements. The woman's mind, for instance, works with the implements of soft, tender arms, attractive face and form, and, perhaps, through the consciousness of her function and history as a wife and mother. A man's mind works through the implements of strong, hard arms, a muscular body, and a history as a husband and father. Behind the implements, however, the mind is the same.

---

2. Dreiser is probably referring to the period from 1893 to 1898 when he was courting his first wife, Sara Osborne White Dreiser.

A man, therefore, can depict woman if he remembers and imagines the media through which the woman's mind works."

"You use the realistic method of depicting men and women, rather than any other. Why?"

"Well—" and he again sat up on the edge of his chair as his mind concentrated on the answer. "That opens up an interesting question to me. I use the realistic method because, like every one else, I have to respond to world currents. At this time the world current flows to realistic representation, and will for some time do so more and more. In time, however, it will turn back to romanticism.

"Furthermore, the literature of every nation reflects the temperament of its people—some literatures more than others. Now the American temperament essentially calls for realistic interpretation. We can't be said to have a literature that reflects us as we are at present. In the past there were Cooper to picture the passing Indian, Bret Harte and Mark Twain to depict the West of '49, 'Uncle Tom's Cabin' to picture the ante-bellum South, and so on. But the America of to-day, with its big financial combinations, its tremendous industrial developments, and the significant changes in our attitudes toward men and women, has not been sufficiently depicted as yet. It demands a fearless, realistic presentation."

"How about William Dean Howells's work?"

"I'm afraid I can't accept 'Silas Lapham' and the others. They don't tell about the insides of modern conditions boldly and trenchantly enough. They are still under the handicap of American prudery—afraid of frank speaking about many things that move real men and women."[3]

"What handicap has prudery placed upon the development of literature here?"

"Why, prudery taboos the discussion of sex relations. And the keynote in a man's or a woman's life is to be found in sex relations. Writing a realistic novel without bringing in sex relation is like trying to build a serviceable house without doors and windows. But Americans are beginning to realize this, and I see the change has begun and is making rapid progress."

"When and with whom did you first notice the change?"

"Well, I remember back in 1888, when I read H. B. Fuller's 'With the Procession,' I said to myself, 'Why, this is like Chicago or New York. It is like what I see about me.' Then came Norris's 'McTeague,' Brand Whitlock's 'Thirteenth District,' and Will Irwin's 'Story of Eva'—all strik-

---

3. Dreiser wrote positively about Howells's fiction in reviews and interviews of the later 1890s; by this date, however, he had adopted the position, which he held for the remainder of his life, that Howells's novels were limited because of his observance of Victorian proprieties.

ing the same note.[4] But the critics with one accord damned the books and their authors as immoral because they dared to speak out frankly about real relations of men and women.

"Nevertheless, I felt that this was the kind of work I myself had to do. So I wrote 'Sister Carrie,' and left the first part of it with a publisher for reading. When I came for his decision, I found that not only would he have nothing to do with my book, but that he would have almost as little to do with me. I was a dog, it seems, who was trying to tear down that beautiful American reserve. The critics felt the same way about me. That was as late as ten years ago.

"Then came the recognition in America of such books as Tolstoy's 'Anna Karenina,' of H. G. Wells,[5] and other writers who brought the big change with them. To-day, 'Jennie Gerhardt,' which is even franker than 'Sister Carrie,' is received with hardly a word of protest for its plain speaking.

"And"—the recollection of past opposition seemed to rouse for a moment his fighting temper—"whether critics and publishers like it or not, I am going to keep on telling the truth as I see it, no matter what becomes of my books, or me, even"—flicking his handkerchief out determinedly—"if I have to go back to editing a woman's magazine."

In both "Sister Carrie" and "Jennie Gerhardt" the theme is like that of Hardy's "Tess of the D'Urbervilles." The notable difference between Mr. Dreiser's and Mr. Hardy's stories is the violent and tragic end of Tess. The interviewer pointed out the difference to Mr. Dreiser.

"Well, that's just what I resent in 'Tess,'" Mr. Dreiser responded. "I got the jolt of my life when I read that Tess, the soft, yielding, loving woman, could plunge a knife into a man's heart. The book is otherwise splendid art— but I can't go the conclusion!"[6]

"Then you think that Tess's story should have ended as Carrie's and Jennie's did—without a climax?"

"Do stories in real life always end with a climax?" Mr. Dreiser demanded. "No; there's too much of the retribution idea in such endings—retribution

---

4. Dreiser cites Henry Blake Fuller (1857–1929), *With the Procession* (1885); Frank Norris, *McTeague* (1899); and Brand Whitlock (1869–1934), *The Thirteenth District* (1902). Either Dreiser or the interviewer has confused the writer Will Irwin (1873–1948) with Will Payne (1865–1954), the author of *Story of Eva* (1901). Dreiser often offered these relatively little-known novels by Fuller and Whitlock (along with Hervey White's *Quicksand*) as important precursors of American realism. It was his reading of Norris's *McTeague* on its publication that led him to submit *Sister Carrie* to the new firm of Doubleday, Page, which had published *McTeague* and where Norris worked as a reader.

5. Best known for science fiction, the novelist H. G. Wells (1866–1946) also wrote realistic novels, including *Ann Veronica* (1909), a story of a girl who defies conventional morality by running off with the man she loves.

6. This reading is shown as printed; perhaps Dreiser said "I can't go with the conclusion."

for the 'sins' of such girls as Tess, Carrie, and Jennie. These girls did not sin. There's no such thing as sin to me. We grow largely through error. At any rate, I don't believe that retribution or Nemesis is at all as inevitable in life as in books."

"But some of your own characters seem pursued by Nemesis—Hurstwood, for example, and Jennie Gerhardt's father."

"Oh, the Greek furies are as real to-day as they were in Greek tragedy. But why they hunt those whom they do none of us can say. The same course of life will bring the furies in one case and happiness in others. We have no volition in the matter—we can neither avoid them nor invoke them. Life is arbitrary and to most of us chaotic."

"You don't impress one in your books as looking at life pessimistically. It doesn't seem ugly to you."

"Far, far from it. Everything—*everything* in life and on earth seems beautiful to me. There's no angle from which one cannot see beauty in what is even looked upon as ugly. Every street in New York, for example, no matter how ugly it is considered, seems to sing a song—its own song. I remember having that same feeling even about a slimy little alley I once came across.

"And what is more," went on Mr. Dreiser, "Life needs no embellishment to make it appear beautiful or romantic. To me, realism is more romantic than romanticism itself. And it is not only certain parts of life that I find beautiful. I see the romance of it best when I see all of it. That is why I find that I have to use broad canvases in my stories."

The talk was drifting away from the ordinary channels of an interview. Perhaps it was the Hudson River below and the Palisades, both half hidden in a soft, white mist, that led the novelist to talk quietly of the great unknown infinite facts behind the curtain of seeming things.[7] For when the afternoon sun and a wind cleared the mist off, and showed again the beautiful prospect below, both Mr. Dreiser and the interviewer emerged from the mood of the abstract and found that the thirty minutes allotted to the interview had stretched themselves unnoticed to several hours.

7. The interview took place in Dreiser's Upper West Side apartment, at 3609 Broadway, which had a view of the Hudson.

Novels to Reflect Real Life
That Is What Theodore Dreiser Would Have
The American Temperament Not Expressed Properly
in Present Day Fiction Thinks the Author of
"Jennie Gerhardt"—New Literary Standards
*

New York Sun, 21 November 1911, p. 9.

Aware that *Jennie Gerhardt* was vulnerable to the same charges of immorality that led to the suppression of *Sister Carrie*, interviewers frequently asked Dreiser to explain his realistic treatment of life in his novels. Often, as in this interview, his response focused on noting the reading public's admiration of Russian, French, and British authors whose realistic novels had captured the national temperaments of their countries and then arguing that the American temperament could be captured only in novels that presented life as truly as it was shown in contemporary newspapers and magazines. The interview was reprinted as "A Realist in American Fiction" in the *Denver Times*, 23 November 1911, p. 20.

When the English novelist Arnold Bennett came to this country the other day and said he considered Theodore Dreiser a leading representative American novelist, as truly reflecting current literary tendencies, he called attention by the remark to subtle changes in literature, illustrated by the case of Mr. Dreiser.[1] For the latter's "Sister Carrie" when it appeared less than a decade ago, was quickly suppressed by its publishers, neither an old nor a markedly conservative [ho]use, because it represented too realistic, too grim a type of fiction, and only about 500 copies of the book lived among a little group of followers.[2] Now his "Jennie Gerhardt," of the same realistic type, has just appeared from the house of Harpers.

Whatever may be the real significance of the work of the American re-

1. See p. 14, n. 1.
2. See p. 1, headnote.

alist in American fiction, his explanations cannot but be interesting. However, he is not anxious to explain; like Robert Herrick, he would much rather let his work alone speak for itself.[3] But when cornered he tentatively ventures an explanation, the while nervously folding and refolding his already much folded handkerchief; sitting quietly in a stationary armchair in a fashion which somehow or other constantly calls to mind the nervous, rocking chair habit of Sister Carrie; twisting the ring which he wears on his forefinger—and it is probably as illuminating a point as one could mention in regard to the author that he can wear a ring on his forefinger with an air of sincerity, so to speak, with no suggestion of affectation.

"I fell down," he admits. "That is, my novel was suppressed. And I didn't offer another to the public for years.

"Perhaps I could have written an unobjectionable, a desirable book if I'd tried. But I didn't try. And I never will. Why in the name of truth and art should I stoop to such travesty? Why shouldn't I do my best, both by myself and by the thing I profess to work for?

"For what have we all against this literature of ours that we won't let it express itself truly, naturally? Great American novels can't be written while we refuse to countenance the true expression of the American temperament; while we refuse to hear of what goes on in the cities to-day—except by reading in the newspapers and the magazines. And let me say that for real worth in what literature is supposed to stand for, to-day's newspapers and magazines are so far ahead of all the novels that have been published that there is no comparison. For they are vital, dramatic, true presentations of the life that is being lived to-day.

"Why can't that thing be put into our novels—supposed to reflect life? Lord knows—I don't. I know that we hold up our hands in awed admiration of what Russia has achieved in the way of a national literature—a vital expression of the national temperament. I know that we exclaim at the French masters for what they have done to immortalize and perpetuate their own peculiar national temperament. England too has had her honored craftsmen—all of whom we honor and respect for what they have done.

"But as for ourselves—Lord help us! Have we no temperament to be expressed? Look around you, go through the country; the question answers itself. And yet we don't want to read about it in books, the only worth while thing of the age to read about now or in time to come. We don't want such books on our shelves—the while we eagerly find places for the French mas-

---

3. A social realist like Dreiser, Herrick (1868–1938) was known for his aloofness. His early novel, *The Web of Life* (1900), is often compared to *Sister Carrie*.

ters, the Russian masters and what not, lamenting that we have not such in our own dear land.

"Certain of the earlier reflections of temperament have not been without their representation. There is Hawthorne and his 'Twice Told Tales,' which I should name even before his 'The Scarlet Letter,' Harriet Beecher Stowe and her 'Uncle Tom's Cabin,' Mark Twain and his 'Tom Sawyer,' and Bret Harte in a part of his work.

"Poe of course is a reflection of nothing but himself—that strange genius which might properly have been met with in any age or any country. And works like those of W. D. Howells, no matter of how much distinction in themselves, have absolutely no place in a reckoning of this sort. For Mr. Howells won't see American life as it is lived; he doesn't want to see it.[4]

"His is like the attitude of a family which I once visited. I mentioned a certain episode. 'We don't talk of that,' I was told. The fact existed, was known to exist; but it was not recognized.

"So that great stretch of country which is universally called to mind by the term 'American,' in which a real and a throbbing life exists, has been allowed no literary expression. If one wanted to put finger on the name of the man who first recognized this, strove to work true to his ideals and pioneered the way to a real American expression of American life, I should say put it on the name of Henry B. Fuller.

"I remember reading his 'With the Procession' back in '88, I believe. Then I read Frank Norris's 'McTeague,' and Hervey White's 'Quicksand,' and Brand Whitlock's 'The Thirteenth District.'[5] These are all names of pioneers who were blazing the trail in the ten years or so immediately following my reading of—"

Mr. Dreiser then realizes he has said more than in his first guarded moments he had intended to say, but having said it, he sticks by it.

"What's the use, anyway, of trying to do anything unless you try to do it the way that strikes you as being right? I don't care if the public doesn't want to read my books, if the publishers don't want to publish them.

"I'll write them the way I know they ought to be written. And I'll not starve. I'll go back to editing first." And he accompanies the threat with a forceful gesture which prominently involves finger ring and handkerchief.

For a man who protests he cannot talk seriously about his work, cannot even seriously think about it, unless actually at it, pen in hand, the author

4. See p. 16, n. 3.
5. See p. 17, n. 4.

of "Jennie Gerhardt" manages to achieve an air of enthusiasm, and savagery even, if occasion demands.

He maintains that his conception of life when he is seriously at work is entirely different from his attitude toward life when going about ordinary workaday matters; that he does not realize the hows and the whys and the facts of present day existence until he starts into the actual writing of them.

"But how can that be?"

"I don't know, but it is."

"How can you be sure then that your viewpoint when writing is the accurate one?"

"I don't know, but it is."

"How do you know it is?"

"Because it is. It is."

And there you are.

Anyway, the author says he does not like to explain. "What is the purpose of fiction?" he repeats. "Well, what is the purpose of the Hudson River out there? What is the purpose of anything? Everything just naturally manifests itself—or should do so naturally. Books are only forced expressions of individuality moulded by their times and environments. Of course they reflect tendencies, for they are temporal in their conditions of making, and fashions of making change."

"And must they be true?" he asked. "Naturally; for to be worth while they must be both artistic and humanitarian, and nothing could be thus and not be true. And ultimately the truth wins. So fundamentally every worldly success is artistic and humanitarian." Which discloses an admiration on the part of the author for a certain Mr. Woolworth, a commercial genius who conceived the notion of operating five and ten cent stores.[6]

"I don't know the man," he says. "I don't know whether the idea that he has first of all done a beautiful, artistic and humanitarian thing has ever entered his head. But he has—and he has achieved a great success. Think!

"Scores of manufacturers annually overproduce along certain lines. They are glad to sacrifice on these, for even a small per cent is a profit above dead loss. At the other end are the millions of the poor, anxious for the necessities and the pretty trifles which they have not enough money to buy in the usual departments. Along comes the middleman with his great idea. He buys the stock of overproduction and brings salve to the manufacturer, and he buys at a price which brings these articles within the range of the poor, for a price ridiculous and never before heard of—five or ten cents.

6. The American merchant Frank W. Woolworth (1852–1919) opened his first five-and-ten-cent store in 1879. By the time of this interview, there were over one thousand stores throughout the United States and several foreign countries.

"Now of course I don't know the man nor the real facts of his case. But they must be something like this and he has done a truly beautiful, artistic, humanitarian thing. The matter may be beside the question, but it shows at any rate that all successful things have these basic elements."

Mr. Dreiser, who in addition to saving up his seriousness to use when he works, saves up a lot of strength and works hard and long, already has ready a successor to "Jennie Gerhardt," and others under way. They are all realistic exploitations of the same idea. For he'll write no other kind, even if he has to go back to editing.

Theodore Dreiser
The Author of "Jennie Gerhardt" Repudiates Jenny and Talks about His New Book—His Impressions Abroad

BY MONTROSE J. MOSES

*

New York Times Review of Books, 23 June 1912, pp. 377–78.

From November 1911 to April 1912 Dreiser toured Europe after receiving an advance from Century Company for three articles on the trip. He received an advance from Harper's on his forthcoming novel *The Financier* as well, for the trip was also intended to let him research Charles T. Yerkes (1837–1905), the model for the novel's hero; Yerkes had lived in Europe during the last years of his life. Montrose J. Moses (1878–1934) was an author and editor of books on drama as well as a critic.

To Theodore Dreiser, "Jennie Gerhardt" is an accomplishment of the past. He declares that he will never write another book like it; that such a type of woman no longer appeals artistically to him. But at present, it is very probable that he feels this simply because he is so deeply immersed in a volume he is writing for the Century Company on his recent travels abroad.[1] He certainly trailed through the Continent with the enthusiasm of a boy, exhibiting a freshness of vision which bids fair to produce a book of impressions by no means stereotyped. And there is small doubt that some of his varied experiences will figure in the first of a three-volumed novel, "The Financier," which in August will be published by the Harpers.[2]

In one paragraph, I am trying to detail all the news it took me several hours to extract, for Mr. Dreiser approached his work only after he had taken a flying trip through Europe. And this personally conducted tour led me to

---

1. Dreiser's contract for the articles also gave Century Company an option on a book he would write about his trip. Both the articles and the book, *A Traveler at Forty*, were published in 1913.

2. It was not until later in the summer that Dreiser acceded to Harper's request that each of the volumes in the Cowperwood trilogy bear a distinctive title.

believe that in "The Financier," the scenes of which will be laid in Philadelphia, Chicago, and London, with the persistent accompaniment of New York, there will be some minor touches of Paris and Monte Carlo.

Mr. Dreiser looked very much like the Man from Home during his talk. Seated in a rocking chair, which moved back and forth whenever we were traveling fastest, he every now and then emphasized a point with his goldrimmed glasses, in between whiles folding his handkerchief four times in length and then rolling it into a tight ball to clinch an argument. Above average height, with a decided stoop, he is altogether a serious looking personage. If seen on the street, he may be quickly identified by a characteristic stride, which is such an excellent excuse for a man to let his mind wander in the busy thoroughfares. Slow but sure of speech, Mr. Dreiser is modern in taste and poetic in feeling. These two qualities will assuredly mark the book of travel when it appears. And there is a fund of humor in this tourist guide. How many times during his talk did he chuckle in good-natured memory, and when he chuckled, the chair rocked in unison, and the handkerchief unrolled itself in expansive accord!

"Why did I go abroad?" he asked himself. "So as to satisfy an almost constant desire to see the five or six largest cities in the world. And to contrast them with New York! My, my, my—what a highly individualized place Paris is, with its walls hugging an eight-story life! And what a contrast there is outside those walls—as sparse and as poor as Bayonne! But go anywhere you please inside, and all life is vital; you see brisk Frenchmen on the streets. So much of the city reminded me, not of Third Avenue here, or Seventh or Lenox, but of this smart and comfortable west side.[3] What courage, hope, and enthusiasm there is in France!

"Yes, I went to the cafés, for the food is good. But I couldn't see that it was any more garish there than what you see at Shanley's. Everything is far more artistically done, the rooms being small in comparison with the Knickerbocker Hotel, for instance.[4] I should say that the Paris restaurants are one-quarter the size of those in America. It is a strange fact that the well-dressed Frenchman is so common that that he scarcely ever attracts attention. He is likely to come from any quarter. It is the women who are remarkable. It would seem as though a man wouldn't be seen with any but a striking looking woman. I am sure that there are many tragedies hidden away, where a woman couldn't afford to look well and perforce felt obliged to stay away. For there is vital interest in women; there is the spirit of contrast all around you; the atmosphere is tense with it!

3. Dreiser was living in an Upper West Side apartment at the time of the interview (see p. 18, note 7).

4. Shanley's, a famous New York City restaurant, and the Knickerbocker Hotel were located in Times Square.

"Paris, the city of champagne, not of ordinary wine! In the restaurants, cheek by jowl with you, are Spaniard, Russian, and all the color of Europe. Coon shouters regale the crowds,[5] colored balloons fill the air, there is a crazy sense of delight! Everything tends to create fervor. The night life has no appreciable effect upon the day life of Paris. You know how mosquitos bite until the victim becomes immune. I verily believe that the average Parisian is hardly aware that the restaurants are there.

"Of course the very fact that Paris is awhirl would indicate that the French temperament is quite on the surface. But the Frenchman is not more sexual than the American, who is very deceptive. We can't tell what fires burn beneath the Chinese exterior of the average New York business man. The American doesn't look what he does. You know our expression, 'Don't get gay'?"—here Mr. Dreiser leaned forward, smiling broadly and waving his handkerchief free of its wrinkles so as to begin the folding again—"Well, the Frenchman says, 'Get gay,' and he eats with one hand, leaving the other one free to demonstrate with.

"Gestures, Lord! how they do wave and chatter! I remember asking a cabby the way to a certain place. He felt first, clasped his hands to his fore-head, shrugged his shoulders, snapped his fingers, and all that sort of thing. Then he called a second cabby to help him, and he went through similar agonies. And not content with that, a third cabby was hailed. Until finally I was the centre of a jabbering trio. Suddenly one of them thought where the place was. Imagine me the victim of a chorus of 'oui, oui, oui.' Would an American taximan do that? These French drivers are artistically inde-pendent. I remember calling one to take me to the Bois, but my lord didn't care to go there, and so off he drove, leaving me to wait by the curb until a cabby came along who did care to go to the Bois. I have walked along many a day, watching the drivers dusting their little carriages and fixing flowers in their horses' rosettes."

Our conversation led us to the subject of art, for from what Mr. Dreiser let fall I inferred that in "The Financier" the collecting instinct of a Mor-gan or of a Frick will have some play.[6]

"Art! there's to be a great deal about art in my book—that beauty which has been shut out so long, like the pottery in Nero's Palace. The rich dis-play is absolutely endless. When I reached Rome, I was not there long be-fore I began to realize that there the remains one sees are native, and fit in

5. By "coon shouters" Dreiser probably means Negro singers. He refers to them in *A Trav-eler at Forty* in a more detailed discussion of the restaurant scene he is describing here (pp. 221–24).

6. The banker John Pierpont Morgan (1837–1913) and the industrialist Henry Clay Frick (1849–1919) were both renowned art collectors.

with the climate, while the painting in Rome is not as impressive as it is in Florence.

"America is being judged very closely by the English, who in a way like us, though they say no. They seem to resent our false, blatant, strident vulgarity. They are civil and well mannered, even on their trams. But here in America there is the divine right for any one to insult you. You know, I rather like it, for it gives us the divine right to slap insolence in the face and go our way.

"I'm half German," Mr. Dreiser confessed, "so I'm not going to say a word right now about what I think of the Kaiser's country. But I must confess that I don't care for the 'I'll eat you up' attitude of the nation. My one great impression was that the soldiers are wonderful in their appearance, and I often speculated as to whether some of them, in their spic-and-spanness, wanted to be quite as nice looking as they are. I distinctly felt the desire for war with England, and let me tell you, there'll be some war if they do fight! Do I believe in the peace movement? I would, if life were peaceful, but is it?"

The handkerchief was now quite bedraggled looking, so Mr. Dreiser discarded it for his glasses, which conducted him through his discussion of his work.

"You may think it strange that I am avoiding New York as the locale of 'The Financier'," he averred. "I haven't struck the city of cities yet, but I have a novel stored away for it. I'm going to write about it some day. But now I'm crazy about Chicago with its great personality. The only reason my book is to be in three volumes is that 500,000 words couldn't conveniently be put into one. It is all about American conditions, the rich and poor figuring equally, and the working problem in Chicago being discussed. As for the English part, you will hear much of English convention and English civility. But Chicago is my love; I don't believe any one could be crazier over a girl than I am over that city. You know I came from Indiana, but for eight years I was a newspaper man in Chicago, and then turned to New York via Toledo, Cleveland, and Pittsburgh. I've started many magazines, Every Month, Smith's Magazine, the Broadway Magazine,[7] and I organized—or disorganized, as you will—the staff of The Delineator.

"It was just after 'Sister Carrie' was completed that I began to work on 'Jennie.' I can't dash off manuscript; I hate to push the pencil. If a thing doesn't grip me, if it is not vital to me at once, it is very difficult for me to go on. That was the fate of 'Jennie.' The only reason the book ever got

7. Dreiser was a reporter in Chicago for only five or six months (not eight years), and he did not "start" *Smith's* or *Broadway* but rather initiated new editorial policies when he became the editor of these magazines—*Smith's* in April 1905 and *Broadway* in April 1906.

finished was that, begun during my free-lance days, it weighed heavily on my conscience. I hate to leave a piece of work undone.

"Maybe I sound disloyal, but Jennie's temperament does not appeal to me any longer. I found, however, when I came to finish it, that I had to be true to the first part of the book—in other words, to the character—rather than to my personal likes. That is why I didn't shift the key. Structurally the book is sound, I believe. But in the new novel, the note of the plot will come from the man, and man shall be the centre of the next three or four novels. It would have to be a most remarkable woman for me to write a book about one after Jennie! Possibly that is because I know more about women now.

"You may call 'Jennie' sordid if you will, but there is a certain charm even in sordidness, if it is used with art. A marvelous story might be laid in Fall River or in Jersey City. I have been asked over and over again what I believe realism to be, and I only say that you will find the reply in your own temperament. You can't answer life in a book. No one can solve anything in a single piece of literature. I think I'm a believer in art for art's sake. It's impossible to say that conditions can ever be perfectly moral, so long as there are differing temperaments. And from the same pot—meaning the same era—you get the religionist and the anti-religionist. Nature grows all types. They are all using up good land. One is supposed by his goodness to triumph and he doesn't; another is supposed by his wickedness to destroy and he doesn't. There are weeds and flowers in the same spot, and whether we get the weeds out depends on the gardener. I believe in being what I am; in expressing what I feel!

"I have never encouraged all that talk about the American novel. Of course, I'm a citizen of this country, and I suppose there is a certain race temperament that we cannot escape. But isn't Mme. Bovary as true in Louisville as elsewhere? The only thing that race difference does is to make you palatable to the land in which you are born. My one ambition is to represent my world, to conform to the large, truthful lines of life. And if I do that, no matter whether my characters live in Columbus, Ohio, or not, I will be true everywhere.

"I have written about nine short stories, but it's hard work. I need a large canvas. As I said, before I can go on I have to get a huge enthusiasm, and a short story is too small for the necessary run before the jump. I know that I am ultra-serious, that some people who meet me think I am too heavy. If I could, I'd get away from that; I'd rather be something else than I am, but I can't. And so you will find 'The Financier' serious.

"The book is going to create a great amount of comment. The first volume is the segment of a much larger thing. I've read through nearly every book that has been written on financial conditions—Hyde's book, Lawson's book—and the rest.[8] And it all seemed to me that they had only nibbled at the barrel of cheese. If the searchlight on this new book of mine is blistering, in the endeavor to see whether my statements are valid, I can only say that I have taken no end of care to verify my data. In my day I have written on trade conditions, and I have interviewed financiers. As to the truthfulness of my data there can be no question. But I am not a critic; I'm not quarreling with life, even though life is sad. I take my own misfortunes with less agony than I do other people's. Everything that is may not be all right, but it is beautiful. Life's all right if you are all right yourself physically."

The economy of space alone prevents me from continuing. Mr. Dreiser had something to say of Frank Norris's "McTeague" and Henry B. Fuller's "With the Procession," two of his favorite books.[9] He had equally as much to say about publishing conditions, and about the fate of three-volumed novels. And when we parted at the door he eulogized postcards and the service they were to him while he was abroad. He may be serious, and, as he says, sometimes ponderous, but by the rocking of his chair at emphatic moments, by the squeezing of the bedraggled handkerchief whenever an experience pleased him, by the hearty laugh, I should say that Theodore Dreiser is not as lacking in humor as his walk would suggest. In observation he goes a brisk trot.

8. Dreiser appears to be referring to Henry M. Hyde's novel *The Buccaneers: A Story of the Black Flag in Business* (1904) and Thomas W. Lawson's *Frenzied Finance* (1903), an exposé of the Amalgamated Copper Company.

9. See p. 17, n. 4.

Theodore Dreiser on the Novel
The Author of "Jennie Gerhardt" Takes a Pessimistic View of the Modern Novel—"What New Form Will Succeed It?" He Asks

*

New York Evening Sun, 28 September 1912, p. 7.

Several circumstances can account for Dreiser's comments here on his fatigue and the future of the novel. In August and September he had been working hard at editing *The Financier* to meet Harper's deadline for fall publication, a process that included deciding where to make extensive cuts to an excessively long text. At the same time, because he was having financial difficulties, he had to be concerned about the public's response to his new novel. The interview was reprinted as "Theodore Dreiser Warns Prolific Novelists; Says Writer Folk Should Take Vacations" in the *Terre Haute Star*, 27 October 1912, p. 6.

Theodore Dreiser, author of "Sister Carrie," "Jennie Gerhardt" and the newly published novel "The Financier," sat discussing the drift of modern literature over a cup of tea. Sunlight danced through the yellowing foliage and in at the window, but Mr. Dreiser was in a pessimistic mood and would not be comforted by tea, sunshine or conversation.

"It is possible," said Theodore Dreiser, and he looked very sad over it, "that the public will always continue to love defective psychology. In that case, there will continue to be room for the scrub playwright, the hack novelist and the half-baked picture painter. But, on the other hand, if there should be an intellectual evolution from the defective psychology of to-day to a correct psychology, there will be a renaissance of literature. The novel may disappear as a form, and a new form of literary expression succeed it. Perhaps the mammoth of realism will finally sink into the mud by its own weight, to be superseded by the five-toed horse of symbolism, as the mammoth of the paleozoic age was succeeded by a smaller and more useful animal. In that case, literature will get somewhere.

"I am tired of my job, you know. Everybody gets tired of his job now and then—farmers and mechanics and writer people—everybody! I feel as if it would be such a rest to do something commonplace. The next vacation I take I am going to be a conductor on a street car or else work in a tobacco factory.

"Yes, I am perfectly in earnest," he added. "The last long vacation I took I spent nine months as a laborer working for the New York Central with a pick and shovel; I laid cobblestones in White Plains and dug ditches down the railroad tracks.[1] The reason that this literary life is so enervating is that we are all playing with chestnuts. The old forms have been done to death, and they are not worth two whoops any more. Balzac wrote forty or fifty novels about as well as it can be done. What's the use of repeating the old forms after that? Did you ever stop to think that the novel really burst forth upon the world practically a fully developed and perfect form and that it has not been improved upon to any extent?

"'Clarissa Harlowe' was among the first English novels, and we have never gone very much beyond it.[2] Then there was Defoe's 'Moll Flanders'; no one has ever beaten that old story of the prostitute and the thief. I am unable to see, as some do, that Arnold Bennett, although he is having a great vogue just now, does as good work as was left us by Balzac and Thackeray and Tolstoy. Nor does Wells, in my opinion, come up to their mark. He fails to organize his stories as well, though he presents the right material."[3]

At this point Mr. Dreiser pushed back his teacup and, pulling out a big white pocket handkerchief, held it out in front of him by the two upper corners. He carefully rolled it up, then methodically folding it back and forth in one hand, he began rolling it into a little hard round ball with the other. He did it all very solemnly and unconsciously. It is a little habit that helps him to think, and he has never figured out how many times a day he shakes that handkerchief out to roll it up all over again.

"The trouble is," he continued earnestly, "that the novel has been over-worked, and I should not be surprised if it disappears as a type, just as other things have. Why, do you realize the way the printing presses are pouring off novels? We now have them by the ton. Twelve hundred different novels published in this country last year. That would be too much, even if they were all good. Life gets tired of anything. Civilization changes, governments change. Literature must change to keep up. The trouble is that we have been too much concerned with externals and the optical evidences of things, and

1. To help himself recover from a nervous breakdown, Dreiser worked for the New York Central from early June to Christmas Day 1903, a period of nearly seven months.
2. The correct title of the novel by Samuel Richardson (1689–1761) is *Clarissa, or, The History of a Young Lady* (8 vols., 1747–49).
3. See p. 17, n. 5.

have not organized into literature that which we know. Now, along with our research into chemistry and biology and the composition of things, why not investigate what causes thought and frame that into books? There are two phases, the actual thinking and the mood which precedes or succeeds the thinking. That mood is really the interesting part and we know comparatively nothing about it. People are going to get tired of stories which merely tell that Jennie got breakfast and John went to his office and Jim kicked the cat.

"Was it Matthew Arnold or Pater who wrote that some day we are going to realize that the most interesting and dramatic situation in the world is the spectacle of an old man seated by a table thinking?[4] Ibsen tried it with the drama,[5] and perhaps the next person will be able to do even better. To any thinking man to-day there is nothing so dreary as the present state of the stage. Brieux is dull except in spots; Ibsen and Shaw are the best. But great heavens, think of the worst! It has gotten so that I find it impossible to go to the theater any more. You can always bet on it that there will be some jarring intellectual flaw in the play. Take 'Alias Jimmy Valentine,' a great success.[6] Yet could you accept such a situation and such a sacrifice as real? When you came outside and looked at the trolley car going by didn't you realize how artificial was the thrill that the play gave you? You don't want artificial thrills any more than you want artificial diamonds in the place of real ones, or rabbit pelts for sealskins."

Mr. Dreiser hesitated when it came to prophesying what might succeed the novel.

"Why be definite," he pleaded, "when it's so silly to be definite or positive about anything? How can I know what's going to succeed the novel? If I knew I would write it. I would do it if I could, but a person must have real inventive genius to think of a new way of doing anything, and I do not claim that. It is so much easier to do things the way they always have been done."

At this point Mr. Dreiser showed how much of a conservative he can be. If he does not always talk as one, he looks it. He is a big man. His hair is sprinkled with gray, and he has gray eyes behind gold rimmed glasses. He wears gray clothes and gray ties—not a gentle gray but a massive steel gray that makes you think of strength and power.

Questioned as to the possibility of post-impressionists in literature as well

4. The author of the statement on a "spectacle of an old man" has not been identified.

5. The *New York Sun* prints this name as "Hasen"; it has been emended to "Ibsen" on the basis of context and the *Terre Haute Star,* which prints it as "Ibsen."

6. *Alias Jimmy Valentine,* adapted by Paul Armstrong (1869–1915) from an O. Henry (1862–1910) story, was a 1910 melodrama about a reformed safecracker who risks imprisonment by using his criminal skills to rescue his employer's daughter when she becomes trapped in a bank vault.

as in painting he said, "They present a realer realism than has ever before been portrayed. No, I do not think that post-impressionism is realer than reality. They simply strip away the outlines and show a thing unmodified by mood or temperament. It is like looking at a world without any atmosphere. But I am not at all sure that the evolution of literature is going to follow along parallel lines to those that the post-impressionists are working out for art.[7] When it comes to the forms of the future, I simply do not know.

"For myself, I have often thought that I should like to write a volume to be called 'The Sealed Book' with this warning printed on the outside, 'Don't read this book unless you have the special kind of guts that will stand for it.' And the book should be—oh, perhaps an absolutely accurate biography, not a lot of elusive imaginings and romanticism, but a literal transcript of life as it is. Jean Jacques Rousseau perhaps came the nearest to writing such a book. He tried to write it in his confessions but he was looking at his life through his own temperament, which made it impossible for him to see it truly. It would take the mental acumen of an Emerson and the picture-drawing power of a Dickens (some great, large-minded outsider) to write a book of life as it really is. It must be someone who can show the facts of life with great art, with the illuminating flashes that show not only the concentrated filth at the bottom but the wonder and mystery of the ideals at the top. It must be some one who has a keen desire to look with his eyes right into the sun, even though he knows that it may blind him."

7. The English art critic and painter Roger Fry (1866–1934) coined the term *postimpressionism* to describe the work of painters, particularly Paul Cézanne (1839–1906), Paul Gauguin (1848–1903), and Vincent van Gogh (1853–90), who depicted reality starkly but also often with considerable distortion of visual representation.

Theodore Dreiser Now Turns to High Finance
Not to Make a Fortune, but to Frame
His Forthcoming Novel
No Change of Method
New Study Will Be as Suggestively Analytical
as Its Predecessors

*

New York Sun, 19 October 1912, pt. 2, p. 3

The race for wealth at the pace set in America has interested Theodore Dreiser, novelist and philosopher. The author of "Jennie Gerhardt" and "Sister Carrie" has been devoting a long period of thought and study to a dramatic picture of exploitation and high finance, particularly in the reckless years following the civil war.

In his forthcoming novel, "The Financier," which is to be issued on October 24 by his publishers, Harper & Brothers, Mr. Dreiser traces the evolution of a "Napoleon of Finance" from small beginnings before the war to vast dealings which include banks and street railways and close alliance with politics.

His book covers a wide field, and those who know Mr. Dreiser's work know the characteristic breadth and force of his treatment. The new field which he has entered has piqued the curiosity of readers who have learned to regard him as the leading exponent of the newer school of realistic art, and an interview was sought with the author of "Jennie Gerhardt" in order to obtain some information as to his new book, "The Financier." The title clearly indicated a distinct difference in theme from his former books, and this prompted the first question.

"Have you not changed your field of work, Mr. Dreiser?"

"Yes, to a certain extent. But 'Sister Carrie' came very near being a man's book, and I think if I had it to do over that I would now make it one. Nevertheless as it is I think it gives satisfactory evidence that my tendency was to make an elaborate study of a man.

"In 'The Financier' I have not taken a man so much as I have a condition, although any one who follows the detailed study of Cowperwood's life would fancy perhaps that it was more a man than a condition that I was after. It has always struck me that America since the civil war in its financial and constructive tendencies has represented more the natural action of the human mind when it is stripped of convention, theory, prejudice and belief of any kind than almost any period in the world's history.

"In Rome around the date of the accession of the emperors we have an illustration of the strange, forceful ruthlessness of the human mind when it has freed itself from old faiths and illusions, and has not accepted any new ones. There you got mental action spurred by desire, ambition, vanity, without any of the moderating influences which we are prone to admire—sympathy, tenderness and fair play.

"Many of the emperors were murdered, as the ordinary schoolboy knows, and thereafter the world passed into the shadowy realm of religious belief which endured until the Renaissance. Thereafter the amazing figure of mediaeval Italy appeared, including such astounding personalities as Machiavelli, Alexander VI, Cesare Borgia and others. There again you have direct action of the human mind untrammelled by our so-called sense of justice and unmodified in the matter of ambition by any faith or any fear.

"There have been other periods, but few so glitteringly significant until we arrive at the year 1865 A.D. and thereafter. Then here in America we began to breed a race of giants acting directly, wholly financial in their operations, because finance was the one direct avenue to power and magnificence.

"Such men as Rockefeller, H. H. Rogers, Jay Gould, William H. Vanderbilt, E. H. Harriman and perhaps Russell Sage, are conspicuous examples. They knew no law and they would smile with contempt on any one who did. I do not think that the mind of H. H. Rogers or John D. Rockefeller or E. H. Harriman was far removed from that of either Alexander VI, Cesare Borgia, Machiavelli, or to go back to the Roman Empire, any one of twenty Roman emperors, including Galba and Nero.

"Our giants have been strong, eager, enthusiastic and without compunction. They have taken where they could, and silenced their victims with a bludgeon or ignored their cries. It is nothing new in the world; it will never be old or new. It will be simply different. New times make new methods and new conditions. Our Americans have looked at what they wished to do and have proceeded without let or hindrance to secure it.

"It is this atmosphere that I have begun to indicate in 'The Financier.' That book is not a complete picture. The full matter, if it could be condensed into one volume, would give possibly an interesting and I hope dramatic interpretation of what has been and still is happening. If I had the time and strength I would select other characters, illustrating the same tendency under other conditions. If this is a change from my older method, then I have changed."

"What is the theme of 'The Financier,'" asked the interviewer.

"I have fairly indicated it in just what I have said. The locale is Philadelphia, the period from 1847 to 1873, the character a national type, the conditions not different except in detail from those that have occurred in San Francisco, St. Louis, Boston, Chicago, Philadelphia and New York. I only hope they are accurate. Aside from the few specific facts with which most of us are familiar the color and the characters of the story are created out of whole cloth.

"I spent some time in Philadelphia studying the location of the scenes and familiarizing myself with the machinery of local government, but beyond that I guessed, as I had a right to do.[1] The political atmosphere is simply typical, not accurate. The historical dates, in the main, are correct. I spent most of my time reading of financial characters of one kind and another in order to familiarize myself with the workings of finance sufficiently to make it intelligent without giving so much accurate detail that nobody would read it."[2]

"Is this typical, do you think, of American finance in connection with public service?"

"Fairly so, yes. I believe there have been many worse conditions than I have described. The machinations of Cowperwood are child's play so far as the Philadelphia end of this story is concerned as compared with the subtle manipulation of financiers in other cities, and even in Philadelphia at a slightly later period."

"Does your book attempt to picture the civil war?"

"Not at all. Most of the financiers of whom Cowperwood is a fair representative were not interested in the civil war nor the question of slavery or any matter of human right. They were concerned as to what avenues of personal profit the war might open to them. P. D. Armour, for instance, got his start by realizing that because of the war pork would be in great demand. It went I think to $9 a barrel. Consequently he stored pork until he had a corner and found himself rich.[3] That is but a single instance. I drew on the civil

---

1. Dreiser lived in Philadelphia from July 1902 to February 1903 while seeking to recover from a nervous breakdown, but there is no record that he spent time in the city while doing research for *The Financier*. While he was researching and writing the novel, much of his information on Philadelphia came from correspondence with Joseph Hornor Coates (1849–1930), a Philadelphia editor and publisher whom he befriended when he lived in the city (see n. 5 to this interview).

2. See pp. 28–29 and n. 4 to this interview.

3. Dreiser interviewed the Chicago meatpacking industrialist Philip D. Armour (1832–1901) for *Success* magazine in 1898 ("Life Stories of Successful Men—No. 10, Philip D.

war just enough to show that this was the attitude that was taken. And the introduction of the figure of Lincoln is merely to prove what I have just said."

"Did not your preparation for 'The Financier' require a great deal of time?"

"In all about a year. My greatest difficulty was in acquiring a working knowledge of finance and getting accurately the mental point of view of the proper character. I found a history called a 'Day by Day History of Philadelphia' to be of considerable value and the biographies and autobiographies of such men as Daniel Drew, Jay Cooke and others.[4]

"I owe really a great debt of gratitude to a private collection of newspaper clippings that was open to me and which covered many phases of the data I was seeking.[5] It was no trouble to indicate the atmosphere of Philadelphia, although I have never lived there.[6] Most of the histories of that city give a very good picture. My greatest difficulty was in making the machinery of my story work so that it gives a sense of movement and not of a vast complicated structure without life."

"What will be the character of your next book?"

"I shall probably follow the evolution indicated in 'The Financier.' Naturally a story which deals with finance and which has it beginning since '73 and carries its life to the present hour, or nearly so, would be more involved, more ruthless and more orgiastically magnificent than one located between 1847 and 1873. But I do not know that it would be more human or have more of an intellectual or passional appeal."

Armour," *Success* 1 [Oct. 1898]: 3–4; repr., Dreiser, *Selected Magazine Articles of Theodore Dreiser*, vol. 1, ed. Yoshinobu Hakutani [Rutherford, N.J.: Fairleigh Dickinson University Press, 1985], 120–29).

4. Drew (1797–1879) was a notorious speculator associated with stock market and railroad scandals, and Cooke (1821–1905) was a banker who marketed government bonds during the Civil War and financed construction of western railroads. Dreiser's use of Ellis P. Oberholtzer's *Jay Cooke: Financier of the Civil War* (1907) has been well documented, and he probably used Bouck White's *Book of Daniel Drew* (1910) as well. The author and publisher of the *Day by Day History of Philadelphia* have not been identified; Dreiser may have been referring to the detailed work by J. T. Scharf and Thompson Westcott entitled *History of Philadelphia 1609–1884*, 3 vols. (Philadelphia: L. H. Everts, 1884).

5. Dreiser is referring to clippings about Yerkes, primarily from the *Philadelphia Public Ledger*, made available to him through Joseph Hornor Coates (see n. 1 to this interview).

6. Dreiser had in fact lived in Philadelphia in 1902 and 1903 (see n. 1 to this interview).

Dreiser on Need of Liberty in Writing

New York Sun, 29 November 1913, Literary Section, p. 4.

Before the book's publication in November 1913, editors at the Century Company had cut *A Traveller at Forty* extensively for moral and other reasons, which may account for Dreiser's complaints about artistic freedom in this interview. Also notable are his views on woman suffrage and his description of his writing methods.

Theodore Dreiser, author of "A Traveller at Forty," and the interviewer, who had been sent to question him on various subjects, foregathered in a large crowded room where the telegraphic returns from the Harvard-Yale football game were being received. The coherence of the interview was somewhat impaired by shouts of "Wow!" "Eat 'em up, Yale!" "Touch down! Touch down!" "Three long Harvards and three times three for Brickley!"[1]

"Who have accomplished the most in American literature?" asked Mr. Dreiser. "The pagans. Hawthorne—pure pagan, Poe—pagan. Thoreau—pagan. Even Emerson thought as a pagan, but he contrived to play a constant New England obbligato that made him acceptable among—"

"Yow-ipp!" shouted eight hundred enthusiasts as the football was carried down the field for a 15-yard gain. After one or two attempts to get the interview under way, author and interviewer sought the peaceful quiet of upper Fifth avenue of a Saturday afternoon and finally plunged into Central Park, where Mr. Dreiser's ideas came from him with less interruption.

"Ever since I began writing," continued Mr. Dreiser, "I have had the feeling of being pushed back. Somebody has always been telling me that I must not write about life as I see it. 'Don't do it. You mustn't say that. Keep back.' I wrote 'Sister Carrie' about thirteen years ago and when a thousand copies were printed, bound and ready to be put out, the publisher decided to suppress the book. The reason given was that it was immoral, but in that same

---

1. A fullback, Charley Brickley kicked five field goals to lead Harvard to a 15–5 victory over Yale on 22 November 1913. The location of the telegraphic broadcast of the game in New York has not been identified.

year the same publisher brought out 'An Englishwoman's Love Letters' and Zola's 'Fecundity.'[2]

"My opposition has been from a third party, a critic, a publisher, a clergyman, somebody who sets up as a judge of what I should say to the public. I consider this all wrong. Every art has what may be called the rules of the game. I am not averse to obeying the rules of the game, not in the least; but what I resent is having a third party break in between me and the public. The deal is between the writer and the reader and is not a three cornered game.

"I don't at all believe that democracy will strangle art. Democracy cannot wipe out differences between high and low, rich and poor, strength and weakness, big brain and little brain. The color of life which fascinates me so much is just as vivid to-day as it was under princes and kings. In the chapters of 'A Traveller at Forty,' which were published in the *Century,* I tried to catch the color of life in London, Paris and elsewhere, and the whole book is an attempt along this line.[3]

"Of course in art, the color of life, speaking more literally, can be expressed by a painter who sees. The *Century* is doing some excellent work in this line. The public has a right to look to the *Century* for leadership in art."

In "A Traveller at Forty" and indeed in his previous books which have all been fiction Mr. Dreiser shows himself to be an appreciater of women. It was natural, therefore, that he should be asked his opinion on woman suffrage.[4]

"Women surely have a look-in already in the game of life. No woman, with even the slightest equipment of charm need feel herself powerless under the present arrangement. In this struggle that is going on for the vote," he said, "the women may conquer the men. If they do beat the men, then I say let them have the vote. If they are the stronger, then they are entitled to it. But I tell you there are individual men whom women will never get the better of.

"Yes I think women will get the vote in America, but it won't do them any good. They will get it and then they will neglect or abuse it, and conditions will be exactly the same again.

2. *An Englishwoman's Love-Letters,* by Laurence Housman (1865–1959), is the story of a girl whose suitor leaves her when he discovers that she is his half-sister, and Zola's novel focuses on the theme of human procreation. Doubleday, Page and Company published both books in 1900.

3. Thirteen chapters of the book appeared in *Century* magazine in August, September, and October 1913.

4. By November 1913 women had received the vote in ten Western states, and strengthened by the inclusion of working-class women and men's support groups, the suffrage movement had become much more aggressive on the national level. On 3 March, for instance, the day before the inauguration of Woodrow Wilson, over 5,000 women marched in the nation's capital to call attention to their cause.

"No, I was not inspired to become a writer by some European or American novelist's work. It was through an intimate friend of mine with whom I was living. This friend, the city editor of a newspaper, kept dingdonging at me, saying I must write a novel.[5] He wouldn't take no for an answer. Finally I managed to get 'Sister Carrie' finished. I have been very fortunate in having about me from that time on a group of friends who believe in me and who have been interested in my writing. Without my friends probably I should never have written at all. This latest book, 'A Traveller at Forty,' is written around the personality of a man whom I call in the book Barfleur, a most extraordinary, charming, cultured man of the world who not only made this book possible but put me in contact with European people and conditions in the most skillful and pleasant way.[6]

"No, I do not begin by writing a scenario of a novel. I have the general plan in my head and take it at the beginning and carry it through as best I can. Sometimes the story changes and reforms itself. Sometimes I destroy whole sections of the novel and begin again. I find I can write many hours consecutively without rest.

"Look at that man," suddenly exclaimed Mr. Dreiser, gazing at a young man of the period wearing the very latest advertised style of collar, a very small mustache and a hat tipped back from his forehead. "I wonder what that kind of man thinks of. It is a well defined type. I have seen hundreds of them here in New York. I wonder what is going on in his head. How does he spend his time? What are his amusements? I should like to know."

A further study of this type was impossible at the moment, but the interviewer had received a definite impression of the artistic and human curiosity of the writer, whose gaze had in it an absorptive quality that might mean [a] later extraordinarily accurate painting of this particular type of American.

In conversation Mr. Dreiser appears temperate, cool, absolutely honest, truth loving, with none of the affectations of speech and manner that sometimes cling to the successful novelist. His point of view is not always a humorous one, but he has a splendid capacity for laughter that racks his large frame. When an idea amuses him his laughter gathers slowly, gradually reaches a gorgeous climax and slowly tapers off to gravity again. He has a thoroughgoing scorn for conventions.

"What we need," he said, "is absolute liberty. There are countless forms of life besides man. The animals and the trees have no Ten Commandments and they seem to get on pretty well."

5. The friend was Arthur Henry, who was the city editor of the *Toledo Blade*. He was living in New York with Dreiser and his wife when Dreiser began the novel in September of 1899.

6. Barfleur is the pseudonym Dreiser used for Grant Richards (1872–1948), the London publisher who arranged his tour of Europe and served as his guide.

Theo. Dreiser—Radical
Author of "Sister Carrie" and His Views of Life

By Albert Mordell

*

Philadelphia Record, 7 December 1913, pt. 3, p. 8.

Late 1913 found Dreiser in the midst of the most prolific period of his career, having begun or completed four novels and a number of works in other forms since returning to full-time authorship in 1910. His aggressive defense of a realistic aesthetic in the interview is perhaps related to his inability to derive a satisfactory income from this productivity. Albert Mordell (1885–1965) was a Philadelphia-based journalist and critic. His book *The Erotic Motive in Literature* (1919) was widely discussed.

Arnold Bennett considers "Sister Carrie," by Theodore Dreiser, the best American novel of the past twenty years,[1] yet the number of American readers who know Dreiser is not large. He is not one of our "popular" novelists, but he is certainly one of our most interesting novelists. His "Jennie Gerhardt" is captivating. Intellect, life and originality are reflected in the book.

I met Dreiser recently in his studio in the heart of New York.[2] The subject immediately turned to the value of the realistic novel.

I was myself in full sympathy with realism, but I gave some arguments in favor of romanticism in order to draw Dreiser out.

Away with Hypocrisy

"I cannot understand this outcry against realism," he said. "Let us look at life as it is. Why should we hide the darker side? We ought to do away with this pretense and hypocrisy. Most people have trouble, in this world; why shouldn't they be described? As a rule the game"—the word "game" was a favorite word of Dreiser's for life—"is pretty hard. Of course most of my

1. See p. 14, n. 1.
2. Probably the studio apartment of Kirah Markham, at 23 West Fifty-eighth Street, where Dreiser was living sporadically at the time.

characters have anxieties, just as people do in life. They lead lives that the conventions do not sanction; so do many people about us. Are they right or wrong? It's a question whether the game is worth it. If it isn't, if disaster follows, well, that's the end of it. Anyhow it may have been worth while trying. It often puzzles me how men who have had lives full of misfortune rise up in arms against novels because these do not show the game as rosy, sunny. People want you to lie to them. Now look at the old literature. Doesn't the realistic art alone survive out of all this old mass of writing? In fact, weren't all these old accounts of wars, blood and thunder realism? Just because it all happened a thousand or two thousand years ago in another country it is supposed to be romantic; if the domestic wars, for example, of our time and country are written up, then it is called realism. The only difference between romanticism and realism is locality and time."

Mr. Dreiser became so serious in his talk that I had to remind him that I was not one of those who disagreed with him.

Big American Novels

"What, in your opinion, are some of the big American realistic novels?" I asked.

"'With the Procession,' by Henry Fuller; 'The Outcast Manufacturers,' by Charles Fort; 'Quicksands,' by Hervey White."[3]

"I haven't heard of any of them," I commented. I doubted if others knew any more about them than I did.

"These men will come into their own some day, but I should also add Frank Norris' 'McTeague,' David Graham Phillips' 'Hungry Heart,' Brand Whitlock's 'Thirteenth District,' and Edith Wharton's 'House of Mirth,' the greatest novel I ever read by an American woman. George Eliot's 'Adam Bede' is a big thing."

This made me curious as to Mr. Dreiser's views on the English novelists.

"I suppose you don't care for Scott," I remarked.

"I don't want to go back on Scott. I remember my boyhood days when I fed on him, and I am an admirer of Dickens. But these old novelists and Thackeray do not tell us everything. They are sentimental and tell us usually about our better side. The two big novelists in England today are Hardy and Moore. I believe Hardy is not greatly admired by the English, but he is a master mind, his works are beautiful, and of Moore I can't forget his 'Evelyn Innes.'"

3. For Fuller, see p. 17, n. 4. The other novels are Charles Fort (1874–1932), *The Outcast Manufacturers* (1909); and Hervey White, *Quicksand* (not *Quicksands*) (1900). Of these figures, Fort, an idosyncratic philosopher as well as a novelist, was almost entirely unknown; Dreiser sought for many years to gain recognition for his work.

Admires French Writers

"How about the French writers, Mr. Dreiser, say Flaubert and Balzac?"

"I admire them both immensely. They are realists; they give us life with its disillusionments; they show us the game as it is."

"What is your attitude toward the sex novels of today, of which so many are being written?" I continued.[4]

"I suppose certain celibates need them. They are the result of a puritanical view of life. There is a market for them just as there is for butter and eggs. I am not opposed to them, but I don't read them."

"However, your own belief is that literature should follow life as it is?" I supplemented.

"Yes," Mr. Dreiser replied, "and since most lives are failures literature ought to show us that. No, I am not a pessimist; I am not even sentimentally aroused by suffering. I sympathize with struggling merit more than I do with poverty in general. When I had my troubles I thought I was just one of the few. Why, do you know that 95 percent of the men in business are not successes? Both the conventional and unconventional lead unhappy lives. My own characters, who defy the moral conventions, are not happy. Yes, life is a game and often the best men get the worst of it. The most successful are often the least gifted, and literature should show us the facts as they are."

Dreiser's New Novel

"Are you working on anything new?" I asked further.

"Yes, I am writing a sequel to 'The Financier,' called 'The Titan,' to appear in February. Then there will be a third and last part called 'The Stoic.' I hope some day to condense 'The Financier.'[5] We have never yet had a history of the financier in American fiction. I am told there are many Nietzschean views in this book, though I have read little of Nietzsche.[6] My disposition is to see divinity in the individual, and yet show the evil things

---

4. In 1913 magazines and newspapers often published articles and editorials on the frank treatment of sexual matters in recent plays, stories in magazines, and novels. The "sex novel" usually cited in these discussions was *Hagar Revelly*, by the social reformer Daniel Carson Goodman (1883–?), a story about the downfall of a New York shop girl published in January 1913.

5. Dreiser believed that *The Financier* had been insufficiently edited by Harper's because of the firm's desire to rush the book into print. He published a condensed version of the novel in 1927.

6. Most of Dreiser's awareness of the ideas of the German philosopher Friedrich Nietzsche (1844–1900) came through H. L. Mencken, who was a Nietzsche enthusiast.

in him. I think for myself, I do not accept anything, neither church, state or the marriage institution as final. You will find some of my views of life scattered through my book, 'A Traveler at Forty,' which has just come out."

"How is it that between the years 1901 and 1911, the dates of 'Sister Carrie' and 'Jennie Gerhardt,' you published nothing?" I inquired.

"Well, you know 'Sister Carrie' was withdrawn because the publisher's wife thought it immoral.[7] No publisher would handle me. I became [an] editor of magazines and finally I edited the Butterick publications. I was either occupied earning a living or nursing my broken nerves. I lived in different cities and I found life hard."

From the Middle West

Mr. Dreiser is a man of 42. He was born in the Middle West; had a college education and spent several years as a newspaperman. In his late twenties he published articles in many of the magazines. He became known in 1907, when the novel "Sister Carrie" was published the second time, and it is only within the last two years he has become really famous. As editor of The Delineator he organized the Child Rescue Association, which did good work. He is known in Philadelphia, where he lived in 1904.[8]

His novels belong to radical literature. He is subjective in his art, though he is not as much so as novelists London, Sinclair and Whitman are in "Martin Eden," "Love's Pilgrimage" and "Predestined," respectively, all of them autobiographical novelists.[9]

Whatever be the final opinion of Mr. Dreiser's trilogy, most critics are all agreed that he has in his first two novels given us feminine types as living and immortal as Hetty Sorrel, Tess, Madame Bovary, Eveylyn Innes and Nana.[10] He has also brought profound ideas into our fiction.

7. See p. 2, n. 3.

8. Dreiser lived in Philadelphia not in 1904 but rather from July 1902 to February 1903 while seeking to recover from a nervous breakdown.

9. Jack London (1876–1916), *Martin Eden* (1909); Upton Sinclair (1878–1968), *Love's Pilgrimage* (1911); Stephen French Whitman (1880–1948), *Predestined: A Novel of New York Life* (1910).

10. Named are the heroines of George Eliot's *Adam Bede* (1859), Thomas Hardy's *Tess of the D'Urbervilles* (1891), Gustave Flaubert's *Madame Bovary* (1856), George Moore's *Evelyn Innes* (not Eveylyn) (1898), and Emile Zola's *Nana* (1880).

Author Criticises Orthodox Editors
"Man with an Idea" Looked upon as Dangerous,
Says Theodore Dreiser—Thinks Democracy
Restrains American Literature

*

Philadelphia Public Ledger, 26 April 1914, p. 7.

In February 1914, after the plates were prepared and sheets for 10,000 copies were printed, Harper's decided not to publish *The Titan*. By the end of March, with the aid of friends, Dreiser was able to interest John Lane in publishing the novel, but his problems with Harper's may have been the reason for his angry outburst in this interview against a democracy in which editors try to please the "prejudices and stupidity of the multitude."

"A man with an idea is dangerous; if he displays sincerity in his support of that idea he is looked upon as a criminal." So said Theodore Dreiser, the novelist, last night.[1]

In America, he said, the opposition to any thoughtfully conceived work of fiction was deplorably evident.

And Mr. Dreiser's nature will brook no flimsy compromises. He is an individualist and steadfastly refuses to mar the strength of his work by complying with what he considers the arbitrary demands of carping editors. The democratization of culture in the United States, he believes, is responsible for "the discouragingly low standard of current literature on this side of the Atlantic." He adds:

That there is a certain class of readers in this country eager to accept literary productions of genuine merit is evidenced by the increasing demand for the writings of Continental writers, such as Anatole France, for example. Yet this portion of the reading public does not seem to be sufficiently conspicuous to convince publishers of the advisability of devoting themselves to serious fiction.

1. Dreiser had rented a room at 4142 Parkside Avenue in Philadelphia at the time of this interview.

Mr. Dreiser is opposed to Democracy—at least in the ordinary sense of the term. In Socialism he sees a sincere but sadly misguided movement. An intellectual aristocracy, he holds, would be the form of Government nearest approaching the ideal.

The novelist pointed out, in discussing this theme, that all the truly progressive movements in the world's history have been led by individualists, men who thought and acted for themselves, rather than in accordance with the precepts of others. The unquestioning adherence to the Constitution manifested by most Americans he referred to in tones of ironic pity. He continued:

Noteworthy achievements in the fine arts are retarded in our country because we put shackles on our intellects. In mechanical discovery we lead the world, for the very apparent reason that in that department of human activity we have no absurd restrictions. The man who is improving a flying machine, or an electrical appliance does not have the spectre of public disapproval continually before him. He can work with a free mind. But suppose he wishes to paint a picture, or compose an opera, or write a book! Then he is required to comply with rigorous restrictions. And we are all only too familiar with the results.

The tendency here is to put the pyramid on its apex, to discard the opinions of those at the highest point of the intellectual scale for the prejudices and stupidity of the multitude. Everything is for the vast, ruling majority. No wonder that Europe laughs at us. The idea that all men are created equal is one of the fundamental errors of our system of Government. For to the distinguishing mind it is quite apparent that the degree of intellectual endowment with which individuals come into this world varies enormously. But to level down is the cry of mediocrity everywhere.

The typically American delight in ostentatious display, mechanical music, red automobiles, said the novelist, sometimes made him feel that a return to actual barbarism would soon be at hand.

Business Overlords of America Greatest, Most Powerful Men since Days of Old Rome They Have Made History as Well as Money, Says Theodore Dreiser, and Thinking in Terms of a Continent Have Figured in a Tremendous Romance of Unscrupulous Success

By Marguerite Mooers Marshall

*

New York Evening World, 18 June 1914, p. 3.

Marguerite Mooers Marshall (1887–1964) was a New York journalist and the author of an epistolary novel entitled *Drift* (1911). The interview was reprinted as "Business and Morality Are to Be Separate" in the *Rochester Union and Advertiser*, 10 July 1914, p. 2.

Since the making of the Roman Empire the world has held no men so great as the business overlords of America.

That is Theodore Dreiser's estimate; that is why he has given us "The Titan" and "The Financier," two of a prospective trilogy, with an American business genius as hero of the plot—or villain, if you like it better so.

Arnold Bennett, W. J. Locke and other critics of distinction name Mr. Dreiser as the greatest living American novelist.[1] It's not difficult to quarrel with his manner; he is detailed, catalogue-ish, and his English can be gratingly unmelodious. But in his matter I know of no American who follows more sincerely George Moore's splendid dictum, "To be ashamed only of being ashamed!"[2] His men and women, now passion-torn, now fatalistically quiescent, make our fictional lay-figures more artificial than ever. And if some of us wish he would take more pains to adorn a tale, we may at least be thankful that he refuses to point a moral!

1. See p. 12, and p. 14, n. 1.
2. The source of Moore's statement has not been identified.

Meanwhile, his conception of the American business man is distinctly interesting, and as far removed as possible from the European sneer at the "money-making machine." Over orangeade and molasses caramels we talked yesterday afternoon in Mr. Dreiser's summer writing-room, which is a Staten Island veranda, set just above the bay and swept by keen salt winds. Mrs. Dreiser, a charming woman with bands of soft brown hair and slanting brown eyes, was ready to supply orangeade or smiles whenever the conversation became particularly candid and emphatic.[3]

"The business man as you see him is primarily an expression of the will-to-power?" I asked Mr. Dreiser when our rocking chairs were comfortably placed. (I know whence the heroine of "Sister Carrie" derived her fondness for that article of furniture.)

Business Is Swiftest and Surest Road to Power

"Each of us is an expression of the will-to-power," he replied. "But in America business is still the swiftest, surest method of attaining great power.

"When I was a boy, and I think the case holds true now, the natural, inevitable thing for the ambitious young man was to go into business. The ideal of everybody was to be president, vice-president or secretary and treasurer, of something. It never occurred to anybody that greatness could be achieved as a writer, a musician, an artist. Therefore all the potentially great men poured into business, and that fact, combined with the wonderful opportunities, the things waiting to be done, gave the United States a group of men the like of which has not been seen since Roman days.

"They were men who thought in terms of a continent," Mr. Dreiser continued, a light of enthusiasm in his blue-gray eyes, deep set under heavy brows. He is a man who looks every day of his forty-odd years, and who looks more the realistic novelist than the editor of a woman's magazine, a past performance of his. He has a long, heavily built body, a swarthy skin and a rugged, irregularly featured face, across which a wide, wise smile is constantly flashing.

It came now as he added, "I am certain that the mind of the great merchant is conscious of the poetry of his work. He has something that men want and he sends it to them everywhere. From Alaska to Mexico, from Massachusetts to the Philippines, he makes himself known to men, for he supplies what they need, whether it's oil or tobacco or steel rails. The romance of it is tremendous.

3. Dreiser was living on Staten Island with his sister, Mame, during the summer of 1914, and she was probably the hostess. Dreiser's wife, Sara "Jug" White, had red hair and was living in New York City.

Captain of Industry Proof of Great Mind

"The people who talk about 'money-making machines' ought to stop and think of what American business men have accomplished. It takes mind, and a fine quality of mind, to think out and build up the industrial enterprises of this country. When old Commodore Vanderbilt had a dream that there must be a railroad between New York and Chicago, it was a wonderful dream! When Rockefeller decided that he must own all the oil in the country, he showed that he had a remarkable brain."

"But the type of all-conquering business man of which you have written is frankly unscrupulous, is he not?" I questioned.

Mr. Dreiser sat bolt upright and his right hand shot out in a rotary gesture which is evidently a favorite of his.

"Nature is unscrupulous!" he exclaimed. "She takes her own way, regardless of the suffering caused, and the fittest survive. And in each one of us lingers this instinct of nature. In the weak it is mostly drowned under the rain of ethical exhortation poured on them from the beginning. In the strong unmorality triumphs. And to-day America is great not because of, but in spite of, her pieties and her moralities.

"In them, however," he added more calmly, "lies another reason for her particular sort of greatness. Business and morality can so easily be kept in separate compartments.

Religion and Ethics out of Business Life

"The fact that you believe or disbelieve in certain accepted forms of religion is in no way concerned with the fact that you have wire nails to sell me. On the other hand, your religion and ethics are inextricably mixed up with self-expression in art or letters.

"Because of our narrow-minded intolerance, the men who might have given us an American art have followed the line of least resistance and gone into business. There they could do as they pleased and yet conform to all the prejudices of the community. In fact, most of the great business men of the last half-century have been church members and moral husbands.

"But how they did get away with it in their chosen line!" Mr. Dreiser spoke with retrospective appreciation while his fingers absent-mindedly laid in pleats a large square linen handkerchief.

"What were the laws of a State, what was the Constitution of the United States, to old Commodore Vanderbilt? He passed like a comet that comes no one knows whence, but goes whither it will. We said, 'Men are equal.' He and his peers knew that men are unequal. We said, "This is a democracy.' And the great financiers built up an oligarchy under our very noses. What did they care for the verdict of history? They WERE history!"

"You remind me of Bernard Shaw's explanation of Napoleon," I remarked—"that he was great because for himself he suspended the ordinary laws of conventionality and morality, while keeping them in operation for other people."

Great American of Future a Bureaucrat

"Well, but on the whole those men have been a blessing to the rest of us," defended Mr. Dreiser. "They have given opportunities to all of us that we shouldn't have had without them. It's because of Vanderbilt that we can now ride to Chicago in eighteen hours. It's because of Rockefeller that we get oil at the present price. We would pay more if there were a hundred competing companies.

"It's as foolish to attempt to judge these men by the ordinary code as to apply that to a thunder storm or any other natural phenomenon. Each did what he had to do. If he had faltered a stronger man would have ridden over him. Despite all the muckraking, most of us have a secret admiration for these business giants."

"Will the future great men of America be like them?" I asked.

"No," said Mr. Dreiser promptly, rolling his pleated handkerchief into a neat little ball. "We are now clamoring for a perfect democracy. We plan to elect good government officials and then put all the power in their hands. Very well. The ambitious young men will soon see clearly that they can obtain most power as government officials, and they will all study law and get themselves elected to office. Then the greatest Americans will be bureaucrats. The passion for regulation of everything and everybody is already upon us."

For the sake of those who listen to commencement orators I ventured a final question. "What's going to happen to the altruists, the people with a love for humanity? Have they no chance of greatness?"

"They always get the worst of it," the novelist-philosopher vouchsafed, cheerfully. "If you offer to bear the other fellow's burdens he'll let you, every time."

Dreadfully materialistic, of course. But—well, have you found that it works differently?

No More Free Ads for Racy Novels
Successor to Anthony Comstock Has New Plan of Uplift

*

New York Tribune, 20 August 1916, pp. 1, 3.

Dreiser's novel *The "Genius"* was published by John Lane Company in October 1915, and despite mixed reviews, over 7,500 copies were sold by the following summer. Then, on 25 July 1916, John S. Sumner, who succeeded Anthony Comstock as the leader of the New York Society for the Suppression of Vice, threatened the novel's publisher with prosecution if it did not stop selling the novel and remove over ninety passages he found obscene. In this interview, granted shortly after Sumner's action, Dreiser expresses his frustration with Puritan thought in America that will not allow the publication of realistic works similar to those being published in Russia and other European countries.

John S. Sumner, successor to the late Anthony Comstock in the Society for the Suppression of Vice, has worked out a new method of censoring literature which does not conform to the society's standard of propriety. He is trying out the plan on Theodore Dreiser's novel, "The Genius," published last year.

The essential feature of the new method is to get rid of objectionable publications without giving the authors and publishers the benefit of free advertising, such as followed Mr. Comstock's attacks on the picture "September Morn"[1] and the novel "Hagar Revelly."[2]

In the latter case there was a spectacular raid of the publisher's shop, in which the proprietor was arrested, taken to court and tried with great vigor,

---

1. *September Morn* (1912), a painting by the French artist Paul Chabas (1869–1937), depicts a nude young woman bathing in a stream. In 1913 police in Chicago ordered an art store to remove a print of the work from its window, and a few months later, in New York, Anthony Comstock tried but failed to get the original removed from the window of an art gallery. The controversies made the painting famous, and over 7,000,000 reproductions were sold.

2. Because *Hagar Revelly* (see p. 43, n. 4) contains a number of seduction scenes that Anthony Comstock found obscene, he had the publisher, Michael Kennerley, arrested and copies of the book impounded in September 1913. Kennerley fought the ban and was acquitted in a federal court.

but no success. The only results were columns of free press notices and an increase in sales. It is to avoid this that Mr. Sumner has adopted his new method, the aim of which is to persuade the publisher to agree voluntarily to suppress or expurgate the publication objected to.

"I do not care to say exactly what steps are to be taken, because I do not think publicity of these things does any good," Mr. Sumner said yesterday. "We are in consultation with the publishers of 'The Genius,' and if we succeed nothing will be said about the case, as our purpose is only to suppress what we consider evil."

Author Gives His Views

J. Jefferson Jones, jr., literary manager of the John Lane Company, publishers of the "The Genius," also refused to discuss the matter, but Theodore Dreiser, the author, paused yesterday in the composition of his next book in his study at 165 West Tenth Street,[3] to give his side of the triangle. A list of seventy-five pages which the vice society considers "lewd," and seventeen "profane," has been filed with the publishers.

"I don't know what action the John Lane Company will take," Mr. Dreiser said, "but they have been asked to destroy the plates of the book. A list of the pages objected to has been placed with them. But I can say there will be no suppression of the book nor will the plates be destroyed, because, if the publishers should wish to accede to the demand, which I don't believe they will, I will get out an injunction to prevent them.

"The John Lane Company agreed to pay me a royalty of 20 per cent on all copies of the book sold, so that I have a live interest in the continued sale of the book and will, therefore, take action. To me the issue is a contest that goes down to the very roots of thought in this country. Are we going to succumb to Puritan thought, or is it possible for the United States to accept a world standard of thinking?

"In the United States we are always talking about the great American novel. How, I want to ask intelligent men, are we going to produce that?

Asks if This Is Free Country

"Are we going to do it by adopting the world standard of criticism which has permitted the publication of Flaubert, Balzac and others in France; Tolstoy in Russia; Moore, Bennett and others in England; and Strindberg and Ibsen in Norway and Sweden? Or are we going to let Major Funkel-

3. Dreiser lived at this Greenwich Village address from July 1914 through September 1919.

hauser,[4] who obtained the withdrawal of Shakespeare's 'Antony and Cleopatra' in Chicago—are we going to allow him and Mr. Sumner to read and decide how far our minds shall go?

"Is this a free country? Is an artist to be allowed to interpret life as he sees it, or is he to conform to a car conductor standard of literature? There is something just absolutely sickly about the whole mental attitude of this country. These people haven't the brains to read 'The Genius' and understand what metaphysical import is back of it.

"They don't see anything as a whole or in its relationship to life as a whole. They see that on page, say 78, there is a reference to a stocking or a leg, and that is 'lewd' to them. They just paw over the pages, and it means nothing to them that the incident may end in the most terrible tragedy in the world."

Mr. Dreiser[5] said he had a plan afoot to publish all his works in foreign languages and let "America be damned." If a work comes from Russia, he said it is accepted.

"If my name were Dreisershefsky and I said I came from Warsaw I'd have no trouble," he said. "But I come from Indiana, so good night!"

4. A major in the Illinois National Guard, Metellius C. Funkhouser (not Funkelhauser) was appointed second deputy police commissioner by Chicago mayor Carter Harrison and put in charge of a morals squad assigned the task of eliminating prostitution and other vice in Chicago's notorious South Side levee district. While visiting Chicago in the spring of 1914, Dreiser spoke out against Funkhouser's censorship powers, noting that "a big city is not a teacup to be seasoned by old maids" ("City Censored to Death, Says Author," *Chicago Daily Journal*, 18 March 1914, p. 1).

5. The printed text reads "Mr. Sumner," but the statement is clearly Dreiser's.

Theodore Dreiser Deplores Suppression of His Novel, "The Genius," by Vice Agent
In a Talk with a Sunday Eagle Writer the Author Explains His View of Life and Draws the Line between Truth and Pornography

By Berenice C. Skidelsky

*

Brooklyn Daily Eagle, 26 May 1918, [sect. 3], pp. 2, 5.

The suppression of *The "Genius"* had been going on for almost two years without resolution at the time of this interview. In it, the journalist Berenice Skidelsky summarizes events during those months and provides Dreiser with the opportunity to speak on the importance of intellectual freedom and the immorality of best sellers.

In October of 1916[1] the John Lane Company presented to the public "The Genius," by Theodore Dreiser, generally accredited by critics one of the greatest of American novelists. The public, or the reading part of it, primed for appreciation by conversancy with earlier works, gave the book a ready hearing, and, though here and there a dissenting voice was heard, the consensus among critics whose names have come to have weight in their particular field—names like James Huneker and Henry Mencken and Lawrence Gilman—was that "The Genius" embodied many of the qualities which constitute the essence of "greatness" as the term is applied to works of literature.[2]

For almost a year the sale flourished. In July of 1917,[3] however, John Sumner of the New York Society for the Suppression of Vice, walked into the offices of the publishers and demanded that the book be withdrawn from

---

1. The novel was published in October 1915, not 1916.

2. Huneker (1860–1921) and Gilman (1878–1939) were music, dramatic, and literary critics for, respectively, the *New York Sun* and the *North American Review*.

3. Sumner made his demands in July 1916, not 1917.

distribution. He had received letters, he said, protesting against its "salacious and profane passages"; he had read the book, he added, and he felt that the protests were justifiable. He did not deny that the work was powerful, and that personally he had liked it. But, he declared, falling into the hands of children or of persons of perverted impulses, it would be instrumental in doing much harm; the children and the persons of perverted impulses must at all hazards be shielded, and therefore the book must be rendered inaccessible.

The publishers, knowing that their visitor was legally empowered to make his demand, wasted little time in futile expostulation. The book was withdrawn; but simultaneously a firm of noted lawyers was retained to handle the matter of legal protest against the ruling of the vice suppressors. This firm associated itself with another firm, of which Joseph S. Auerbach, to whose lot fell the pleading of the case, is a member.[4]

Analyzed from Moral and Literary Viewpoints

On May 1 of this year Mr. Auerbach appeared before the Appellate Division of the New York Supreme Court with a forceful and scholarly argument (which will be presented in its entirety in the June issue of the North American Review),[5] wherein he analyzed the book from moral and literary standpoints, giving a careful and comprehensive outline of the story, and quoting at great length excerpts substantiating his stand that "The Genius" is no mere aggregation of "pornographic and blasphemous" sentiments, as had been alleged, but a work justified by its absolute fidelity to life.

"The whole preposterous campaign that has been carried on against such books as 'The Genius,'" he declared, "finds its excuse in the shallow notion that the adult must be fed on the same kind of mental food as the child. Inasmuch as indolent parents betray a trust toward their children by not standing sentinel over their course of reading and intellectual and moral training until they reach mature age, a book intended for thoughtful persons must be suppressed by some vice society, lest the susceptible young be contaminated by contact with it! In disregard of the accepted rule of law and common sense, the application of a general principle is to be measured by and subordinated to the possibility of an individual hardship!"

The five judges who listened to the appeal are now deliberating upon the merits of the case. Should their decision be unfavorable to Mr. Dreiser's

4. Skidelsky appears to be confused here. Auerbach was a member of the law firm of John B. Stanchfield and Louis Levy, which was the "firm of noted lawyers" that agreed to argue Dreiser's case a few months after The "Genius" was withdrawn.

5. A lengthy extract appeared in the June 1918 issue, not the entire argument.

side, it will be carried to a higher court.[6] But the author and his friends, personal and literary, are hoping that such procedure will not be necessary.

The story about which the dispute centers is, briefly, that of a young man, Eugene Witla by name, from a small Middle Western town, who chafes under the restricted confines of his environment and who goes to Chicago to give freer play to his not clearly formulated but nonetheless imperative ambitions. His experiences are varied in his attempts to gain a livelihood, and they are interspersed with amorous ones, among which one eventually culminates in a reluctant marriage. His similar experiences in New York, Philadelphia, Paris and smaller cities to which destiny leads him are depicted with all the power of the keen psychologist. The lure of beautiful women is one of the most potent influences in Witla's life. Like Thomas Hardy's hero in "The Well-Beloved,"[7] he is forever discovering in some woman the elusive qualities of that peculiar charm his nature craves, forever being disillusioned. The need of women in his life is neither physical nor spiritual, but both; and the double and sometimes more or less conflicting urge is admirably handled by Mr. Dreiser. There is much of the idealistic and much of the intellectual in Witla's composition, and these not infrequently give battle to the undeniably very strong sensual element. He longs to evolve some firm foundation upon which to base a plan of conduct; but though his search for a modus vivendi is an honest one, his only reward is to be plunged more and more deeply into skepticism. "He was going round in a ring," the author says, "asking questions of this proposition and that: Are you true? And are you true? And are you true? And all the while he was apparently not getting anywhere."

Inter-Action of Temperament

Perhaps in all literature there is no more careful and subtle study of that unformulable thing called inter-action of temperament than Dreiser's treatment of the relation between Witla and Angela, his wife. For this alone, the lover of good literature would give place to "The Genius" on his bookshelves.

The close of the book sees Witla, a widower with a baby daughter, disciplined by his experiences, largely master of himself, yet more than ever conscious of the eternal mystery of life, the impenetrability of ultimate truth.

6. In July 1918 the New York Appellate Court dismissed the case, ruling that, since there had been no prosecution, they could not render an opinion. As a result of this decision and Lane's refusal to test Sumner's threat, no copies of The "Genius" were sold until 1923, when Boni and Liveright published the novel after buying the rights from Lane.

7. The hero of Hardy's novel is the sculptor Jocelyn Pierston, who falls in love with three generations of women from the same family while searching for the perfect form in woman. It was first published serially in 1892.

"Overhead were the stars," writes Dreiser in closing, "Orion's majestic belt and those mystic constellations that make Dippers, Bears and that remote cloudy formation known as the Milky Way.

"'Where in all this in substance,' he thought, rubbing his hand through his hair, 'is Angela? Where in substance will be that which is me? What a sweet welter life is—how rich, how tender, how grim, how like a colorful symphony!'

"Great art dreams welled up into his soul as he viewed the sparkling depths of space.

"'The sound of the wind—how fine it is tonight,' he thought.

"Then he went quietly in and closed the door."

The entire philosophy of Theodore Dreiser is intimated in one passage of "The Genius," and some sympathetic understanding is necessary, even though there is not acquiescence, in order to grasp what Dreiser stands for and what has gained for him a place in the opinion of discriminating critics among notable writers of this period.

"He was always thinking in his private conscience," Dreiser writes of Witla, "that life was somehow bigger and subtler and darker than any given theory or order of living. It might well be worth while for a man or woman to be honest and moral within a given condition or quality of society, but it did not matter at all in the ultimate substance and composition of the universe. Any form or order of society which hoped to endure must have individuals . . . who would conform to the highest standards and theories of that society, and when found they were admirable; but they meant nothing in the shifting subtle forces of Nature. They were just accidental harmonies blossoming out of something which meant everything here to this order, nothing to the universe at large."

It is this constant sense of the cosmic and the eternal, overshadowing and modifying interpretation of the earthly and the immediate, that colors all his work.

What Dreiser Says of It

Commenting upon this point in a recent interview with the writer, Mr. Dreiser said:

"As I see it, life—the technique or method of living—is not a fact but an agreement. And in that can be traced the roots of most protests such as this which has been raised against 'The Genius,' and of which there are innumerable counterparts in literary history. There seems to be an uneasy, smouldering fear lest the points of the agreement be nullified; a fear that what has been achieved may be destroyed.

"And what would seem to corroborate that analysis of motive is the fact that only when a so-called 'objectionable' work is sincere and above vulgarity in its intention do people get excited about it. Some of the plays presented on the stage today, the moving pictures, the musical comedies, though seemingly in need of censorship, evade it. I confess I am puzzled about some of the plays that get on—I don't understand the psychology back of their acceptation by the Vice Commission in view of the general stand that it takes. Perhaps it is their brevity—the fact that they are quickly over, and that the points perhaps condemnable (from the censors' standpoint) are passed almost before there is time fully to grasp them. It may be that; as I said before, I am at a loss to get at their actual motives.

"The fate of the novel, though, seems to bring it more within the grasp and the investigation of censors and vice commissions than any other form of art. A novel is a full spiritual transcript of characters; because of its logic and its philosophy, there is no escape from its true significance. It relentlessly shows all facets of life, being the most leisurely of all literary forms."

The Case of "Sister Carrie"

Mr. Dreiser is almost a fatalist in his belief that a special destiny—his, it happens incidentally—lies in wait to place obstacles in the way of certain creative artists, as far as having their work accepted is concerned. He told of the experience of his first novel, "Sister Carrie," which in 1900, upon the recommendation of Frank Norris and other literary notables, was accepted by the Doubleday, Page Company, and the contract duly drawn up and signed.

"Then," said Mr. Dreiser, "the publishers suddenly experienced a change of heart, and notified me that they would not publish the book. Of course, had I known as much then as I do now, or as I did even five years later, about the publishing world, I would simply have acquiesced to the altered decision and looked for publishers elsewhere. I have no doubt I would have found them. But instead, acting on some advice given me, I insisted, as I was within my rights in doing, upon a fulfillment of the contract. The company, then, had no alternative other than to abide by it; they did it in the letter, by publishing something less than 2,000 volumes, but they failed in the spirit, by storing the books in their basement, and making no effort whatever to bring them before the public.

"About seven years later, as part of the firm of B. W. Dodge & Co., I purchased the plates and the already printed copies, and brought out the book."

"Did the reception given it by the public back up the conscience qualms of the original publishers?" he was asked.

"No," said Mr. Dreiser. "The book found an audience and called forth no protests."

Mr. Dreiser feels no resentment against those who do not like his books; it is the most natural thing in the world, he declared, that persons should be divided in their opinions about them, for he sees in that division an expression of the inevitable friction of ideas inseparable from man's relation with man, and unquestionably an important element in furthering human growth. He is barricaded by an impregnable self-realization against hurt from lack of general approval.

"I have my following," he said, "and that is all anyone could expect. More than that, it is all anyone could possibly want. It would be absurd to desire unanimous approval. It isn't necessary. But what I do feel is that—"

Mr. Dreiser paused, to formulate the point clearly.

"That your following ought to be allowed to 'follow' unmolested?" interposed his visitor.

"Well—yes, something like that," responded Mr. Dreiser. "If there are mature minds who want what I have to give, I object to its being forbidden them because a handful of persons, whose competence to judge might well be questioned, feel that it isn't good mental food for children!

Called Poe "a Failure"

"I'm not thinking only of myself in this matter. A few weeks ago I happened to see an article, prominently featured in a prominent newspaper, which was a rabid attack upon Edgar Allan Poe and which summed him up as a failure. Poe, perhaps the most precious heritage of the land: A failure!"

Mr. Dreiser's voice shook with honest indignation.

"Poe, with his vision, with his ingenuity, with his intuition, with his wonderful gift of rhythm, was proclaimed a failure by some obscure individual quite incapable of understanding Poe!

"Frankly, I think it high time that persons who know and care about good literature should take some firm stand in the direction of a censorship of critics, and drive off the boards the petty yelpers to whom the Poes of literature are failures. College professors, with academic bias and in a great many cases little knowledge of the relation between literature and life, discourse learnedly on literary values, shaping and incidentally vitiating the taste of the average reader, with whom, by reason of their positions, their dictums carry weight."

According to Mr. Dreiser, the end devoutly to be wished is to be done with illusion, to substitute for it the strength and virility which will face the facts of life in stark fearlessness, to strike off the paralyzing fetters of what Hardy has called "timid obsequiousness to tradition."[8]

"If we don't," was Mr. Dreiser's warning, "if something doesn't happen to encompass the intellectual emancipation of the race and to break the hide-bound tradition which is its enemy, man will go to seed. Our universities today, which ought to be the center of the move toward freedom, are in reality grossly misnamed, for they have degenerated largely into technical institutions. If a man opens his mouth to express an opinion which doesn't conform to certain set notions, he is thrown out. In Heaven's name, then, where does the 'university' phase of the institution come in? If they want to pursue that kind of policy, let them—but then let them at least call things by their right names, and not use a term supposed to be all-inclusive as a title for something in which the free pursuit of truth has no place!"

The inculcation of dogma, religious or otherwise, in the minds of the young is another thing which Mr. Dreiser regards as a menace. "It is dreadful to think of shackles being forged," he said, with profound conviction, "which are going to hold the mind that ought to fling its doors wide open to light and truth in a vise-like grip of timidity utterly precluding initiative. There's little enough inherent moral courage, as it is!"

Why Gorki Was Shunned

In relation to this, Mr. Dreiser spoke of the visit paid to this country by Maxim Gorki a number of years ago, and of the ill reception accorded him by men of literary prominence in this country because of their disapproval of his private life—"men like Mark Twain," said Mr. Dreiser, "who in his 'What Is Man?' showed much greater vision than he dared give practical expression to, when it came right down to concrete situation, such as extending the hand of welcome to Gorki.[9]

"And, indeed, that incident of Gorki's reception was much more far-reaching in its effects than most persons have any idea. Gorki, who heads one of the most powerful papers in Russia, and who does much to mold public thought, is using his power to spread his own distrust of America."

"Don't you think there is a certain amount of economic determinism in most persons' fear of being guilty of non-conformity?" Mr. Dreiser was asked.

8. The source of Hardy's statement has not been identified.

9. Twain was the chairman of a committee of literary notables who had planned a dinner to honor Gorki (1868–1936) upon his arrival in New York in April 1906 to raise money for the Russian Revolution. The dinner was canceled when newspapers revealed that Gorki had traveled to the United States with a Russian actress with whom he was living instead of his wife. Twain's essay "What Is Man?" was published posthumously in 1917.

"Unquestionably," he said. "But if they care more for their security than they do for the vindication of their principles, it is regrettable. Of course, if that constitutes their 'pursuit of happiness'—man's alleged right to it is a good bit of a joke as the world stands today!—I suppose they have a right to choose their method. Personally, though I don't know whether you'd call it 'happiness' or not, what I want is the freedom to look life squarely in the face, and to understand its intricacies, and to reflect what I see. That is my 'pursuit of happiness,' and that is what the vice commission says I have no right to do."

The True Vision of Life

When it comes to immorality in books, said Mr. Dreiser, the so-called "best seller" type of fiction is vicious in the extreme.

"These books are nothing short of disastrous in their effects," he said, "for they are calculated to bring about mental incompetence by giving an utterly distorted vision of life, and thus unfitting their readers to meet and to understand the manifold phases of reality."

The suppression of "The Genius" has roused much protest among men and women of literary standing. H. G. Wells, Arnold Bennett, W. L. George, William J. Locke and Hugh Walpole are among the English writers who cabled their expression of disapproval, and the American list includes many familiar names.[10]

The experience of Mr. Dreiser's book has been that of many works which today are counted among the classics of literature. Prominent among them is "Madame Bovary," by Gustave Flaubert—a title which appears in practically every list of "world's greatest novels," and which, had the censors of his day had their will, would not have appeared in lists of best or worst! Flaubert, writing in 1880 to Guy de Maupassant concerning a projected suppression of some work of the latter,[11] says: "Are we to be subject to the whim of every court in French territory, including the colonies? To whom

10. Largely through the efforts of H. L. Mencken, 458 names appeared on a protest that the Authors' League of America issued against the suppression. The cable from the English writers, sent on 13 September 1916 to the John Lane Company, read: "We regard The Genius as a work of high literary merit and sympathize with the Authors League of America in their protest against its suppression." It was signed by Wells (see p. 17, n. 5), Bennett (see p. 14, n. 1), Locke (see p. 12, n. 2), and the novelists Hugh Walpole (1884–1941) and E. Temple Thurston (1879–1933). The name of the novelist W. L. George (1882–1926) was added later.

11. The letter was sent from Flaubert (1821–80) to de Maupassant (1850–93) on 19 February 1880 in response to a threat of prosecution de Maupassant had faced over the publication of a poem that was considered an outrage to morality.

are we responsible, pray? How ought we to write? . . . I can understand why a man should be prosecuted for writing a political article; although I defy all the courts to show what good such a prosecution has ever done. But to prosecute a man for a piece of literature, or a poem—seems to me absurd. . . . Utter, then, to your accuser your denunciations against all the Greek and Roman classics, so that he may be persuaded to suppress these also, from Aristophanes to gentle Horace and tender Virgil; those also of foreign lands, Shakespeare, Goethe, Byron, Cervantes, and in our own country, Rabelais, the fount of French literature. You may add Chateaubriand and Moliere and the great Corneille, and Father La Fontaine and Voltaire and Rousseau. Add to these the fairy tales of Perrault.

"A man mounts toward the height of Olympus, his face is lit with a celestial ray, his heart is full of hope, of aspiration toward the beautiful, the divine; he is already half transported to the sky; but a wretched jailer's hand drags him back into the gutter. If you hold converse with the muse they take you for a debaucher of girls. . . . And they will make you stand, my friend, at the bar with thieves, and you will hear a fellow read your verses, stumbling over the feet, and re-read them, laying stress on some words, to which he will give a double meaning, and some of them he will repeat over several times, like Citizen Pinard with his 'Note his mention of her ankle. Gentlemen, think of it, her ankle!'

"But surely all this is impossible. You will not be prosecuted; you will not be condemned. There has been some blunder, some misunderstanding. The Chancellor will interfere. The glorious days of the Restoration have not yet returned.

"Yet who knows? Earth has its boundaries, but human stupidity is limitless."

Dreiser Favors Federal Control; Hits Financiers

*

The Huntington Press (Ind.), 18 June 1919, p. 1.

Dreiser was in Indiana visiting May Calvert Baker (1864–1941), his seventh-grade teacher, whom he had praised in *A Hoosier Holiday* for her kindness to him when he was growing up in Warsaw.

Theodore Dreiser, distinguished Hoosier author, who is visiting in this city, a man with liberal ideas and a real American, holds chief interest in the welfare of the mass of American people. Democratic in his ideas and an advocate of a broader democracy for the peoples of the world, his idea is that the working man should be more closely related to, and more deeply interested in, the government under which he lives.

When questioned as to his views on the League of Nations he said that he was in favor of a league of nations but thought that Germany should be admitted to the league, saying that it could not be a league of nations without Germany. He believed that the people of Germany should have a chance to work out their own plan of government just as the people of the United States did in 1776.

Favors Government Control

Mr. Dreiser is in favor of government control of public utilities and does not think that the government was given a fair trial in its operation of railroads and other utilities during the war.[1] It is his opinion that the inefficiency in the operation of these utilities is a result of a propaganda carried on by those to whose interest it would be for government control to fail. Mr. Dreiser cited as an illustration of his point the telephone service of New York City, which has been under the control of Postmaster General Burleson.[2]

1. During World War I the federal government created several agencies, including a railroad administration, to control segments of the economy essential to the war effort.
2. Albert Sidney Burleson (1863–1937) was the postmaster general under the Wilson administration and chairman of the United States Telegraph and Telephone Administration when these utilities were under federal control, from July 1918 to August 1919.

"You could sit at the telephone for five minutes before one of the central girls would condescend to ask what number you were calling," said Mr. Dreiser, "and yet people are told and believe it, that service is poor because the telephones are under government control."

"I cannot understand," said Mr. Dreiser, "why it is that the American people without thinking for themselves, will believe that government control of railroads is a failure merely because they have read that statement in some paper controlled by the moneyed interests of the nation."

Land of Promise is Myth

In speaking of America as "the land of promise where any person may become a Rockefeller or the head of the nation" Mr. Dreiser said: "That idea is a myth; it is an illusion kept alive by Wall Street in order to deceive the working class of people into believing that they are living under an ideal government that is the best in the world. Why the rank and file of the people of this nation have no chance under the sun of ever becoming a Rockefeller, unless one of them is a heaven-born genius or a brilliant crook. It isn't even a gamble because the cards are stacked from the top and the ordinary man has no chance at all and will have no chance until he begins to think for himself and calls for a new deal.

"The rank and file of the people of this nation have no more chance for worldly advancement than the people of any other nation. The ordinary man is forced to think and act as the moneyed class of the nation see fit. If he attempts to do some original thinking and begins to air his opinions he is thrown in jail for a Bolshevik, and as a result we have the public allowing the corporation newspapers to do their thinking for them. In order for the ordinary man to climb in life he must agree with the powers that be or he is ostracized in the business world."

He cited cases from his own personal observation where this condition was true and stated that he did not think that there would be any great social uplift for the masses until this condition was remedied in this country. He said that the public was taught to believe that the government was some noble, high-minded institution above reproach but that in reality it was as susceptible to flaws as the government of any other nation.

Mr. Dreiser spoke in glowing terms of Indiana as to climate and scenery and stated that he would like to spend much of his time here if possible.

Noted Novelist Visits in City
Theodore Dreiser, Native of Indiana,
Seeks Rest in "Old Stamping Ground"
Working on a New Book
Criticized for Realism and Challenge to "Puritanical
Sentiment," but Works Gain in Popularity

*

Indianapolis Star, 27 June 1919, p. 5.

Dreiser's second stop during his trip to Indiana was in Indianapolis, where he visited John M. Maxwell (1866–1929), a journalist with the *Indianapolis Star* who had been Dreiser's mentor when Dreiser began his newspaper career in Chicago. It was probably Maxwell who arranged for this interview, which, from the subjects covered, seems intended to make Dreiser's name and works better known in his native state.

Theodore Dreiser of New York, novelist, essayist and playwright, is in Indianapolis for a week as the guest of Addison Parry at Golden Hill.[1] Mr. Dreiser is the author of "The Titan," "The Financier," "The Genius," "Sister Carrie," "Jennie Gerhardt," "A Traveller at Forty," "A Hoosier Holiday," "Plays Natural and Supernatural" and other books. He is a Hoosier, having been born in Terre Haute in 1871, attending school at Warsaw and for a short time at Indiana University. He is a brother of Paul Dresser, the Indiana song writer whose ballad "On the Banks of the Wabash" is the song of the state. The name was originally "Dreiser" and Mr. Dreiser sticks to the first spelling, his brother making slight modification of it for song writing purposes.

"I am trying to get a couple of months rest," said Mr. Dreiser, "and so I came to my ancient stamping grounds to look up old-time friends and to refresh my sight with scenes of my early days. Indiana is my state. I need

---

1. Parry was John M. Maxwell's nephew. Dreiser had accepted an invitation to stay with the Parry family during his visit.

rest for I was knocked down by an automobile in New York a few weeks ago,[2] sustaining a fracture of two ribs. I want to try to forget how severely it hurt every time I sneezed. What a memory.

Finds Plenty to Do

"Yes, I find plenty to do. Just as fast as I finish one book another vista of work opens up and the trouble is not [to] write, but to find time to write about the things that one would like to write about. Life is so full of effects of evershifting color that he who seeks to 'hold the mirror up to nature,' so to speak, has an illimitable field to select from. Just [at] present I am at work on a new book of essays, 'The King Is Naked,'[3] based on the old story of the King who insisted that should he go down the street naked and at the same time declare that he was fully clothed, the fawning sycophantic character of the masses worshiping at the throne of alleged greatness would be such that the general populace would cheerily chortle, 'Yes, the King is clothed!' But as will be remembered, a small boy happened to come along, his bright good soul unabashed and unsoiled by the influences and environmental conditions that tend to make us all more or less intellectual cowards, and this brave little lad saw things as they are and he pointed the finger of shame at the King. So I am trying to be that 'brave little lad' in my coming book of essays. I want to chip off one little tiny piece, if I can, of the leaden weight that keeps men's eyes closed to the truth. And yet I shall only be roundly scored for my pains. People do not like to have their myths destroyed. A smiling, agreeable lie is so much nicer to travel with than rough, rugged truth. But it is the truth that makes men free. A lie won't do when a human being is brought to the operating table. The doctor must know the truth and the patient learns it at the expense of extreme suffering."

Criticised for Realism

Mr. Dreiser's books have been criticised for their realism and for the point blank manner in which the moral set out by some of them challenges so-called "Puritanical sentiment." Numerous efforts have been made by vice-societies and other agencies to suppress his books, but so far the activities of the objectors have not been successful. His fame continues to grow and

2. Dreiser had been hit by a car on 11 May while crossing Columbus Circle in New York City.

3. "The King Is Naked" was a working title Dreiser had given to a collection of essays and reading plays on which he was working at the time of the interview. The collection was published under the title *Hey Rub-A-Dub-Dub* in January 1920.

it was only recently that "Mercure de France," the leading critical publication of Paris, said of him and his works, "Dreiser is the only living American writer that continental Europe will consider."

"I have no objection to criticism," said Mr. Dreiser. "Proper criticism is valuable. It is our opponents who strengthen us, not the flattering words of our friends who like us too well to point out our shortcomings. So they can criticise all they want to in my case, just so my books continue to sell. I have my audience in this old world of ours. While it is necessary for us all to keep the dollar in mind, primarily, as with most other writers, I do not write for money. I write to achieve some kind of a result. Charles Read with his books reformed the insane asylum and prison methods in England[4] and Charles Dickens with his "Oliver Twist" laughed the old-time pauper asylum with its cruelties off the stage of England. A book should not be written unless it has some such mission. If one does not like my grammar, please let him like the thought sought to be set forth by the bad grammar, if it is insisted that I indulge in such. But for grammar I do not know of a worse grammarian than Shakespeare, who deliberately violated all accepted canons of style and rhetoric and violated them so desperately that none, except perhaps myself, has had the temerity to imitate him." At which last remark Mr. Dreiser laughed heartily.

Paid for Not Telling Truth

"For the last year," he continued, "I have been liberally paid for not telling the 'truth.' I wrote a play called the "The Hand of the Potter," and twice it has been accepted for stage publication and twice declined, the forfeits amounting to $2,000.[5] Yet there is not a single thing wrong with the play except that it tells the 'truth.' Its dramatic power has never been challenged but, alas, it deals with a story of mental and physical delinquency. The supreme object of the play is to impress the necessity of watching and removing human defectives of dangerous tendencies instead of letting them wander around until by some sadistic act, anguish and life-long unhappiness is

4. Reade (not Read) (1814–84) was a British dramatist and novelist. Two of his "reforming" novels were *Christie Johnston* (1853) and *Hard Cash* (1863), which sought the reform of prisons and lunatic asylums, respectively.

5. *The Hand of the Potter* is a four-act play about a young man who sexually molests and then kills a young girl. Prior to its publication in September 1919, Dreiser had received payment for two options for its production, but in neither case were the options forfeited because of censorship. In the first instance the producer Arthur Hopkins (1878–1950) gave up his option when he was unable to satisfy Dreiser by setting a date for a Broadway production; in the second, Charles Coburn (1877–1961) sold his option back to Dreiser when a play his company had launched in 1918 became the smash hit of the Broadway season.

brought to the innocent. I do not preach in the play; the sermon is taught by the play itself. Managers are drawn to the manuscript as the moth flutters around the light. They want to but do not dare. Puritanical sentiment again. Shall we never shake off the shackles of false reasoning? Will man never look himself squarely in the face and recognize himself to be nothing more than an evolutionary product? Until he does recognize that truth, his every act may be directed toward disaster, for unless the premises on which reasoning is based is right, all deductions that flow from the premises will be just as false as the premise itself. Our first great duty then is to learn to think. I am trying to think myself and trying to teach others how to think."

Mr. Dreiser will remain in Indianapolis for about a week and then continue his trip West. He plans to be absent from New York until after hot weather.

America and Her Jews

By Berenice C. Skidelsky

Jewish Advocate (Boston), 5 February 1920, p. 7.

The journalist Berenice Skidelsky probably sought out Dreiser's observations on American Jews in this interview because the central characters in his controversial play *The Hand of the Potter* were members of
a Jewish family living in the Upper East Side of New York City. Since
the play was published in September 1919, and Dreiser left New York
on 8 October to live in California, the interview must have been held
in the late summer or early fall of that year. It was reprinted as "'As Yeast
Added to the Nation's Making': Theodore Dreiser, North American
Novelist, Gives His Impression of the Jews," in *New York Jewish News*,
12 February 1920.

Theodore Dreiser, foremost novelist of America—or one of the foremost,
if one distrusts superlatives—keen observer of men, close student of human
values, and sensitive interpreter of human relations, declares that the Jews
of America are as yeast added to the other ingredients in the nation's making. He sees in them an indispensable leaven for the satisfactory rising and
formation of the mass. It is a peculiar radical buoyancy that he recognizes
which points for him the analogy.

In the Semitic nature, as Mr. Dreiser sees it, there are qualities of warmth,
of sweetness, of almost childlike enthusiasm, that radiate love of life, and
stimulate zest for living in all contiguous peoples.

"The Jews are ecstatically in love with life," he said in a recent interview.
"Their interest in all things is intense. They are essentially artists,
transfiguring the commonplace with a glow of hope, and seeing in the hum-
drum everyday the stepping-stone to a larger and more vigorous life toward
which they are always reaching out."

It is because the Jew is incessantly, irrepressibly dynamic, said Mr. Dreiser, that no amount of anti-Semitic prejudice nor ostracism can nullify his
influence.

"Look at the sidewalks on the East Side, at any minute of the day," he said. "They fairly teem with life. Here one finds none of that quiescence observable in other sections of the city. Strongly magnetized by life, the people of the East Side are forever out of doors, forever seeking human contacts, the more completely to sense the fullness of life. One visualizes the Jew as darting around like a waterbug, in a hundred eager directions, fearful lest something elude. The rich, exuberant nature seeks nothing less than the whole of life."

Even in business, Mr. Dreiser declared, the race shows a rare quality of imagination.

"The Jew sees possibilities in a nickel," he said, "which wouldn't be apparent to others in a hundred dollars. He has a natural reluctance to be employed; with ever so little capital, plus much imagination, he embarks perilously but courageously upon a business of his own. It may be on an absurdly small scale—no more than a pushcart or a peddler's basket, perhaps—but it fires his imagination with visions of unhampered opportunity such as no regular pay envelope could offer."

That attitude of mind, or rather of spirit, said Mr. Dreiser, working in a community, stirs it to a fuller courage and a freer endeavor. It makes for commercial progress, and at the same time it introduces poetry into business.

"The place of the Jew in art," he went on, "is too well established to need discussion. They are patrons—creators—interpreters. Jewish artists in the field of painting, music, the stage, are not only numerous, but are richly represented in the highest places.

"All of this direction and achievement is expression of a warm, perfectly legitimate sensuality, inherent in the Jewish temperament, and pregnant with color and vitality. It is an Oriental quality which, infused into the comparative rigidity of the Western peoples, lends them a greater flexibility and thereby offers promise of a richer life.

"It will be an advantageous day for the non-Jewish world when realization of that fact sweeps away the present obstacle of ostracism and persecution."

Cruel Words, Theodore Dreiser!
Famous Novelist Comes Out of Hiding;
Pours Sarcasm on Los Angeles, Our Artistic
Pretensions and Our Far-Famed Climate

BY EDITH MILLICENT RYAN

✳

Los Angeles Sunday Times, 17 September 1922, pt. 3, pp. 13, 15.

Dreiser met Helen Richardson in the middle of September 1919, and less than a month later he moved with her to Los Angeles, where he resided until October 1922. While living there he attempted to keep his address a secret by providing only a post office box number to his friends and others, which explains Ryan's extensive comments on the way she located him.

Theodore Dreiser did not say "Well, I'll be—," but he looked it. The writer, who is the most free-handed of American authors in dispensing with shock absorbers in his formidable list of novels, short stories, plays, essays, philosophical dissertations, books of travel, poems and what not, received a large-sized healthy shock the other day when he opened his door and had to admit to the caller that he was Dreiser.

"But how the—?" he began. "Why, this is the first time my bell has been rung since I came out here. Now tell me how did you find out where I was?"

His visitor agreed to tell him all about it if he would promise in exchange to be equally communicative about certain things she wished to know. A bargain was struck and then Dreiser said:

"Don't tell a soul. Not the name of the street, nor the town. I don't want anybody to know. I don't want to see anybody. Not a body. Was trekked to death in New York and don't want another procession of ants out here. I'm going back, just as soon as I can rent this house. Nobody knows who I am in this little place, not even the people next door. And I've been here a year.[1]

---

1. Dreiser and Helen had bought a home at 625 N. Columbus in Glendale.

"Cruel Words,
Theodore Dreiser!"
Los Angeles Sunday Times,
17 September 1922, Part 3,
pp. 13, 15.

Theodore Dreiser—An Impression by Flora Smith

The Esthetic Hollywood Mr. Dreiser Expected

Hollywood as Mr. Dreiser Says He Found It

Can't Write and Do Society

"I'm not a hermit. Nor mysterious. But you know there are a lot of people that regard writing as a sort of picnic. They flock. Want to know how you do it. Want to see you at it. It all takes up time. It leads nowhere. Let people get wind of you and it means invitations. Society is a business in itself. I can't manage it and do my work, too. Why, under the sun, then, is there anything strange about keeping it dark where you are!"

Mr. Dreiser, who has a box at the post office, has accordingly kept his address as secret as the Sphinx her ancestry. Apparently when those occasions in business have arisen where he must part with his signature in the town where he is residing, the process is a hurried affair amiably aiding his predilections for incognito. Unknown at a garage where we paused, a corner grocery store, two real estate offices, a bank, at the next place inquiry dispatched a girl who returned with a slip of paper on which was written all of Theodore Dreiser's name except the final r, street number, following. It was on the chance that Dreise and Drieser were the same that brought us to the author's delightful cottage. This much we'll say. It has the best manicured lawn in the neighborhood. The life of a weed is short, for Dreiser cuts the grass about once a day with a trowel in his pocket. This implement was kept busy while he talked of cabbages and kings, for while the conversation opened in the living-room of the cottage, prospective renters soon called to look at the house and Dreiser said "we'll duck" and led the way through the kitchen into the back yard.

Athens of the West! Huh!

Mr. Dreiser does not claim to have made a thorough diagnosis of the case of Los Angeles and Hollywood. Evidently a guileless curiosity brought him thither. Waldo Frank[2] had told him of an artist colony at Santa Fe. Some one else at Greenwich Village warbled about all the artists that were leaving for Los Angeles, the "Athens of the West."

"Whoever imagines that Los Angeles is the Athens of the West must have a good bootlegger," said Dreiser who added some expressive expletives that might not pass the printer. "There is no literary kick about Los Angeles. It would not be well to say it—Los Angeles takes everything to heart in the nature of comparison—but San Francisco is far ahead of it artistically. There one is stimulated, but here. . . ."

---

2. The novelist Frank (1889–1967) was an acquaintance of Dreiser's in Greenwich Village and an editor of *Seven Arts*, which published Dreiser's critique of American culture entitled "Life, Art and America" in February 1917.

"Well, you know everyone comes out to Los Angeles for only one thing—a good time. It's beautiful all right—is there anything lovelier than this little town?—the climate is fine, why it's a Riviera and some day will have a population of 2,000,000, perhaps 4,000,000, and then it will be a larger Riviera. And that's all. There's a lot of hoi polloi—scads of them.

Yearns for Struggle

"It's too soft out here. Perhaps the climate is the reason. I don't know. But most people you meet are only looking for three meals a day and a dance somewhere at night. That satisfies them entirely. I want to be back where there is struggle. Those are the people that interest me. I live on the edge of Greenwich Village—not that I mingle in their life. I don't. I have my friends, of course. But I prefer to wander around the west side of New York, where the toilers are. I like to mingle with them. That's health. I don't care about idlers, or tourists, or the hum drum, or artistic pretenders that flock out here, or the rich who tell you—and that is all they have to tell—how they did it. They would have interested me when they were struggling.

"There is no art in Los Angeles and Hollywood. And there never will be. You hear about the so-called great artists who are out here. But who are they? Who among the writers? The screen has attracted certain writers who want the money it offers, but not those men with ideals of art and spiritual convictions, who are not coming out here. And won't come. They would not want a mess made of their work. I myself would not want my 'Jennie Gerhardt' botched up on the screen.[3] I would have my ideas as to how it should be done. But when an author mixes in, he gets laughed at and is only ridiculous. What does he accomplish?"

Mr. Dreiser, back in Greenwich Village, heard the world of motion-pictures spoken of as one of enchantment. So naturally in this year he has been out here, he visited a number of studios and saw the whole works.

"The only thing you can say of the motion-picture business is that it is a great enterprise," he declared. "It really is that. But an art? No. It is simply a commercial organization. There is no artistic atmosphere in picture-making. It's just a lot of people tramping around.

Rough on Movies

"When the thing is finished, to whom should the credit go? In the first place the producer hunts around for some vehicle, fishes up some book or a script

3. Dreiser later changed his mind: in 1932 he sold Paramount the film rights to *Jennie Gerhardt*. See pp. 264–65.

is manufactured by a hack, then someone reads it, next it is put into continuity, then the director has a whack at it and we must not leave out the cameramen, art director, title writer, cutter and last, but not least, the actor. Who emerges out of the process as the haloed centerpiece? You can't say it is one person more than another. Not the actor, for he has no creative opportunity. He does what the director tells him and what is the director? What does he know?

"The credit in a play goes to playwright and actor. The work on the speaking stage can be conceived in an artistic atmosphere, especially with men like Belasco and Arthur Hopkins at the helm.[4] The playwright puts forth creative ideas, the actor again, such a man for instance as John Barrymore, reads the play from a creative viewpoint and acts the role accordingly. The motion-picture actor rarely even sees an entire script, knowing often nothing when he stands before the camera of what he is expected to do.

Charley? Charley? Pish!

"I can't see how it ever will be an art. It could be. It isn't impossible, but I doubt it. Name the artists in the industry in America. Griffith has done some things, but Lubitch has accomplished the same, and a lot more.[5] What are the De Milles, who are Allan Holubar and Allen Dwan or any other directors.[6] Name the actors who are great artists. Charlie Chaplin isn't a great artist. Fairbanks is doing good work, there is Barrymore always, his "Dr. Jekyll and Mr. Hyde" was immense,[7] but name any American films off hand that stand up besides "One Arabian Night," "Passion," "Deception," "Dr. Caligari's Cabinet."[8] All our pictures are produced on an absolutely commercial basis.

"Lubitch is a great artist and has produced great pictures. His coming over here to make a series of pictures may have constructive influence. But will

4. David Belasco (1854–1931) and Hopkins were New York theatrical producers. In 1917 Hopkins paid Dreiser for an option to produce *The Hand of the Potter* (see p. 70, n. 5).

5. Ernst Lubitsch (not Lubitch) (1892–1947) was a German film director who had achieved international acclaim for his comedies and historical dramas.

6. Holubar (1888–1923) was a Hollywood actor who later turned to directing films. Allan (not Allen) Dwan (1885–1981) had directed numerous Hollywood films by the time of this interview, including many starring Douglas Fairbanks. Helen Richardson had a part in one of the films he was directing in the spring of 1922 (Dreiser, *American Diaries, 1902–1926*, ed. Thomas P. Riggio [Philadelphia: University of Pennsylvania Press, 1982], 386–88).

7. *Dr. Jekyll and Mr. Hyde* (1920) starred John Barrymore (1882–1942).

8. *One Arabian Night* (1920), *Passion* (1919) and *Deception* (1920) were the English titles of German films directed by Ernst Lubitsch (see n. 5 to this interview). *The Cabinet of Dr. Caligari* (not *Dr. Caligari's Cabinet*) (1920) was a German expressionist film that had greatly impressed Dreiser when he saw it on its release in the United States.

he be allowed to have his own way, to carry out his ideals? I am skeptical.[9] We are not an artistic nation. All we care about is to be rich and powerful. Supposing pictures were produced that were art, where could 20,000 theaters be obtained that would show them?

We Have No Ideals

"Here and there are a few that care very vitally about art. The majority does not. The one aim of existence is to obtain everything that contributes to the ease of life. That is the chief thing. We have no national ideals. That is why we are always fearful of the Japanese peril, because that little country has ideals. The United States today is a continuation of old Rome. The Roman knew two things—money-getting and war. Any knowledge he had of art he learned from the Greeks. They only spread their knowledge in a limited quarter because their pupils were a few sons of the rich. They were responsible for our renaissance and the revival. The Romans contributed nothing. The fabric they built up was only a piece of cheese.

"We have Roman types, plenty of them, in our United States. On the streets you see them, in banks, everywhere in business. Mark Hanna,[10] I always said, was Marcus Aurelius all over again and President Arthur's face was on many an old Roman coin. Old Rome was the beginning of what we have now. For all their pretensions as art patrons, the Romans didn't care a hang about art any more than the Americans do. You can't have art if you don't think. Most people are not able to think and the rest won't unless they are forced to. A man must be absolutely up against it to use his brains. The Greeks had the art of thinking. They did not pass it on. When anyone speaks of Los Angeles as the Athens of the West when there is no Athens anywhere, it is too laughable.

No Place for Artist

"There is no place for the artist. Mention anyone from any age, Sappho, Horace, Dante, Michael Angelo, Shakespeare, and how easily would they achieve success today in Los Angeles or anywhere in this country. They would have a lovely scramble to get a meal ticket. Who would care about them? Who would help them? To gain success—money, success in litera-

9. Lubitsch came to Hollywood at the request of Mary Pickford in 1922, and, contrary to Dreiser's fears, was very successful in directing films that were praised for "the Lubitsch touch."

10. Hanna (1837–1904) was an Ohio industrialist and political adviser to William McKinley when McKinley was governor of Ohio and president. From 1900 to 1904 Hanna served as a U.S. senator.

ture—a new writer gets an audience when he is sensational. Shakespeare would have a fat chance to monopolize the limelight were he writing his plays today."

Mr. Dreiser is not mourning over a world that is out of joint.

"It is wrong and it can't be righted," he says cheerfully. "When you know that, the unalterableness isn't going to cause you any tears. I don't worry about it. One could lose his mind if he took it to heart. I don't care a damn about the masses. It is the individual that concerns me.

"And that brings me to this wonder. We have about 120,000,000 people in the United States and millions are out of work. I pick up a newspaper and read some pleasant little patter about the mother idea, how noble is the woman who has fourteen to eighty-seven progeny to her credit and how splendid to emulate her example. More people! Good heavens! When there isn't work enough for 7,000,000 or more in this country, why increase the population to more millions of mutts and lobs? What are they for, what are they doing, what could they do?"

Dreiser had found no answer out here in Los Angeles and Hollywood, where he has viewed an aimless procession going nowhere. With his dynamic energy he confesses that the climate of Southern California is lowering that energy. He does not propose to be exposed to the contagion. The much exploited luridity of Hollywood, where he lived for a short time, he found anything but highly colored, it was only prosily tame.[11] To be sure, there was always a picture being shot near his window that excited him quite as if the village band were passing by, but the mild excitement interfered with his five hours a day at his typewriter.[12] Herein is the secret of his incognito in the small town whose view enchants him—we shall not say whether it be the ocean flowing by his front door, mountains at the back, or the jutting walls of a canyon at the side, for we agreed not to give him away—the author has finished a novel while out here and is now reading the proofs.[13] He doesn't say what it is about, but it is a departure.

Will he come back to Los Angeles?

11. From April through August 1920 Dreiser and Helen lived at 588 N. Larchmont Street in Hollywood, in a neighborhood where there were a number of studios (Dreiser, *American Diaries, 1902–1926*, 311).

12. Dreiser did not type. All his manuscripts were handwritten and then given to a typist.

13. At the time of the interview Dreiser was probably reading the proofs of *Newspaper Days*, a volume in his autobiography that was published in December 1922 under the title *A Book About Myself*. He did not finish a novel while living in Los Angeles.

Too Artificial and Tame

Dreiser doesn't say yes or no. The climate he claims is enervating and yet there is something agreeable about it, too. No scene would hold him forever. Curiosity brought him here. It has been satisfied. He expected something real, but found a passing show, hoped for something artistically vital and landed among a bunch of lotus eaters. It was too anemic for him, he confesses.

Theodore Dreiser is a difficult person to reduce to the confines of an interview. He is dynamic and flashing with a mind like a volcano in constant state of eruption pouring out a lava stream of ideas. He uses his brain every minute, a brain that keeps turning out a freshly created product. In the last analysis he is not a critical carper.

"I see things this way," he said once.

The impression he leaves is that of an absolutely healthy man, and except for his dislike of Los Angeles, full of sanity and honest vision. He is cast in the mold of an athlete. He radiates normality. There is considerable of the colossus, the titan about Dreiser with a lively think tank added. He is a combination of virile forces, the agile discus thrower, a fleet Marathon runner, a romantic Siegfried. He neither mocks, curses, derides nor explodes, though translating his dynamics into mere words it might sound that way. Dreiser is an idealist. He admits it, but says such a conception of him, such a classification, would make America laugh.

What deflected him from standardized processes of thinking?

"God and nature," laughs Dreiser, who began at the age of 17 years to refuse to follow the path of least resistance mentally and to see things as he saw them.

His excursion out here does not represent to him a wasted year. He has enough ideas to stock a book, but not the kind he cares to write.

"Would I write a book about studio life?" Pause and expletives, "Not I."

A Bookman's Day Book
Monday, Dec. 18

By Burton Rascoe

*

New York Tribune, 24 December 1922, sect. 6, p. 22.

Burton Rascoe (1892–1957) was an editor, critic, and journalist who became Dreiser's friend and defender. In 1925 he published *Theodore Dreiser* (New York: Robert M. McBride), the first book-length assessment of Dreiser's works.

This afternoon went to see Theodore Dreiser, who has come on from Hollywood for the winter and is living in St. Luke's Place,[1] next door to Sherwood Anderson. Although we had exchanged brief notes from time to time for several years, I had never met Dreiser until to-day. He is more youthful looking than I expected him to be, remembering that he published "Sister Carrie" more than twenty years ago. He is tall, without superfluous flesh and only slightly stooped. His hair is gray, his eyes deep-set, his cheeks so full as to seem puffy, his lips thick. He has no gestures and is the most immobile writer I ever saw, apparently capable of sitting at ease for an hour without moving a muscle. His voice is well modulated, soft and without any nasal quality. He speaks slowly, with the average stammer, and there is a certain air of humility and gentleness in his bearing. I got from him the same sort of impression of dogged, persistent honesty, sincerity, frankness and hungry curiosity about life that I get from his writings. He greeted me with the friendly casualness one has toward friends of long standing. He had a sheaf of manuscript in his hand, and after he had got a match for my cigarette (he doesn't smoke) he sat down and explained in a timid and bashful manner that he had been writing poems and that he was anxious to know what I thought of them. He said he would like to send the batch of poems he has

1. Dreiser had taken an apartment at 16 St. Luke's Place in Greenwich Village.

written over a long period of years[2] and have me make frank notes of comment on each one.

"They are free verse sort of things," he said. "Just moods and impressions and attempts to get into a few words something I feel about the color and beauty and strangeness of life. I have been writing them off and on for years. I don't know whether they are any good or not, but they are things I had to write just the way they are written."

I asked him to read some of them to me, knowing that I had been much more sympathetic toward Sherwood Anderson's "Mid-American Chants" after hearing Sherwood recite them than I had upon reading them in "The Little Review";[3] but Dreiser picked out five and handed them to me. I had almost wanted to laugh when he told me he was writing poetry, so redundant, cacophonous and deficient in word values is he in his prose; but these strange pieces had life and heart in them, like his plodding, cumbrous novels, and moreover, they have the impress of authentic poetic emotion. Here was ineluctable sadness with a poignancy in no way rhetorical, glimpses of beauty caught in images from life in a city street—astonishing things, really, yet somehow in character, somehow the sort of fumbling grasps of poetic essentials one would expect of him did one ever think of him expressing himself in verse, free or otherwise.

He works daily, he told me, from 10 until 3 or 4, uninterruptedly and without lunching. He is still writing "The Bulwark," the third volume of the trilogy which includes "The Financier" and "The Titan,"[4] and he has also written eight of a series of fifteen portraits of women,[5] which is to be a companion volume to "Twelve Men." That book, "Twelve Men," he said, is apparently the best liked of all his books. More copies of it have been sent to him for his signature than of all the others combined.

He recited to me without bitterness, indeed with an amused resignation, the rebuffs he had had, the difficulties he still encounters in finding a market for his writings, the hostility of the reviewers, the trenchant personal abuse that has been heaped upon him gratuitously by critics, the hard time he has had in making a living. Of the series of fine and original portraits in "Twelve Men" he was able to dispose of only one to a magazine, although, he said, "I hawked them all in every editorial office.[6] Everybody said they were no good

2. A limited edition of Dreiser's poems entitled *Moods: Cadenced and Declaimed* was published in 1926. A regular edition under the same title appeared in 1928.

3. Anderson's poems were also in free verse.

4. *The Stoic*, not *The Bulwark*, is the third volume of the trilogy.

5. These portraits were published in 1929 as *A Gallery of Women*.

6. Actually, seven of the portraits had appeared in magazines prior to their publication in *Twelve Men*. Perhaps Dreiser is referring to the new and revised versions he prepared for the book, for he was able to sell only one of them to a magazine.

until after they came out in book form and critics here and there began to praise them. Then editors wanted me to write more like them."

Dreiser's tenacity of purpose in the face of all possible odds against him has been not the least noble aspect of his writing career. Against a storm of critical derision, moral indignation, the hounding of the vice society, rejection slips, insufficient financial returns, discouragement and abuse, he has made no compromise whatever; he has expressed himself unequivocably, sincerely, as he felt. He is at once a proud and humble man, without arrogance or a sense of martyrdom, driven by a desire to write of life as he sees and knows it as well and as truthfully as he can. He moved, a pathmaker, with heavy, crunching, powerful steps, through the brambles and thickets of American literary prejudice, making way for a host of more graceful but less powerful writers who follow him, and who in the blithe heedlessness of youth will never be properly grateful for the work he has done until it turns out, as it reasonably may, that he has done not the most artistic but the most significant work of his period in America's age of democratic industrialism, that it was his genius which most accurately reflected peculiar aspects of that age.

Literary Censorship Bunk and Hokum, Says Theodore Dreiser
Author of Suppressed Novels Certain Men Are Responsible for Latest Agitation Declares Women Have Time to Find Beauty in This World Flays Vice Organizations Blames Movement on Crass Ignorance and Stupidity, and Tells Why

By Elisabeth Smith

*

New York Evening Telegram, 4 March 1923, p. 5.

In March 1923, largely through the lobbying of the New York Society for the Suppression of Vice and a newly formed Clean Books League, a clean books bill was introduced in the New York State legislature that was intended to nullify the legal arguments and defense strategies that had been used against charges of obscenity. This new attempt at strengthening the censors' hand led to the following interview with Dreiser. The interview was reprinted as "Fears 'Snooper' Government if Censors Get in Saddle" in the *New York Evening Mail*, 10 March 1923, p. 3, and excerpts were reprinted as "The Question of Literary Censorship" in the *Independent* 110 (17 Mar. 1923): 191.

Are we to have literary censorship which will be a candle-snuffer of condemnation extinguishing the flame of genius?

Are we to have literary censorship which will be a shielding screen from evil, making for morality in the land and protecting home and hearth?

Choose for yourself the way to couch the question. The issue remains, however stated, and is pertinent at this time, when Supreme Court Justice

John Ford[1] and other prominent persons are promoting sentiment in favor of the enactment of literary censorship legislation.

We went to see Theodore Dreiser, that veteran crusader against censorship, who has been more or less involved in its toils for the last twenty-three years since his "Sister Carrie" was first suppressed at the instigation of John S. Sumner.[2] "Sister Carrie" has long since been adjudged to possess unusual literary merit, but Mr. Dreiser has not forgotten that its suppression closed the office of every publishing house against him, and at the same time was glad to take a far from elevating $15-a-week job.

Today the censorship rash has broken out anew, and its apostles—to change the figure of speech—are playing the censorship scales in all eight octaves.

However numerous and fervent these apostles may be, Theodore Dreiser feels assured of this:—

Men, not women, make up their ranks.

Men for Censorship

In the picturesque words of Mr. Dreiser:—

"The average woman knows that associations for suppressing vice are fool things, and even the ignorant woman suspects that all this talk about the evil arising from knowledge is bunk and hokum.

"The men of the country, however, are all for it."

In his home in that little portion of Leroy street which suddenly and strangely calls itself St. Luke's place, down in Greenwich Village, Mr. Dreiser sat before an old-fashioned marble fireplace of other days and discussed the question of censorship, its whys and wherefores and his opinion of America in general.

A tall man is Theodore Dreiser, with something more than a suggestion of rough-hewn grimness that borders on gauntness about his face. When he talks, however, the listener forgets this and the somewhat abrupt manner of speech which he seems to have at first meeting.

During the hour which we spent with Mr. Dreiser, he was quiet in speech and gesture, no matter how forceful was his language at times to drive home his point. His hands were never still for a moment, however, and he unceasingly plaited and replaited and folded and refolded into a diminutive

1. A justice of the Supreme Court of New York, Ford (1862–1941) was the founder and head of the Clean Books League.

2. Sumner, the executive secretary of the New York Society for the Suppression of Vice, did not instigate the suppression of *Sister Carrie*; see p. 1.

square a pocket handkerchief. There was a burning desire on our part to ask him the psychology back of that plaited and folded handkerchief, but we did not dare.

"Censorship? Say that for me it is a chestnut," was the way in which this novelist and essayist, who sometimes has been termed the American Zola, began the conversation.

"It is the men, not the women, who are responsible for the censorship talk," he continued. "There are millions of"—using a descriptive adjective of forceful and uncomplimentary profanity—"women in America today. There are many whose altar is a shop window and whose god is a pair of silk stockings. Yet a woman has time to snoop around and find beauty in the world the way a man has not. If she has any brains at all she has the leisure time in which to sharpen them.

Women Are Pagans

"Women are all pagans. When it comes right down to it, they do not believe in anything but their own destinies. Their temperament is for artistic things. Their sympathy is for the beautiful.

"Women may be active in church reform, in the anti-saloon league movement, in suffrage, but they do not attack literature because they know its value and beauty.

"Why is it that the proposed noble body who are to look out for our literary morals do not go after our plays and our movies? I have seen movies that would curl your hair, in spite of the motion picture censorship we are supposed to have. 'One Arabian Night' is such a picture.[3] I am not saying that there is anything in it or any other picture that should be suppressed, but I do say that there are more things there to attract the censors than in the books that have been attacked.

"Why attack books? Why books?

"Take 'Hamlet.' Look what it gets away with and the censors have nothing to say. I do not wish to jump on Shakespeare, but why don't they raid 'Hamlet'?

"It was this fellow Sumner who caused the suppression of my 'Sister Carrie.' He had at that time just been appointed secretary of the Society for the Suppression of Vice, and he was looking for a way to get his name

---

3. Released in the United States in 1921, this German film tells the story of a elderly sheik who has a beautiful dancer brought to his harem and then kills her because she is attracted to his son. Ernst Lubitsch (see p. 75, n. 5) acted in and directed the film.

in the papers.[4] When he found how well he succeeded, he was flattered and looked around to see how he could keep it up.

"Those who appear in such movements have a burning desire to earn their $5,000 or $6,000 a year and to be talked about in the same breath that the names of men of genius are mentioned.

"I personally have contemplated horse-whipping"—naming a well-known agitator of literary morals. "He needs a good licking. But to denounce him as I am doing this minute through a decent medium will be swell fun for him. He will like it.

"This country is a peculiar land. I don't know what to think of it. Every one quietly acquiesces to every measure that is taken. Consider prohibition, for instance.

Under Lock and Key

"If a girl under sixteen goes out and tries to get a copy of the books that were brought up in the courts last year and which were exonerated, the chances are ten to one she cannot get it unless she has the cash to buy it.[5] She cannot get it at the public library across from my home here.

"If a person of mature years goes into a library and asks for a copy of, say, Anatole France's 'Isle of the Penguins,' he is asked the warning question:—

"'You know this is a book of questionable morality?'[6]

"'We know it, but, for God's sake, let us have it,' is our answer, and then we are given the book from a special shelf, where it has been placed under lock and key. All my books in Chicago libraries were placed in safes. At any rate, they were safe from fire.

"That same girl who might not be able to get the book she was after will probably get it some way if she cannot at the public library. If she can't get it she can get the thing she is looking for by going to the Art Museum and

4. See n. 2 to this interview. The actions Dreiser describes were those Sumner took in the suppression of *The "Genius,"* not *Sister Carrie* (see pp. 51–52).

5. Among the books that were brought to court by Sumner and exonerated in 1922 were an English-language translation of *The Satyricon,* by Gaius Petronius Arbiter (fl. first century A.D.); *A Young Girl's Diary* (1921), by an anonymous Austrian girl and with an introduction by Sigmund Freud; *Casanova's Homecoming* (1922), by Arthur Schnitzler (1862–1931); and *Women in Love* (1920), by D. H. Lawrence (1885–1930). Justice Ford formed the Clean Books League after a circulating library sent a copy of *Women in Love* to his sixteen-year-old daughter (see n. 1 to this interview).

6. *Penguin Island* (not *Isle of the Penguins*) (1908) is a satirical history of civilization. Dreiser is probably referring to France's depiction of women in his novel as promiscuous temptresses who pretend to be virtuous.

looking at some of the pictures there. That will satisfy her just as well, if she but knew it.

"The censors cannot really attack the movies because such enormous amounts of money are back of them. They cannot attack the biggest publishers. They know if they attack a wealthy corporation they will have eighteen detectives and seventy-five lawyers on their trail. I know an instance where such an attack was attempted and this was exactly what happened. The attack immediately stopped. The would-be censor was afraid."

At this point we interrupted Mr. Dreiser to ask the why of censorship, whether its motive was underlying Puritanism or altruism or what.

His answer was that it was crass ignorance and stupidity.

"Look at the intellectual level of Iowa, Kansas, Nebraska and other rural districts," he said. "Why, it is so low, it is simply beyond belief. The greater part of the United States of America is not able to think.

Men Talk Like Kids

"It has material prosperity, beautiful homes, machinery galore, and yet the majority of its people have the mentality of a European or Asiatic peasant. They are concerned with their little marriages, their little deaths. National or artistic problems have no place in their lives.

"Take any large, successful organization. Listen to them talk. When they do not talk business, their conversation is like that of children—boys of nine or ten. They know nothing of art, of science, of religion. Literature is the last thing they know anything about.

"Make an intelligent remark to them and they look like a pancake because it happened that you did not tell them a funny story.

"This country has wealth and leisure that is as H.G. Wells[7] says, staggering. But its people simply do not think. They are carried away by nuts and fool ideas.

"You can slam its young people into universities with their classrooms and laboratories, and when they come out all they can talk about is Babe Ruth.

"It is a hopeless country for intellectuals and thinking people. The only thing they can do is to make an existence among themselves, to have a free masonry of their own from which the rest are excluded."

"The Genius," probably Mr. Dreiser's most talked of book, is to be reprinted by the Metropolitan Magazine, and later a new edition is to be is-

7. See p. 17, n. 5.

sued in book form.[8] This has been one of Mr. Dreiser's suppressed novels which has occasioned much comment.

"It will be printed exactly as it was first written," Mr. Dreiser explained. "This time, if necessary, it will be fought out in the courts. Before it was suppressed without proper court action."

8. An abridged version appeared in the *Metropolitan Magazine* in 1923 (56 [Feb.–Mar.], 57 [Apr.–Sept.], and 58 [Oct.–Nov.]), and the new edition was issued by Boni and Liveright in August 1923. Neither of these reprintings had the changes demanded by Sumner.

Mr. Dreiser Passes Judgment on American Literature
"We Have No Substance Today. We Have Very Little Today"

By Rose C. Feld

*

New York Times Book Review, 23 December 1923, p. 7.

Rose Feld was a young journalist who had previously been assigned interviews with Robert Frost and Edgar Lee Masters. Commenting on this interview to W. A. Swanberg, she recalled that Dreiser asked her "very personal questions": "Was I married? Did I have a fiancé? Was I interested in men? Did I like to go out to theaters and entertainment? There was an air of tension about him. I could see that if I gave him the slightest encouragement the situation could grow embarrassing. I adopted an attitude of severest reserve" (W. A. Swanberg, *Dreiser* [New York: Scribner's, 1965], 280).

H. G. Wells, Arnold Bennett, D. H. Lawrence, Hugh Walpole, Joseph Conrad, Gilbert Cannan,[1] these, says Theodore Dreiser, are the reigning American novelists.

"Americans?" he was asked.

"American," he replied and smiled sardonically.

It all came up in an interview in which he spoke as frankly and amazingly about many things, pseudo-realism in America, faulty criticism, sex and the domination of the Anglo-Saxon ideal.

The writer called him on the telephone to make definite the appointment he had promised.

"Come along right now," he said, and gave his address.

The house was one of a one-pattern row on a street near Washington Square.[2] There were several names on the door-plate, but not that of Theo-

---

1. See p. 17, n. 5, for Wells; p. 14 for Bennett; and p. 61, n. 10, for Walpole. Gilbert Cannan (1884–1955) was another English novelist and a playwright. *Round the Corner* (1913), his best novel, was suppressed by the Library Association in England because of its frankness.

2. In September Dreiser had moved into two rooms in the Rhinelander Gardens apartments at 118 West Eleventh Street in Greenwich Village.

"Theodore Dreiser:
A Caricature Drawn
from Life by Wyncie King."
From "Mr. Dreiser Passes
Judgment on American
Literature," *New York Times
Book Review,* 23 December
1923, p. 7.

dore Dreiser. Yet the address was correct. We rang and apologized to the middle-aged woman in boudoir cap and slippers who opened the door. We explained that we were certain we were wrong, but would she help us. Theodore Dreiser did live there, she told us—one flight down. She directed us down a row of dark stairs. We saw an open door and wandered through it. A heavy man, with open vest and shirtsleeves, was sitting at a dining room table. Again we apologized and made inquiries.

"Oh, him," he said, and led us out to the next door. We knocked. A voice answered, and the man in shirtsleeves shuffled off. Mr. Dreiser invited us in. The room was on the street floor, one flight down from the stoop. Years ago, when the house had been inhabited by its original owners, it was probably the dining room. There was nothing conspicuous about it. It certainly did not look like the home of a writing man. In the corner was a washstand with the intimacies of toilet frankly displayed. There was a huge lump of coal in the grate. On the mantelpiece above it sat a fat Buddha. A couch, a table, a couple of chairs and a few books completed the furnishings. It was quite evident that this author was not being pampered. In the course of the interview the reason for it became obvious! The house belonged to his sister.[3] Sisters, like valets, never let their perspectives grow dim.

3. The Rhinelander Gardens were managed, not owned, by Dreiser's sister Mame and her husband.

Throughout the entire interview Mr. Dreiser never once gave the impression that he was nervous. His mind wasn't. Yet his hands kept playing with his handkerchief, which he continually folded and unfolded in accordion fashion. We started him off on the subject of realism and the rest was easy.

"Realism," he said, "is not literature; it is life. That is where most of our present-day writers are making their big mistake. They set out to write a novel of realism and then proceed to ignore life entirely. They choose one dark, dank, ugly corner of life and spend themselves lavishly upon it, forgetting that life consists of many corners and many open spaces. The realistic novel of America is not the torpid, sick neurasthenic novel. Life in America is not like that. It may be like that in Russia, or places where poverty is resignedly accepted as the lot of a mass of the people, but not here, not here. A foreign writer once said to me that people can't be poor in America. They can't stay poor. There is always a push upward. He was right. In the same manner the life, or the soul if you will, of an individual needn't stay poor. If the home life is rotten, the individual can get out. He gets some joy out of his job, his friendships, the whirl of action about him. What I am driving at is the fact that the portrayal of American life does not lend itself to Russian atmosphere, to a Dostoyefsky plot, to Gorki treatment.

"Yet if a stranger in this country decided to get the spirit of the people—the life of the people—through our present day novels, or, say, a goodly number of them, what would he think? This is a people that spends its hours in miserable suffering and useless agonizing. Take Evelyn Scott's 'Narrow House' for one, take a newer book, 'Undertow,' for another.[4] Take Ben Hecht's 'Gargoyles.'[5] These are examples that come to my mind. The first peoples her book with characters that show an intense poverty of physical comforts and a bitter poverty of soul. All hate each other, and they continue living together. It's like locking a lot of people into a pen and torturing them. If that is typical of the United States, I never saw it. It may be true of other countries but it's not true here.

"The same is true of 'Undertow.' The children hate the father, the father hates the children, all hate themselves. They continue to live in a weird dark cellar of life, groping about in anguish, yet not making any effort to get out of the dark and the terror. Now I may be as ignorant as a pig, but

---

4. *The Narrow House* (not *Narrow House*) (1921), by Scott (1893–1963), was the first novel in a trilogy on three generations of a family. It focuses on a housewife reduced to domestic duties in a loveless marriage and her daughter-in-law victimized by society's overemphasis on beauty in women. *Undertow* (1923), by Henry K. Marks (1883–?), narrates the downfall of a family intimidated by a domineering father. Dreiser had reviewed the novel for the *New York Evening Post Literary Review* (17 Nov. 1923, p. 255).

5. *Gargoyles* (1922), by Hecht (1894–1964), is an attack on puritan morality in the early 1920s.

again I say that is not American realism. Ben Hecht does the same. It's as though these people consciously made up their minds not to give a picture—a realistic picture—of American life, but to paint something dark and sombre and drab and call that realism. And they paint on a ten-inch canvas.

"I confess there is something interesting about their canvases, small cornered as they are. Their distortions remind you of a Van Gogh, a Gauguin or a Cezanne. You can't tell whether the little canvas depicts Spring, Summer, Autumn or Winter. But it's rather attractive, repellently attractive. I suppose you can call it distorted realism if you are inclined to be kind. Yet the objection there would be, again, that the canvas is not large enough. A person's life cannot be told in a niggardly image of elongations twisting in pain.

"At any rate, one can not get away from the fact that right now we seem to be supporting a school of this new kind of writing. Whether or not there will ever be a master of this school or whether it will grow or die out, I can't tell. It's interesting to watch, however.

"Another school apart from this one and tagging after realism that has come before is the type of novel that fashions itself after Frank Norris. 'West of the Water Tower' is a case in point. Another is Ethel M. Kelly's 'Heart's Blood.'[6] Brevity seems to be the essence of these writers. They use the short-story technique. There doesn't seem to be a person today who is interested in writing a well-rounded life picture.

"Life is larger than they paint it. It's really more gorgeous. If you want a great scene you can't get it in a miniature. The great realistic novels of the past, 'The Idiot,' 'Anna Karenina,' 'Madame Bovary,' 'The Brothers Karamazov,' could they have been written in the so-called present style of realism? Their authors needed breadth and length. They took the trouble to make their picture complete. The little canvases of today will never displace the larger ones of yesterday. They can't."

There was a pause. The handkerchief was let out and again folded meticulously. Mr. Dreiser went on:

"Form is another curse under which American writers are suffering. The critics are greatly to blame for this. A man writes a novel and how is it reviewed?

"'This book is a masterpiece. The hero is described in one sentence.' In other words, the critics don't give two straws about the substance of the book,

---

6. *West of the Water Tower* (1923), a novel about small-town sexual standards, was written by Homer Croy (1883–1965). *Heart's Blood* (1923), by Kelley (not Kelly) (1878–?), deals with a puritanical Cape Cod girl who becomes disillusioned when the man she has befriended and loved for many years divorces his wife and marries another woman instead of her. Both authors were friends of Dreiser and had been his assistants during his years as a magazine editor.

but confine themselves to singing a paean of praise about its style. What happens as a direct result of this? Every young writer who wants to make a mark confines himself to form and lets the substance go. They strive after a quality of description, an alliterative feeling, 'Gertrude Stein' stuff that all the world considered a joke when it was born and now scrape to it so sedulously. The effect is the thing, the right word, the short sentence. And they're dishonest about it. They pretend at the same time to tell you a story, a life story. They don't.

"Walter Pater was interested in style but he was honest. He spent himself without measure to get the right word, the right feeling. When you pick up 'Marius the Epicurean' today you stick to it not because of its substance, for that is very modest, but because of the form.[7] If you are interested in getting a story—and are honest—you lay the book down and turn to somebody who was equally lavish in giving you details of action.

"We have no Walter Paters today. We have no substance today. We have very little today."

Again a pause punctuated by the white action of his nervous hands.

"I don't like to be criticizing American letters so bitterly, but there are so many things wrong with them. Take Irvin Cobb's statement about sex the other day.[8] He said he was sick of the 'garbage' of the younger writers, who act as though they had just discovered sex. He said, I believe, that it gives him great pleasure to lose himself in a book of Emerson Hough or Rex Beach[9] after reading their drivel. Or words to that effect. And the American public swallowed his statement in toto and felt very much better after taking the dose. Here was a man after their own heart.

"I, too, am sick of the exaggeration of sex in our novels of today. But the person who ignores sex is as much of a fool as the person who over-emphasizes it. You can't write a novel of realism and let sex out of the picture even as you can't write a novel full of sex and call it realism. Cobb said that our younger novelists are writing about sex as if sex had just been discovered. As a matter of fact it has just been discovered in American life and letters.

"Up to about 1900 this country was trying to make it appear that there was no such thing as sex. On the one hand there were people who acted, publicly at least, as though sex was something of which they had no knowledge. On the other hand, there were people who considered sex only in the light of crime. American life was built on untruths of this sort. 'The Scarlet

7. Pater's book, a philosophical romance, was published in 1885.
8. Cobb (1876–1944), a journalist and humorist, was on the staff of *Cosmopolitan Magazine* at the time of this interview. The source of his statement has not been identified.
9. Hough (1857–1923) and Beach (1877–1949) wrote historical romances set in the West and adventure stories set in the Klondike and other regions, respectively.

Letter' was produced out of the feeling engendered by this blindness to things as they are. Even today you can pick up a paper and read of communities rising in wrath over the presence of a 'Fancy Woman.' It happened in Georgia only several weeks ago. She was publicly horsewhipped and driven out. We're full of that kind of hypocrisy.

"It's hypocritical because just as long as it's hidden nobody does anything about it. People take it for granted that certain things exist. But let a thing lift itself up in the eye of the public and what happens? A storm of abuse and a public horsewhipping. There are places today in the United States where the drama of 'The Scarlet Letter' could be re-enacted. Americans love that kind of thing. They like to see communities aroused to wipe out an evil which every man in his heart knows that he can privately condone. We're a nation of reformers. We like to set examples for our neighbors.

"Many of the younger writers disgusted with this sniveling hypocrisy have swung to the other extreme and do nothing but talk sex from cover to cover. I don't know which is worse. Neither is the truth. Neither is giving the subject its real value in life. Does it take a Frenchman or a Russian or a German to get his proportions straight? I don't know. What I do know is that they have produced and are producing art and we are not. We're not.

"Hamlin Garland, Will Paine, Stephen Crane, Henry B. Fuller, Frank Norris, Brand Whitlock[10]—these are some of the real people who could have made a real contribution to American literature if they hadn't been discouraged by the great American fear. Take Brand Whitlock. He can write. But when it comes to writing about women he falls down. He doesn't know how to treat them. They've got to fit into the picture of American idealism. Therefore he always has his men kiss the heroine's hand or touch the hem of her garment. That's not realism. That's not life. Put Brand Whitlock in France or Russia and he'd be a real writer. It's more national than individual, this fear, this reticence."

He looked around his place and smiled. It wasn't hard to imagine of what he was thinking.

"What's the cause of this thing you call fear of looking at the truth? Is it our youth?" he was asked.

"No. No. I don't think so. It's because we take our social keynote from England. And England isn't young. She's old. She's grown old in the tradition that certain things aren't done or spoken about—in public. We follow blindly because we have such a stupid, unreasonable respect for everything English. We don't admit it in so many words. We admit very few truths. But who are the reigning American novelists of today? H. G. Wells, Arnold

10. For Payne (not Paine), Fuller, and Whitlock, see p. 17, n. 4.

Bennett, D. H. Lawrence, Hugh Walpole, Joseph Conrad, Gilbert Cannan. Yes, American. We have no respect for ourselves, for our own thoughts. We have to follow in the footsteps of those who know.

"That's what's put the damper on our own realists. England which writes in English doesn't do certain things. Therefore we can't do them. That's simple. And yet if we had any sense we'd appreciate that England is not famous for her realistic interpretation of herself. Who are the realists of England? Fielding, Smollett, Swift, Shaw, Moore. The first three are rarely mentioned by the man or woman of culture in England and the last two are out of it in polite society.

"Right now England is as poor as we in literature. And yet, and yet, we take our cue from her. Not from France and not from Russia. Not the Russia of the present, if you please, but the Russia of yesterday, the Russia of the great realists. Realism isn't one thing, it is many things. It is life as expressed by the temperament of the writer.

"Turgenev gives you one picture, somber but full; Gogol another, a laughing one; Tolstoy worked in pain and gives you a novel like 'Anna Karenina,' which is a moral bellyache; Dostoevski paints with a feeling of amazement that things can be as they are; Tchekoff is interested in the artistic problem. Each, however, spares himself no toil in making the picture complete and true.

"But we, we can't do this thing. We can't. Our god is respectability and he says certain things aren't done, or if done, aren't spoken about."

Dreiser Wants to Know More about Us
The Famous Novelist Asks Questions about the Jews—
and Answers Some
Why "The Hand of the Potter" Was Written
in a Jewish Setting

By J[ean] J[affe]

*

The Day (New York), 13 April 1924.

I imagined all along that meeting Theodore Dreiser, the great American novelist, would mean meeting a prototype of some of his heroes; at any rate the hero of his autobiographical "Book about Myself."

I thought when on my way to meet him that he would explain the reason (as he sees it) for the suppression of "The Genius" some years ago; that he would expatiate on the frequently misunderstood characters of "The Financier"; that he would account for the consanguinuity of some of the figures of "The Twelve Men";[1] that he would elaborate on the validity of the facts governing "The Hand of the Potter," his play of Jewish life. I was very eager to receive some good and sound truisms about journalism as offered so copiously in the "Book about Myself."

When I finally met Mr. Dreiser he neither explained nor advised.

He asked questions:

From the moment I entered his simple, book-furnished room and saw the big towering, reticent, dignified, wistful Mr. Dreiser, my expectations were relegated to the background. He was not the newspaperman of his autobiography, nor the alert and scheming financier, nor the young master who misled Jennie Gerhardt. He seemed to me like a proud intelligent woman who after giving birth to several children becomes bigger, superior, and more majestic (quite a droll simile for the very manly Mr. Dreiser).

Before I ventured on my "whys and wherefores," my host asked:

"How many Yiddish dailies are there in New York? What is the nature of them? etc., etc., etc."

---

1. The title is simply *Twelve Men*, not *The Twelve Men*.

I explained employing figures, numbers, adjectives, etc.

He went on: "Is that newly Jewish populated section in Brooklyn as great as the East Side?"

I tried to the best of my ability to compare the two, distinguishing their characteristics, the improvement of the former upon the latter, etc.

These questions, I was impressed, seemed to be lurking in Mr. Dreiser's mind a long time, waiting to be answered. And I, fortunate and unfortunate one, was called upon now.

"What do those garish signboards all along the East Side mean when they say 'First Tovler Monster Ball,' or the like?"

And I resorted to what I knew of the intricacies of the various Jewish societies and "Landsmannschaften," which are dotted all over the city denoting congregations of individuals, of common nativity, trade, or inclinations.

There was one question, however, which I would not relinquish. It was about the "Hand of the Potter."

This play was produced at the Provincetown Theatre, New York, about three years ago with a competent cast and ran some months.[2]

It is a play which deals with an immigrant Jewish family in the Ghetto, whose existence is drab and made unbearable by the gulf between the parents, who retain their pious faith and traditions, and the children, who could not be content with these and have no legitimate chance nor ability to adopt other spiritual channels. The squalor of their tenement, the lack of ideals, dignity and respect; the absence of light and love therein drive the children to the street. The greatest victim of circumstances is the eldest son. Through disreputable associations and a good deal of "knocking about," he lost his sense for beauty and love. He is bereft of all the finer feelings and sensibilities. The plot revolves about him. The story begins as it ends, in helpless misery.

"Did you have a special reason or motive for placing the plot of the 'Hand of the Potter' in a Jewish background?"

"No! There was absolutely nothing insinuating or vicious about it. It simply found that atmosphere and those surroundings suitable for what I had to say. In order to make sure that I did nothing erroneous or invidious, or misrepresented any point, I had the manuscript read and reread by several Jewish people before publishing or producing it."

Mr. Dreiser proceeded: "Who are the Jewish writers in America today most popular among the Jews?"

---

2. Produced by the Provincetown Players, *The Hand of the Potter* opened at their McDougal Street Playhouse in Greenwich Village on 5 December 1921 and ran for three weeks.

I enumerated Raisin, Asch, Yehoash, Kahn, Kobrin, Hirschbein, etc.[3]

He knew of Asch and his "God of Vengeance."[4] He commented on its merits as a work of dramatic import and his fine and keen analysis of a Jewish soul. He also knew of Pinsky and his works.[5]

From the amazingly great amount of information which Mr. Dreiser has about Jewish life in New York, from the subtle points he seems to have gathered from study and observation, together with his power of perception of detail and color, we can expect from him some day the American novel on the Jew in America.

3. The Yiddish writers listed are the poet Abraham Reisen (not Raisin) (1876–1953); the dramatist and novelist Sholem Asch (1880–1957); the poet Solomon Bloomgarden (1870–1927), who wrote under the pen name "Yehoash"; the dramatist Leon Kobrin (1873–1946); and the dramatist Peretz Hirshbein (1880–1948). Kahn has not been identified; the name may be a misspelled reference to Abraham Cahan (1860–1951), a novelist and the founding editor of the *Jewish Daily Forward.*

4. Written in Yiddish, *The God of Vengeance* (1907), by Sholem Asch, tells of a brothel owner who cries out against God's vindictiveness when his attempt to bribe God into protecting his daughter's purity fails. The play was translated into English in 1918 and performed on stage in New York in 1923.

5. David Pinsky (1872–1959) was a dramatist. Many of his plays had been translated from Yiddish into English in the decade prior to this interview.

Clean Book Bill Slays Freedom, Insists Dreiser
Hampers Flow of Literature and Forges Weapon for Intolerant Detractors, Novelist Declares Fiction to Be 'Throttled' Censorship, He Adds, Shunts Artists to Side Streets While Mediocrity Passes

*

New York Herald Tribune, 27 January 1925, p. 4.

After a proposed clean book bill was defeated in the New York State legislature in 1923, the Clean Books League and its supporters introduced a similar bill in each of the decade's remaining years. This interview was held a few weeks after the bill was reintroduced in 1925.

Theodore Dreiser denounced the pending clean book bill yesterday as a subtle, two-edged menace to liberty. Rousing himself from his usual calm despondency over the state of the republic, the novelist called all believers in the old American traditions to the ramparts to repel censorship.

"Besides hampering free production of great literature," said Mr. Dreiser, "this bill would forge a weapon for every powerful and intolerant institution that resents criticism. It would make it possible to suppress a work, irrespective of its moral effect, if they persuaded a jury that one paragraph was obscene."

Speaks from Experience

"Once establish the precedent," he continued, "that a book may be destroyed because twelve citizens hold a fragment sexually improper, what is to prevent the Church, the chambers of commerce or other influential agencies from searching out such a fragment to silence a detractor?"

Mr. Dreiser is familiar with censorship. Two of his novels—"Sister Carrie" and "The 'Genius'"—were suppressed and excluded from public libraries. That was several years ago, and now they sell freely and steadily, due to a shift in censors' standards. At that early time Mr. Dreiser was bitter against suppression because of its restrictive effect on artists.

To-day, however, he is more alarmed over what he regards as the hidden potentialities of the new bill for shackling all free expression than he is over the right of the literary man to deal frankly with sex. He sees it as another insidious assault on the older American virtues of outspokenness and individualism; another attempt at organized control of public opinion.

Worst of all, in Dreiser's mind, is the fact that the attempt should be made in New York.

Sees Menace to Freedom

"This city," he observed, "is the last refuge of the free, truthful man in America. Here the intelligent artist, the man who resents the rigorous regimenting of life going on elsewhere, can huddle into a group and express himself without regard to his neighbors or the Ku-Klux Klan or the corner banker.

"They know, these reformers, Justice Ford and Mr. Sumner[1] and the rest, that their attempts to fasten censorship on us will keep the truthful artist in the side street while the procession of mediocrity passes, with bands playing, down the main highway.

"What they do not know, perhaps, is that their bill would make every novelist, every poet, every social critic the prey of institutions that hold themselves above criticism. They may not know it, but their bill would throttle the free expression of social, political, religious and economic theories in fiction form. That is why every American who believes in free speech, whether it agrees with his views or not, should oppose this double-edged instrument."

Although Mr. Dreiser is forthright over what he sees as the decline of American courage since Colonial and pioneer days, he is a gentle Jeremiah. There is no anger in his voice, even when he talks about the people who harried him in his early authorship.

Finds No Solace Abroad

"I am, with respect to my country, like a man," he said, "who thinks that he hates all his relatives. But every once in a while one of them dies and he goes to the funeral and he finds that they aren't a bad set, after all—perhaps just weak and foolish, as he is.

"It's a hard place for an intelligent man to work. That is why so many

1. See p. 83, n. 1, for Ford and p. 51, headnote, for Sumner.

American literary men have gone abroad to live. But I can't live over there. Europeans are strangers and Americans are my people. I am of the soil, of the blood. I have little in common with a European. Our traditions are different. Why, we can't even deride the same things! When I make fun of Broadway actors, Congressmen or ladies' literary clubs he looks at me blankly.

"But there's nothing doing out there," the novelist continued, waving in the direction of his native Indiana and the rest of the interior. "Courage to think for themselves and to be different has passed out. I can't live anywhere but in New York. I've tried it often when I wanted to get away to write a book.

Pities Middle Class

"You can live all right if all you want to talk about is your next door neighbor's cabbages, his motor car or the radio. Even the American gift of friendliness, which foreign visitors talk so much about, is a delusion. They are friendly to strangers, so they can find out if they think 'all right.' If they do, they ask them to join the Knights of Pythias or the country club; if they do not, they try to injure their credit.

"Many a time when I have been living quietly in a small town somewhere men have come to me at night—professors, lawyers or maybe doctors—and told me the most amazing tales of their intellectual exile. They have no one to talk to; if they express ideas contrary to the ones prevailing in their community they are hunted down savagely."

These people—the average middle class American type—do not love their country, Mr. Dreiser asserts. The intellectuals, who see its faults; the poets, who feel for it, and the Jews of native birth, do.

"I believe, although many people won't agree," he said, "that the Jews understand and love this country better than the old so-called Anglo-Saxon stock. They sink deep roots here, they appreciate the material opportunities and they try to give something in return. And look how the Klan treats them!"

But, after all, the author ended sardonically, perhaps the mass of the people is happier under a strictly material civilization.

"Sometimes I think," he ventured, "that it is better for the people to think alike and to accept the existing order unquestioningly than it is to have them disturbed. Maybe the perfect state of the future is one in which most of the people will have motor cars, radio sets and nearby motion picture theaters and no libraries and no doubts.

"Geniuses and artists are freaks, anyway. They upset old ideas. Perhaps the instinct of the people in trying to put them down is sound."

See America, Says Dreiser
Artist's Greatest Opportunity Is Here, Writer Believes

By Susan Frances Hunter

*

New York World, 5 April 1925, sect. 3, pp. 1, 9.

To show whether Dreiser's ideas on life and living have changed in the twenty-five years since the publication of *Sister Carrie*, Hunter elicits his thoughts on a wide variety of topics, including marriage, living conditions in the 1920s, birth control, war, and the importance of beauty and suffering in life.

While the great drama "Sins of the Stage" is being enacted by theatrical and court officials in New York,[1] a few blocks away an artist proclaims America the greatest field of opportunity in the world for art. Here is the chance to produce that which will startle, amaze, and destroy the criticism so often hurled about Puritan America repressing her artists, he declares. Perhaps better than any one else he is in a position to know whereof he speaks.

Several years ago, about a quarter of a century, to be exact, Theodore Dreiser wrote books which were described as being bad, so bad they were almost immediately suppressed. Strangely enough, his publisher's conscience seemed to have been even worse affected than his critics. But without the quiver of an eyelash, apparently, Theodore Dreiser went his way, found a new publisher and continued his writing. The debt he owes his critics to-day has reached such proportions he will never be able to pay them. They established him. Because they dangled him in front of their readers as a distorter of ideals, dubbing him a pervert, young America ran at him, devoured his books and spread the flame of his fame.

While teachers, preachers, vice squads, and District Attorneys toil to

1. On 14 February 1925 New York's district attorney and police commissioner, along with John S. Sumner and an Episcopalian minister, launched a crusade to clean up immorality on the New York stage. The censorship battle with theater owners and producers received considerable press coverage as the city officials sought agreement on the use of citizen play juries instead of courts to rule on complaints about plays.

Theodore Dreiser   Drawn by William Auerbach-Levy

"See America, Says Dreiser," *New York World*, 5 April 1925, Section 3, pp. 1, 9.

clear away vice-spreading nets, Mr. Dreiser goes calmly on writing his books describing life as he sees it. If there is such a thing as a scientific novelist, the application fits him in that he seems merely to report what he finds in human nature. Going so quietly along his way, saying so little when the storm raged highest among the censors, has given an impression of something hidden, dark, and mysterious about Mr. Dreiser.

Rumor declared he lived in a basement apartment, wore trousers held up by one gallus and a nail, used the skeleton of an old piano for a desk[2] and caught his stories from the dark, damp, dingy atmosphere in which he lived. It may have been here that he found the courage to be the first American to produce the type of writing for which Balzac, Tolstoy, Flaubert and De Maupassant are famous. It is suggested that Mr. Dreiser is responsible for the flood of realistic literature with which this country has been flooded of late years.

Calling to see Mr. Dreiser a few days ago we found a great many of these ideas erroneous. He does not look as if he had ever lived in a cellar. Rather he looks as if he had always lived as he does now, where sunshine floods his windows, open sky stretches before him and all around is comfort and cleanliness. A clear eye, a radiant complexion, muscles evidently hard, give him the appearance of rugged health. Snow-white hair makes him appear more than his fifty-four years. One or two nervous habits indicate that he is not

2. Dreiser did in fact use a desk made from his brother Paul Dresser's rosewood piano.

always as calm as he appears. He frequently presses his hair backward in the manner of a small boy training his hair. His hands seem always to be moving, constantly holding something. This time it was a handkerchief which was continually folded and refolded as a seamstress prepares a fluted ruffle. In a two-hour interview it was probably folded a thousand times.

Somewhere Mr. Dreiser hinted that clothes have a distinct philosophy.[3] It is perfectly evident, however, that he does not give much attention to his appearance. Not that he was expected to be clothed in royal purple in his studio, for here he was in the regulation artist's smock, but observation of his tie, his socks, his handkerchief gave the impression that he spends mighty little of the royalties from his books for clothes.

His apartment was very simply furnished. There was no great array of art objects or rich hangings here. Rather there was an almost painful simplicity of things—at least it was so to a woman. Or was it simply the lack of a woman's hand to arrange it?[4] Strips of carpet instead of rugs covered most of the floor. Two bookcases, one evidently built by a poor carpenter—probably a great writer—were filled with interesting books. Among these were the works of Shaw, Flaubert, Ibsen and Tolstoy. A piano nearby raised the thought that it might have been the one formerly disemboweled for desk use. If so, it had now been re-emboweled for natural service.

Evidently conditions had changed since he wrote "Sister Carrie" thirty years ago. Had his ideas changed too and were his opinions about life and living different to-day? What could a quarter of a century do to one, especially with a World War coming in this period? Then he told me how he felt and how he sees things to-day.

"Not cocksure about anything," was the way he put it. "We don't know why we are here or where we are going, and to suggest that we do is asinine. The man with convictions is painful to me. In all my wrestling, jostling, swatting contact with the world I saw a great deal of heartache, much unfulfilled desire, but nothing was made perfectly clear to me except that we suffer and continue to exist.

"Forces control us about which we can know nothing. There may be a council of gods which we will never know. There is no evidence of just one God in spite of all the churches proclaim.

"As for myself, some days I feel there is a God and other days I know there isn't. My observation and experience lead me to believe that there is scarcely

3. Dreiser's discussion of clothes appears in chapter 1 of *Sister Carrie* in a paragraph beginning, "A woman should some day write the complete philosophy of clothes."

4. In January 1925 Dreiser and Helen Richardson moved to an apartment at 1799 Bedford Avenue in Brooklyn, and in March he rented an office in the Guardian Life Building on Union Square in New York City. This interview was probably held in his New York office.

a so-called sane, right, merciful, true just solution to anything. Brute force sits empurpled and laughs a throaty laugh.

"The church is responsible for the institution of marriage as it exists today. It was set up for the benefit of the church and should be immediately scrapped. It is a continuous source of trouble, not sacred or a sacrament. It is, instead, an outrage to make two people live together if they don't want to, and the rank and file is going forward to greater freedom in spite of all the handicaps the church sets up."

That he had exercised this freedom himself was pretty generally known. The evidence of lack of a woman's hand about his apartment, which had now become more pronounced by a close-up view of the window draperies,[5] which showed that either he or some other bad seamstress had made them, confirmed the theory of a bachelor life. But as he talked, one had the feeling that he would not mind a personal question.

"Would you mind telling me about your marriage, Mr. Dreiser?" I asked.

"My wife and I were separated after nine years of married life because I could not do my work under the conditions which existed," he stated very simply.[6]

Certainly none of his views about life have seemed very optimistic, but his philosophy about the individual living his life, as it seemed he must, brought up the question of a possible Utopia for each of us.

"Even workingmen can live like kings to-day," he announced. "But life isn't any more pleasant than it was in the days described in Boccaccio's 'Decameron.'[7]

Here I sat back disappointed, hoping to hear him say that in a few years we would all be living like kings, writers as well as workingmen. Instead he began talking about the Romans.

"They thought Rome was perfect in her days of glory. There were no greater number of them complaining than our own Bolshevists and Socialists who rave today about living conditions. After all, the extreme optimist needs only to look at the condition of the mill people in Fall River or some other factory town.[8] The same is true in other countries.

---

5. The original text reads "a close-up view of the home of the window draperies."

6. In 1926 Dreiser told his attorney that he had separated from his wife on 1 October 1910, which was almost twelve years after their marriage on 28 December 1898. In fact, however, he had continued to live with her intermittently until he moved to Greenwich Village in 1914.

7. *The Decameron* (1349–51), by Giovanni Boccaccio (1313–75), is a collection of tales narrated by three men and seven women who have left Florence to escape the Black Death of 1348, an epidemic of bubonic plague that killed one-quarter to three-quarters of the population of Europe. Dreiser is probably referring to the ravages of the plague that are described in the frame story.

8. By the early 1920s competition from the South and the failure to make technological

"What have we to-day to make life as hummingly interesting as that described by Plutarch when armies held sway? People were kept busy manufacturing all the things that the army needed. Life to-day in one hundred American cities where people do the same thing day in and day out is not so interesting as it was in the past.

"A greater number do have time for pleasure and are able to secure more comforts, but the degree of pleasure is perhaps not so high. The very size of many families makes life a terrible problem. The need of birth control is a necessity.[9] The idea of some parents that they must have many children is damned nonsense. They should be permitted to have only the number they can take proper care of. The State should regulate this."

Mr. Dreiser was one of thirteen children left to make their own way by the early death of their father.[10] He managed to get in some time at the Indiana State University.[11]

"Do you think wars are caused by overpopulation?" I inquired.

"No, not necessarily," he replied. "War will always be because it is an instinct. Stage a battle and see how quickly seats sell. Contests are conditional with human nature. Everybody is fighting somebody else all the time. If this is inherent in little things, it is more so in big ones."

Mr. Dreiser might be said to have waged a little war of his own for recognition of his work. His weapons have been indifference and persistence. The odds have certainly seemed against him, but the other day he made an assertion that every ambitious, daring young man or woman might well consider.

"This country," he declared, "is the greatest field of opportunity in the world for the artist. Here is the chance to produce that which will startle us. Literally thousands of people have an amazing desire to write realistic books. The odd thing is that most of them want to indict life, not picture it in its ordinary beauty.

"Even a scrubwoman shows this in her love for the pot of red flowers on the fire escape. This alone will penetrate her soul more fully and provoke her

---

improvements in the textile industry had led to unemployment and miserable living conditions among the people who had worked in the mills in Fall River, Massachusetts, and other New England factory towns.

9. The related issues of population size and birth control were hotly debated during the 1920s. On the one hand, the Roman Catholic Church and European governments concerned about diminishing populations argued against birth control. On the other, feminists and social and political liberals strongly supported it. As early as 1921 Dreiser supported Margaret Sanger (1883–1966) in her efforts to legalize birth control in America.

10. The interviewer is in error here. Dreiser was twenty-nine when his father died on Christmas Day 1900.

11. Dreiser attended Indiana University in Bloomington during the 1889–90 school year.

dreams as nothing else she meets all day. To be shut off from beauty entirely is what makes us suffer most poignantly. What is lacking in the experience of these young writers to make them think there is no beauty in life?"

In connection with the discussion of beauty it was a temptation to question him as to how much money could change the color of living. Instead, he was asked about labor and capital, which, after all, is not so far away from beauty.

"If making comfort and money possible for millions of people is good, then big organizations are a good thing," he replied. "For a long while I believed that capital would send the country to the devil, but in spite of my bellyaches, the country progresses. As for me, a lot of money would be a damned nuisance. The business of taking care of it would leave no time for my writing. With an average of six hours a day for a year or more on each book I write, there would be mighty little time for bookkeeping."

A bookkeeper would probably be another nuisance and hamper the story he carries in his mind, sometimes for ten years, before he sets it down. Writing is not an easy task to Mr. Dreiser, but one he labors over as did Flaubert.

Broadway gets little praise from Mr. Dreiser. There is nothing there that will last. Nothing that compares with Moliere or any of the old masters. And the play is the most lasting of all forms of literature, he believes. "The Little Clay Cart,"[12] 2,000 years old, and the old Grecian plays show what a hold this form of writing has on people, he thinks. Of his own work, he likes best some of his short stories. But the durable quality in his work does not interest him so much as being able to portray things to satisfy himself. There is little written to-day that will live, he thinks.

"How about Shaw and his writing?" seemed a natural question here.

"Mr. Shaw's writings will live," he declared. "Shaw himself, however, is a clown in the form of an artist, content only to swing from the trapeze or chandelier. He is, I believe, the greatest living writer.

"I do not read much. Just enough to feel the tendency of the times. In D. H. Lawrence I find some interest from his being original, especially in 'Sons and Lovers.' The question of sex with him and many others seems to predominate. My idea of this phenomenon is that of Freud. If the love life is distorted or fails to bring the happiness people expect from it, nature assists by bringing out some other trait, usually developing the talent one is most gifted with. I believe the greatest work of artists has been largely determined by this.

12. *The Little Clay Cart* is a Sanskrit play of unknown authorship. Its date of composition is also unknown, with scholars dating it anywhere from the third century B.C. to approximately A.D. 150. Dreiser may have read about or seen a December 1924 production of the play at the Neighborhood Playhouse in New York.

"It is only by suffering that we grow, anyway. It seems that achievement requires first that we suffer. The flower must first be crushed before it gives its sweetest perfume, and so with us and our work."

And now the interview was ending. His thoughts had been given as though he sat looking and told what he saw as the crowd passed by. It was quite evident that all that mattered was that he should tell truly what he had seen.

If all the money in the world had been poured at his feet, I feel sure he would still work six hours a day. His only contentment is to lose himself in his work. This he could do as well in a dungeon as in palace. In trying to discover a reason for his existence he has found none, but he must keep going on anyway. He believes that each of us stands near a precipice similar to the one over which Hurstwood in "Sister Carrie" stumbled. "Beating a cat for being a cat will not change it" rather sums[13] up his belief of life.

"The American Tragedy" is the title of his next novel shortly to come from the press. It will revolve around the living conditions in this country.

13. The original text reads "gums" here.

Glimpses of Interesting Americans: Theodore Dreiser

By WALTER TITTLE

*

Century 110 (Aug. 1925): 441–47.

Walter Tittle (1883–1966) was a painter, etcher, and magazine illustrator who in 1925 published a dozen interviews with American writers, humorists, and prominent political figures under the general heading "Glimpses of Interesting Americans." Along with each text he included a portrait of the subject that he had sketched while conducting the interview. For this interview Tittle had Dreiser comment on the difficulties facing artists and the work of contemporary writers while he sketched.

On a blustery day during one of our January blizzards[1] I wended my way with difficulty to a quaint row of old houses in Eleventh Street. Crossing the snow-filled front garden, I mounted the steps of a lower balcony, a distinguishing feature of this old terrace being that balconies for every floor cover its entire facade. Ringing the bell marked Dreiser, I was soon confronted by the object of my quest. The author of "The Genius" bade me enter.

This tall, broad, blond man offered an exterior different from the one I was expecting. I had seen fairly accurate photographs and had forgotten them, and for no particular reason had visualized a dark, nervously tormented eccentric, not resembling in the slightest degree the quiet, deliberate, and apparently phlegmatic reality. He told me that one writer had given a most unflattering description of his head, which he repeated in part to me, the adjective "lumpy" assuming prominence in it.[2] I agreed that, for the lower part of his face, this might apply, and the description might even assume a general accuracy were it not for the keen and piercing expression of eyes and the powerfully modeled forehead above them. They proclaimed

1. Dreiser signed the sketch that Tittle made during the interview and dated it "Jan 27–1925."
2. The writer was Harris Merton Lyon (1883–1916). He had worked for Dreiser in 1906 when he was editing the *Broadway Magazine*, and the two remained friends until Lyon's early death. Lyon's description of Dreiser appeared in *Reedy's Mirror* 23 (21 Aug. 1914): 7–8.

Sketch by Walter Tittle. From "Glimpses of Interesting Americans: Theodore Dreiser," *Century* 110 (Aug. 1925): 441–47.

that there was nothing lumpy about the brains of their possessor, at any rate. A safe remark was this, in view of the quality of the work that has come from his pen, and I was regaled with additional proof in the talk that followed.

I expressed a hope, as I started my sketch, that my hand and pencil would serve me well. I was considerably fatigued from a long period of strenuous work, and remarked that the complicated life of the present time, particularly in New York, levied a physical tax upon us that was at times depressing.

"We all suffer from it," he said. "I was greatly surprised at a confession from that jovial and apparently irrepressible man, Senator Depew, that he had fought against gloom and a tendency toward morbid depression all his life.[3] The late F. W. Woolworth gave me a similar account of himself.[4] If darlings of the gods of success like these have this difficulty, we need not be surprised at our own drab moments."

The mention of Mr. Depew brought comment upon the increase of the

3. Chauncey Depew (1834–1928) had been president of the New York Central Railroad from 1885 to 1899 and a U.S. senator from New York from 1899 to 1911. Dreiser may have had Depew in mind because he had recently written an article about him ("Chauncey M. Depew," *Hearst's International-Cosmopolitan* 79 [July 1925]: 86–87, 183–85).

4. It is not known when Dreiser met Woolworth. He told an interviewer in 1911 that he did not know him (see p. 22).

average of longevity that has become so marked in spite of modern complications of existence. Greater knowledge in matters of medicine and hygiene have raised the expectancy for us all. We cited several cases of men of very great age who are still among the most active figures in the affairs of the day.

"I read but recently in a newspaper," Mr. Dreiser said, "of a California woman, aged ninety-one, who brought suit against a widow of ninety for alleged alienation of the affections of her husband, a youth of ninety-three. What could be more hopeful for the race than that?"

"With this wonderful tendency already developing, and Dr. Voronoff and his gland operations to assist, Mr. Shaw's dream in 'Back to Methuselah' should become a reality," I said.[5] "In a London club some time ago I was treated to the spectacle, at once pitiful and humorous, of two very old men eagerly discussing the possibilities of Voronoff's experiments."

"I fear," he said, "that this operation is merely a happy thought born of a deep desire."

I was greatly pleased with my sitter's optimistic and philosophical attitude toward the difficulties that the present commercial age, turning from interest in the arts and crafts, offers to devotees of these lines of endeavor. In the Middle Ages art and exquisite craftsmanship assumed the proportions of a major industry, with great cathedrals and palaces being built, and workers with brush and chisel in keen demand for their adornment. Art was as vital a necessity as railroads now are, and the demand for it just as insistent. Life, too, was simple, and artists of all kinds worked without the interruptions of our present squirrel-cage existence.

"In spite of these difficulties we can, even now, do pretty much as we will," was the reply. "Many of the greatest figures of the past faced difficulties that were well-nigh insurmountable. Balzac was always in debt, and had to dodge his creditors by any subterfuge that he could invent. Villon was constantly being locked up or buffeted from place to place in danger of his life.[6] I sat in the square near the old meat market in Haarlem and counted fourteen expensive cars, years ago when automobiles were rare, drawn up in front of the museum where Franz Hals's pictures were to be seen. And this three hundred years after the death of a man who was repeatedly incarcerated for drunkenness and vagrancy. He was in utter poverty at the end.[7] Poe had

5. Serge Voronoff (1866–1951) was a Russian physician living in Paris who was known for his experiments on rejuvenation involving the grafting of animal glands on human beings. In *Back to Methuselah* (1921) George Bernard Shaw includes longevity in the play's speculative fantasies about human life in the future.

6. Because of his involvement in brawls and other illegal escapades, the French poet François Villon (1431–?) spent much of his known life under arrest or wandering to escape arrest.

7. Frans (not Franz) Hals (1580?–1666) was a Dutch portrait painter. Dreiser's description of Hals's character was based on biographies of the artist that were highly inaccurate.

nothing; he lived a life of direst misery and poverty, but his life was enormously great. Success and money have nothing to do with greatness. I envy Poe. I envy Whitman, living in his lousy old house in Camden. He had a gift! Why should he bother about money?

"One must sacrifice to achieve one's work. The things that people buy with money are usually impediments, anyway. Society was delighted to meet Shaw when he possessed one suit and a brown flannel shirt. He had no money, so he dismissed sartorial obligations. People were eager to associate with him on any terms. Supposing Shaw had had money. That would have been pathetic. He was far better as a man who possessed one suit and wrote for whatever he could get. He had a gift. That was better than anything else that could be given him. One can do what one chooses, even in these days. I find nothing wrong with this commercial age. What I have I got out of it."

"Would you have got more in another age?"

"Perhaps more, but of a different kind. I think it is better to be one of a few artists than one of many, as in past ages. If you were choosing, which would you prefer to be: a wholesale grocer with a comfortable place in society or Villon? I have often thought how amusing a spectacle would result, if in some place there was a counter for spirits to choose their lives before entering the world. Many would select paths of least resistance, but some would gladly claim the difficult existences, arguing, 'If I do so, I will have this great gift.' The gift of genius is worth whatever of hardship that accompanies it.

"This recalls to me the yearnings of a man I once knew who had made several millions in business. The money did not satisfy him completely: having acquired it, his dearest desire was to write a great play. He struggled hard, but the results he achieved were commonplace. He amused me greatly by declaring that he would give two million dollars if he could have written 'Hamlet' or some such great play that would live."[8]

I laughed at this naïveté, and remarked:

"He seemed to think, then, that in cold cash he possessed the equivalent!"

"Exactly," was the answer. "He underpriced it very much according to my way of thinking."

"The chance to survive and live of even great art is pretty much of a gamble," I remarked. "Carelessness, accidents, and fluctuations in existing

Modern scholars have discovered that the reports about his being a drunkard were based on mistaken identity and that the tales of vagrancy are without foundation.

8. Probably Joseph G. Robin (1876?–1929), who was a wealthy banker when Dreiser met him in 1908. Dreiser published a character sketch of him in *Twelve Men* under the title "'Vanity, Vanity,' Saith the Preacher" and later wrote an introduction to *Gaius Gracchus*, one of two plays Robin published in the early 1920s under the pseudonym Odin Gregory.

tastes have destroyed and caused to be lost forever many of the great products of the past."

"Yes," he replied, "think of the burning of the great library at Alexandria alone.[9] The chance of survival is very remote for most artists and writers. Stevenson is already starting to fade, and, more recently, who now reads Richard Harding Davis and David Graham Phillips?[10] Both were prominent in the bibliography of their times."

"Who, living to-day, will be remembered, do you think?" I inquired.

"Maybe Rockefeller.[11] He is really a wonderful man. He is an enigma. He claims to be a Baptist, but has universal conceptions, and acts on them."

"You think they are his own?"

"Well, it seems odd that the man should have done exactly the right thing so often. In business he had a success that points to genius, and since, in his charities, the same thing is indicated. He knows how to select men, and can be measured by the ability of the men he selects. Harper of the Chicago University seemed to attract him, and his first great endowment resulted, and since he has continued with such men as Flexner.[12] This supposedly hard-headed business man surrounds himself with dreamers; he evidently likes them and speaks their language. The same was true of the elder Armour and Dr. Gunsaulus.[13] They measured each other, much as a man is measured by the wife he chooses."

"Who, in your opinion, writes well to-day?" I asked.

"Almost no one in America," he replied. "Anatole France was a great writer, and Maeterlinck. D'Annunzio is another.[14] There is a considerable

9. Historians once believed that the most famous library of antiquity, the Alexandrian Library in Egypt, was destroyed by fire in 47 B.C. when Julius Caesar was besieged in Alexandria. The story is now known to be apocryphal.

10. Davis (1864–1916) was a well-known correspondent for New York papers as well as the author of short stories, novels, and plays. Phillips (1867–1911) was also a journalist but is best known for his muckraking fiction. His greatest novel, published posthumously, was *Susan Lenox: Her Fall and Rise* (1917).

11. John D. Rockefeller (1839–1937), whose Standard Oil Trust made him one of the richest men in America, was also known for his simple lifestyle and his philanthropy.

12. Rockefeller was the major benefactor to the University of Chicago in 1892 and endowed the Rockefeller Institute for Medical Research in New York in 1901. William Rainey Harper (1856–1906) was the president of the University of Chicago at the time of Rockefeller's gift, and Simon Flexner (1863–1946) became the director of the Institute for Medical Research in 1903.

13. With the aid of the Chicago meatpacking industrialist Philip D. Armour (see p. 36, n. 3), Frank W. Gunsaulus (1856–1921) established the Armour Institute of Technology in 1893. Dreiser interviewed Gunsaulus for *Success* magazine in 1898 ("A Leader of Young Mankind, Frank W. Gunsaulus," *Success* 2 [2 Dec. 1898]: 23–24).

14. Along with citing the French novelist and poet France (1844–1924), Dreiser names the Belgian poet and dramatist Maurice Maeterlinck (1862–1949) and the Italian novelist, poet, and dramatist Gabriele D'Annunzio (1836–1938).

list of writers who might have been great. Some recent ones in our own country gave promise of greatness in their early works, and then were led away. One of them said to me: 'I know I could have done it, but I lacked the courage. I could not stick it out.' There are too many easy and remunerative paths to tempt them to-day. On the whole, however, I think our literary product is an improvement over the past."

"But do you think our present writers compare well with the Concord school, or contemporary English ones with the mid-Victorian group?" The answer was only partial, and came in the form of a negative statement:

"The Concord school is really very thin, with the exception of Emerson. Hawthorne was only about seventy-five per cent. as great as his reputation. Anatole France could have made 'The Scarlet Letter' a hundred per cent. performance. Hawthorne got only about three fourths of its possibilities. Conrad was a great writer, and it is easy to see why so many people do not understand him. The average reader demands a lot of plot and incident. Conrad was really a painter. His plots were mere threads on which to hang a series of paintings. Most of his novels are collections of pictures, made understandable by moods, temperament, and movement of given characters. For me the greatest of all modern writers were the Russians. Dostoyevsky, in that supreme work, 'Crime and Punishment,' really had no plot at all. The whole thing is draped upon a structure as simple as a proposition in Euclid. It is boiled down to utter simplicity."

I made some notes of his remarks as I sketched, and asked if there were any particular subjects upon which he would like to be quoted.

"No; far be it from me to interfere with you. I shall be interested in reading the impression that I have given you; some that have been written in the past were pretty hard on me. I don't care at all about that, however. You have a free rein. What have you heard about me in the past? What impression of me did you have before we met?"

"Well," I replied, smiling, "I had only a vague picture of you as a sort of wild and eccentric person who had written some able novels that were supposed, in some instances, to be quite naughty."

"Just what I thought!" He laughed heartily. "I am supposed to be the lowest of the low, the vilest of human beings. Say what you please about me, but give also a portrait of me as I appeared in my contact with you."

"I have had an awfully good time with you," I said, "and no basis for muck-raking; but as I expect to be in Europe when the article appears and beyond present possibility of a 'beating up' or anything of that sort, you had better worry a bit."

"Don't mind me," he said. "Write it to please yourself, and good luck to you!"

A Visit with Theodore Dreiser

By Isaac Goldberg

*

Haldeman-Julius Monthly 5 (Oct. 1925): 448–52.

Dr. Isaac Goldberg was a Boston-based author and critic who published a biography of H. L. Mencken entitled *The Man Mencken* in 1925. In August Dreiser had sent Goldberg a reminiscence of Mencken that was included in the book.

There is sometimes a symbolism in the atmosphere that surrounds the men you visit. During the past few days I have been in New York, seeing this fellow and that, attending this theater and that, comporting myself most methodically if un-Methodistically. You call on Nathan,[1] let us say, in his bachelor apartments at the Royalton: a spacious room bathed in twilight, comfortably full of books, disquietingly well supplied with drinking glasses. By the window, a writing table fairly laden with lead pencils. Strewn about, objets d'art. A perfect setting for the nonchalant wisdom of the man, in which his pleasant baritone rings out harmoniously and softly. Or you are closeted for more than three hours with Mencken in The Algonquin across the way. Not too near the rialto downstairs; agreeably far from the madding crowd of buzzing literati. For Mencken is not one of the Algonquin boys. Five floors up their voices are not heard. He began to stay at that hotel, I believe, some time before it became associated with the literary crowd that now forgathers there.[2] At Baltimore, his home town, which he boosts with all the fervor that he condemns in the professional booster of other towns, he is the business man as scholar. In New York, which he has written against with a similar fervor, he is the scholar as business man. His parlor, bedroom and bath are practical places. His face is that of a practical editor alert for

1. George Jean Nathan (1882–1958) was an author, a drama critic, and, with H. L. Mencken, an editor of *Smart Set* and *American Mercury*.
2. In the 1920s the dining room of the Algonquin Hotel in New York City became an informal meeting place for a group of writers, known as the Algonquin Round Table, that included Franklin P. Adams, Dorothy Parker, Robert Benchley, and George S. Kaufman.

subscriptions. In moments of confidence it takes on an unholy glow—a real glow that shines with a blend of malice and magnanimity. I know of no picture, really, that conveys anything like a genuine impression of a man, and I have seen pictures of him from his third month through every stage of his varied and restless career. If you think Mencken is a sybarite, get that idea right out of your head. He is one of the hardest working men in the United States and thrives on the exercise. Condemn him to luxurious inactivity and you'd kill him.

I started, however, to speak of Theodore Dreiser. I had never met him before, and, you know, first meetings with great men are in a way a minor ordeal. No matter how well you know their works, no matter how glibly your own tongue can work, there is ice to be broken and there are times when a tongue makes a poor ax. My appointment was for the evening. Dreiser, who is finishing his new book, "An American Tragedy," in a specially rented New York office, lives in Brooklyn, which is also the base of my visits to Gotham. Accordingly I showed up at this place, ready for the regular chat about books and people. Drawing up alongside the curb I caught sight of an ungainly figure bent over an automobile. A charming lady was giving the car a drink.[3] I had seen that powerful masculine face before in pictures, and wondered what Dreiser (if it were really he) could be doing out here, preparing for a spin, when he had arranged to see me at that very hour. Perhaps he was trying to escape me. If so, I couldn't very well blame him. Talking books to a man after he has been stuck all day in an office room writing them is hardly his proper notion of relaxation, especially when there is a pretty driver at the wheel.

"Pardon me," I ventured. "Is this Mr. Dreiser?"

It was, and a heavy hand was extended to meet my own. But what about that automobile? Had I broken up a party? On the contrary, as it soon appeared, I was to make one of it. There was to be no evening of book chat in an apartment. This was to be a flying interview, open-airy, informal, with Dreiser and I seated in the rear and the fair charioteer guiding us through the open spaces of Brooklyn's seemingly endless thoroughfares.

Dreiser is the flesh and bone of his books. He is their living image, just as they are his. The man is tall and husky, a lumbering fellow who towers above you. As "formless" as his mastodonic novels, he is as living. There is no suggestion of stupid manner; he puts on no literary "dog." He has no clean-cut formula for life, which he greets in much the same informal, unstudied manner as he employs with an intrusive caller on the hunt for personal contacts.

---

3. The driver was Helen Richardson, who was living with Dreiser at the apartment in Brooklyn.

Well, there we sat in a machine that, fortunately for me, did not speed too rapidly; otherwise I'd have been numbed to the knees after an hour and a half of it through the cool night air. Dreiser, on the other hand, no cap on, disdained the use of his top-coat (which served me most agreeably as a blanket) and kept his jacket open to the breeze. An open-airy fellow for you.

Open-airy in his thinking, too. Most men, after a busy life spent in meeting new situations, manage to settle down into a mental routine that spells for them a sort of recumbency. Not Dreiser. His sense of wonder at the spectacle of the world is as fresh as ever. He has no fear of speculating upon the works behind the face of the clock. It would be fatuous of me, on the strength (or weakness) of this meeting, to say whether Dreiser has the metaphysical cast of mind; to argue, as does Mencken, from the closing chapters of "The Genius," Dreiser believes in all the hocus-pocus that engages the thoughts of Eugene Witla. This however, I am ready to say: that Dreiser has the true novelist's faculty of penetrating into his characters, however diverse they may be. Let us take "The Genius" again as example; I refer to it because, though written some eight years ago, it is the latest of his republished books, having at last won the right to reading which the smut-seekers sought to deny.[4] I choose it also because it is a much maligned work. To me, fresh from perusal of it, it is not half so bad as Mencken has made it out in his fine essay upon the man.[5] To be sure it is a hulk of a book, meandering, plowing its way through fields of irrelevancy and verbiage; and yet, somehow or other, this is no merely inert mass of words; and yet, somehow or other this mastodon lives, moves, convinces. Eugene Witla may not, in all his habits, be a commendable character, but he is a living one. His wife Angela may repel us with her arbitrary insistence upon a dead form, but she is no fictional automaton. Read the book as simple tale, and there are many moments when you are hard put to it to place your sympathies entirely with him or with her. Such a reaction to the book is Dreiser's reaction to life. Like all of us, he has his own marked prejudices and predilections, but he is no judge, sitting pompously on some soaring cloud, meting out rewards and punishments.

We spoke of many things; among them, naturally, the contemporary novel, about which Dreiser is quite optimistic. Never, he thought, were so many good novels being written or was good writing so widespread. The drama, he agreed, was not a vehicle solely for ideas, but an emotional conflict. (This, apropos of Mencken's peculiar attitude toward the stage, which

4. *The "Genius"* was written in 1910–11, not "some eight years ago." It was first published in 1915 and republished in 1923 (see p. 87, n. 8).

5. Goldberg is probably referring to Mencken's essay on Dreiser in *A Book of Prefaces* (New York: Knopf, 1917).

he believes to demolish by betraying its intellectual poverty.[6] But then, Mencken is not the most trustworthy of guides when it comes to emotional expansion; he flouts it, mistrusts it, perhaps fears it.) It would surprise many readers to learn that Dreiser—"the American Zola"—is not familiar with Zola's works; Thomas Hardy, on the other hand, he regards with an esteem that is deep and unaffected. It was easy to drift from the modern novel into psycho-analysis, and here Dreiser is alive with innumerable intuitions. Yet don't let me give you the notion that the novelist is a literatus on parade. His conversation, on the contrary, is just what it should be, strangely enough—conversational. It is liberally besprinkled with "d'you see?" and "don't you know?" It is suddenly interrupted by tangential flights, or by a passing distraction, such as directing the silent but listening driver on the seat ahead of us.

Another of his admirations is Havelock Ellis—the sanity of the man, his broad tolerance, his all-embracing sympathies.[7] Dreiser is surprised to learn that Ellis began as a poet, as will be most of Ellis' admirers when his collection of youthful verse reaches these shores. I go on chatting about Ellis and his wife, Edith; about the too-little known James Hinton.[8] All the while my hope is that Dreiser will somehow get to talking about himself, but that is easier hoped than achieved. At last I ask him point blank about his latest novel, "An American Tragedy." It appears that the book is on the verge of completion, and that it deals with the career of a luxury-loving youngster to whom all gratification of his impulses has been denied. Through a long train of strange circumstances he goes to execution for a crime which it is difficult to say that he has or has not committed. Surely something to wait for.

Dreiser is not an improviser. He carries his plots around with him for year after year before setting pen to paper. (Really pen, not typewriter, as the typewriter irks him.) Thus he had "Jennie Gerhardt" all done in his mind for fully ten years before he wrote the novel down.[9] By the time he is ready to begin writing, he sees the book as plainly as if it were a tree rising up before his eyes. Root, trunk, branches, twigs, so to speak, are all there; it is only the leaves that require to be sketched in.

6. Goldberg may mean that Dreiser "believes [Mencken's attitude is] to demolish [the drama] by betraying its intellectual poverty."

7. Ellis (1859–1939) was an English physician and pioneer in sexology best known for his *Studies in the Psychology of Sex* (6 vols., 1897–1910).

8. Hinton (1822–75) was an English ear surgeon who spent much of his life speculating on and writing about philosophical issues related to the reconciliation of science and religion and to the unification of knowledge.

9. Goldberg is wrong about the composition of *Jennie Gerhardt*. Dreiser began the novel in 1901 and stopped working on it in late 1902 or early 1903. He returned to it fully in late 1910 after resigning as editor of the *Delineator* and finished it in early 1911.

By this time we have come back to his apartment. It is filled with a warmth that is most gratifying after an hour and a half of evening breezes. A simple, inviting place, as much as I saw of it, with books cheerfully yet not too plentifully in evidence; on the walls, a few paintings of striking style, a couple of which might have been made by Eugene Witla in the early days of his rugged lines and strength of inner vision. Beer is served, and I, who believe in cakes and ale, politely refuse; I'm not a drinker, and hence a determined opponent of Prohibition. Dreiser eyes the cap of foam critically and drinks the glass down. We chat about Freud and nervous breakdowns, and Dreiser relates one that he experienced—a rather queer one, in which his physical make-up was seemingly unaffected, except that he lost weight. With him it took the form of an aching desire to be forever on the move, to travel hither and yon; perhaps it was what the Spaniards call the nostalgia "del mas alla"—the homesickness for the beyond, the desire to be in the other place, wherever that other place may happen to be. At any rate, it lasted a few years and left him, when it had spent its force, stronger at a low weight than he had been at his heaviest.[10]

I listen to the man talk on about his tastes in music, among which is an unashamed fondness for Grieg. His preferences reveal a decided interest in the emotional vagaries of the art rather than in its technical problems. Here, of course, he is intuitively right. He, the novelist, and I, the writer of words, agree on the spot that music is the greatest of the arts. Not the science of music, but the passional immediacy of it—its freedom from the tramelling necessity of such definite symbols as words, its wealth of primal sounds with which to paint, as with so much colors, upon that intangible canvas which is our body and soul. And this affable fellow, this dreaded realist, the speculating liver, is the bugaboo of the Vice Societies, who strain at a "Genius" and swallow the commercial smut of the magazine stands! Dreiser feels no discoverable rancor against the vice crusaders. It puzzles him, however, that the almost unadulterated dirt of the growing number of flapper magazines should pass muster, while sober transcriptions from life should be pounced upon and hounded out of print. Again, of course, he is right. The filthy little publications to which I refer are concocted with no other purpose than to feed the natural curiosity of adolescence. Instead of bringing to that appetite the food of truth, of vision, of reality, of scientific knowledge, they whet it with literary cantharides, with smelly aphrodisiacs in print, with "romance" as glamorous as false, with stereotyped situation and response, with

10. Dreiser had gone through a period of wandering in 1902 and 1903 while suffering from neurasthenia.

obscenity that is doubly indecent for the skill with which it manages to keep on the hither side of the legal letter, while violating the spirit.[11]

These lines suggest a fight that will have to be fought more than once again. As often as the war-cry sounds, so often will the name of Dreiser be invoked as the first of our contemporaries to have met the enemy and conquered him by the strategy of virtually ignoring him.

I am not given to trusting first impressions, especially when one has had but a couple of hours in which to assemble them. Yet as I rode and talked with Dreiser on this rare night, I could not help feeling that this man was very much a boy. Perhaps his capless, coatless, ambling manner reinforced the impression, yet I am sure it is rooted in something deeper than external appearance. Something in Dreiser, whatever it is, does not seem to have grown old. It has the defects and the qualities of the youth that has been preserved, but it is youth. There were moments when his face—a big, battered, asymmetrical face—suggested a prize-fighter just emerging from the ring—vulnerable but victorious. Transpose that metaphor from pugilism to life itself, and you have a fair image of the man. Life has battered him in many an encounter, yet he retains a sweetness that must be fed by some inner source. Lately he surprised many of his friends by suddenly appearing in gay raiment that would move Sherwood Anderson to envy. More surprised still were they when they looked through "The Nation" of April 15 and found there Dreiser's cheerful essay upon art in America.[12] Far from souring, the man takes on a healthy smile. Cherchez la femme? Perhaps. But there's a man about the house, too, when you talk to Dreiser.

11. The flapper magazines described by Goldberg had become extremely popular in the early 1920s. Their contents generally consisted of supposedly true stories about the personal experiences of wives and flappers, in which sex played a major role. More commonly referred to as confession magazines, the best known included Macfadden Publishing's *True Story* and *True Romances*, Dell Publishing's *I Confess,* and Fawcett Publications' *True Confessions*.

12. "America and the Artist," *Nation* 120 (15 Apr. 1925): 423–25.

Master of Creative Art Discusses Modern Problems
An Afternoon Chat

By Flora Merrill

*

Success 9 (Nov. 1925): 21, 109.

"That is why we need a scientific commission appointed to get down to brass tacks and study people's weaknesses—what they are up against—and consider the natural and material interests of people.

"Such a code would not need to be enforced by Law. It would be the experiences of people doing one thing or another and you could be guided by them or not just as you wished!

"It would appeal to their common sense—and soak in as *fact*.

"It would work because what Law is there about the Ten Commandments? They are just stated and appeal to your common sense. No one is going to say it's outrageous to honor your father and your mother. If you can, you will!"

"Do you think, Mr. Dreiser, that marriage as established by present law and convention is a success? Is this so-called new freedom going to result in something different from the present marriage relation?" I asked.

"They tell me there are just as many marriages as there ever were," he answered, "and that considering the total population they last about as well. I think there have always been an enormous number of mistakes.

"*Love leads blindly*, imagining it sees something that isn't there. In a year or two it too frequently finds out that the ideal was only a dream—but there is the home, furniture payments, a couple of children and general attachments which spring up around a scene.

"There is also the opinion of the natives and your relatives! All those things which might be called fixation complexes—and you are all set and so go on with it.

"*In the long run, however, most people get hungry for a sympathetic and intelligent contact with some one person.*

"After the first flare of youth dies down, they begin to feel the need of fixation, having something that is their own.

"Most people get to the time when they no longer want to knock about.

I know of scores of men and women who have lived five or six years together and then said: 'Darn it. I can't leave this man or woman.' and so they have called it a day.

"This need of a companionship that is *fixed* and definite is the true basis of marriage—and it's on this leg only that it is going to stand.

"All the rest is slave-driving by public opinion.

"People are terrorized into accepting conditions they hate or would be better off without because they haven't courage."

"Marriage must always have some form," Mr. Dreiser insisted. "There will always be many men and women who are specially drawn to one another, as is rather obvious, and the attachment will have a more or less durable quality. *It's a chemic condition which doesn't change very much!*"

"I do think this," he announced, "society may get disturbed for a while, but conditions will eventually sober down. Whether or not the Law or the Church compels it, there will be a standardized union into which people will fall *because they want to.* They always have!

"There was such a thing as marriage long before the Church came along with its sacramentary rules and regulations."

To the question: *"Has God ever bound two people together?"* Mr. Dreiser retorted.

"If you want to say that Nature is ruled by a God then you can say that the God of Nature has bound two people together—but there again your Nature is working through chemical laws, which are voiceless.

"If you want to call it the Law of God, all right! But if you want to call it chemistry and the natural law in the physical world, all right—and that's what I would call it. Jacques Loeb would call it a mechanistic process.[1]

"Frankly, I'm strong for birth control," Mr. Dreiser added, "and if the world had any sense it would be spread before the people.[2] If there was ever a worth while issue, it is *intelligent* birth. We all have the right to be intelligently born.

"I believe that an intelligent practice of birth control would solve many marriage difficulties.

"Morality encourages itself. It neither needs encouragement or discouragement. It is entirely self-sustaining. If there is one thing which takes care of itself in this world, it should be morality without let or hindrance.

1. Loeb (1859–1924) was a physiologist and the director of the Rockefeller Institute for Medical Research from 1910 until his death. His belief that life phenomena could be explained by physico-chemical laws, which he presented in *The Mechanistic Conception of Life* (1912) and other writings, greatly influenced Dreiser's thoughts and vocabulary on human behavior, particularly during the years he was working on *An American Tragedy*.

2. See p. 105, n. 9.

"The United States now has about every known process with which to make people *good by law*," Mr. Dreiser complained. "It is getting to a point where a man is afraid to take his hat off without permission. Out in Indiana your breath can cause your arrest—it is legal proof you are a bootlegger.

"Every bungleheaded, destroying movement the world has ever known has told the human mind what it *can* and *cannot think*. That is what happened in the Middle Ages.

"If the law starts to do our thinking for us, we'll soon have a country of Robots!"

"You may not make people *better* by laws, Mr. Dreiser," I agreed, "but don't you think it would be possible to make them more *comfortable* by law?

"We pension admirals, generals, policemen and firemen, so why wouldn't it be a good thing to establish some of this economic security before the age of usefulness is passed? Why shouldn't an author, for example, have society provide for his leisure in which to do creative work?"

"*As long as a person isn't helpless, he should shift for himself*," Mr. Dreiser contended. "He ought to have to worry a little. Anyone who thinks he shouldn't is a fool.

"I don't mean a person should worry up to the point of going to an asylum, but the struggle to survive makes us step lively and make a good showing.

"It is monkeying with machinery when you begin to take care of people, or when you urge upon them a lot of humanitarian schemes which encourage them to lie down and quit trying.

"Don't forget that the world got this far in the game without much humanitarianism. If it's an interesting place, it's so by reason of the fact that people have had to step lively to get anything."

Any suggestion that "*Sister Carrie*" might have been a still better book could he have written it wholly free of economic worry, met with no sympathy from its author.

"No, I have had plenty of elbow room," he said. "*I think life is brutal, but if you decrease that iron condition that has made the world what it is, it is going to become less snappy, less colorful!*

"The best way you can help me or anybody who does anything is to reward *us*—and not the man who does nothing.

"Put the emphasis on the person who does something. The fellow who backs himself does more to make life interesting for the public than ten thousand of those you take care of.

"Strong people aren't around looking for something for nothing—they resent it, but the dub is always ready. He'll take everything you can give and more.

"Economic conditions in this country are very different from what they were twenty years ago. Then my sympathy was aroused for the steel workers in Pittsburgh because I didn't think they were getting a square deal. That is very different from charity.

"Enormous fortunes were then being built up at the expense of the poor man.

"*To-day it isn't like that!*

"The laborer no longer needs your sympathy or mine. If he can't get five dollars a day, he'd rather beg on the street.

"My sympathy is naturally with the fellow who is trying to do something and is up against it, not with the fellow who is drawing down a lot without making any effort.

"*There is poverty in the United States, but it hits the middle class.* Newspaper people, for instance, and all the classes who aren't organized. If there were a union for authors, I'd be glad to join it and make no bones about it. I'd like a chance to get my rights—I haven't had them yet!

"I dislike the mass laws that try to reach the people by the millions. Misery is special and personal. When misfortune knocks at your door, it's *your door* and you have to attend to it.

"*If one is so small that he can see misery and do nothing to help, why he is just scum.*

"I think most people go to the front for someone. Few people can sit back and say that it doesn't concern them."

Still giving his handkerchief rough treatment, Theodore Dreiser continued cheerfully:

"*Life has always been worth living to me.* I like it as it *is!*

"That may be because I have a good appetite, certain unsatisfied desires and still see a few things here and there I wouldn't mind picking off as I go along.

"*So life isn't as dull as it might be.* I suppose if I didn't have a chance, and there wasn't another loaf of bread in the bread box or any kind of kick from anything, I'd think life wasn't worth living, but I can only speak for myself.

"In spite of myself I may become one of the fundamentalists," he observed. "My new book is *absolutely moral!* It will come out this Fall and is another little piece of humor that I'm offering the public, cheerfully entitled, 'An American Tragedy.' Readers may even think it teaches a good lesson.

"Who knows? I may be called to confer upon the state of the country—and be sent as ambassador to England.

"I may become so respectable that a brass band will be sent to meet me upon my return—but then again I may not.

"I am afraid there's a manuscript in the trunk over there that's a little dangerous.[3]

"*Just as soon as I get a good first-class coat of whitewash, it's pretty certain to begin to rain.*

"But I like my new book—I wouldn't write one I didn't like even for a coat of whitewash."

Twenty-five years ago, Theodore Dreiser wrote a book which shocked our mothers, roused the ire of the critics, and was the beginning of the censors' long devotion to Mr. Dreiser. The author's only answer to the indignant public, critics and censors was to continue writing about life *as he saw it*.

When "Sister Carrie" was an eleven-year old book, his "Jennie Gerhardt" was published, and again he was denounced.

Public opinion didn't remain calm, however, and when "The Financier" and "The Titan" appeared with a hero who was a world-famous traction magnate and an international Don Juan, it was pretty generally believed that the author must be a terrible man.

He laid bare spots in life that politer contemporaries ignored. He said things about sex and marriage that barred his books from the libraries and excited the censors. He showed life in all of it sordidness, the exploitation of underpaid labor, and the corrupting devices of the mastodons who through chicanery and dishonesty amassed their fortunes.

To-day, Theodore Dreiser's hair is white, but his attitude toward life is young, and he grins at the position in American letters to which Fate and the censors have forced him, which, after all, is a rather lonely plane.

As Sherwood Anderson has written: ". . . because of him, those who follow will never have to face the road through the wilderness of Puritan denial, the road that Dreiser faced alone."[4]

He didn't come into vogue in the company of a group of young fellow artists—the benefits derived from mud-slinging rather than log-rolling were his lot.

I asked him how it happened that he chose Brooklyn as a residence and a place like Union Square for his writing.[5]

"Oh, that was just a big mistake," he grinned. "Going to Brooklyn was a fluke. Snow lured me. It gave one of the churches a Christmas card effect, and the neighborhood a peaceful, Yuletide appearance.

3. Dreiser may be referring to the first volume in his autobiography. He finished the manuscript in 1916 but withheld publication because of its graphic discussion of family matters, including his and his sisters' sexual adventures. He later revised the manuscript and published it as *Dawn* in 1931 (see p. 148 and p. 148, n. 6).

4. Merrill is paraphrasing Anderson's concluding paragraph in his sketch of Dreiser published in *Little Review* 3 (Apr. 1916): 5.

5. See p. 103, n. 4.

"But I have near died since the windows were opened, with all the automobiles in the world going by.

"The Christmas spirit of good-will vanished when along came Spring and eight million automobiles. I went to the City of Churches and homes in order to write in peace—but I am going back to Manhattan where it's quiet!"

Theodore Dreiser in Berlin Arranging
Novel's Translation
American Author Makes Plea for
United States of Europe

*

Chicago Tribune and Daily News (Berlin edition), 14 August 1926, p. 1.

Suddenly affluent from the commercial success of *An American Trag-edy* and the sale of movie rights to the novel, Dreiser and Helen Richardson sailed for Europe on 22 June 1926 to go sightseeing, meet with publishers, do research for the third volume of the Cowperwood trilogy, and visit with writers and other European notables. Traveling as husband and wife, they toured Norway, Sweden, Denmark, Germany, Czechoslovakia, Austria, Hungary, France, and England before return-ing to the United States on 22 October.

Theodore Dreiser, the trenchant American novelist, whom that country chose to ignore for a quarter of a century because of the "moral turpitude" of one the characters in his first published book, is in Berlin.

He has come to Europe to complete the arrangements for the transla-tion of his latest novel, "An American Tragedy," which has had an imme-diate widespread success, into Swedish, Danish, German, Hungarian and French. The popularity of the book, which has been dramatized by Patrick Kearney and will be produced this Fall on the New York stage by Horace Liveright,[1] has somewhat puzzled its author. "It is not as good as 'Sister Carrie,'" he said on Friday, when being interviewed at the Palast Hotel, "nor a bit better than 'The Financier' or 'The Titan,' and there is no moral or spiritual difference between the content of it and my other books, but the public has decided it will take to this one."

1. The production opened on Broadway on 11 October 1926 and ran for 216 performances. Patrick Kearney (1893?–1933) was a young actor turned playwright whose only other four-act play before being hired to dramatize *An American Tragedy* was *A Man's Man* (1925). The producer Horace Liveright (1886–1933) was also Dreiser's publisher. It was his idea to bring Dreiser's novel to the stage.

"A Rank Fatalist"

When asked how he happened to become an author, Mr. Dreiser laughed and said he just "blundered into it." He said he was a "fatalist of the rankest kind" and that "you do what you can, and are what you are."

"I had no more intention of being an author than a coal heaver," he went on. "I had been a reporter in St. Louis and Philadelphia and then was the editor of a magazine in New York. The management thought I was making a poor job of it and pitched me out. I then wrote articles, essays and opinions for a living, but I had no idea of becoming an author.

"At this time I had a friend who wanted to be a short story writer and he wanted somebody to encourage him, so he suggested that we write a story together. I balked at this, as I had never written a story, but he insisted that I start writing, so he could, and he drove me through it. When it was all over, I couldn't believe it. I thought it was a rotten story. To my astonishment, it was sold for $100, but my friend's was returned.[2]

"But he was not through. He had the idea of writing a novel and wanted me to write one at the same time. I wrote down the title 'Sister Carrie' and then went on writing the story. I quit it three times, for four months at a stretch, dropping it for good each time, but this fellow couldn't work unless I did, and he urged me on. He made money on his novel,[3] but I almost starved to death on mine," he concluded.

Mr. Dreiser's long years of struggle for recognition have not changed his idea of values, however. He believes that poverty is an incentive to production to an artist, and forces the best in him out.

In the next breath the intrepid scribe from New York inquired about a Berlin restaurant where[4] a good beefsteak could be had for breakfast, in place of soft rolls and pastry.

Commenting in his forceful style on the present state of nationalistic querulousness in Europe, he said he could "see no such solution for the problems of Europe unless all the war debts were dropped and the nations formed an accord of the United States of Europe. If they do not do this, the war is not over and they will have another fine butchery. These little countries are the curse of God."

2. The friend was Arthur Henry, a Toledo, Ohio, newspaper editor. As a result of Henry's encouragement, Dreiser wrote four stories while visiting him in the summer of 1899, but none of them was published before 1901 (see Donald Pizer, *The Novels of Theodore Dreiser: A Critical Study* [Minneapolis: University of Minnesota Press, 1976], 3–6).

3. Henry's novel was *A Princess of Arcady*, which, like *Sister Carrie*, was published by Doubleday, Page and Company in 1900.

4. The original text reads, "scribe where abouts New York inquired the in Berlin of a restaurant where."

A book of his prose poems called "Moods" has just been published by Boni & Liveright, and this Fall "Chains," a book of short stories which has just been finished, will be issued.[5] He is now working on a new novel.

5. A limited edition of *Moods: Cadenced and Declaimed* was published in July 1926. *Chains* was not issued until April 1927.

A Great American Writer Is in Paris

By Victor Llona

*

Les Nouvelles Littéraires, 25 September, 1926, pp. 1–2.
Translated from the French by Carol Pizer.

Victor Llona was the translator for a French edition of *An American Tragedy* published in 1932. In addition to conducting this interview during Dreiser's visit to Paris, he took him on a tour of the homes of Victor Hugo and Honoré de Balzac.[1]

In 1923, when a translation of "Twelve Men" appeared, I tried to sketch, for the readers of *Nouvelles Littéraires*, a portrait of Theodore Dreiser, novelist, poet, essayist, and playwright, of whom H. L. Mencken rightly says that he dominates the literary landscape of the United States like a solitary and majestic peak. In a short article, however, it is impossible to study in depth a personality as rich, as vigorous, as varied, as this one. To convince the French public of the writer's importance, it would have been necessary for his most outstanding works, at least the ones best known to his compatriots, to have been translated into our language. If "Sister Carrie," "Jennie Gerhardt," "The Financier," "The Titan," and "The Genius" had already appeared in France, there would be no need to repeat that Theodore Dreiser is one of the greatest novelists of our era—certainly the most powerful and the most moving since Thomas Hardy. The difficulty of publishing such long works at the present time has made our editors hesitate. But since the resounding success of "An American Tragedy"—a true consecration in which the critics and the public have shown themselves to be unanimous— the hesitation is no longer permitted. With this formidable novel—I would say "this masterpiece" if I weren't afraid of appearing to write a panegyric— Dreiser is going to conquer the world as he has conquered America.

To quote Mr. Mencken again, Dreiser has expressed "the essential trag-

---

1. See Llona's account of Dreiser's visit in Llona, "Sightseeing in Paris with Theodore Dreiser," ed. Ernest Kroll and Margaret Kroll, *Yale Review* 76 (June 1987): 374–79.

edy of Woman" in his first two novels, "Sister Carrie" and "Jennie Gerhardt."
He traced the tragedy of Desire—desire for fame, for money, for love—in the
vast triptych of which two panels, "The Financier" and "The Titan," depict
the rise of a businessman and the third, "The Genius," that of an artist amidst
the blows and the favors of fortune. But the businessman and the painter realize that success leaves nothing but a bit of ashes in their hands. Love is an
agonizingly painful illusion that time or circumstances serve to thwart if they
don't destroy it. Finally, in "An American Tragedy," this fertile novelist has
given us the tragedy of Fate, which places a weak and ambitious young man,
a hedonist without energy, before a heart-breaking problem. The son of wandering preachers, Clyde Griffiths revolts against the bizarre and miserable life
that his parents force him to lead. He manages to create a fairly satisfactory
situation for himself. In order to marry a wealthy society girl with whom he
has fallen in love, however, he needs to rid himself of a mistress whom he
has made pregnant. He contemplates eliminating the obstacle through murder. Chance takes charge of executing the act while leaving the appearance
of an intentional crime. And human justice weighs down on the young man,
while his family continues the monotonous and useless crusade, the pathetic
preaching from which their unfortunate son had drawn the seeds of the discontent that will lead him to the electric chair.

Theodore Dreiser spent eleven years composing this 900-page account—
one that will perhaps mark the apogee of his career—which in any case
contains the essence of his knowledge of human nature, of his direct art,
simple like all that is truly great, disdainful of compromise. I do not know
anything that can be compared to this epic of sorrow, of the temptations
and weaknesses of the human heart, except perhaps "Crime and Punishment," naturally with allowances made for the difference between the two
authors' temperaments. On the part of the American, no mysticism, good
health, a constant equilibrium; his pity, contained and therefore more trou-
bling, is not exteriorized—it springs up spontaneously in the reader's soul
from the spectacle of the games of chance shredding poor human mice with
indifferent claws. In this Dreiser makes us think again of Flaubert, who,
impassive at least in appearance, wished to be only the impartial recorder
of destiny's judgments. Such is, it seems to me, the man who used ax blows
to clear a path across the jungle of Puritan prejudices for new generations
of Americans, the man who has made possible the frankness of expression,
the quite personal and autochthonous art, of a Sherwood Anderson, of a
Sinclair Lewis, of a Dos Passos, of an Ernest Hemingway, of the charming
and delicate Scott Fitzgerald.

I was anxious to welcome Theodore Dreiser during his stay in Paris. He
received me in a peaceful and quaint hotel on the Left Bank. This setting

seems too narrow a frame for a personality as physically and morally powerful as this one. Since I cannot place this great American in his proper mi-
lieu here, I would like to install him before a background that is violently
foreign to him. From the contrast we might draw some unexpected effects,
an indirect and therefore more revelatory enlightning. I suggest a walk in
the Luxembourg gardens, which are quite near. The royal garden accepts
under its foliage, surrounds with its statues of queens, the distinguished son
of a new race and unfolds before his eyes a noble landscape, the honor of
the capital of an ancient nation. On the terrace that overlooks the gardens
in which, in this season, dahlias weave a sumptuous symphony of colors,
before the pond that reflects the huge sun and the tiny sails, before the palace of Marie de Medici, Dreiser bends his great height a bit, inclines his
forehead crowned with gray hair, and contemplates for a long time the peaceful spectacle that stretches before him. Then he invites me to sit down, and
I see in the softness of his blue eyes that he is touched by such majestic and
serene beauty.

"This is the second time that I have been to Paris. I spent some time here
before the war, and I have the sensation of having been the witness of a
totally bygone era. The beauty of the city remains; people have not yet
damaged it too much.[2] But the winds of change, this kind of itch that today pushes men to move, spoils my joy of traveling in Europe again. I have
just spent several weeks in the Scandinavian countries and in Germany,
Austria, Czechoslovakia. Everywhere streams of tourists, amid their tour
buses, everywhere the noisy, indiscreet invasion that seems so useless, for
will these people ever understand?"

The chair attendant comes over and berates us.

"Do we have to order something? I'd be happy to have some beer."

"Later, if you wish. This woman only wants a small fee for the use of her
chairs. Later I'll take you to a café where the beer is more drinkable."

"With pleasure. I like beer—undoubtedly because of my German-Dutch
origins. But you know, I've just come from Munich, where the beer is excellent. In any case it would be ungracious of me to be difficult. The junk
that our illegal purveyors of alcohol make us drink in America offers no
attraction other than that of breaking a wicked law."

"Actually, I was meaning to ask you what effects prohibition has had on
American morality."

"Later, please. First I'd rather forestall the literary question that I see
looming over the horizon. Yes, a French writer, a giant, had a determining

2. Dreiser first visited Paris in 1912. For his description of Paris during that visit, see chapters 21–24 in *A Traveler at Forty* (1913) and his comments in the interview with Montrose J.
Moses (pp. 25–26).

influence on my intellectual development. The thunderclap that set fire to the powder keg. I tell the story in the attempt at autobiography that I called "A Book About Myself." A boy anxious and haunted by I don't know what vague but urgent promptings, I went one day to the public library in Pittsburgh (Pennsylvania). I came across a translation of Honoré de Balzac. What enchantment! The discovery of a world whose existence I had suspected. I went through the whole work. I devoured it with a formidable appetite and satisfaction.[3] 'Here is life,' I said to myself, 'the multiform and tragicomic drama of humanity. The setting of the action could just as well be Pittsburgh, Chicago, New York, as this Paris that I am unfamiliar with but that this genius of a man just revealed to me. But in truth the human heart must be the same in Pittsburgh as in Paris. Ah! To become the Balzac of America!' The unrealistic reveries of a young man. I consider, however, that chance made me read Balzac at the most favorable moment. It is between eighteen and thirty years of age that a man must become acquainted with this prodigious novelist. Later, his romanticism rings false, his style seems bombastic, his eternal and so often childish digressions exhaust and disappoint a more highly developed intellect. But what an inspiration for an aspiring writer!

"Later I experienced the influence of Dostoyevsky, but above all that of the great English philosophers, Huxley, John Stuart Mill, Wallace, especially Spencer.[4] These, with the German Haeckel,[5] naturally, confirmed me in my materialism, a materialism in which, by the way, I think I give the spirit more than its due. When all is said and done, we find ourselves before this dilemma: was the spirit placed in us by a conscious Creator, or is it simply the effect of the chemical reactions of the gases that make up our person?

"My books, in which man is the plaything of blind and implacable fates, reveal well enough which of these two explanations I personally have chosen. And then I have the example of the Greeks; they said everything, and better than anybody else. And the Romans, inspired by the Greeks! When Marcus Aurelius speaks, his voice seems to be that of a man of today. There is the undeniable mark of greatness.

"The same for Cervantes and Shakespeare. What do they say, if not what our heart has always intuited before the mysteries of pain and love?

"Other French authors? Certainly. France is a seemingly inexhaustible

3. See chapter 62 in *A Book About Myself* (1922), which was later republished as *A History of Myself: Newspaper Days* (1931). The book he read was a translation of Balzac's novel *The Wild Ass's Skin* (1831).

4. The individuals mentioned are Thomas Huxley (1825–95), John Stuart Mill (1806–73), Alfred Russel Wallace (1823–1913), and Herbert Spencer (1820–1903).

5. Ernst Haeckel (1834–1919) was an evolutionary biologist whose popular work *The Riddle of the Universe at the Close of the Nineteenth Century* (1900) gave mechanistic explanations of life similar to those Dreiser discovered in the works of Jacques Loeb (see p. 121, n. 1).

mine of profoundly human geniuses. At the hazard of memory, which will undoubtedly not serve me well, I cite the gigantic Rabelais. He was apparently the curé of a little village near Paris. No, but can you visualize Rabelais confessing the good women of his parish?"

Dreiser laughed aloud, hiding his mouth with his hand, with a frank, young, and infinitely attractive laugh. Theodore Dreiser has a sense of humor—this sense that, for Anglo-Saxons, is the redeeming virtue par excellence.

"Montaigne? Yes. A good curio maker. I mean that, retired to his chateau due to laziness, lassitude, or disappointment, this keen philosopher entertained himself by assembling his thoughts in a shimmering and varied mosaic. But—no doubt it's the fault of the translator, for I don't know French—his book gives me the impression of slowness and marking time.

"What did you say? The French lack aptitude for the novel? But the authors of "Madame Bovary" and "Madame Chrysanthème," of "Manon Lescaut," of "Les Misérables," as so many other 'romances' that I could cite—all these were French.[6] Is there anything more beautiful in literature than Anatole France's "Thaïs," more touching than the "Crime of Sylvestre Bonnard"?[7] I don't think that the 'English novel' is all that much the novel par excellence.

"Maupassant, another great artist. He had a 'sex complex,' but how many writers are obsessed by this complex, which, in the United States, has become the most obnoxious conversational cliché. Maupassant is undergoing an eclipse in France, you tell me. Don't worry about it. One day he will receive the justice due to him. After their deaths, all great writers undergo a period of waiting on the threshold of definitive glory, even and especially those who have experienced transitory and fleeting glory during their lifetime. They emerge from this antechamber with their true greatness fully recognized, a recognition that they will retain through time. Look, when I left New York, Ibsen was playing simultaneously in five theaters. When I arrived in Oslo, I was curious to see him played in his native language. Well, no Ibsen was playing in Olso. And the person that I asked to show me his house gave me the address with indifference. Similarly, I've heard that last year in Paris, at a *Pen Club* dinner, when the Norwegian novelist Johan Bojer[8] got up to propose a toast to 'one of the greatest French writers, Guy de Maupassant,' everyone was surprised. Do you grasp the irony of all this?

6. Along with mentioning the novels of Flaubert and Hugo, Dreiser cites *Madame Chrysanthème* (1888), by Pierre Loti (1850–1923), and *Manon Lescaut* (1731), by Abbé Prévost (1697–1793).

7. *The Crime of Sylvestre Bonnard* (1881) was also written by Anatole France.

8. Bojer (1872–1959) is best known for his novel *Den store hunger* (1916; trans., *The Great Hunger*, 1919).

"Zola? Some people have done me the honor of comparing me to him. However, I've read only six of his little short stories, which were certainly remarkable. And very recently I wanted to familiarize myself with his famous "Nana." Well—but perhaps it's again the fault of an inadequate translator—I couldn't continue reading the book. It seemed terribly crude.

"But let's go have this beer you were talking about earlier." We sat down not far from the Odeon, in a quiet café that has a history as illustrious as its name.

"Prohibition has struck a blow at American morality that I don't know how it will recover from. From the literary and artistic point of view, this has given us a freedom that we've never enjoyed before. But the respect for the law has been profoundly compromised. Having learned to disdain, to violate, a law that his instinct finds bad, the American ceases to respect the others whenever they annoy him a bit. From that emerges the state of anarchy that we live in and that makes of life in the United States something as violent and as bloody as our adventure films. In the midst of these excesses, the American soul searches desperately for a new ethic. I strongly doubt that it will eventually find one that conforms to reason."

A conversation with Theodore Dreiser could not but terminate on a note of lofty and disenchanted pessimism.

"England Gone America Mad,"
Dreiser Says on Return Here
Author Declares Britons Can't Sleep for
Worrying over Wealth, Resources and Prestige of U.S.;
Finds That Paris Is Dead, but Does Not Envy Us

*

New York Herald Tribune, 23 October 1926, p. 7.

"England is America-mad. The English girl imitates the dress of the America girl—no longer that of the French girl. The ambitious English boy plans to go to America. The English press froths with discussion of America. The English can't sleep with thinking about America. They envy our wealth, our resources, our youth, our spirit, our prestige. They envy us the very American continent itself—forgetting meanwhile their own very real superiorities: their more intelligent government, their finer statesmanship, their calm and civilized life, their honorable tradition."

So said Theodore Dreiser, author of "An American Tragedy," on his return from Europe yesterday. He dismissed ship news reporters at the deck with a brusque "I refuse even to pass the time of day," but finally gave an interview to the Herald Tribune at his hotel last night.

"Paris is dead—the old Paris, the lovely city with its delicate aromatic patina, its tradition of the Louis, of Napoleon, of the Empire," Mr. Dreiser said. "That Paris was crushed by the war, run over by automobiles, trod on by the ready-made shoes of standardization. Its Seine is full of scows and barges, its streets are full of motor trucks, its shops are full of products of the machine age. Its people are discouraged. It is unpleasant to be in Paris now, just as it is unpleasant to be in a room where people are crying. And yet the youth of France, unlike the youth of England, never thinks of going to America. The French are incurably French and France for them is the world."

Asked about Bernard Shaw, whom he saw in London, Dreiser said, "Oh, he's always the same, whether in his articles, in his plays, or at luncheon— witty, delightful, flashing with ideas. He reminds me of H. L. Mencken. In spite of Mencken's contempt for the theater the two men have many points of contact, though neither would like to admit it.

"Mencken says Shaw is a moralist, a preacher, but what has he been doing himself all his life except trying to reform American letters and the American boob? If Mencken were taken away from his American boob for one year he would die of homesickness."

Dreiser's view of America's future is a gloomy one. "America is curiously indifferent to its fate," he said. "Our leaders are merely cheer leaders. None of our politicians has the courage to deal with, none of our newspapers has the courage to discuss, really fundamental issues such as the Catholic question, the Negro question, the money-power question or even the liquor question. We are too cowardly or too stupid to face them. We can't help being prosperous now, with our vast natural resources. But wait until population increases to the bare subsistence level. Then America will meet her first test."

Dreiser Says Jury Systems Fail
in "Knife Edge" Criminal Cases
His "Tragedy" Traces Evils of "Careerism"
Novelist Uses Typical Case to Show How
Ambition, Seduction and Murder
Are Everyday American Tragedies

By Phil D. Stong

*

Denver Post, 28 November 1926, p. 24.

Best known as an author of books both for children and for adults, Phil
D. Stong (1899–1957) worked as a journalist in New York City from
1925 to 1932. This interview was syndicated by the North American
Newspaper Alliance and appeared in the *New Haven (Conn.) Register*
on the same date.

New York, Nov. 27.—Ambition, seduction, murder—these are the elements
of the typical American tragedy, according to Theodore Dreiser, America's
great realistic writer—America's greatest realistic writer, many would say.

His novel, "An American Tragedy," is taken, he says, from one of a pro-
fusion of similar cases to be found in the chronicles of American crime. It
is the crime which American thought and American life make characteris-
tically American.

Clyde Griffiths, his hero, is a literary, but rather faithful, re-incarnation
of an unfortunate who "fried" on the electric chair in Sing Sing several years
ago.[1] His case was a cause celebre of the time. But "An American Tragedy,"
says its author, is something more than an artistic representation of a crime,
its causes and consequences. It is a study in justice.

Clyde Griffiths would never have gone to the electric chair from a jury

1. Dreiser's source for his novel was the murder of Grace Brown by Chester Gillette in
upstate New York in July 1906. Gillette was tried and convicted in late 1906 and executed at
Sing Sing in March 1908.

on which Theodore Dreiser sat. Nor would he have gone scot free. Fifteen years in the penitentiary perhaps, or a life term with recommendations for clemency, would have been a just sentence, as human justice is assessed, for Clyde Griffiths, and, inferentially, for that young man executed some years ago in Sing Sing.

"The intent of 'An American Tragedy' is to show that the snap judgments of juries are inadequate in those knife-edge cases where justice is not to be found plainly to the right or to the left; where there is a subtler distinction to be made than one between black and white," says Mr. Dreiser.

"There is a saying, 'To know all is to forgive.' 'An American Tragedy' attempts to tell, not all, but a good deal more than the jury knew, of what might have been the facts of a famous murder case in New York state."

Says Juries Are Often Adequate

Casually, almost as an afterthought, Mr. Dreiser adds: "We can never know all the facts about any case, of course. But we can know much more, in most cases, than was considered by the jury which sentenced the prototype of Clyde Griffiths to death. We can investigate these things intelligently and judge them reflectively. There are decisions which casually chosen juries of men, unused to judge human motives and actions, are ludicrously unfit to render.

"In the courtroom they are placed under conflicting prejudicial influences. The superficial data of the case are hurried before them, first in the false light of one bias; then in the false light of another. They hurry out of the court and render a decision under pressure, in haste—a snap judgment.

"Justice, except by chance, is an improbable outcome of such a process. We can never do much more than compromise with our ignorance on such things, of course. But under this system the most delicate implications, knife-edge divisions of morality, are settled with a hurried yes or no."

Mr. Dreiser's reflections on "An American Tragedy" followed his first viewing of the play made from his book.

He had been in Europe when "An American Tragedy," dramatized by Patrick Kearney, and produced by Horace Liveright,[2] opened in a New York theater. A few days after his return, recently, he attended the play—one of the strangest successes that ever "packed them in" week after week.

His great bulk more than filling his aisle seat, his fingers playing restlessly with a handkerchief, the impassive author sat unrecognized and calmly watched his creatures suffer and die. Clyde Griffiths, young, enthusiastic, ingenuous, started out on the career his wealthy uncle had given him to

2. See p. 126, n. 1.

dream of. Lonely for the time with only his ambitions, and always weak, Clyde got a girl in his uncle's factory "into trouble."

Scenes slipped past almost cinematographically. Clyde struggled to release himself from his responsibility to the girl, for Sondra, wealthy and socially influential, had shown him love and success on the same path.

Upsets Boat to Drown Girl

Clyde considered a murder in keeping with his weakness. The factory girl could not swim—he would take her boating and simply upset the boat.

Clyde's arrest followed in a mountain camp where he was holidaying with Sondra and her set. The trial presented a prosecutor inspired to cheap eloquence by the possibility of political advancement and Clyde swearing to his lawyer that he had intended to upset the boat but had lost his nerve so that what he had planned and failed to execute had occurred at last, by accident.

The last episode in the death cell showed Clyde still uncertain whether the fate he awaited was a just one or not. The audience left convinced of nothing in regard to the crime. Perhaps Clyde deserved death—perhaps— he swore that he did not himself know whether he was a murderer or not.

Almost unrelieved tragedy, uniformly somber, in places startlingly ugly, the play is counted one of the half dozen big successes of the year, in company with a comedy, a revue or two and such queer companions. The answer is that it leaves its impress on its auditor's conversation for days—if not on his moods. It has a powerful retrospective flavor, and a sharp one. It is a dash of bitters, or tabasco, in the sirupy theatrical ladle of legs, wisecracks, and polite intellectualism. Curiosity leads many to the play; a serpentine fascination holds them.

The author of the book was deep in a consideration of technical phases of the production the next day at his hotel.[3] A gray and white room, almost bleak, a little above Columbus Circle, a gray and white man, formally polite, but rather evidently thru with an American tragedy as a human problem and impatient at being dragged from his technical study of an American tragedy as a play.

The author whose slow, indifferent, progress to the standing of a classic master has been such a "success" story as he would grin at, talked on justice. His eyes, dark under heavy brows, cold and curious, fastened on a point in space, or stared at the floor, as tho he were watching the capers of microbes; capers of which he did not approve but too unimportant for his reproach.

3. Dreiser stayed at the Hotel Pasadena on Broadway and Sixty-first Street in New York when he returned from Europe on 22 October. Since he attended a performance of the stage production shortly after his return, the interview must have been held in late October.

The blacksmith's biceps is large, one expects it; the fighter's hands are large, one expects that; it is several minutes before one notices that Dreiser's head is too heavy even for his powerful, rather well-proportioned body. His full lips, a little sullen, pout back from strong, white teeth which clip off his words; a schoolboy pompadour staggers back from the high, over-crammed forehead, with a certain air of pugnacity.

The machine had ground out a number of ideas on justice, precisely, at a rate neither slow nor fast—clear expressions, simple words—and it stopped with gruff definition. You must drop in another question or you will not get any more ideas out of the mechanism.

Scores of Similar Cases

There are no preliminary twistings or grindings. Mr. Dreiser sits on his straight chair rather stiffly, watching his microbes with a certain petulance, and the machine in his head ejects ideas in a pleasant barytone.

"Of course, because it is a typical American tragedy. There have been scores of cases like it—such and such a case down south,"[4] a dozen cases are named out of hand. "It happens time and again in America. I considered this case and the other but the one I chose seemed to me to embody most clearly the elements which make these crimes typically American.

"A young man starts out after a career, untrained, unqualified, unedu-cated—with a high school education or even less. He's filled with the com-mon dope of success that is injected into all classes and conditions of people in this country.

"What he means by building a career is a sort of undefined hopefulness. He has no intelligent notion of building a career, or carefully laying the struc-ture, of working for years at the foundations. He has neither the intelligence nor the training for planning. He doesn't mean by building a career what J. Pierpont Morgan would mean, starting in life. It doesn't occur to him that careers and skyscrapers have to be constructed with the same patience, the same forethought, the same disregard of immediate results. A skyscraper begins by going many yards underground.

"What he means by building a career, I suppose, is chiefly luck. Of all

4. Dreiser probably named a case in Charleston, South Carolina, in 1900, in which a man shot his lover in order to marry a Charleston society girl. Dreiser cited this and several other typical cases in the first of a series of articles on the 1934 Robert Edwards case (Dreiser, "I Find the Real American Tragedy," *Mystery Magazine* 11 [Feb. 1935]: 9–11, 88–90; repr., *Re-sources for American Literary Study* 2 [Spring 1972]: 5–17; and Dreiser, *Theodore Dreiser: A Selection of Uncollected Prose*, ed. Donald Pizer [Detroit: Wayne State University Press, 1977], 291–99). The specific case in Charleston has not been identified.

the kinds of luck, the kind most favored by romance is luck in love. The poor young man loves and is beloved by the boss' daughter; he marries her; he makes good in his father-in-law's business.

Cites "Fatalism of Europe"

"Think of the stories that have been written about that. Think of the novels and stories—the thousands of them—why, I know even poems—they've written poems on that theme—poems—

"That is American. It doesn't happen in Europe—it isn't written about on every hand in every month's crop of magazines, in every month's books, as it is here. There's no climber class in Europe. If you're born a duke there's no need to have aspirations; if you're not, it's virtually impossible that you'll ever be one.

"That's the first of it. The young man gets entangled with some girl and then he finds some way to help his chances by an opportune marriage. That's the rest of it. In that situation young men do various things. Sometimes they kill the girl. That's why you can find fifty—a hundred cases, precisely identical in their main phases, in American criminal history.

"That complication, too, is American. In Europe, a young man in that situation, supposing that he could be marrying into an upper class, would do nothing whatever about the girl. Suppose she came around to this man and his new friends—'This man seduced me!' He'd simply say, 'Of course I did—you and fifty others—what of it?'

"It could happen nowhere else, you know, as it has happened in America. It's a typically American tragedy, you know—dozens, scores of cases—all following the same main lines. Before writing 'An American Tragedy' I went carefully over the evidence in fifty cases or more—all similar—there was this preacher[5]—that young doctor who used some sort of pills[6]—all suddenly

5. The preacher was Clarence Richesen (?–1912). In 1911, while serving as a minister in Hyannis on Cape Cod, Richesen had an affair with one of his parishioners and, when she became pregnant, promised to marry her. However, after he moved to Cambridge and found an opportunity to better himself by marrying someone else, he poisoned his lover by giving her pills that he claimed would abort the pregnancy. After his arrest, Richesen confessed to the murder and was electrocuted. Shortly before he turned to the Chester Gillette case as the source for *An American Tragedy*, Dreiser had written six chapters for a novel based on the Richesen case (Pizer, *The Novels of Theodore Dreiser* [see p. 127, n. 2], 364n11).

6. Dreiser is referring to Carlyle Harris (1868–93). As a young medical student (not a doctor) in 1890, Harris secretly wed a girl. A year later, when he was being pressured to make the marriage public, he poisoned her because he was afraid his family would disinherit him for marrying below his social status. Dreiser learned about this case in 1894 when he met Harris's mother, who believed her son was innocent. By then, however, Harris had been convicted of first-degree murder and executed in the electric chair.

seeing the promised land of success ahead—involved with some woman—taking the criminal way out."

The machine stopped again. The calm, curious eyes, staring out of some emotionless Nirvana into which a little discontent had entered, sought the next question.

"Oh, the Hall-Mills case was altogether different. I discarded it at once. Plain sexual murder.[7]

"No, not another facet of the same circumstances—well, perhaps. But without the elements which make 'An American Tragedy' a typical American tragedy. Different because of its state of development. They don't know who the murderer was, of course, but the facts are fairly plain, you know—it wouldn't have done at all, altogether different."

The machine continues for a moment of its own volition, in reference to nothing, if you will. "A woman always believes that she has made a man's career, no matter what it is or what she is. She always expects a certain gratitude from him, appreciation from the world, if she's done no more than live with him—"

Author Pleased with Play

"The play? It was an experience for me to see a work that took me years to do, 300,000 words to unfold, and two volumes to contain, packed into twelve scenes and two hours of dialog. I believe that Kearney has picked out the salient and vital points of the story and planned their continuity as well as anyone could have done.

"The characterizations are different from those I had pictured myself, of course. But they pleased me immensely. One man's idea of the person behind certain behavior is one thing—another man's is another. The exact persons to live out an America tragedy may as well be Liveright's and Goodman's[8] as mine. They do bring out the things in the story quite as well as the originals would if the originals could be incarnated from print and thought and put in the roles. Every person's idea of the living characters of the book would be different from every other person's. The ideas of those who cast the play and mine are different. But those of the director and the

7. In 1922 the bodies of the Reverend Edward Wheeler Hall (1882–1922) and Eleanor Mills (1888–1922), a singer in his church's choir, were found in a compromising position under a tree in a lover's lane outside New Brunswick, New Jersey. Both had been shot, Mrs. Mills's throat had been cut, and love letters from Mills to Hall were scattered over and around the bodies. No one was indicted for the murders until 1926, when Hall's wife and her two brothers were charged, tried, and acquitted in one of the more sensational trials in the 1920s. The case remains unsolved.

8. Edward Goodman (1888?–1962) was the director of the stage production.

producer are just as successful and good as mine—they say the things I said and live the things I wrote."

It would have been indecent to keep Mr. Dreiser longer from the things that were calling for him. The interview was over. The great master had been kind, courteous—he had not stinted work or thought.

Now he was almost cordial, however, almost brisk. Just the exact moment that courtesy required of lingering at the apartment door—then the door closed. Behind it, it was not hard to picture him, at whatever activity, free again, his mind at last at the desired clinic of the drama; almost happy to be done with outworn reflections on man's little recognition that justice is unattainable; almost enthusiastic over new curiosities not yet pursued to the ultimate impasse.

A Neighborly Call on Theodore Dreiser
An American Novelist Talks about Himself and the Work of His Fellow-Writers of Fiction

BY JEAN WEST MAURY

*

Boston Evening Transcript, 29 January 1927, Book Section, p. 1.

Jean West Maury, a journalist and writer of children's books, was a reviewer and columnist for the literary section of the *Boston Evening Transcript*. A much condensed version of the interview appeared earlier as "In the Workshop of an American Realist" in *Literary Digest International Book Review* 4 (Mar. 1926): 223–24.

My appointment was for one o'clock and I had been warned that I must be on time. Mr. Dreiser was not to be disturbed beforehand, nor could be kept waiting. It was, therefore, one o'clock to the second when I knocked at a door whose upper panel of glass was covered by an impressionistic painting which effectually obscured the view within from the viewers without. Theodore Dreiser himself opened the door, not very wide, evidently surprised to see two when he had expected but one. Martha Ostenso was the other.[1] He eyed us both rather truculently, reminding me of an overgrown country schoolboy, suddenly called upon by his teacher for a Friday afternoon before visitors "speech" when he doesn't know a thing "by heart." However, since we had got into the room, he seemed to decide to make the best of it.

"Take a chair," he ordered. "Take a chair a-piece."

We could not have taken more than that for, as I recall, there were only two chairs in the room—and a flat-topped desk and several packing boxes. Miss Ostenso refused to be seated. "I can't stay," she said, with the enviable

---

1. Ostenso (1900–1963) was a Norwegian-born author of novels depicting Scandinavian immigrant life in the Midwest. Her *Wild Geese* (1925), mentioned later in the interview, was her first novel and remains her best-known work.

blush that marks her unpainted youth and freshness. "I just wanted to see how you looked when you weren't eating!"

"Eh? What?" queried the mystified Mr. Dreiser.

Miss Ostenso hurriedly explained that she had often seen the author in a little French restaurant where she liked to go for dinner. "Besides" she added, visibly embarrassed, but pluckily determined, "I've always wanted to meet you."

Bravely, if not quite fearlessly, she looked up at him, a small Brunhilde without her armor. Dreiser, big, hulking, impressive, one hand in the pocket of his loose gray coat, even the stripes of his shirt—he wore no waistcoat—aggressive, looked down at her.

"Yes?" he growled, but his gray eyes had grown warm and friendly, very kind. "Well, how do I look when I'm not eating?"

"As if you wondered why I wanted to know," spoke Miss Ostenso, and departed.

She's a dear. Mr. Dreiser did not say this in words. He did not need to. His eyes, as he turned from the door that had just closed behind the amazing young author of "Wild Geese," said it for him. He apologized for the disorder of the room, explained that he was in the midst of packing for a trip to Florida,[2] and we sat down, I before the flat-topped desk, he beside the window. At once he began to question me.

"How long have you lived in New England? . . . Do you like it? . . . Don't you find Boston different from all other cities, and the New England countryside different from and lovelier than any other part of the United States?"

He was still alive to his first impressions of New England, derived from a marvelous trolley trip he had made for a magazine years and years ago.[3] He had been charmed with everything he had seen. He loved it all, he said, the old-established look of everything, the incomparable quiet and beauty of the elm and beech-shaded roads and streets, the lovely individual homes each set in its own grounds, large or small, surrounded by its own trees, its own smooth lawn, its own flowering plants and radiantly green shrubs.

"Those New England villages had an unspeakable appeal for me," he declared. "I've never forgotten it. Except for two or three places in the old South, there's nothing else in our country that seems to me so nearly what it means to be. There's no pretense about a New England village."

2. After completing *An American Tragedy* Dreiser left for a Florida vacation on 8 December 1925. This fact plus the reference to his Guardian Life Building office (see n. 12 to this interview) helps to date the time of this interview as late November 1925.

3. "From New York to Boston by Trolley," *Ainslee's* 4 (Aug. 1899): 74–84; repr., Dreiser, *Selected Magazine Articles of Theodore Dreiser*, vol. 2, ed. Yoshinobu Hakutani (Rutherford, N.J.: Fairleigh Dickinson University Press, 1987), 91–100.

He got into some of the little fishing villages on the sea. "I should like to live in one of those fishing villages. I almost wish," he admitted, "that I had been born in one of them. I could have loved it so. But all New England villages are charming. They get under your skin. There is about them something you don't get even in the villages and small towns of New York or Pennsylvania, and certainly nowhere in the Middle West, something that speaks of a sequestered family life, of respect for tradition and of a self respect too deep for ostentation."

His personally conducted discussion of New England led by natural steps, too numerous to be retraced here, to religion. He expressed much interest in the growth of the Roman Catholic Church in Boston.

"I was brought up in that faith," he explained. "I made my last confession when I was seventeen. In the confessional I told the priest I was reading Carlyle's French Revolution, and that I had read some of Macaulay and Michelet. He objected. He said the Church did not approve of such books for the young. I asked him if that meant the Church wanted to control my thinking. He said: 'Of course the Church is not trying to control your mind; the Church wants to advise you, to help you.'" He left the confessional more than ever determined to read the books he had mentioned, and resolved never to make another confession of his sins. "Of course," he added, "that meant my religion was gone. It left me rather up in the air, but it was very nice air. The unhappy part about it was that it grieved my father. He lived and died a devout Roman Catholic. To him the Pope was always infallible.

"My mother came from a family of Mennonites that afterward branched off into Dunkards, and later into the United Brethren of Chicago. My mother was never religious. Because she was very much in love with my father, at least then, she consented to be baptized in his faith, and promised to have all children born of her union with my father baptized Catholics. She kept her promise. But she was never at heart a true Catholic. She had a beautiful character—a beautiful Pagan soul—but she was never religious."

Perhaps this curious combination of faith and non-belief on the part of his parents, which must have meant a continual clashing of influence, explains much that seems otherwise inexplicable in the character and work of Theodore Dreiser.

From his early childhood, Dreiser was always trying to find a reasonable explanation for all he was expected to believe. This greatly disturbed and annoyed his father, but not his mother. "My mother was always with me in spirit," he said. "She made up to me for all the rest of my troubles. She was a broad-gauged woman. Just to know she was with me in my search for the truth was sufficient to make life look pretty good. She had a beautiful soul."

He has no quarrel with any religion. "I have great respect for people's beliefs," he said, "whether sensible or not."

He said that with many people religion was an instinct. "For the most part, a man must have something outside his own strength to lean upon, but I think the choice of his religion should be left to the individual. I do not think religion should be organized and forced upon any people, in the name of Christ, of Buddha, of Mahomet, or of any other leader. That sort of thing dragoons men into acting as if they had been born evil. I do not believe it. I do not think the average man is at all rotten. If you swept away all existing religions everywhere, gave humanity a clean slate tomorrow, I do not believe the average man would be one whit the worse off. He'd probably have a brand new religion within a week, but while he was without he would have behaved just as well.

"Look at the Chinese. They have never had a religion. Confucianism? That is not a religion in the sense that it 'binds the spiritual nature to a supernatural being,' which is, I believe, the first definition of the word. Mohammedanism, perhaps, and Buddhism a bit, with a touch here and there of Christianity, but not enough of all of them put together really to encompass them as a people. The Chinese have lived four or five thousand years without a religion. And look at them. They have the oldest and surest civilization in all the world."

All the time he was talking he was twisting his handkerchief, shaking it out, plaiting it into tiny folds, shaking it out again. I rather liked the business with the handkerchief; it seemed somehow characteristic. The Chinese, he assured me, were not an evil people.

"They could not have lived and increased as they have done for these thousands of years if they were an evil people," he added. "They are not a race of murderers; they take care of their children, and of their parents and their relatives. If the continuity and progress of a race depended upon its adherence to any set religion, the Chinese long ago would have been as extinct as the Toltecs. Instead of that they outnumber the people of any other race. They have produced great men, great women, great books, great works of art. Chinese art, compared with the art of any people or any time, is beautiful—and it has nothing to do with religion."

He was busy plaiting the handkerchief again with both hands, absently, all his attention centered on his defense of the religionless Chinese. Suddenly the hands were still. One, holding the handkerchief, was on his knee; the other lay on the arm of his chair.

"What is good? What is bad?" he asked, and seemed actually to wait, in all courtesy, for the answers he did not get and had no right to expect. "It may be good for you to do something, to have something, and bad for me to let you do or have that particular thing. Both of us can't have what we want. . . . I lean more to the mechanistic side. If you put your hand in a buzz saw it's pretty apt to be cut off. If I get excited, I pay for it. Still, I think no one should be shut off from any experience he wants to undergo. No one should be kept from trying to find out the truth for himself. I do not think that it should be said to the human mind about anything: 'All that is now a closed book; there is nothing more to be learned.'

"The religion that appeals to me as the most reasonable of all religions is that interpreted and taught by Elias Hicks, a Quaker. Hicks believed that every individual must have his own revelation of the truth. He believed there was a divine instinct in every man, something that told him to sit still and listen. His Book of Discipline is ideal for human guidance, if human beings could ever successfully follow an ideal."[4]

Of his newspaper work Mr. Dreiser tells us at length in "A Book About Myself." That work took him through many adventures and experiences that he has since been able to turn to account in his fiction, but it left him, at the last, full of bitterness. That was in New York when, after an almost spectacular career as a newspaperman in St. Louis, and no mean success in other cities, he found himself unable to get an opportunity to show what he could do. It was the best thing that could have happened to him, but it did not seem so to him at the time. He called it "a messy and heartless world" with which he had to work.

Reference to "A Book About Myself" brought from him the statement that the title was none of his choosing. "My publishers plastered that title on it," he said. "It is the second volume of a series of four, and I had called it 'Newspaper Days.'[5] I don't see anything wrong with that for a title, do you? Yes, I have the first of the series written. The manuscript is in an old tin trunk with a lot of other unpublished stuff. I am not sure that it will ever be published. Too much family stuff in it. I have not submitted it to my family, nor to my publishers, but I don't think I have any right to publish it."[6]

At my request he showed me some of his poems. They sounded a bit Whitmanic, but seemed to me better, cleaner, more musical than anything

4. Hicks (1748–1830), a New York farmer and Quaker leader, played a major role in the schism of American Quakerism into two branches during the 1820s. It is not clear, however, what Dreiser means by his reference to Hicks's "Book of Discipline." Books of Discipline are not the work of any one author but rather collections of testimony concerning Quaker belief and experience prepared by specific Quaker meetings—the Philadelphia Book of Discipline, for example. Dreiser became interested in Quakerism in early 1914 when he consulted a number of Quaker works in preparation for writing *The Bulwark*, a novel of Pennsylvania Quaker life.

5. In 1931 Liveright republished *A Book About Myself* under the title *A History of Myself: Newspaper Days*.

6. Dreiser is referring to the manuscript of *Dawn*, which he indeed did publish in 1931, though only after cutting it and disguising the names of family members.

I had ever seen of Whitman's. I said so. In a moment he was at my throat, growling like an angry bulldog.

"They can't touch Whitman," he declared, belligerently. "Not Whitman's poetry. Much of Whitman's writing was not poetry at all—it was beautiful prose-philosophy. But when Whitman begins to sing, he sings! Have you read Whitman? Very few who condemn him have really read Whitman. Have you read his 'When I Heard the Learned Astronomer?' No? Have you read 'The Noiseless, Patient Spider?' Those are two of the loveliest things ever written. And there is the one beginning, 'A child asked me what is the grass.' I can't tell you how beautiful those things are. Don't argue about Whitman. Read him."

Looking back on it now it seems to me that he was more concerned in having Whitman properly appreciated than he was in putting himself, or his poetry—which, now that I have read Whitman, I still think is better than Whitman's poetry—or anything else he had written, in the most favorable light. And yet there are those who think of Dreiser as a bloated egotist.

Because of the too realistic nature of his writing, his calm matter-of-fact way of opening up a rose to show the slug at its heart, Dreiser has had no end of trouble getting his books before the public. One of his books was once rejected by the publishers after it was in type.[7] "The Genius" (which title Sophia Kerr has recently used for a short story)[8] was withdrawn from publication after it had been out a year. He has always had trouble finding a publisher for his plays. One of them, "The Hand of the Potter," all of his old publishers declined. His present publishers, Boni and Liveright, asked him for one of his books. He had a book ready, took it to the inquiring publishers and with the book-manuscript, the manuscript for "The Hand of the Potter."

"They didn't want the play," he admitted, with his funny, oblique grin. "'No play, no book,' I told 'em, so they took the play."

All of Dreiser's fiction has been attacked by critics, in and out of print. Libraries decline to carry some of his printed works. Even "An American Tragedy" is banned by some libraries. Others are kept by some libraries only "for hall use." One wonders a little if all this censorship has not made sales for his books, and created a more or less morbid interest in his writings that only time can sift and settle in its true proportions.

7. Dreiser's novel *The Titan* was in final page proof in early 1914 when its publisher, Harper's, withdrew the book. (It was published by John Lane later that year.) Harper's had apparently received information that Dreiser's portrayal of Beatrice Fleming might provoke a libel suit in Great Britain, since the character was based on Emilie Grigsby, a woman still prominent in English society.

8. Sophie (not Sophia) Kerr (1880–1965) was a prolific writer for popular magazines. Her story "The Genius" appeared in the *Saturday Evening Post* 198 (30 Jan. 1926): 40–41.

He feels adverse criticism rather acutely, I think. Not of himself personally. That he does not mind in the least. He will give you a little book in which his friends say all sorts of unflattering things about his personal appearance. "Long, loosely put together," says Harris Merton Lyon, in his description of Dreiser,[9] "with design obtuse, blunted or slack where in most individuals nature makes for acuteness and tautness. A lolling gate, a lolling head; unbeautiful, unarresting, prematurely grizzled. A loose mouth, chin blunted and rather small; bluish grey eyes, large lolling eyes, perhaps neurotic and meaning nothing, save perhaps in anger. Simply a tall, ungainly, unlovely man with something of the cast of Oliver Goldsmith's features. Something lumpish, something rankly vegetable is evoked. What? A huge rutabaga; a colossal, pith-stricken radish." Rankly overdrawn as this is, Mr. Dreiser does not mind it in the least. But he resents the attacks upon his books.

"I have been hounded," he said "ever since I began to write. It was started by three women. One in Denver, one in Chicago, and one other woman, started to pound and to hammer. From 1903 to 1915 a woman on the Chicago Tribune never stopped pounding me. Jesus! Every time anything of mine would come out she'd do a handspring. The other two would join her, and the hissing and squawking could be heard from coast to coast.[10] And now nearly everybody takes a lick or a jab at me."

But they don't all jab to hurt. If all that has been said for and against the writings of Mr. Dreiser could be got together, it is pretty safe to say that the for would outweigh the against.

As a writer, he looks upon himself as a recorder of life as it is. He writes of it as he sees it, the good along with the bad, the mighty with the simple, the evil with the righteous, the dull with the interesting. He leaves the reader to make his own deductions. It is rather odd that he has never drawn into his fiction a character so delightful as his good friend Barfleur about whom he writes so charmingly in his "A Traveler at Forty,"[11] or, for that matter, that he has never created a character in fiction so lovable as the Theodore Dreiser he so naively depicts in that same book.

Just as he put Europe as he saw it into his one book of travel, so does he put life as he sees it into all his fiction. He knows his books will not

9. Lyon's pen portrait of Dreiser appeared initially in *Reedy's Mirror* (see p. 108, n. 2). It was republished in 1917 in the John Lane publicity pamphlet *Theodore Dreiser: America's Foremost Novelist*, from which Maury quotes.

10. The *Chicago Tribune* reviewer appears to be Elia W. Peattie (1862–1935), who published three negative reviews of Dreiser's work in the *Tribune* beginning in 1911, and the "other woman" is probably Mrs. N. P. Dawson, who, between 1913 and 1922, wrote eight negative reviews of Dreiser's books for the *New York Globe and Commercial Advertiser*. The Denver reviewer has not been identified.

11. See p. 40, n. 6.

have a popular appeal. He does not write them for the money he will get out of them.

"I don't give a damn about money," he said in his slow, convincing way. "I have never formulated a single commercial scheme in my life. I've had to work, and I've made money, but I've never known how to keep it. Money doesn't mean much to me."

His room, high up in a downtown office building where he does most of his writing,[12] certainly has in it none of the showy "trappings of wealth." Some books, notably an old and worn set of Encyclopedia Britannica, which he says he uses a lot, and the necessary place to sit and work, make up the furnishings of that room. He reads enormously when he is not at work on a book or a play, goes often to the theater, which he loves, and spends a lot of time at the Museum of Art.

"I could stand days at a time before some of those great paintings in the Museum of Art," he said. "I don't spend much time now looking at reproductions. You can't get the artist's personality from a copy as you can from an original. I had to learn that for myself. I had seen and been thrilled a thousand times by copies of Botticelli's Primavera, but my first look at the original in the old city of Florence almost took my breath away. As I stood looking at it I seemed to feel what the artist was dreaming away back in the Middle Ages.

"I can't define what it is that gets into the original of a work of art other than a personality. Whatever it is, it is the thing that makes a great picture. Take Whistler's study of his mother, or any one of his portraits, or his etchings along the Thames. You think the copies are beautiful, but when you see these pictures in the original, you know that the copies, no matter how perfect, lack something. It is Whistler's personality. It is something that can't be copied. No reproduction can quite get his nice arrangement of details, his delicate perceptions of light and shade. But, more than anything else, it is Whistler's indescribable feeling for life itself that one gets from his originals and misses in the copies of his work. I think a great artist puts something of his own soul on every canvas he paints. That is why those great originals are so precious, so priceless.

"It is the same with a great sculptor. When I saw Michelangelo's 'Dusk and Dawn,' his 'Night and Day' as he himself had left them, the tears came to my eyes. I can't describe them. I can only feel them. Curious how anything so without form and substance as darkness and light could be so livingly portrayed in marble.

12. Dreiser rented an office in the Guardian Life Building on Union Square from March to the end of November 1925.

"How full life was for Michelangelo! If he had lived a thousand years it would not have given him time to express all that life meant to him. So much of his work was not finished, not because he did not want to finish what he began, but because he did not have time. Artists and sculptors living after him, borrowed his ideas. Some of them have borrowed only part of his ideas, without completing them for themselves. Rodin, seeing some of Michelangelo's unfinished figures, borrowed the uncompleted expression of the idea and gave the world 'The Thinker,' a copy of 'The Duke of Urbino,' no more, no less."

Mr. Dreiser writes of these unfinished pieces of the great sculptor's works in "A Traveler at Forty," calling them "strange, unfolding thoughts, half hewn out of the rock."

He is greatly interested in the work of American artists. "Back in the 'nineties," he said. "I belonged to the Salmagundi Club, where such men as George Inness, Bruce Crane, and J. Francis Murphy used to come and talk.[13] A lot of distinguished artists, or men whose work afterward made them famous, belonged to that club. But America had not acknowledged their existence. You couldn't talk about American art then. To hear our critics and art collectors of that period was to hear that the United States could not produce art. Foreigners were the only artists. The George Innesses that now bring $20,000 sold then, when they were purchased at all, at $1,000. The work of many of the others now to be found in the Metropolitan Museum of Art, and eagerly sought after by collectors, could not then be sold at all."

While he is gripped by his admiration for the work of the old masters, he has no quarrel with the ultra-modernists. "Certainly I don't object to them or to their work because they are impressionists. The new method may express a great deal of temperament. Any method an artist finds adequate and intelligent is the method for him."

Going from art and artists to writing and writers he said that perhaps too many books were being written, but that the average book, for all of that, was very well constructed. "I am considering the average book technically," he explained. "You respect technique up to a certain point. The thing that makes a book live is the same thing that makes any other work of art live—the personality that is put into it. Why does Emily Bronte live? You have only to read "Wuthering Heights" to know. . . . There has been more palaver about Poe dead than about all of us who are alive. The books about Poe

13. Dreiser joined the Salmagundi Club, on West Twelfth Street, in early 1898, and lived there for several months. The membership of the club consisted largely of writers and artists. Crane (1857–1937) and Murphy (1853–1921) were minor landscape painters. Because Inness, a major landscape artist, died in 1894, Dreiser could not have known him, but he probably knew his son, George Inness Jr. (1853–1926), who was also a landscape painter.

would make a little library all by themselves. The value of a man's work is not measured by its quantity but by its quality. Think of the books written by E. P. Roe, and who ever thinks of E. P. Roe?"[14]

Asked how he accounted for the revival of interest in Blake, he said that he had not noticed there was a revival. "I think it is more a steady growth of interest. Blake gave us something that we are coming more and more to appreciate. There is something—in his books and in his drawings—to feed upon. What could be more appealing in its beauty and simplicity than his: 'Why should I be bound to thee, O my lovely myrtle tree'? Blake's life was a tragedy from beginning to end. The world will never forgive that piece of cheese, William Haley, who kept Blake's nose to the grindstone for what should have been some of the most productive years of Blake's life.[15] Imagine starting out with a poetic temperament, a soul inspired to do beautiful things, and a hand and brain ready to put those beautiful things into shape and color, and then having to take orders and do merely mechanical work. Blake was a great man, but it has taken nearly a hundred years for the world really to begin to appreciate his greatness. No, it isn't a 'revival' of interest; it is an awakening."

Dostoievsky's "Crime and Punishment" he considers the most impressive book he ever read "for sheer mental revelation." "Madame Bovary" he calls one of the great books of the world, while "Thaïs"[16] has "beauty as moving and soothing as anything ever written."

He holds that a writer is at his best when he writes about things with which he is thoroughly familiar, especially if he writes fiction. "Thomas Hardy," he said, "has become a universal novelist by writing, wonderfully and well, of his own little neck o' the woods in England."

Of our own writers he spoke first of Edith Wharton. "I think highly of Edith Wharton. She knows her ground, and she knows how to cover it. I like the matter and the manner of that man Cabell.[17] We have some good writers. 'My Antonia' and 'The Lost Lady' are fine books.[18] The man who promised to produce the greatest American novels died when he was just beginning to show what he could do. That was Frank Norris. In 'McTeague'

14. Roe (1838–88) was a popular sentimental novelist. His most well known book was *Barriers Burned Away* (1872).

15. Hayley (not Haley) (1745–1820) was a minor poet and country squire who employed Blake from 1800 to 1803 but who completely misunderstood the nature of Blake's art and thought.

16. *Thaïs* (1890) is a historical novel by Anatole France.

17. The Virginian novelist James Branch Cabell (1879–1958) gained notoriety during the 1920s because of the sexual suggestiveness of much of his fiction. His *Jurgen* (1919) was widely condemned and banned.

18. These are two novels (1918 and 1923, respectively) by Willa Cather (1876–1947).

he had a great novel. How the critics howled when that book came out! How they leaped upon him tooth and nail! Sherwood Anderson, in 'Many Marriages,' is almost great. He seems to think he needs to tell a story, but he doesn't. Plot for him is not necessary. He has an idea, and he writes out of that idea. And what he writes is interesting.

"Nearly everybody has one story to tell. Nearly everybody of normal intelligence has one book he might write. What so many writers in the United States do is to write one book that is really good. It is drawn from their heart's blood, and because of its source it is vital. Into it the writer puts all that is himself. It represents his entire experience with life. When it is written, he has exhausted his material. He should stop. Such a writer has no ability to interpret life as it comes to and is lived by others. He cannot put himself in another's place; he cannot envisage the life of another.

"There are other one-book writers who are so because they lack courage, or industry, or need money. Harold Frederic wrote one book. It was a fine book, very effective, very true. It was denounced.[19] He decided to reform. After that he wrote nothing but drivel. Not long ago I made a list of twenty or twenty-five men and women writers like that. They had proved they could write, but they were afraid to go on. They were spiritual cowards.

"O. Henry was a man of genius. He wrote two or three great stories, full of sweetness, beautiful with understanding, happy with laughter. If I were dealing with his stuff I'd cut out all the rest. He should live, and he would live, by those stories and those alone. He wanted to stop writing after he had written them, but he was forced to go on. His publishers subsidized him—bribed him with twenty cents a word. That in itself was enough to make a man who needed money—and O. Henry nearly always needed money—spoil any good short story. How can a man who needs money stop at five thousand words when by stringing his idea out to ten thousand words he can get another thousand dollars for it? It takes a very great genius to dig hard for a new idea when he can make as much by stretching out an old.

"Ambrose Bierce? Why mention him? He is a stylist—nothing more."

19. It is not clear whether Dreiser is alluding to Frederic's initial novel, *Seth Brother's Wife* (1887), which was his most realistic work but financially unsuccessful, or *The Damnation of Theron Ware* (1896), which was controversial in its portrayal of religion. Dreiser frequently praised the latter, but Frederic wrote only two novels after it.

An Interview with Theodore Dreiser in Which He Discusses Errant Youth
American Novelist Blames Hidebound Conventional Morality for the Negative Confusion That Pervades American Youth—the Confusion Born of a Heritage Gone Wrong
That Heritage, the Puritan Influence, Is Our Greatest Possession, but Like All Great Possessions, Capable of Becoming Our Greatest Menace

By Philip Emerson Wood

*

Philadelphia Public Ledger, 3 July 1927, Magazine Section, p. 7.

The following paragraphs were printed as a headnote above Wood's byline. They explain why Wood asked Dreiser about the problems facing youth in the 1920s and list some of the questions he must have asked prior to or during the interview.

Is the tragic dilemma of youth today—if such a dilemma exists, as the moralists and philosophers tell us—due to the clash between Reality and Illusion, the head-on collision between Truth and Romance?

Are youthful crime waves, student suicides, mental smash-ups and moral collapses to be accounted for on the ground that youth is hopelessly engaged in the pursuit of a pot of gold at the end of an impossible rainbow, and the romantic fiction that good fortune will appear on the scene in any crisis?

If cold facts and ideals are to be reconciled, what philosophy of life must be evolved for youth in an age of super-sophistication?

Theodore Dreiser, the American novelist, wrote a book around this theme a little time back. It was done into a play that countless thousands of Americans have seen—the pitiful story of an American boy gone wrong and coming ruefully to an ignoble death in the electric chair.

This man should have some answers for the queries listed above. And he has, as the following interview demonstrates. He says "we must learn to adopt the compromise of tolerance, which is as cleansing as laughter and as fruitful as good orchards."

The astonishing success of Dreiser's masterpiece, "An American Tragedy," proceeding, as it has, from its first edition as a novel, through six triumphant months as a play on Broadway[1] and still persisting as one of the six bestsellers, testifies to a breadth of public interest that would justify many inquiries.

Having both read the book and seen the play, I had two excellent reasons poignantly to appreciate this epic as American fiction's superlative tragedy of youth; but I wanted to know why Dreiser had written it in the first place. And I wanted to learn from Dreiser—and this for purposes of sharing—just what monstrous fault lies at the bottom of this terrible story; what sin of commission or of omission constitutes the greatest American tragedy. And I wanted his remedy.

The great novelist proved to be a big, boyish man of middle age, a man of leonine head, massive shoulders and delicate, tapering hands, who welcomed me with such genuine cordiality as actually to seem pleased at my intrusion.

"You take your ashtray, and I'll eat my candy," he said, seating himself in the other chair, "and we'll have a wonderful time." So, while he held his sweet chocolate in one hand and the other occupied itself with a handkerchief, we conversed to the perpetual accompaniment of a nervously rocked rocking-chair—one sign of an active mind.

"I wrote it," he said, "because I had to. That is why I have written all of my books: because they demand to be written. And that, incidentally, is justification enough for any writer so willingly a medium for art as to be both regardless of the market and fearless of the censor. You have quoted John Drinkwater as saying, in his 'Estimate of Swinburne,' that the true poet is mastered by his song;[2] that must be so; I am sure, at any rate, that the same is characteristic of the true novelist—that the real story-teller is mastered by his story.

"As regards the story of Clyde Griffiths, I'm frank to admit that I was mastered for ten sympathetic years, and that for more than two of those I

1. See p. 126, n. 1.
2. John Drinkwater (1882–1937) was an English poet, dramatist, and critic. The correct title of his study of the English poet Algernon Charles Swinburne (1837–1909) was *Swinburne; An Estimate* (1913).

sat at that table every single day from 9 in the morning until after midnight obediently spinning the yarn.

"I was possessed of a frenzy for sketching—or so it seemed to me at the time, so great was my haste—moment after moment, detail after detail, of that tragic experience, fearful that if I omitted a single fragment of the mosaic the total effect might be ruined.

"After which came the considerable task of editing, when the medium becomes the mentor and therefore additionally responsible for the brain child intrusted to his care. Because I never once intruded upon this book my own point of view or interpretation or philosophy, nor even indulged myself the relief of painting a word-picture here or there—liberties I have felt free to take with other books I have written. When the job was done the result seemed so foreign to me that I simply couldn't adjust myself to it at all.

"It struck me as being just a monumental failure. If it had been so adjudged by the world I would have been disappointed, naturally; but I should still have had the compensation of knowing I had done my best, and there is a certain success in that.

"But that, of course, is not all. To say that I wrote 'An American Tragedy' because I had to do so is only half an answer to your question. What you want to learn, obviously, is that which specifically commanded me— that particular vibration which found such complete response in me as to force me to listen long; that poignant chord which sounded over those ten years with such sustained intensity as to compel me to speak.

"Well, as a matter of fact, it was no single note, but a repetition; it was a sequence of tragedies so insistent as to achieve the terrible beauty of a dreadful monotone. For, you see, Clyde Griffiths' experience was not unique: it was typical; Clyde himself is not unique: he is a prototype. There were any number of youths victimized by a condition which I shall attempt to explain whom I might have chosen for my unfortunate hero as profitably as I chose Chester Gillette, that luckless lad who murdered one sweetheart in favor of another in upper New York State those several years ago.[3]

"There was a minister down in Massachusetts,[4] there was a farmhand in Colorado,[5] there was a student only recently in Minnesota.[6] Day by day,

3. See p. 137, n. 1.

4. See p. 141, n. 5.

5. The murder case involving a farmhand in Colorado has not been identified.

6. A murder case involving a student in Minnesota has not been identified, but it is possible that Dreiser was thinking of William Orpet, a student at the University of Wisconsin. In a trial in 1916 Orpet was acquitted of the charge of poisoning a former lover who claimed she was pregnant when she learned he was engaged to another girl. The Orpet case was one of the typical cases he cited in his first article on the Robert Edwards case of 1934 (see p. 140, n. 4).

week by week, year by year, sufferers from Clyde's malady passed in dismal parade across the headlines of the newspapers, and I witnessed their passage with increasing pity. Ultimately, when I became painfully conscious of the imperviousness with which, nationally, we dismiss youthful crime waves, student suicides and such in our hectic search for excitement and indulgence of ourselves in material prosperity, I fled to my desk.

"Clyde Griffiths, the prototype, was the victim of a prevalent confusion— the confusion born of a heritage gone wrong. That heritage is the Puritan influence, our greatest possession, to my mind, but, like all great possessions, capable, if not properly utilized, of becoming our greatest menace. This to a large extent has happened. It went wrong when its strength was misspent in a clinging to its repressions in an effort to resist the tides of change.

"As a result, American youth was left high and dry, with neither dependable foothold upon reality nor hopeful glimpse of promised fields—neither solid establishment in wise traditions nor the conception of a properly enriched future. Clyde, for instance, was the product of a dogmatic religious atmosphere that took no account of actuality, and the victim of a harsh actuality that made no allowance for vague beginnings. Between the two his life, untutored to compromise, was lost.

"Lacking the positive endowment of a backbone background, he was incapable of facing the issue of his conflict; lacking the vision that is the reward of living, he was incapable even of realizing that it existed. So he was left a negative. And he sought the negative solution, which is escape: sought to destroy the beautiful truth that was Roberta so that he might follow the bright vision that was Sondra. He took Roberta out in a boat, vacillating as to whether to drown her or not, but his very vacillation is only a reflection of the conflict between illusion and reality that was visited upon him by his early training and environment. He was incapable of a positive decisiveness even at the crisis, and confided his problem to circumstance. It is my sad conviction that this same negativeness has a sad analogy in all the tragedies of contemporary American life.

"In the same boat with Clyde, figuratively speaking, are innumerable young Americans desperately believing that there is a pot of gold at the end of an impossible rainbow.

"The scion of wealth who imagines he can buy happiness; the flapper who dreams she can exchange her beauty for a palace and live happily ever after; the choir-singer who lets her passion robe her shepherd with heroic dimensions, dismissing life itself in her frenzy to live the deception, and— saddest of all—the student suicide, so confused by intellectual bankruptcy as not to be able to meet and dispose of pessimism.

"Obviously, there is some fundamental error, and I believe it happens to be a unifying one. A certain influence has exerted itself upon one and all—from the young explorer in crime to the saddest of willing victims of delusion. It is a romantic fiction, desperately clutched at through the negative darkness; the fiction of Fortune's appearing on the scene at the crisis and giving something for nothing. And the reason for this, the darkness itself, so to speak, constitutes what we might call—if tragedies were not so analogous to the pound of feathers and the pound of lead—the greatest American tragedy.

"This I believe to be hidebound conventional morality. Like a huge cloud, it has settled over us to suffocate us as it has blinded. It has fastened upon our puritanical virility and rendered it ineffective. Now, personally, I feel that we have nothing so vital and vigorous as that Puritan strain, if we will only shake off the shackles of misinterpretation. We must be worthy of it. When the Puritan fathers left the meads of Britain to batten on the granite moors of New England, it was imperative for them to employ a rigid code in the enforcement of their purpose. But the experience seems to have resulted in a focusing upon the rigidity at the expense of all purpose. So that today, with our frontiers broken and our commercial prosperity established and secured, we have a condition pitifully divorced from imperative purpose and burdened with decayed repressions. We have a nation relaxed into the pursuit of pleasure, with no hard necessity to keep its nose to the grindstone, and we have only a succession of prohibitions brought bluntly to challenge the release of inhibitions naturally subsequent upon leisure and enjoyment.

"We have been guilty of mass thought, mass action, mass judgment too long; we have made a fetish of generalizations. What is right for the many—we have taken the dictum over from Puritan days to an epoch to which it does not apply—is right for the few; what is a sin in the throng we adjudge to be a sin in the individual. Such reasoning has always been erroneous, but in our busy and more intensive ancestors it was at least excusable: its adoption eliminated involved considerations of the individual when community interests were all-demanding.

"Today we should be able to correct the error. Conscious that no civilization ever has survived except through its individuals, we should indulge ourselves the profitable experiment of adopting latitudes that would permit of individual development. We should assume the wisdom, though we have it not, of letting youth be young first, so that it may proceed naturally to a development broader and more vigorous and more accomplishing than our own.

"Let me sketch, briefly, the contrast in a different setting. A friend of mine—a Russian—was approached by his daughter with a confession that would have shocked and dismayed the average American parent. This father, though, did not weigh the issue on the scales of an impervious moral-ity, but simply asked, 'Do you think you have acted wisely?' To him it was a matter of practicality rooted in ethics rather than one of morals derived from precedent. That, however, was due to his peculiar heritage. But the inci-dent is enough to indicate that, to older civilizations if not to our own, the ethical side of the matter deserves consideration. It may be argued that it indicates, also, a decadent attitude toward something of tremendous impor-tance; but personally I tend to accept the evidences of artistic and cultural accomplishment in other, older civilizations as testifying to something more beautiful, more aspirant and more enduring than decadence."

He had risen and was looking out of the window, down upon a shrunken multitude moving antlike below. There was a certain apprehensiveness in his attitude that suggested to me that he might be waiting for my question. So I asked it. He answered with slow, deliberate conclusiveness.

"What is the remedy?" he repeated. "Anything but escape. Anything but a fatuous attempt to destroy our precious if perilous legacy in a chasing of the bubble of illusory deliverance. We cannot change; we should not want to. We can only improve, refine. Depending upon our very Puritan influence for the positiveness we must realize in order to direct that influence prop-erly and profitably, we must bring definite and progressive order to the nega-tive and forgetful chaos. Then we must build up, on the foundations of that order, new structures worthy of our new dreams.

"We cannot become Russians, and that should be as gratifying to us as it probably is to the Russians. But we can at least consider all other peoples, and how they toil not with inner conflict, neither do they spin confusing skeins of youthful bewilderment. We can consider them, and we can be accepting of their valuable contributions, always remembering that such contributions are valuable only as we apply them to our vast intrinsic store.

"We must learn, first, foremost and persistently, to adopt the compro-mise of tolerance, which is as cleansing as laughter and as fruitful as good orchards are. Taking all foreign contributions and refining them in the cru-cible of our national experience, and applying the result to our enriched intrinsic possessions, we will find ourselves arrived at new and worthy pur-poses. And to achieve a purpose is to approach a destiny."

Theodore Dreiser Here on Way to Study
Results of Sovietism

*

New York Herald Tribune (Paris edition), 27 October 1927, pp. 1, 10.

On 11 October 1927 Dreiser received an invitation from the Soviet government to attend the tenth anniversary celebration of the Bolshevik Revolution in Moscow, which took place 3–10 November. After receiving assurances that all his expenses would be paid and that he would be allowed to travel freely throughout Russia for a month or more, he left New York on 19 October and spent some time in Paris and Berlin before arriving in Russia on 3 November.

Theodore Dreiser, the American novelist, arrived in Paris yesterday on the way to Russia, professing a wide-open mind and only a vague idea of what he will see and learn in the next two months as a guest of the Soviet Government. He will be a strange guest, an ignored guest, free to tramp about the country and scrutinize the people, customs, policies and ideals as he wills. He will be an experiment.

The first week of next month is the tenth anniversary of the Russian revolution.

This, then, is the experiment: 1,500 intelligent persons from other nations, writers, painters, bankers, Government experts, diplomats, laborers, industrialists, are going to Russia in small groups to look upon the fruits of ten years of Sovietism. There will be no conducted tours, no lectures, no printed propaganda. The guests may roam the country as they will, or hive themselves up in Moscow. At the end of two months they will return to their native countries free to tell their fellows what they saw and learned, be it favorable or otherwise.[1] The Soviets are content to rest their case with their guests. Mr. Dreiser will lead the party from the United States.[2]

1. Although 1,500 persons of the types described were invited, there is no evidence that they all were offered the opportunity promised Dreiser to roam the country at will or to stay for two months. Probably Dreiser described what he was to be allowed to do, and the interviewer assumed that the same arrangements were made for the other visitors.

2. Dreiser did not lead the American delegation, but he was told that he would have more of his expenses paid than most of the other delegates (see Dreiser, *Dreiser's Russian Diary*, ed.

The novelist is going both as a student of economics and as a culturist, his ideals divided between the conceptions of the artist and the worker. He knows, he confesses candidly, little about Russia. Some of his views are those of 1919, when Russia was a lawless, starving, violent nation of people spinning about in quest of something they were not sure about. Others are strictly up-to-date, especially as concerns Russian literature.

"I have read all I could on Russia," Mr. Dreiser said yesterday. "Russian literature shows the country to be dynamic, bubbling, spiritually alive. The literature, for example, is pre-eminent because of its naturalistic approach. Read Dostoievsky, Gogol, Checkov—great men! Now about their mode of living and their government.

"An artist flourishes under adverse conditions. Success has bought off at least 90 per cent of those persons whose artistic concepts would otherwise have been correct, those writers who were potentially worth while. But security has its values. Where the economic scheme insures economic security, then you have a people less selfish."

He was asked if he knew that Upton Sinclair was the most popular writer read in Russia.

Understands Sinclair's Popularity

"That is quite understandable," he replied. "People like to have their ideals confirmed for them. He does it in his works. I can see that he would be."[3]

"Have you any preconceived notions of Lenin and Trotzky?"

"Trotzky, I am informed by people who knew him when he was here, is a zealot, a sort of Christ of the economists. Lenin, I am also informed, was a remarkable man, a broadgauged man, a genius of government. That is all the notion I have."

He then was told that a recent interview with him indicated that his trip to Russia was to examine its possibilities as a place to work, since he no longer found it possible to work in New York.

"That is positively incorrect," he said. "You can't pry me out of New York. I've worked there. I hope I always will."

Mr. Dreiser said he would not write about Russia while there, and no novel about it when he returned.[4] "You can't invade a country and write

---

Thomas P. Riggio and James L. W. West III [Philadelphia: University of Pennsylvania Press, 1996], 29).

3. A convert to socialism, Sinclair (1878–1968) focused on the exploitation of workers and other evils of capitalism in many of his novels and other writings. His best-known novel was *The Jungle* (1906).

4. In fact, Dreiser did write about Russia, first in a diary he kept while there (published as *Dreiser's Russian Diary*; see n. 2 to this interview) and, when he returned, in a syndicated series

of it understandingly," he explained. "You can't write much of anything that way."

An "Individualist"

"I am an individualist," the writer continued. "They of Russia in policy and ideals I believe are collectivists. Any nation is entitled to adopt any means whatsoever to move away from misery. If Russia is really moving away from misery I am with them, and I don't care what the world thinks. If that's their ideal then I say, 'Go ahead.' And about propaganda. It's all right in some instances. Take the 'Confessions of St. Augustine' and 'Uncle Tom's Cabin.' Were they not critical propaganda?

"Government is a concept. Russia has a dream. Human nature is malleable. Government can exert pressure on the individual and make him a collectivist. I don't care about that. Ideals are what I want. That is my view of Russia. I am interested in it, its change, its ideals, its dreams."

Mr. Dreiser first was invited to Russia by the International Workers' Aid, a sort of "Russian Red Cross," it was explained.[5] He was hesitant, preferring a more formal invitation from the Government.

On the status of American society today Mr. Dreiser delivered himself as follows:—

"Religionists control America. The American people, like the Germans, the English and the Russians, think religiously. But in America religion is a much more vital factor; in fact it is so vital that the religionist forgets all about himself in attempting to reform the other fellow. Hence the shibboleth of our times 'the American people must be moral—if not by faith, then by law.'

"You see, it's this way," he went on, "when one exalts a religious ideal he forgets all about religion in the contemplation of the ideal. That is what I mean by saying that, while the attitude of the American people is essentially religious, while religion affects and often dictates politics and expresses itself often in fundamentalist crusades against public vice and individual liberty, religion, as such, has very little to do with the life of the religionist.

---

of eleven articles for the North American News Alliance ("Dreiser Looks at Russia," *New York World*, 19–28 Mar. 1927), a magazine article ("Russian Vignettes," *Saturday Evening Post* 200 [28 Apr. 1927]), and a book entitled *Dreiser Looks at Russia* (1928).

5. F. G. Biedenkapp, the executive-secretary of the International Workers' Aid, visited Dreiser on 11 October and extended the Soviet government's invitation to attend the celebration in Moscow. "A Russian Red Cross" was the description Dreiser used for the organization after he was told that its purpose "was to aid workers in all countries" (*Dreiser's Russian Diary* [see n. 2 to this interview], 28).

Points to American Mission

"This leaves the way open for another ideal which is so closely bound to the life of the idealist that it is no longer an ideal but a spring of action. The American thus becomes the apostle of all those essentially material things that can be made bigger and better and at the same time expand the joy of material living.

"What will be the outcome? The attitude is not wholly confined to America; it seems to be permeating the world. The international diffusion of capital and the interlocking of international bonds through investment and finance, it seems to me, must eventually give rise to a financial Caesar, or a financial triumvirate or even a financial oligarchy which must rule the world and upon which will fall the onus of keeping the king's peace."

Mr. Dreiser averred that in the realms of both the novel and the drama America is rapidly coming to the forefront and producing literature of a high quality and essentially American in inspiration and execution.

"Writing is a profession," he said, "and with the large market for literary wares thousands are being attracted into the field. We can't help develop a few good ones. The dominant note is realism and though it is difficult to write a good realistic novel, I believe we are on the point of producing a number of writers who may win international recognition. There's a market for romantic stuff, also, but the best work is being done in realism."

Mr. Dreiser characterized Shaw's "Saint-Joan" as the greatest piece of classic drama he had ever seen and ranked it in the first rank of the world's best dramatic works. He also mentioned a French play, produced in America several years ago, "The Failures," as one of the best things that has been done.[6]

"I have forgotten the author's name," he went on, "and strange to say I don't believe he is recognized at all in France."

Of H. L. Mencken he said that the one-time iconoclast had turned reformer, an apostle of uplift. "Mencken is trying to convert the boob American to accept the advantages of civilization, but he's having a hard time of it. Hence he's got a lucrative job for the rest of his life."

---

6. A play by Henri René Lenormand (1882–1951), *The Failures* (1920) is the story of an impoverished playwright and his wife, an actress. When she engages in prostitution to support them, he murders her and commits suicide. The play was produced by the Theatre Guild at the Garrick Theatre in New York in 1923.

Dreiser back from Russia; Praises Soviet
Novelist Reports Happiness Is More
Widespread Than in America,
with None Lacking Food or Shelter
Liberty Is Less, However
Would Not Starve There, but He Would Be Put
in Room and Told to Go to Work

New York Herald Tribune, 22 February 1928, p. 6.

Dreiser left Russia on 13 January 1928 and, following stops in Paris and London, arrived in New York on 21 February.

After three months in Soviet Russia,[1] Theodore Dreiser returned yesterday singing the praises of communism. There is no Utopia on the steppes, as Dreiser sees conditions in the land of the late czars, but there is much that the United States could copy, for he found in Russia a more general distribution of happiness than was ever managed here. The novelist went abroad as the guest of the communists, but he insisted that this fact did not influence his conclusions.

Dreiser said he found no Elysium, and that some of his observations were under conditions none too pleasant. He found the leaders of the Soviet generally disposed against him because of his nationality.

On his arrival here on the Hamburg-American liner Hamburg, he was told of the bread lines in lower New York.[2]

"It is a disgrace," he remarked. "This country has sent billions abroad.

1. Dreiser was in Russia for a little more than two months (seventy-three days), not three months.

2. A week before Dreiser returned, Bowery missions had reported a significant increase in the number of jobless seeking food and shelter during the previous two months. The headline for the story in the *New York Times* was "Call Breadlines Longest Since 1916" (16 Feb. 1928, p. 21).

Millions of this have been wasted, and are being wasted to-day. Look at the money that is being wasted in this country. Yet we have bread lines! Why, Russia will not let any one starve. If people can't pay their rent the government pays it. The government feeds the hungry. No one is in want."

Would Change American Life

Centralization of wealth in the United States seemed to be the greatest evil to Dreiser. He described America as a land where "slickers" fought for money and when they had it lived for nothing except to take more away from other "slickers."

It is this system that has to change, Dreiser felt. He was convinced that when the result of the Russian experiment becomes better known the so-called capitalistic countries will be forced to meet the Russian plan half way in order to avoid some such cataclysm as upset the old Russian regime.

Dreiser quoted Winston Churchill, Chancellor of the British Exchequer, with whom he talked after leaving Russia, as agreeing with him regarding the "inevitable influence" of the Soviet republic on other nations. He added that Churchill privately favored spending "half of the British treasury" on humanitarian projects, such as those instituted by the Russians, in order to prevent the complete upset of the government.[3]

Dreiser said that were he a Russian citizen his lot would not be anything to shout about. He would not starve—he emphasized that—but he would not have the opulence in which he is now ensconced. He said the Russians would put him in a room and tell him to go to work and that his comfort would be determined by the products of his labors.

Just now in Russia there is no sincere cultivation of the arts, he said, and unless artists turn their talents to propaganda for communism there is little hope of recognition. The authorities there want cheerful things—a reaction to the Russian literature of the last century, he found.

Marked Change in Writings

"They are writing as a result of what they have been through," he said. "It is similar to the change in literature that came with the rise of Christianity. Pagan stories were forgotten and generations passed before they were revived."

Dreiser used the comparison of Sovietism and Christianity advisedly, for when he was asked if the leaders of Russia to-day were fanatics, he replied:

---

3. Ray Long (1878–1935), an acquaintance of Dreiser's and editor of Hearst magazines, made arrangements for Dreiser to have an interview with Churchill while he was in London.

"Of course, it is a religion."

The nation appears healthy, he said, and though not as well clothed as more settled countries seems on the whole a good deal happier.

"When a worker leaves the mines over there at the end of a day's work he comes out smiling," he said. "That means something."

Dreiser Home, Sees Soviet Aims Gaining
Author Thinks Principles of Government Will Spread Even to This Country but in a Different Form He Declares There Is No Bread-Line or Unemployment in Russia—Deplores Coal Strike Here

*

New York Times, 22 February 1928, p. 9.

Theodore Dreiser, author of "An American Tragedy," returned yesterday with Mrs. Dreiser[1] after spending eleven weeks in Russia studying the Soviet regime. He said he was convinced that its fundamental principles are destined to exert a vast change in the social and economic status of the world.

The author said he believes that while America will drift to these principles, they probably will be manifest in another form, since no nation completely takes over the governing methods of another.

It was explained that Mr. Dreiser had been received in Russia as an emissary of American letters and Joseph Stalin placed at his disposal two secretaries who were with him and Mrs. Dreiser for their entire stay, traveling with them wherever they went.[2] The Dreisers returned on the Hamburg-American liner Hamburg.

Varies on Labor Program

The writer regarded as splendid the Soviet program as it is applied to the masses, since every one is guaranteed food, shelter and clothing, but he was at variance with their overemphasis of the importance of labor.

He was asked if he had met Trotsky and replied that he was in Moscow

---

1. Dreiser returned with Helen Richardson, who was often introduced and passed off as Mrs. Dreiser before their marriage in 1944. She joined Dreiser in Paris after he left Russia.

2. Helen did not go to Russia with Dreiser (see previous note). During his tour he traveled with Dr. Sophia Davidovskaya, a physician who was sent by VOKS, the government agency in charge of his visit, to serve as his official guide and watch over his health, and with Ruth Kennell (1893–1977), an American living in Russia who served as his secretary. Kennell later wrote about her trip with Dreiser in *Dreiser and the Soviet Union, 1927–1945: A First-Hand Chronicle* (New York: International, 1969).

at the time of the Russian leader's fall and saw him made a target for a fusillade of overripe tomatoes.[3]

"The Soviet Central Committee, the ruling power in Russia," Mr. Dreiser said, "will not stand for opposition of any character within its ranks. Trotsky and some of his associates in the minority group were in a temper of revolt. Stalin and his group were in the majority. There was nothing left but that Trotsky and his associates be ejected, and though he is a man of tremendous following, he was ejected and exiled. Every Soviet realizes that their strength alone lies in unity, and if there are divisions the scheme must fall."

The writer said that what interested him greatly in Russia is that there is no private property. He said that Stalin lives in a three-room apartment which cost $125 a month and which, like all other apartments, is paid for by the Government.[4]

He was asked if there is not a tendency to adopt capitalistic methods. He said that while Russia already had returned to gold and silver as an exchange, the country seemed apparently determined to centre everything in the nature of property in the Government itself, instead of in individuals and groups of individuals.

When asked what happened to the collector and the connoisseur in Russia, Dreiser said:

"There are none, nor should there be. We people in America have a mania for collecting endless objects. Art and books properly belong where every one can have them, and that is what has happened in Russia with all private collections of art and of libraries."

Distrusts "Big Business"

Dreiser spoke distrustfully of American big business and was bitter on the question of the coal strike in the bituminous mines.[5] He said he held no

3. Dreiser arrived in Russia at the time the power struggle between Joseph Stalin and Leon Trotsky had reached its climax. Trotsky was expelled from the Communist Party while Dreiser was there and banished from Moscow shortly after he left. Although he tried, Dreiser was unable to meet and interview either Stalin or Trotsky, and there is no record in his diary that he ever saw Trotsky, even from a distance as a target for overripe tomatoes.

4. This statement was quickly corrected by Dreiser. In a letter to the editor of the *New York Times* dated 22 February and published on 28 February, Dreiser wrote: "In the interview with me in today's TIMES I am made to say that Joseph Stalin lives in a $125 a month flat with the Government as his landlord. He lives and has his offices in the Kremlin, the guarded official centre of all the principals in the present Central U.S.S.R. control in Moscow. What he pays, if anything, for his three rooms is very likely 10 per cent. of his official wage. And his official wage is 225 rubles per month—say, roughly $112" (p. 24).

5. On 1 April 1927 the United Mine Workers went on strike when operators in the bitu-

communistic convictions, but that such conditions as these point directly to the fact that if American business men do not face their responsibility of assuring the workers the right of shelter, clothing and food, the workers will develop here the same consciousness as they have in Russia.

Mr. Dreiser was surprised to read in the newspapers brought to the liner at quarantine yesterday morning about the labor conditions here.

"I cannot understand," he continued, "why there should be bread lines and unemployment in a nation as rich as America,[6] which in recent years has given $15,000,000,000 to Europe outright and where there is sufficient to provide every human being here with food, shelter and clothing.

"In Europe there are reports of actual poverty all over the United States as the result of stagnant business conditions. Yet nowhere in Russia, regardless of whether the nation is prosperous or not, will you find men without coats standing in bread lines waiting for a hand-out. That is one thing the Soviet has accomplished and which is not a theory but a fact."

The liner was a day late because of head winds and high seas all the way across from the Channel to Sandy Hook, the officer said.[7]

---

minous coal industry refused to negotiate a new contract unless the union accepted a reduction in wages. At the time of this interview the strike was still ongoing, with the plight of striking miners worsening while operators kept the mines open by importing strikebreakers.

6. See p. 165, n. 2.

7. The last paragraph in the text of the interview, which discusses the birth of a baby boy during the ocean voyage, has been omitted.

Dreiser Looks at the Russian Jews
In an Exclusive Interview America's Foremost Novelist Compares His Impressions of Jewish Life in the Soviet Republic and in This Country

By Sulamith Ish-Kishor

*

The Day (New York), 10 February 1929 [p. 1?].

Sulamith Ish-Kishor (1896–1977) was primarily an author of children's books, although she also wrote a number of nonfiction books for adults and articles for periodicals and New York newspapers. In 1935 Dreiser wrote an introduction to her biography of the Roman emperor Hadrian (*Magnificent Hadrian* [New York: Minton, Balch, 1935]), and on his request she wrote an introduction to the revised edition of his poetry, *Moods: Philosophic and Emotional (Cadenced and Declaimed)* (1935).

"There isn't a country in the world where the Jews are as well off as they are right here in America. The general status of the Jewish people is higher in Communist Russia than it was formerly, but the attitude of the Russian people toward them has not changed. As the Jews are natural-born traders, they can't be as happy and comfortable under a system which forbids private profit as under one which is based on individual endeavor. In America we have the ideal conditions for the individual to get ahead of other people if he's able. Most of the Jews I have talked to, here and in Russia, seem to be greatly in favor of the Communist system in Russia, but I don't see any Russian Jews successful in America who are abandoning their business here to go to Russia, unless it's to get concessions."

This is the gist of what Theodore Dreiser, famous novelist and author of "Dreiser Looks at Russia," which is the most comprehensive and readable book about that country today, says on the subject of the Jews and the Soviet Republic.

Sitting in his imposing apartment in the West Fifties,[1] Mr. Dreiser was leaning over his wide desk, stooping his shoulders as large-built men often do. Now he lifted his head briskly and his arresting gray eyes challenged rebuttal.

"The Jews are natural-born traders; for centuries they've been acting as go-betweens. The ancient Phoenicians were of Semitic stock, and they traded all over the old world. It may be something biologically, ethnically, even—who knows—psycho-genetically predestined. Possibly Darwin could have explained it—I do not know. But the fact remains, and you can't take away a race's primary characteristic or bring about a change over-night. There are several colonies of Jewish farmers in the Crimea, I understand, where the settlers get along very well. I've never seen them, but I was told about them. But farming isn't what the average Jew wants to do. Oh, I know there are ever so many idealistic Jews who study all the time and never make a cent, but they're not the active members of the race, the ones you encounter everywhere.

"I'll tell you a story that will give you a fair idea of the problem of the Russian Jew who is trying to adapt himself to present conditions.

"A Jew came to the licensing bureau to ask for permission to do some trading. The man in charge of the bureau said to him:

"'Now look here, why do you want to trade? Why don't you go on a farm instead? We'll give you fifteen acres; we'll give you a horse, a cow, and the necessary machinery for farming. And you won't have to pay any taxes for the first year.'

"'Well of course, that's very nice,' said the Jew. 'But couldn't you let me peddle shoe-strings?'"

Mr. Dreiser laughed heartily and went on:

"The first thing a Russian Jew tries to get is a concession or permission to trade. It's natural; that's what he's been trained for and he knows all about it; he feels lost in anything else. But if he can't get that, he tries to get an official position. They all want to be traders, or else officials! I except, of course, the Jewish artist, scientist, writer, poet, as I except these in any general classification. They are inspired by dreams that are not material and I acclaim them for it. But there are a number of Jews in important state positions in Soviet Russia: M. N. Kantor, head of the Gosizdat (state publications bureau); Mme. Kameneva, head of the Cultural Relations; Mr. Litvinoff, of the Foreign Office,[2] and others. But of course there isn't room

1. In late December 1926 Dreiser and Helen moved into a duplex apartment on the thirteenth and fourteenth floors in the Rodin Studios at 200 West Fifty-seventh Street in New York.
2. Olga Davydovna Kameneva (1881?-1936), was the sister of Leon Trotsky and head of

for all the Jews who want official jobs. If they're told, 'Sorry, we're full up, there's no room for you,' the next thing they are likely to try for is a license to trade at the markets or depots. Once in a while you'll see the police leading away a man who's been trying to trade without a license; they take him to courts and sweat it out of him, and by and by he doesn't want to trade without a license any more. (But there are just as many Gentiles as Jews who try that game.)

"Now I do not assert, because of that, that the Jew cannot be happy in Russia, or that because of certain prejudicial lies, a man or a race cannot find some form of happiness anywhere. But just the same while I was in Russia the thought frequently came to me that because of their rather general instinct for trading and because of Communism's fatal opposition to that instinct, the Jews must needs be unpleasantly[3] affected by it. It would be much the same, I should think, as though I were now never again permitted to write. Not that the general public might not be benefited by that, but alas! My own ingrown instinct is to scribble. And if a Jew desires to trade and is told that he must not—well, you see what I mean. . . .

"On the other hand and, most distinctly, there is no acknowledged anti-Semitism on the part of the Government although it persists among the people, I think. On the contrary, the Government is doing its best to try to help the Jews to adjust themselves to the new order and the so-called discrimination against them applies only to the Jews as members of the bourgeoisie and to the Jews as Orthodox religionists. In short, the Communists are trying to stamp out religion, the Greek Catholic as much as the Jewish or any other. Of course they haven't succeeded; even the children, educated in the Communist schools, are sometimes influenced by the parents and priests and may be found kissing some tenth-rate ikon at a wayside shrine or in a church. Also the old generation complains that the Communist Government makes the children too free, so free indeed that they won't reverence God or their parents and so the elders secretly try to educate the young ones in religion.

"Conversely the Communists charge that the old generations of all the races—Jews, Catholics, Mohammedans, Confucians, Buddhists—are opposing the modern teaching of their schools. And this they fight, of course. But

---

VOKS (the Society for Cultural Relations with Foreigners), the government agency that was in charge of Dreiser's trip to Russia. Maxim Litvinov (not Litvinoff) (1876–1951), a deputy minister of foreign affairs at the time of Dreiser's trip, became the minister of foreign affairs in 1931. M. N. Kantor has not been identified beyond what Dreiser says about him. Dreiser met with Ossip Beskin, the head of the Department of Foreign Literature at Gosizdat, not Kantor, when he visited the publishing house in Moscow (Kennell, *Dreiser and the Soviet Union* [see p. 168, n. 2], 58–59).

3. The original text reads "pleasantly."

truly I believe that there is no animus shown against the Jews as such by the Government; and it refuses to tolerate any outbreak of anti-Semitism on the part of the Russian people.

"But though their social status is thus much improved, and the old fear of sudden violence against person and property is eliminated, they are often more out of place than they were before. Where they come off badly is in the ban on trading; that's the thing they do best, and that's out. They find no satisfaction for their talent for getting ahead of the other fellow. Even if a Jew gets a job as manager of a hotel, there's no chance for him to make any personal profit; if he did manage to get more than his small fixed salary the Government would pretty soon be at his heels. 'Here,' they'd say, 'how do you get money for those fine furs and those magnificent dinners and this luxurious furniture?' The only thing he could do would be to buy the things he wanted and hide them in the cellar in the hope of getting out of Russia some day. A good many people—Gentiles and Jews—try to do that. But that's another thing."

Mr. Dreiser's long right hand, which had been busily moving up and down the edge of the desk as if wiping invisible dust from its polished angles, now closed as he got up—six feet two of Hoosier American, with a broad, oval face, rather ingenuous, and strange gray eyes steeped in a quality that is the opposite of the practical realism characteristic of most of his great works.

"America is the ideal country for the individualist who is capable of getting ahead," his quick, soft voice went on. With decision he added, "I like America and best of all, New York. Look what it's given me—what it gives everybody. You know, Communism isn't independence. It's just the opposite. It's the cutting off of every kind of independence! You've got to obey every law and rule of the community; you've got to swear you'll do it. I have the greatest interest in the Communist experiment; even if it doesn't—as the Komintern is so sure it will—bring heaven on earth in fifty years. Its success is slowly affecting the whole world; it will eventually alter the relations of the other people to their Governments."

Although the book, "Dreiser Looks at Russia," makes no specific reference to the Jewish people, there are, scattered throughout Mr. Dreiser's other works, some interesting references to individual Jews. The following excerpt from his "A Hoosier Holiday" is perhaps most expressive of the light in which this American from Indiana, who probably has had very little contact with Jews, is inclined to regard them.

"For a period of over fifteen years in my life," he says, "at the appearance of every marked change—usually before I have passed from an old set of surroundings to a new—I have met a certain smug, kindly little Jew, always the same Jew, who has greeted me most warmly, held my hand affectionately for a few moments, and wished me well. I have never known him more intimately than that. Our friendship began at a sanatorium at a time when I was quite ill. Thereafter my life changed and I was much better. Since then, as I say, always at the critical moment, he has never failed. I have met him in New York, Chicago, the South, in trains, on shipboard. It is always the same. Only the other day, after an absence of three years, I saw him again. I am not theorizing, I am stating facts. I have a feeling at times, as I say that life is nothing but a repetition of very old circumstances, and that we are practically immortal, only not very conscious of it."[4]

4. *A Hoosier Holiday* (New York: John Lane, 1916), 348.

You Know Mr. Dreiser
The American Tragedian Turns His
Freudian Eyes on Music

By R. H. Wollstein

*

Musical America 49 (25 Feb. 1929): 36–37, 55–56.

Rose Heylbut Wollstein was an author and editor who specialized in interviews with celebrities on topics in music.

A long, lofty, luxurious room, panelled in dark wood, and half-lit by winter light pouring in gray and snow-laden through a tall north window, that framed a scape of jagged and uneven modern buildings beyond; and in a massive carved chair, Theodore Dreiser leaned back his head and talked of music.

There is something revelatory in listening to Dreiser talk, and in watching him. You see a tall man, lithely put together; you see a sculptural head, massive of structure, and with features formed on a large scale and ruggedly, as if hewn laboriously out of rock. Dreiser's face is pallid, and his eyes are light; he has a vast and noble frontal space, and back from it rather than above it, his hair is light, white or fine blond, it doesn't much matter. A veiled look about his countenance suggests a light of startling brightness hidden somewhere beneath.

Dreiser's manner is gentle and mild; almost diffident. His voice is very soft; and a note in it makes you wonder whether at some time, this voice has not called loudly before closed doors. He doesn't talk much, yet he conveys much meaning. While he talked to me, he twisted a handkerchief into quarters and eighths, and sixteenths, and still smaller units; when it was reduced at last to a tight ball, he shook it out, surveyed the design, and began all over again, with the same meticulous precision.

When Dreiser speaks, you actually witness travail and creation. He has a very definite point to make, and he hammers at it, and under it and around it, until it is entirely released. His speech is not fluent, yet he leaves you no doubt as to what it is he means. Often enough, he merely indicates an idea, finishing it by "You know," with a persuasive emphasis on the "You," as though it were the short way of saying: "I want desperately to get this said—so please don't you go adding to the complicatedness of things in general by taking out the wrong meaning." There is a building-sense to his talk: you feel that words are urgent, alive things to him, completing him by producing on the outside a clear picture of the thing that is burning him up on the inside.

"All my life I have had a feeling for music," says Dreiser's soft, hesitant voice, "although I'm not at all technically informed on it. I can't play any instrument—I can't feel the delight of personal performance. I have only one means of expression—words. Nevertheless, technical uninformedness doesn't hinder me from understanding music. The sources of inspiration are identical for all the arts. Man's hunger for emotional release through expression is the sub-structure on which any great artistic endeavor is built, I don't care what its medium. And I can translate the thought of a great symphony or a noble piece of chamber music into my own thought, and take from it the thing I need. The symphonies of Tchaikovsky, for instance, can be translated in many ways; at most, as a profound philosophy of life, and at the very least, as a temperamental reaction to life, without definite philosophy or meditation.

"Besides reflecting the individual thought-processes of the composer, music can express more adroitly and more economically than any other art, the racial and national characteristics from which it springs. Take Grieg. I hear Grieg, and at once I see fjords and ice-capped horns, bleak winter light, and buxom peasant girls in bright dresses. I see Grieg himself, too, hunch-backed and prophetic, struggling to say so much with his music. As a matter of fact, it takes very little material for Grieg to create a mood, compared to the hundreds and hundreds of words Ibsen has to use to say the same thing.

"In like way, the delicacies of Debussy seem to epitomize the light, idealistic temper of the French. Often enough, he says the same pastel and form-lovely things that you find in phases of Watteau's work.[1] Debussy, I think, stands for the exotic dreamer's fancy, for the delicate fugitive of art, for which France has so peculiar a gift. And again, Wagner sums up all the imaginativeness of the Teuton—and he does it best, strangely enough, in Tristan, where the theme is not at all Teutonic but Celtic. I am not a great admirer of Wagner, nevertheless I have to go to him for the perfect expression of German fancy.

1. Dreiser is comparing the music of Debussy to the paintings of the French artist Jean Antoine Watteau (1684–1721).

"I'm not an admirer of Wagner, nor of any other composer of opera. I am opposed to the operatic form as a means of noble artistic expression. I said this back in 1900, when the Metropolitan was at its very peak of perfection, as far as eminence of casts goes, and when general musical opinion inclined to accept opera as Holy Writ more than it does today.[2] I said then—and I still feel—that opera is not harmonious. I don't mean inharmonious in *sound*; rather, inharmonious in those structural proportions necessary for a perfect whole.

"The mechanics of dramatic structure, for instance, often call for pauses after climaxes, that make for uninteresting music. And musical structure often calls for climatic developments that lessen any impression of emotional genuineness in the action. When a tenor draws his sword, and rushes fiery-blooded to the footlights and waits for the orchestra to play the requisite number of introductory bars before he can give his feelings voice—well, that sort of thing doesn't make you feel either comfortable or satisfied.

"Frequently enough, the singer's exotic temperament interferes with the mood of quiet or dreaminess necessary to the action. The only operatic performance that completely satisfied me, without causing me jolts or let-downs, was Pelléas et Mélisande, with Mary Garden.[3] No opera can equal symphonic or chamber music or the unhampered personal projection of a great soloist."

Occupying as he does a unique position in the struggle between the old order and the new, it seemed important to learn Dreiser's views on modern music.

"I take very little delight in modern—or ultra-modern—music. It has not enough poetry or dreaminess. It makes a harsh, cynical business of life, over-looking its beauties. Much of the ultra-modern output is simply ridiculous, by trying so hard to be ahead of the times and prophetic. Perhaps this attitude of advancedness is genuine enough; perhaps it is inspired merely by an active publicity sense. I don't know. But this I do know—unless an attitude of prophecy is backed up by actual genius, the result is not art but carica-ture. Genius *is* prophetic; it doesn't have to try to be. Genius not alone reflects the sum total of its past experience, it looks forward and intimates the future as well. I remember distinctly that the first time I read Dostoievsky I had the sensation of being carried far ahead of my day. I got the same feeling from Freud. But I haven't gotten it from any composer since Debussy.

2. The occasion of Dreiser's statement has not been identified.

3. *Pelléas et Mélisande*, an opera by Debussy, was adapted from a play with the same title by the Belgian poet and dramatist Maurice Maeterlinck (1862–1949). Garden (1874–1967) portrayed Mélisande in the premier of Debussy's opera in 1902 and later in her Chicago debut, where she was the leading soprano from 1910 to 1931.

"Music is behind the other arts—notably writing and sculpture—in finding forms in which to express the modern mind. Our musical standards are still traditional ones. We aren't prepared for the things that are being put before us in modern music. For that reason, there may be more beauty in them than we can see; on the other hand, they may be even shoddier shams than we suppose. Up to thirty years ago, the least show of revolutionariness in art damned a man. Systematized traditionalism held artistic expression fossilized into rigidity.

"Then what happened? A very natural reaction. Like a breath of pure air, the principles of a new freedom came into being in France. Here was revolution on a sound and true basis. But the great and sound and honest revolt soon became swamped with cheap little hangers-on—every loon and lunatic that could write a line or twiddle a note, no matter how imperfectly, 'joined the movement.' And the result, of course, is the artistic confusion we are still fighting to get free of. In music, the struggle isn't anywhere near solved. Music hasn't gotten out of the turmoil into peace and grandeur again. Doubtless a great modern composer will come—some day. He hasn't yet.

"One of the fields where a musical reformer is most needed, is that of the orchestra. Why should the same pat sets of instruments be kept year after year, without amplification or addition? There was objection when the saxophone was introduced into the orchestra. Why? The saxophone is a stirring instrument. The orchestra should be enriched, just as the alphabet should. I can make any number of sounds that I can't put down in writing, simply because there are no letters or symbols to express them with. Why should expression be limited that way? There's no earthly reason why I shouldn't be able to write down by sign or symbol every sound that can be made. And similarly, there is no reason why hundreds of sounds should continue to lie unborn in composers' minds, simply because the proper instrument with which to express them, hasn't yet been used. Something should be done to break down this fenced-in attitude towards instruments.

"As to distinctly non-musical sounds—automobile horns or chains or whistles in music—they leave me profoundly cold and unstirred.[4] I don't say that they haven't a place in music—I simply say that to date, they haven't been used in music in a way worthy to prove their value. Some day a genius may come who will know how to use a little of such mechanical noise to express greatly the spirit of a mechanical age. And there should be great, mighty music when he does come. But he hasn't arrived yet, and instead of being magnificent, a concatenation of mechanical noises proves merely dull.

4. Dreiser may be referring to the *Ballet Mécanique*, by George Antheil (1900–1959), a composition scored for car horns, propellers, and so on, which caused a considerable stir when performed in New York in 1927.

"Of the moderns, I like the Russian school best. The surprising thing about Russia is, that there is no distinctly radical music movement. In spite of the newness and revolutionariness of the government and of everything else, music in Russia is still conventional. The regular European operas and symphonies are being performed in all the large cities, and, as far as I could make it out, no really new native things are being created. The one musical form that they are working out in a new way, is the ballet or pantomime. And that is gorgeous!

"I got the greatest kick out of that. There you have mass movement—mass color—mass spirit, and the most stirring effect of concerted and unified action. They have the National Soviet Ballet School, accommodating some fifteen hundred pupils, ranging in age from three to eighteen. They pay almost nothing for their tuition, and get the best to be had, by way of actual instruction, as well as the richest scenic materials with which to practise their art. This new ballet form is tremendously interesting. I don't say there is any definite political connection between communism in government and mass spectacles on the stage; the two simply seem to have come into a tremendous being together. All the ballets produced in some way glorify the people, or the spirit of humanity, rather than the kings or princelings of orthodox operatic lore.

"Free of religion as they are, these Russians put on Hugo's Notre Dame, exactly as it is written.[5] They leave out nothing, as another country would have to do, because it might offend priests or zealots. They give it like Coq d'Or—pantomime, accompanied by voices off-stage[6]—and I tell you it was like getting to Heaven, to sit there and witness that magnificent, moving mass spectacle. I forgot the cold outside—I forgot I was lonely and in a strange land. There was nothing to do but glory in the ecstasy of it. Nowhere but in Russia could they put on such vivid and human mass-spectacles. And fortunately, Russia is doing it as well as it is possible to do it!

"They haven't any too much money there, but they are able to produce the finest things. It is part of the Russian make-up to venerate art. I know for a fact that men like Stalin—people who actually bear the burden of running the government—are content to work hard for as little as a hundred and twelve dollars a month.[7] They ask no better. But a man who is

5. Dreiser saw a Russian Ballet interpretation of Victor Hugo's *Hunchback of Notre Dame* at the Bolshoi Opera House while he was in Moscow in 1927 (*Dreiser's Russian Diary* [see p. 161, n. 2], 136).

6. *Le coq d'or*, the title under which the Russian impresario Sergei Diaghilev (1872–1929) staged Rimsky-Korsakov's opera *The Golden Cockerel* in Paris and London in 1914. In this production dancers and mimes enacted the plot while singers sat at the side of the stage.

7. See p. 169, n. 4.

recognized as an artist—as a potent factor in building up the country's artistic life, is feted the way royalty used to be, and is paid, proportionately speaking, a higher salary then he would be paid here. I wish we might learn a little of Soviet Russia's reverence for art."

Theodore Dreiser Speaks
An Interview with the Novelist in Which We are Permitted to See Many of His Views and Convictions

By Carol Bird

*

Writer's Monthly 33 (May 1929): 392–98.

In this interview Dreiser discusses at length his views and convictions on the "sex impulse" and censorship.

Theodore Dreiser, one of America's leading and most prolific writers, foresees a rigid form of censorship and suppression as a result of the orgy of sordid plays produced in this country recently.

While the author of "An American Tragedy"—his latest novel, which has also been dramatized[1]—contends that censorship is inevitable, and that Society is justified in protecting itself against a deluge of the vulgar and the obscene, he fears that legal censorship may result in puritanical tyranny in the form of undiscriminating repressive methods. He is of the opinion that the ultra religionist and the rabid reformer, backed by legal authority, may not stop at curbing the cheaply erotic, created for commercial gain only, but may run amuck and invade the field of the truly artistic.

Mr. Dreiser has long been known as an opponent of censorship of art in its various forms. During past "campaigns," and epidemics of suppression, he himself has been a victim of the unwise wielding of censorship power, resulting in its abuse. Two of his well known novels, now widely read and circulated—"The Genius" and "Sister Carrie"—at one time came under the censor's ban, and were taken from the libraries, to be replaced with a change in censorship standards. It is the restrictive and destructive effect on artists and their output which Mr. Dreiser dreads contemplating, but which he

---

1. See p. 126, n. 1.

anticipates as a result of a censorship that does not always differentiate between counterfeit and real art.

He discussed censorship and its abuses and misuses in an interview in his beautiful new studio on Fifty-seventh street, in New York City. He sat at a refectory table in the enormous work-room where he writes his novels, great Cathedral windows letting in a flood of light. Beautiful figures painted in oils, hung on the high walls, bright book bindings, handsome tapestries and oriental rugs, gave warmth and color to a room of exotic atmosphere.

The man who wrote "Jennie Gerhardt," "The Financier," "The Titan," "An American Tragedy," "The Genius," and other novels, is a man of massive bulk, quite in keeping with his works, for they are executed on a somewhat colossal scale. He is of a serious turn of mind, outspoken, forthright. He talked about censorship freely, but impersonally. In this same earnest spirit he spoke of the sex impulse, which he says is so fundamental a part of life that no work of art that attempts to mirror life honestly can be without it.

"With censorship, as with everything else," said he, "there is always the tendency on the part of certain people to go too far. These are the ones without brains, taste or artistic discrimination. And the people who put on sordid, cheap shows, and who publish trashy magazines, books and papers, and the ignorant ones who patronize the obscene shows and buy the trashy 'art' magazines, are the ones who bring about censorship.

"Those who commercialize the bawdy shows know that any discussion of sex pays, for there will always be people who have a morbid curiosity about it. These morbid ones are those whose own lives have been thwarted. Defeated in their natural sex impulse, they satisfy their desires and their needs vicariously—in art, the theatre, statuary, paintings. For we cannot get away from the great and important truth that sex is a fundamental phase of life. It cannot be overlooked or ignored or talked down. And there are always those greedy and unprincipled ones who for money will give the ignorant masses what they crave.

"After all, it is a queer and unnatural mind which is devoid of sex desire. The man without this normal endowment is either erratic or downright insane. Even the Saints were normal in this respect. It was not that St. Anthony had no desires, but that he had them and struggled against them and overcame them, which made him beloved by the Church.

"The real cause of the suppression, or the attempts at suppression, of plays, books, and certain other forms of art, is the kind of sex impulse peculiar to the rather low mental capacities of the masses. Yet it is not the ignorant who create the laws, or take aggressive action in cases of the kind which are now creating so much discussion.

"Those who are doing all the active work for suppression are conservative, cool-headed, cool-blooded individuals who have very decided notions as to what society and morals ought to be. It is the ultra religionist who dictates. And his ire is stirred, his activities launched, because he is offended by what he considers the immoral and vulgar displays of sex. And because he cannot always discriminate, he is frequently offended by the best displays of it. The Venus de Milo, or 'Sex' (the play),[2] it doesn't matter which, to his often frustrated soul—the beautiful work of art and the vulgar drama—both arouse him to immediate and drastic action. To him, 'something must be done about it!'

"It is only very ignorant or terribly over-sexed persons who would be interested in or entertained by a play like 'Sex.' The brothel scenes, which I understand are depicted in it, make certain people laugh, give them a vicarious thrill. If they didn't get a thrill out of it, they wouldn't be there. Naturally, it is just this sort of thing which scratches the moralist most. He sees a vulgar display of this kind, or reads a trashy book written to please the ignorant or the oversexed, and immediately he starts out on his vigorous campaign of suppression.

"'I will do something about this at once,' he tells himself, filled with indignation and disgusted by the crudities and vulgarities he has witnessed. And he proceeds to raid the offensive thing. But having triumphed there, it is not so easy to hold him to his true field. The partially unclothed Venus in the Louvre, 'Jude the Obscure,' of Hardy, 'Madame Bovary'—if any one chances to tell him of them—all come next.

"So, you see, it is not the vulgar fellow who needs sex relief in some form or other who does the suppressing. It is the fellow who is not troubled by the sex impulse who accomplishes it. His well-regulated, cool and calm life goes on without any sex upheavals to work havoc with it. So he works hard, in his moral wrath, to suppress the plays or the books or the pictures which have offended him. And it is the poor fellow who has a different physical make-up who is the one to suffer ultimately.

"Yet Nature is always the same. To a high percentage of people life is based on the sex relationship, and a high percentage of people are controlled by it. It is often the sex desire, and not wisdom or level-headed, far-sighted planning, which throws a man and a woman into marriage. And it is the sex desire, too, which tosses some types of men into the hands of the Church, because their religion and their sex impulse run hand in hand. Then, in the

2. *Sex* was a comedy starring Mae West (1892–1980), who played the role of a good-hearted Montréal prostitute. Written by West under the pseudonym Jane Mast, the play became a hit despite bad reviews after it opened in 1926. Then, forty-two weeks into its run, it received even greater notoriety when authorities raided it and a jury found West guilty of producing a lewd show.

hands of the Church, goaded there by the sex impulse, the victim soon finds that the Church has control over him.

"There is always the same percentage of cool or frigid men and women who never had a strong sex impulse. I suspect that these are in the minority. Of course you cannot look into the hearts of people to learn just how they feel about it. But I fancy there is a larger number of people in this world with strong sex impulses than those with weak or cool ones. This impulse has been present ever since man was an animal, and it will continue to be so until the Creator provides some new methods of producing life on this earth.

"It is true that sex takes many crazy forms. I talked with a well known psychiatrist on this subject not long ago, in connection with the much discussed play, 'The Captive,' of which he disapproved on the ground that it might lure the normal to abnormalities.[3] I did not agree. I know that sex sometimes takes on every imaginable lunatic form, but I do not think such lunacies are contagious. It is only that a too strong yet normal impulse in one sets him before the public. In fact, a little too much of this entirely normal impulse often sets people crazy, throwing them into orgiastic frenzies which, however, are not fatal or contagious. It may make them leap over tables and do all sorts of idiotic things; but then this frenzy attacks animals just as it does human beings. You have only to observe animals, to witness their crazy reactions.

"The sex impulses, unchanged, can be traced down through the ages. If I read history aright, it was this impulse that was responsible for the original form of old Roman and Greek orgies and fantastic celebrations. It took a wild and unrestrained animal form. The Roman and Greek orgiastic dances were lascivious spectacles. There were many wild festivals staged for the worship of Dionysus. The Dionysia was a festival of ecstasy and wild enthusiasm. The people in those days had these outlets for their emotion, and it was through these celebrations that they often sought spiritual purification. Votaries of Bacchus staged drunken revelries, orgies, bacchanalia—all in the name of their religion.

"Then when Christ arrived, and the Christian doctrine went into effect, it proved a powerful deterrent. The God Pan was looked upon as the Devil. He actually became the Devil in the eyes of the Christians. Sex, as one element in the Church saw it, was the root of all evil, an emotion flowing from the Devil. Those who indulged in it were offspring of the Devil. But if that is true, we all have the Devil in us still.

---

3. Because it dealt with lesbianism, *The Captive*, by the French dramatist Eduoard Bourdet (1877–1944), became a controversial play when it opened on Broadway in September 1926.

"The rise of Christianity, and the promulgation of strong moral dogmas, gave rise to these early suppressions. There are accounts of the most ridiculous doings in the Fourth, Fifth and Sixth centuries, in the Middle Ages, when people were swept into the Church like rafts down the river in a flood. These victims of religious doctrines struggled pathetically to overcome sex. There were scourgings, punishments, self-inflicted tortures. They fasted and they prayed and they suffered. The sex impulse must have been pretty strong, to force them to do all the odd things they did in an effort to overcome it.

"What terrible tests they made to prove their invulnerability to the urgings of wicked sex! And these attempts at suppression and repression and the killing of the natural and normal and powerful instinct led to secret vices, the underground and mysterious passages which led to retreats where poor sex-bedeviled souls had taken refuge, running away from life. Balzac threw some light on these goings-on in his writings. He certainly was not blinded to what was taking place all around him.

"We are not any different today than men and women were in the Middle Ages. We have the very same impulses as they had then, only they take different and sometimes new forms. What emerged from all of that long-ago campaigning and attempts at suppression has merely been a new and clearer consciousness and understanding of the beauties of sex. It is the novelist, the poet, the artist, the sculptor, who, realizing the sheer classic beauty involved in sex, gives us all our beautiful forms of art. Sex, in its higher and finer form, is revealed in the semi-erotic music of Wagner, Chopin, Liszt, in our best sculpture, drama, literature.

"On the other hand, it is the more ignorant mind, the undeveloped one, which vainly seeks this beauty of sex in the cheaper magazines, the vulgar plays, the trashy novels, the nude and common photographs. These creations, while they rarely possess so much as a trace of artistic value, still do supply to the semi-literate a taste, a faint vision, just a little sample, though a false one, of the gayety and beauty and ecstasy which is to be found in sex.

"Yet because the desires of the ignorant, and the forms which these desires take, are revolting and offensive to the more refined type of mind, some better educated, more literate persons, try to suppress the amusements and the so-called art forms which appeal to the masses. They always follow and cater to what is called 'the best sentiment of the community.'

"But as soon as you begin suppressing and repressing the natural sex impulse anywhere, it slinks into the cellar and the dark byways. You do not really succeed in suppressing vulgar followers of Dionysus and Bacchus. On the contrary, you simply make him more sly and evasive. He goes into hiding, and then his cravings come to light only when they have taken the form of crimes. Naturally, something has to be done about these poor ignorant ones, for if you let them go the limit they would become altogether too offensive.

"The Old Haymarket here in New York was once a rendezvous for sex.[4] Sex brought people there in the beginning. The Haymarket had what interested the masses. But it was run primarily to make money, and the cheapness of the whole thing was obvious to all except the grossly ignorant. And because those who managed the place had no thought but to make money, everything soon went wild. Murder became rampant. When the underworld didn't like what a man did, it was easy to hire someone to kill him, and dump his body into the river. And thus the Old Haymarket simply had to be put out of commission.

"There are limits to everything, even to sex. Sex cannot, for instance, be given free rein so that it leads to murder. Society is entitled to protection. And that is what it is clamoring for now. And when it so decides, regardless of the soundness of its judgment at the moment, it will have it. And, as in the days of the Puritans, those who do not mentally coincide are none the less compelled to obey. It is not pleasant, but again you cannot sit back and declare that organized society, Puritan or not, is not worth anything. For we must admit, whether we like it or not, that all we are, all the benefits we receive, come from organized society. It protects us, and it will protect itself. The majority is bound to protect itself against the minority. It is true that the majority would and does kill a man like Christ, and it also puts a stop to the actions of a man like Oscar Wilde.[5] But then what is one to do? One cannot refute the majority. Yet when you pause to consider that censorship—a wave of suppression—will not stop to discriminate in its wholesale work of repression, you are forced to sigh painfully, and anxiously await results of the 'reform' movement. Nevertheless, at moments—periods, perhaps—censorship is unescapable. And when you see a play like 'Sex' go, you do not really grieve. I don't, at any rate.

"I once said that the power of censorship is so dangerous, and so impossible to place in ideal hands, that you hate even to talk about it. A mere discussion of the matter is harrowing. If you say to a group of men, religionists or reformers, or whoever serve in the capacity of censors: 'Go and raid the Haymarket, or "Sex," or a cheap and trashy book!' they will not stop there. They are now out for blood, their holy wrath aroused. They will march off to the office of a high-class magazine or launch an attack upon Tolstoy

4. The Haymarket Dance Hall at the corner of Sixth Avenue and Thirtieth Street in New York's Tenderloin district was a famous rendezvous spot for middle-class married men and prostitutes. Opened in 1872, it flourished in the 1880s and 1890s and was finally demolished in 1913.

5. The Irish writer Wilde (1854–1900) was imprisoned for homosexual offenses in 1895.

or Dostoievsky. It would be terrible to see masterpieces ruthlessly emasculated. Or the censors, now grown fanatic, in an orgy of purification, suppression, repression, their reform-instincts aflame, go rushing off to the ballgrounds, and there stop youngsters from playing ball on the Sabbath. Or they prohibit children from playing marbles on that day. Cigarettes and cigars will be attacked next.

"To illustrate what will happen, let me tell you about a man I know who was living in a lumber camp in the South. His work brought him to this isolated spot and he never saw anyone from one week's end to another. He spent his Sundays peacefully smoking in his short-sleeves in front of his little shack in the woods. And as there was a reform wave on, soon he was approached by a committee of citizens who insisted that he dress himself up properly in a white shirt on Sunday. This apparel, they agreed was the only fit and proper kind for a man to wear on the Sabbath day. So this worker in the wilderness was deprived of his one poor little pleasure, his relaxation in his shirt-sleeves.

"And in a certain community of California not so long ago there was a law prohibiting the use of automobiles on Sunday except when these machines carried the occupants to a church, a house of worship. Those are samples of the idiotic form censorship frequently takes. Stir up the censors and you stir up a hornets' nest. After all, these organized censorship committees must earn their salaries. A vice crusader cannot receive $10,000.00 a year without showing some action. He must do something. Thus he pounces on everything and anything that will prove that his committee is justified in existing. Any sort of infraction or imaginary infraction is so much 'gravy' to him.

"True, there are limits to all things, and when art in its every form is abused by the cheap and vulgar demonstrations to which we have been treated lately, society is bound to step in and take a hand. The men greedy to make money, and the ignorant who do not know true art from its cheap and tawdry counterfeit, are responsible for all the trouble. And to these persons, alas, we will owe the reign of a wholesale and indiscriminating censorship, should one come. And there will be many artists of the future who will suffer unjustly if it does.

"I think our salvation—our mental salvation—lies in not keeping things from the human mind. We must face the truth. We must work it out open-eyed and open-minded. Mind is the motive force of the world. If we cannot or will not use our minds, if we must keep them blinded to the truths of life, we might as well cease living. We must stop coddling our minds, making them believe that the sex impulse is not a dominant force in life. We must look facts in the face, and talk things over with ourselves. I cannot believe that such a method of facing the truth will make perverts of any of us."

Theodore Dreiser Gives His Views on Many Things
Author Whose Parents Once Resided in Fort Wayne Asserts That He Still Cherishes His Memories of Indiana—Regards Earth As Reaching a Stage of Over-Population

By Bessie K. Roberts

＊

Fort Wayne News-Sentinel (Ind.), 19 February 1930, pp. 1, 3.

"Fee, fi, fo fum! I smell the blood of another reporter!"

Of course nobody really said any such thing. But it was what I expected to hear at any moment. I was sitting on a luxurious davenport in Theodore Dreiser's New York studio apartment. The room was stately in proportions, rich in its decorative plan. There were books to the ceiling, huge murals, tall chairs, great desk. In short the house of the giant, with everything in the grand manner. Unlike Jack I had arrived to the mansion in the air via the elevator, not the beanstalk.

But the giant had not arrived as yet. He had gone down to earth on an errand and I was awaiting his return, half terrified by the very dimensions of the place. Would he come in with a heavy menacing tread? Would he roar like the giant in the fairy tale?

I looked about me. Above the great mantle was a bust of John Cowper Powys. Dreiser is very fond of Powys I learned later. He speaks of him as Jack.[1] A beautiful portrait of Dreiser placed above a long table is exceptional for the predominance of live blues in background, suit and haberdashery. Above it hangs a rich-toned pagan nude—the reclining figure of a titian-haired woman turning toward an African slave-girl bearing a tray of fruit. High on the opposite wall is a panel of maidens posed in the Egyptian manner. The walls are panelled in dark wood.

And there are thousands of books—Powys, Knut Hamsun, collected works of Frank Norris, Upton Sinclair, James Branch Cabell, "The Great

---

1. Dreiser met Powys (1872–1963), a Welsh novelist, in Greenwich Village during the winter of 1912–13. The two became great admirers of each other's work and lifelong friends.

American Ass—An Autobiography of Puritanism," Mark Twain and count-less others.[2] Quantities of fiction.

The Giant Arrives

When lo! I am discovered. The giant arrived and to my surprise noiselessly. A large quiet man looks at me with deep-set, serious eyes. I feel impelled to give an account of myself. Who am I? Why am I here? I hasten to explain.

For there is no foolishness in a Dreiser interview. It is not easy to gain access to the writer. He feels that he cannot afford to waste his time on futile interviews. They must look promising. They are arranged through his publisher, Horace Liveright, to whom one must submit questions. If the questions strike his fancy the interview is granted.

Theodore Dreiser has a definite connection with Fort Wayne. He told me that his parents lived here about the time of the Civil War, nearly a decade before he was born. His father used to set up woolen mills in various towns in the state, which accounts for the nomadic tendencies of the family.[3] The only woolen mill here during the war was the Henry Rudisill Sons mill, which became the French-Hanna mill. The building is still standing, a four story brick now used as the Schlatter Hardware Company warehouse, on East Superior Street. The drying-ground for the blankets was across the street, where the gas-house stands now.

The most renowned member of the family until Theodore rose to fame, was his brother, Paul Dresser, famous song-writer immortalized by his song "On the Banks of the Wabash." In his book, "Twelve Men," Dreiser gives a highly sympathetic sketch of his brother, who changed his family name. Dreiser evidently has a warm spot in his heart for Indiana. In fact he wrote the chorus of Paul's song himself.[4]

He even handed me the questions I had suggested for the interview, thinking no doubt to aid me in case I lost my wits suddenly and was unable to proceed. But he stuck to the questions only at the start. Mr. Dreiser lights up as he warms to his subject. His viewpoint is detached. He is impressed

2. Hamsun (1859–1952) was a Norwegian novelist who won the Nobel Prize in 1920. *The Great American Ass: An Autobiography,* by Charles L. Edson (1881–?), was published anonymously in 1926. The work is a satiric mock autobiography of a midwesterner raised in a puritanical environment.

3. Paul and Sara Dreiser moved to Ft. Wayne in 1851, shortly after their marriage. The family remained in the city, where Paul Dreiser was employed in a woolen mill, until 1858, when they moved to Terre Haute.

4. Dreiser often made this claim, but its accuracy has been challenged by some scholars; see Richard Dowell, "Dreiser's Contribution to 'On the Banks of the Wabash': A Fiction Writer's Fiction!" *Indiana English Journal* 6 (Fall 1971): 7–13.

with the stupidity, the lack of restraint, the mad conduct of fools. His indictment of the present social order is somewhat scathing. He is not bitter,
however. His is not a personal grudge.

Headed Toward Disaster

"Fewer and better babies—that is the world's crying need today.[5] Society is
living beyond its means. It has too many children, too many insane, too
many defectives, too many slums and too many criminals. This may be all
right as long as we can afford it. But the trouble is we may not always be
able to afford it. We are headed toward disaster.

"The safest and sanest bet is birth control. There are lots more people
in the world than are needed. China and Japan are greatly over-populated.
God knows there are enough Chinamen now. Birth control should be one
of the first considerations of an ideal social plan."

The whole theory of our present maudlin scheme is to save everybody.
Save all the sick, the old, the unfit. But can we afford to do this? Mr. Dreiser thinks not. We are facing certain disaster unless we put our heads together and plan more intelligently.

"Unless the state itself works out a plan similar to the Aristotelian social plan, we, especially in America, are likely to strike a great catastrophe.[6]

"The social organization as a whole should be studied by the colleges.
The approach to the ideal social plan should be an economic one. We cannot afford to go on as we are. Better than any of the automatic checks on
overpopulation such as famine, murder and cannibalism would be the simple
expedient of consciously limiting our birth rate. Parents would be selected
in such a social plan.

"The churches and the other fools will make a mess of things if we are
not careful. It is curious that there is no illustration of a social plan that ever
made a stagger toward working out a sane way to continue itself except the
Athenian group. England borrowed the Aristotelian social scheme and
taught it at Oxford and Cambridge. It was used by the upper classes. Other
nations just flop around getting nowhere. Roosevelt in America yelled about
race suicide in the face of an enormous birth rate. We get worked up about
war and disarmament. But the real peril we take for granted. We do nothing about it.

5. For the related issues of birth control and population size in the 1920s, see p. 105, n. 9.
6. It is not entirely clear what Dreiser means, here and later in the interview, by "the Aristotelian social plan," but he may have been referring to Aristotle's belief that a democratic
society should leave decision making to those who can contribute wise counsel.

State Should Limit Itself

"The intelligent state like the intelligent man should live within its limitations and its means. We could do without lots of people. Even the geniuses come under the head of social entertainment. We could do without Bernard Shaw and even Ed Wynn,[7] although we might not like to.

"Society has a nice little pattern of the family, the father, mother and child or children. And yet we see this pattern going to pieces all around us under the impact of modern life. And who made this plan and decided that it was the best? After all, the human mind is not a fixed but a growing thing. We cannot go on insisting on this pattern."

Even the Ten Commandments are fairweather assertions, he says. It is a marvel to him when people can keep them. But even rigid adherence to their precepts will not avert the disaster that Mr. Dreiser sees headed our way.

"It is easier to keep this family pattern in the small town. But even there one finds defects. Many people feel that they cannot continue to live in the small town. And they become bitter about it after they escape. This is especially true of women and those with the artistic impulse. No doubt the small town is harder on them. They, too, are expected to conform to this set pattern.

"The city, man-made and artificial as it is, allows a more varied life to the individual. It offers a stimulus, especially to the artist, the writer, that the small town does not afford. There is something about the mechanistic defense man has thrown about himself that I like.

Likes New York

"I live away from New York for months at a time. But I am always conscious that I am away from home. I will never live anywhere else now. I like it. I can work best there. It is all very artificial. There is no land. But there are so many of every kind of people. Life is more varied.

"California is ideal for dreaming and idling one's life away. But I can't work when I feel that brilliant southern California sunshine pouring down on me. It is hard to concentrate. I would rather go for a ride with friends. It is an ideal place in which to dream and quit, to do nothing."

Dreiser lived in Hollywood for three years.

As to the bio-chemical reactions of people which Mr. Dreiser emphasizes in his writings, he believes sincerely in this theory. Personalities are undoubtedly changed by winds, rain and climate, even by a cup of coffee.

7. Wynn (1886–1966) was an extremely popular stage comedian of the 1920s and 1930s.

"We cannot deny these chemical reactions. When some people come into the room we are happy. Others make us miserable."

The play, "Rain," illustrates this theory. Dreiser was enthusiastic about this play. And about Jeanne Eagels, who did a fine piece of work in it. He expressed regret at her tragic end which he believed was suicide.[8]

It is better to read science than philosophy, he says. Philosophies change with the variableness of fashions in dress. The laws of science are less mutable. We can get some light from Dewey and James. But we cannot afford to depend too much on these changing views.

Says Art More Enduring

Art is more enduring than philosophy, he believes. The writer who succeeds in giving a true picture of his times has made a permanent contribution to the world.

"Will the modern woman ever return to the cage from which she has escaped?" I asked him.

"My God, I hope not," he said feelingly.

"What is the writer's best preparation for his art?" To this he replied that the lawyer had the best of opportunities to study human nature, to get material for realism in art. And that the physician had the next best chance. Tchekhov, for instance, was a medical man and a great realist.

Dreiser, the great reporter of the American scene, the great realist, has achieved detachment to life. At the same time he has the opportunity to view it as an interested spectator. He needs to climb no magic mountain to achieve detachment. The elevator whisks him to 13 B and there he can view the passing show as from Olympian heights.

Surrounded by Beauty

He is surrounded by beauty, vital, vigorous beauty. And he asks no invisible power to grant him long life to enjoy his blessings. He has no fear nor repugnance at the thought of death. He is ready at any moment to leave it all, not knowing what is to come.

Much of life amuses him. It is really funny. As a spectator he can laugh. He is still fond of the Middle West and of Indiana where his family lived.

---

8. *Rain,* a play set in the South Seas and based on a short story by Somerset Maugham, opened on Broadway in 1922 and ran for two years. Jeanne Eagels (1894–1929) was a great success in the role of the prostitute Sadie Thompson, who wields her sexual power to ensnare a puritanical clergyman; Eagels died in mysterious circumstances.

And that means all of Indiana, for they lived successively in Evansville, Terre Haute, Warsaw and other places.

As he talks thoughtfully he folds his handkerchief into narrow strips and then into little squares. He gives his best attention to what he is saying. He expresses himself with directness and simplicity. He is truly himself.

"Art is more enduring than philosophy. A true picture of our times is a permanent contribution to literature and life."

This explains Dreiser. He has painted a picture of our times. He leaves the deductions to those who can keep pace with the changing styles in such things. And he rests his chance of immortality on this.

Dreiser Talks about Women and Russia
American Novelist Says Unsphinxed Female May Rule Land
Genius in Finance Used Up, No New Schemes; Communism Coming

By Vivian Richardson

*

Dallas Morning News, 18 May 1930, Feature Section, p. 2.

In late March 1930, following a bout with bronchitis the previous winter, Dreiser undertook a lengthy automobile tour of the West, including stops in Tucson, Albuquerque, Santa Fe, and El Paso before reaching Dallas. From Texas he went on to the West Coast (Los Angeles, San Francisco, and Portland) before returning to New York. In the interviews he gave during this journey, Dreiser often spoke harshly about the injustices of American social and political life. He later discussed many of these specific inequities in *Tragic America,* published in December 1931.

Look at him; big shoulders drooping, graying head with thin unruly hair thrust forward turtle-wise, pendulous jowls affixed like palms of fleshy hands to cheek bones, while the grayish eyes hold you with a gentle fire, and he pours the tea.

Theodore Dreiser, dean of American novelists, is talking about women.

"Look at Ruth Snyder.[1] Where have you seen a man with that iron determination to accomplish a given end? Murder—disgrace—child—nothing stopped her. Alexander's mother, too, swept all before her. Queen Elizabeth sacrificed Sussex for admiration, glory, power.[2] Power! Once let a woman taste power and all else is forgotten."

1. A Long Island housewife, Snyder (1895–1928) and her lover were executed in 1928 for the murder of her husband. The sensational case was headline news for many months.

2. Apparently an error for Robert Devereux (1567–1601), the second earl of Essex. Devereux—though a favorite of Elizabeth I—conspired against her and was executed at her command.

"Dreiser Talks about Women and Russia," *Dallas Morning
News*, 18 May 1930, Feature Section, p. 2.

He divides a piece of toast. And we learn that the eternal feminine is
eternally feminine no longer, if she ever was. She is a normal human being
who has got a taste of power and gulps it without a chaser. When the twentieth century uncorked the age-old bottled store of femininity's suppressed
desires, it loosed in America thousands of whirling dynamos of energy that,
operating so long in an arc, have yearly increased in force, and the result is
likely to be a matriarchy.

Madam President. Mamma Chief Justice. Daughter leading armies. Sister with portfolio. And so on.

He takes sugar. And we learn that "democracy is a farce," that "Presi-
dents are chosen three or four years before any citizen votes," that America
is "rapidly approaching Communism" and that whatever happens, "women
are going to play a vital role."

Theodore Dreiser is getting to be an old man now, with the storms of the humanist controversy breaking about his head[3] (little he cares—he likes controversies!), and when he was in Dallas the other day he was tired. He has lost weight, so that the loosely fitting clothes seemed to keep up a special secret rustling of their own, and he moves in them, rather than with them. He had come in a slow, almost lumbering manner across the thick carpet, shoulders heaving, head turning slowly from side to side, and the eyes that appeared to look at nothing observed everything.

"Crowded here," said he. "We can find a restaurant and have tea."

"Why not a woman President?" he resumed the discussion. "I'd vote for her, and probably ask her for a job afterward. In my own lifetime I have seen theories, dogmas, limitations broken down to an extent that is astonishing, a thing that people thought might perhaps have happened in Athens or Rome, but never here. At first this breaking down resulted in a flaming, flamboyant youth, the worst phase of which is over, and we are, as Mr. Harding used to say, getting back to normalcy."

Discard Your Ready Picture

The prime requisite of enjoying the society of Mr. Dreiser in person is the immediate discard of all preconceived notions and pictures of the man behind his books. The calm dispassionateness of his speech is, true, in correlation with the laboratory dissector of human behavior, but where is there about this face, neither so heavy nor so wide as it photographs, above the bow tie of flowered blue crepe an indication of the unconventional creature literary legend advertises? Neither is he, after creating at least two women in literary history so "dumb" that other women have raged and stamped their feet, quite the person one would suspect of naming the female of the genus homo sapiens the most ruthless, indomitable, willful and aspiring being on the face of the earth, and seating her ten or fifteen years hence at the head of the Government.

The one tribute he does not concede her is the ability to hold a man's heart forever. However, he obligingly works this the other way around also.

The Ruling Female

"Women have been virtual rulers a long time. Go back to the founding of this country," he continued. "The pioneers were a huddle of civilization in

3. The New Humanists, a group consisting of academic literary men and philosophers, believed that people can and should use rational choice to control the instinctive sides of their nature. They were therefore opposed to much modern expression, which they felt celebrated the "animal" in man. Two principal figures in the movement, Paul Elmer More

a trackless wilderness, afraid of the Indians, the devil, the great outdoors, everything. To prove their own superiority they created a verbal morality, and their descendants in turn marched all over the country with it. Man being by nature more conventional than woman, she put this code over with hardly a struggle, went scotfree of restrictions herself and,"—a gleam in his eyes—"actually got by with it. They still do. Men seldom rule women. Eighty per cent of the men are ruled by women. Everyone knows cases of men whose talents are capable of bigger things held down to a small town because the women like the bridge club there. Time and again women by sheer pertinacity and force of will induce men into things they don't want to do, had no intention of doing and will regret. I've done them. So has every man. And then we wonder why—WHY—we acquiesced."

Ah! This is more like the creator of "Sister Carrie," of "Jennie Gerhardt"; surely he who "accepted the insult" of being called a realist will go back now and pick up the threads of his earlier literary theme. But no!

"Men never hold women down." (What was it then that happened to patient Jennie?) "If a woman wants a career, she simply takes off her apron, drops the dishwater soap in the woodbox and goes. Home, family nor love can stand in her way."

An "Observer Here Below"

Sometimes as he talks seriously the eyes are amused, or vice versa, an idiosyncrasy that is not only interesting, but pleasing. One comes to watch for it, and like it and be disappointed if some turn of the conversation does not release the change. . . . A waitress hovered over the table, and he fixed her with a solemn eye, but a kind voice:

"Are you in a hurry for us to leave? You want this table for something?"

"Oh no, sir." She retreated rapidly. Irrelevantly he remarked:

"I am glad this is not about books. I am weary of talking books, how to write books, where to write. . . . Why talk about women, either, when there are so many matters that concern both sexes to discuss? I don't know anything about women. I'm simply an observer here below—"

One wonders: "What does he think of when he says below? Simply the sky?" Dreiser doesn't believe in heaven. He doesn't believe in hell. "You know I don't believe in an after life," he said, holding me with the solemn eyes, as matter of fact as if he had announced, "You know I don't eat ice cream cones." Nevertheless the impression was conveyed that he used to

(1864–1937) and Irving Babbitt (1865–1933), had attacked Dreiser in particular in essays of 1928. See also n. 5 to this interview.

startle people into protest with that remark. Now the hovering cubic feet of air seemed aching for a reply.

An "Amazing Futility" in Life

And then he talked of futility. At times he seemed to step mentally out of the role of Theodore Dreiser, aged 59, into that of one of these sad young men who know life is futile because so far they have found it so and moreover have been so informed, and yet can not refrain from looking for and hoping it to be otherwise. Dreiser finds "a futility in existence which is amazing"; and yet later when speaking of the new architecture which he sees springing up at Santa Fe, his eyes glow and his words have beauty and enthusiasm. Or again when commenting on the immensity of Texas and speculating on its future when each point of the star shall have its own giant municipalities until they overlap in territory and almost touch in boundary line—citing exact figures on El Paso, for instance—his words were vibrant, alive, interested.

The fleet greyhounds of his mind escape the lethargy apparently leashing his body in spite of himself.

Genius with Nothing to Do

And he complained that there is nothing new, that all genius in finance was used up years ago, leaving "no new tricks" to do now.

"What need now have we of the Morgans and the Schwabs?[4] I could take 5,000 kids and put them in the important offices of business, and they could run the offices and run them well."

Here again is the chameleon Dreiser. Most readers still have the good old deplorable habit of associating the written word with its author's own personality and opinions—few think of the tawny mustachioed creator of "Madame Bovary" as the simple-hearted good fellow he was, and likewise the most attentive reader of "The 'Genius'" would not suspect its author of caring one whit if adventure is dead, but on the other hand would likely question if for him it ever lived, outside the adventure of "observing with curiosity."

At present he is having a private adventure of his own. Though he had been in Tucson on account of an irritating throat disturbance, there was no particular reason why he should choose to come by Dallas and Houston

4. The reference is to J. P. Morgan Jr. (1867–1943) and Charles M. Schwab (1862–1939). Morgan inherited a great banking firm from his father; Schwab, a protégé of Andrew Carnegie, was the president of Bethlehem Steel Company.

when he is due in Hollywood soon—no reason other than that he is having a good time discovering America for himself.

Turning the Tables

Dreiser sees neither virtue nor pleasure in memory; it is—the lowering brows came lower—"an attribute that makes us less accurate and more garrulous as we grow older." This conclusion apparently would exclude pride or even satisfaction in accomplishment, but when in labeling humanism "University professor show-window stuff," he sat down to write his answer to the charges of Messrs. Babbitt, Van Doren, Canby and others[5] who want to serve America "not necessarily greater, but more gentlemanly or should I say ladylike books," this was his comment:

"I have had a lot of things to do in my life. Now that they are done, I think I will have a little fun. They (the humanists) have insulted me and spat upon me and now I can turn the tables."

Places Reflected in His Voice

There is New York and California and Chicago and wheat fields and coal smoke in the tones of his voice; accents peculiar to places have seeped into his throat and mingled there as the behavior of people sinks into his photographic mind. His manner is utterly natural and unaffected.

Preparing to leave the hotel with newspaper men, he asked:

"Shall I carry a cane?"

"We-ell, do you have to?"

"No. But I want to."

The cane cost $1.50. He told a story about an El Paso reporter who once called it a fashionable cane. Dreiser wrote him it cost $1.50 at a dry goods store. The editor retorted, "It's still a fashionable cane!"

He Knows His Lion Hunters

Dreiser does not pose, or assume hauteur. He arranged himself comfortably in the chair and talked. Especially women—who think he knows too much

---

5. For Babbitt, see n. 3 to this chapter. Henry Seidel Canby (1878–1961), editor of the influential *Saturday Review of Literature*, and Carl Van Doren (1885–1950), a poet and Columbia professor, had just appeared, on 9 May, with Babbitt in a widely reported public discussion of humanism held at Carnegie Hall. Van Doren had spoken in opposition to Babbitt, while Canby occupied a middle position. For Dreiser's "answers" to their charges, see pp. 206–7.

•

about them—are fond of dwelling on his enveloping conceit and yet he is not conceited, but an egoist. The old conception vanishes in favor of this uncomplex, humorous soul (though one finds little enough humor in his books) who wears handkerchiefs crumpled in his pockets, ties a napkin around his neck and eats scrambled eggs from the skillet on the stove (he did in Dallas) if the occasion permits and can sight "yes-men" of literature three paragraphs ahead.

What he retorted, turning away, to one white hope of American litera-ture who caroled, "I agree with you perfectly, Mr. Dreiser," was picturesque enough to become literary history, if only here we didn't have to become what Mr. Dreiser himself terms "ladylike" and translate it simply as "Bosh!"

"You know," he commented on another occasion, "I have been collect-ing for a long time these books by contemporary writers in which univer-sity professors devote a chapter to my work. I have about seventeen or eigh-teen of them now. You know,"—the amused eye glints at a listening professor from Southern Methodist University—"these professors want to rewrite my books. . . ."

Simply a Good Fellow

Such colloquialisms as "scotfree," "turning the tables," the frequent repeti-tion of "you know," "things" as easy designation and "kids" liberally salt his conversation. However, when explaining a matter in which he is very much interested, such as communism, he searches diligently for the right word, although when he finds it, it rarely soars to the six-syllable height usually offered by visiting highbrows to dazzle women's clubs and interviewers.

He is neither uncouth nor excessively polite. I should say that he has reached the exact and most comfortable shade, wherein it is understood that, man or woman, as fellow-inhabitant of the globe, you are entitled to con-sideration, although you probably don't care for the arrangement any more than he does. Man or woman, if you were an acquaintance, he'd call a spade a spade. He held the door to the tearoom and borrowed a dime to tip the waitress. I think he would have borrowed it from a man in the selfsame casual manner.

"I'll pay it back," he said.

He never did. Neither of us expected him to.

"Dumb" Women, Even in Texas

Later some one came back to "Jennie Gerhardt": "How could she have just let life sweep her along without doing anything about it? How could she?

Mr. Dreiser, we don't have that particular, Middle Western, patient type of 'dumb' woman down here. It takes a different turn—"

"Some women are pretty dumb, even in Texas," retorted Mr. Dreiser good-humoredly. "Jennie was a type, of course," he added. "I think people prefer my books according to their own experiences. Many business men tell me they like 'The Financier.' 'A Gallery of Women' probably appeals to the women who have grown up since the war more than 'Jennie' or 'Sister Carrie.'"

Working on New Novel

"A Gallery of Women" is his latest book. "This Madness" appeared serially in a magazine, but has not yet been published in book form.[6] He is working at present on a new novel, "The Bulwark" and some autobiographical material about his earlier life,[7] to supplement a volume already published, "A Book About Myself," of which he added:

"I had called it 'Newspaper Days.' Much to my disgust and without my consent, the publisher changed it to 'A Book About Myself.'"

As, however, he is on his way to Hollywood to do something to talking pictures—he refused to discuss what[8]—and is just now looking around Texas, publication dates of both the novel and the biography are uncertain. Mr. Dreiser often does work when he is traveling; in a round, solid, yet almost feminine hand he writes with a not too fine-pointed pen on page after page of good white paper. He does not use the typewriter.

Wanted to Write Plays

He had, you see, talked about books. When he was young, Theodore Dreiser wanted to write plays. At 23 in Pittsburgh he used to look at the great steel structures rearing their heads in the smoke, and plan to do something that would picture their body and spirit. He saw a play, a tragedy of London, "not a very good play, but it set me thinking," and during his free hours at the newspaper office, he began writing plays.[9] During this period of his

6. This was series of sketches of women that had appeared in *Hearst's International-Cosmopolitan* from February to July 1929. They were never collected in book form.

7. Dreiser worked sporadically on *The Bulwark* from its inception in 1914 but did not complete it until shortly before his death in December 1945 (it was published in March 1946); his autobiography of his early life, *Dawn,* appeared in May 1931.

8. Dreiser's Hollywood agent had informed him that Warner Brothers was interested in several of his novels. Although Dreiser went to Hollywood from Texas, nothing came of the matter.

9. Although Dreiser made an earlier effort at playwriting while a reporter in St. Louis, there is no record of any such effort during his Pittsburgh newspaper days.

life he reread Balzac; probably his first inclination toward the novel was inspired by this Frenchman: "I thought something might be done about America like that." When the showdown came, he was "more or less pushed into writing books instead of plays by others who thought he should."

The "Dreiser Mystery"

His first book, "Sister Carrie," appeared in 1900. Those of the critics who look askance at his schooling—he attended the public schools of Warsaw, Ind., and the University of Indiana, his home State—every now and then profess themselves perennially amazed at what they term the "Dreiser Mystery," i.e., after the publication of "Sister Carrie," it was eleven years until he wrote another book. But upon the heels of "Jennie Gerhardt," came "The Financier" (1912), "A Traveler at Forty" (1913), "The Titan" (1914), "The Genius" (1915), and so on a book or plays or short stories every year, with one exception, until "The American Tragedy" and "A Gallery of Women." How to explain it, they question: After the eleven-year silence, to become so prolific?

Dreiser doesn't help them very much. Well—he was busy; he became a novelist after "a series of editorships"; there was Ev'ry Month, Broadway Magazine, Smith's Magazine and the Delineator, with its two offspring, and in 1907 he organized the National Child Rescue Campaign.[10]

Determined Women

And so at length back to the ladies (not without having been shooed away from communism for the nonce):

"Many a woman is holding down an important job for which some man gets credit. . . . Mrs. McCormick is a good example of ruthless feminine intelligence. . . .[11] I mentioned Mrs. Snyder—the picture of her determination arrested the world. Turned in some other direction, such will might have been constructive. Your own Mrs. Ferguson—I understand that she was the power behind the throne even before she was Governor,"—which will probably be news to Mrs. Ferguson.[12]

10. In 1907, shortly after becoming the editor of *The Delineator*, Dreiser founded the Child Rescue Campaign, which sought homes for orphans. The campaign received a great deal of national attention.

11. Katherine Dexter McCormick (1875–1967) was a social activist and philanthropist who fought for suffrage and birth control rights for women. She helped to found the League of Women Voters in 1920.

12. Miriam A. Ferguson (1875–1961) was the wife of the flamboyant former Texas governor James Ferguson. After he was impeached, removed from office, and prevented by law from

As women delve deeper into politics, which he thinks should interest them because of the intrigue and managing, they will become more proficient; he cites the case of Russian women who since "Anna Karenina," an individualist if there ever was one (exactly Tolstoi's point, of course), have advanced through education from almost the estate of the Biblical woman to active citizens and warriors. Girls in a Russian school are taught military tactics with actual field practice in throwing grenades, etc.

After All, Why Not?

Personally he should not object to that intangible something which some men term the ignominy of petticoat rule. The width of the channel separating male and female does not appear so broad to him as to others who ignore the Mendelian law and its "mere chemical change," illustrating how narrow is the dividing line. The usual contention that women "lose their heads" more readily in crises is "nonsense."

"Why not a Ruth McCormick as secretary to the general committee instead of a Mr. Stalin?"

The Pot and the Kettle

Dreiser shifts in his chair. He leans forward. He is back on the subject of communism. "Dreiser Looks at Russia," was the published outcome of his visit to that country through an invitation from the Soviet Government. Challenge any of its workings, and Mr. Dreiser is ready with an answer, and the calm face with its indoor complexion becomes animated. He does not, for instance, condone the Soviet's preachment of communism through what is no less than a gigantic scheme of censorship, as he made clear in the book, and while in Dallas further pointed out that perhaps there is a case of pot and kettle near at home.

He sees the humanist clan endeavoring to censor literature by deleting—perhaps it would be more "ladylike" to say ignoring—all that "does not appeal to what even then (thirty years ago) was dubbed—I quote—'the better thought.'" Dreiser, who has never been one to squelch what he sees, ugly or beautiful, is told that writers now must approach life "in a gentlemanly spirit" and cater to "conservative thought." This strikes him as very, very interesting. So does the fact that the "dogmatic culture" of New England is "being invaded in a strong manner by the Catholic Church." And he needs

---

running again, she was elected governor in 1924 and served one term. It was widely believed that he ran the state during her tenure as governor.

must point out, though it rings with a personal echo, that "the aristocracy of Yale and Harvard is after all a very limited affair—they censor everything but themselves. Themselves they do not censor."

He mentioned another case where censorship in America came into play as regards the Chinese-Russian Railroad, which the Russians now control. Before they regained control, a most significant battle took place after which an offer of mediation appeared ridiculous. No word of this battle appeared in American newspapers, said Mr. Dreiser, although the offer of mediation was recorded.[13]

The If and When of Communism in America

Mr. Dreiser is not the first to see America on the verge of communism, nor will he be by any means the last. Anyone can look at the increasing centralization of industry and vision not so far away either an oligarchy of wealth, the representatives of which, according to Mr. Dreiser, "might just as well be a communist council sitting in Moscow, for all the difference there is," or State control, which is communism.

"If," he explained, "unemployment is kept down until dissatisfaction is not felt, the solution is obvious. But if the powers of finance spend the money America pours into the coffers abroad in an attempt to become world magnates at the expense of American comfort—presto, a revolution. In this country it would take only from 51 to 55 per cent of the population—for Americans are the most dangerous persons in the world with a gun—to turn the tables."

He spoke with derision of a recent parade of convicts singing hymns through the streets of Chicago as an "attempt to reduce Americans to an humble state of mind."

"In Moscow," he added, where one may see a hearse hauling bales of hay when it is not otherwise occupied "there is not the feel of the fear of poverty that you notice right here in Dallas. . . . Yes—America would make a much more workable communism, economically and scientifically, than Russia."

13. China and the USSR frequently quarreled over control of the railroads in northeastern China during the 1920s. Dreiser may be referring to a 1924 incident in which the two countries agreed that the Soviet Union was to purchase the China Eastern Railroad in Manchuria, with the railroad then to be run under joint management of the two countries. But the USSR soon gained control of the management board and thus of the railroad.

The "Great American Tragedy" Himself

Ah, well, perhaps the innermost Dreiser is a dreamer after all—a most likable, human, personable and neat dreamer, for all his cold dissection of life on paper. The literary storms have beat about his head for many a year, as they beat about Flaubert—who also hated being called a realist—and of Zola, but if Dreiser has not the exquisitely crystalline precision of the former, neither has he a moral to preach as had the latter. They have called Dreiser himself the great American tragedy because he never troubled to avail himself of the prescribed amount of academic erudition. They say he is not scholarly: "Just as he was preparing to read his way to the root of matters, the war came along and he was adopted by a set of young intellectuals who believed there was nothing back of 1914 anyhow. They raised him up—thus he remains." To which the Dallas News Book Page adds that he "is at once America's worst writer and greatest novelist."

Complained of "Tyranny of Things"

He talked, for instance, a great deal and seriously about the tyranny of Things:

"You buy new shoes. You don't need new shoes. You buy a new car. You do not want a new car, you do not need one. You buy a country place: When I was young I wanted a country place. At 30 perhaps I would have enjoyed it. When I got it 30 years later, it cost me $150,000, and I didn't want to live in it anyhow."—The tragedy of which (as they see it) is—Columbus discovering Oak Cliff![14]—Zeno had the same idea some centuries ago.[15]

There were those in Dallas who smiled when he, Dreiser, called Hamsun morbid,[16] and yet who has not snored over Balzac, or Dostoievsky! Certainly an American has the right to choose his own sleeping potion. . . .

As He Sees Life

It seems after all we shall have to accept Mr. Dreiser at his own valuation, which constituted a paragraph of his recent reply to the humanists:[17]

14. Oak Cliff was a prosperous suburb of Dallas.

15. Zeno of Citium (ca. 336–264 B.C.) founded Stoicism, which rejects the passionate pursuit of goals.

16. For Hamsun, see p. 190, n. 2.; Dreiser is perhaps referring specifically to Hamsun's dour *Growth of the Soil* (1921), which received much attention in America.

17. Richardson is quoting from Harry Hansen's column "The First Reader" in the *New York World* for 9 May 1930, p. 11, in which Hansen reprints a telegram sent by Dreiser to the Discussion Guild, the organizers of the program. Portions of the passage also appear in Dreiser's article "The New Humanism," *Thinker* 2 (July 1930): 8–12.

"Personally I appear to be charged with being a realist. I accept the insult, but with reservations. For I fear I do not run true to type—do not run with any clan. Rather I see myself as a highly temperamental individual compelled to see life through the various veils or fogs of my own lacks, predilections and what you will, yet seeking honestly always to set down that which I imagine I see.

"I am told by some that it agrees with what they see. By others not. But what I think I see is beauty and ugliness, mystery and some little clarity, in minor things, tenderness and terrific brutality, ignorance sodden and hopeless and some admirable wisdom, malice and charity, honesty and dishonesty, aspiration and complete and discouraging insensitivity and indifference. Yet altogether contriving a gay, restless and in the main fascinating picture from which but few of us, however great our ills or complaints are prepared to step out. In fact it is not less but more of this inexplicable and often more bitter than sweet brew that we desire—to seize the best of it and escape the worst.

"In addition, it is not any petty scribe, but life itself which makes the often grim and terrible tales to which Dr. Babbitt and his Humanists object. . . ."

Every One Still Happy

And having accepted this, we can sit back and see every one happy: The professorial group secure in their contention that a more scholarly Dreiser could have written better books, and Mr. Dreiser himself just as safe in his retort that they can not prove it. Who knows—he might have written worse ones.

—While the rest of us can be content with pictures of him ambling out in the Dallas shopping district to buy a blue shirt, wearing it later and feeling the cloth meditatively between thumb and forefinger (as men do) when some one remarks on it, stopping to chat to a newspaper man on the street about what is going to happen to Texas, and saying "You know"—in that thin, anomalous voice dripping casually from the almost mobile lips: "You know—"

In his room were a number of books: "What is Love?" "Chemistry of Medicine," his own privately published poem, "Epitaph," and "Trader Horn."[18] Personally I shall always suspect him of carrying a worn volume of "Treasure Island" in his coat pocket, and subconsciously wondering why something interesting doesn't happen to him. But—as for the latter—don't we all?

18. The works are *What Is Love?* a novel by E. M. Delafield (1890–1943); *Epitaph,* a privately printed poem by Dreiser (Heron Press, 1930); and *Trader Horn: Being the Life and Works of Alfred Aloysius Horn* (1927), published anonymously by Ethelreda Lewis (1875–1946). No book entitled *Chemistry of Medicine* has ever been published; Richardson is perhaps referring to *Chemistry in Medicine* (1929), by Julius Oscar Stieglitz (1867–1937).

Theodore Dreiser Discounts Intermarriage
Famed Novelist, Author of "American Tragedy," "The 'Genius,'" Sees Unions between Jew and Non-Jew as Unimportant Phenomena— Hits "Jewish Crybabying for Justice"

By Raymond Dannenbaum

*

Jewish Journal 3 (4 June 1930): 3, 16.

Dreiser was in San Francisco principally to visit the imprisoned radical labor leader Tom Mooney, for whom he was seeking a pardon. The *Jewish Journal* was an organ of Reform Judaism in the San Francisco area.

"The Jews are one of the greatest races which ever stood on earth!

"Jews are marked by a strong feeling for the conservation and use of power.

"They've always yelled about Justice, but with the thought of making things easier for themselves.

"Reform Judaism is the only tolerable kind of Judaism.

"You don't want Zionism!"

These are some of the startling beliefs of Theodore Dreiser, author of the "American Tragedy" and "The Genius." When interviewed at the Hotel Mark Hopkins in San Francisco Dreiser didn't mince words. The great American novelist, one of the fathers of our current liberalism, continued:

Don't Want Zionism

"You Jews don't really want Zionism. You don't care a fig for nationalism. You want to be everywhere like gypsies. You want to be a race which envelops the earth. You'd like to have your fingers in every pie."

His eyes flared when I shot the question—"Do you believe in intermarriage?"

"Rot," he retorted, "The idea of the Jews blending with other races is a joke. No doubt a certain percentage always will, just as certain individuals always have married outside their racial boundaries. If two persons fall in love, it doesn't matter what the racial difference may imply. They eventually follow their own sweet wills.

John Is Different

"You know," he went on, in his quietly forceful manner, "most people won't admit following their own wills but in the end they always do. We're always finding out that John isn't the kind of man we thought him. I think it's d——— fortunate that we do!

"It's an amazing thing that the individual manages to live his own life in response to his own ideas, despite the threat of jails, and mores. Occasionally one is caught, and his fellows attempt to ostracize him. But they themselves are pointing the moral with one hand, while a free hand behind the back indulges in a variety of unconventional and secret gestures!"

Has Bronzed Face

He paused for a moment. I had an opportunity to carefully inspect his bronzed face. I noticed that although he spoke vehemently but quietly, and seemed to possess great repose, nevertheless his mind and body were taut. The tension expressed itself when he took out a fresh white handkerchief, relieved it of its ironed folds, and meticulously folded it into long tucks, of which eventually he devised an accordionlike structure. Then this great observer of the frailities of mankind undid his linen masterpiece, and proceeded to evolve yet more fantastic structures of this humble toy.

He returned with a jerk to intermarriage. "For example," he shot back in reply to my query as to whether clashes were inevitable in such unions, "I've a good friend, a Jew, who's married to an Irish Catholic. They've been married for 15 years—have children. The woman does her best to send them to mass, and occasionally *papa* wants to trot them to a synagogue. But this contest creates no antagonisms—at least no more than are undeniably present in every happy marriage. The children? They won't be either Catholics or Jews . . . and it'll be a d——— sight better for them, too!"

Group Race-Inferiority

Quickly, he switched to another topic: "What astounds me about you Jews," he exploded, "is your feeling of 'race inferiority'—not culturally or as individuals—on the contrary you are sufficiently self-assertive there—but as a group; in your dealings with nations, with problems. It's a kind of public apology for getting on, which has no basis on any score!

"Sixty percent of you are neurotically conscious of opposition. Yet despite it all, you want the heights of power and recognition. You've got to take jolts to achieve them! You see," he smiled, with a chuckle, "this reminds me of a tale told me by a friend, a cavalry officer in the Civil War. During a Northern retreat men were running north as fast as their mounts and their own legs could carry them.

A Hasty Retreat

"My friend was mounted on a good horse, making for home with all his and the horse's might. Despite the horse's speed, an infantryman managed to keep up with the horse, outdistancing the rest of his fleeing fellows. While running at this outstanding pace he kept beseeching my friend at the top of his voice, 'Let me up behind'; to which my friend shouted, 'To h . . . with you, you don't need a horse, you're going as fast as I!'

"Now Jews are like that! You're in the forefront of every movement, and yet you keep shouting for a lift. Why bawl about it?

"Jewish Justice?—Bunk!"

"Justice? The Jew an eternal defender of Justice? Bunk! Jews have always crybabied about Justice, but what they want is Justice for themselves—a special and particularly pro-Jewish Justice. That's not Justice!"

"How do you evaluate the Jew in the world of modern art, commerce?" said I, by way of diverting the interview into more pacific channels. "Commerce? What are you talking about?" he countered. "Jews *invented* commerce! Didn't one member of that old Florentine-Jewish family invent the letter of credit during the middle ages? Didn't Jews discover a way to utilize the benefits of a gold hoard in one place, with a scrap of paper at the other end of Europe?[1] And the Montefiores? And later the Rothschilds?[2] Didn't

---

1. Because of the church's opposition to usury, Jews controlled much of the moneylending in Italy between the thirteenth and sixteenth centuries. The Da Pisa family of Florence in particular played a major role in northern Italian economic life during the sixteenth century. However, since most of the banking activities of Italian Jews centered on lending money

they keep commerce alive with their shrewd brains? And your great Jewish banking firms. Don't they move the wheels of commerce today? There's the answer to your question—are the Jews good in commerce? They invented it, they made it, and they're keeping it going today!

Beautiful Bloch Quintet

"Art? That's another thing. I heard a beautiful quintet of Ernest Bloch's not long ago, in New York.[3] That *is* art, and first rate at that! A Jewish etcher illustrated *My City*.[4] If his manner of catching the essence of New York's skyline with his drypoint better than anyone else I know of is art, then he's an artist, too."

I ventured another question: "What do you think of the Zweigs and their work—*Sergeant Grischa?*"[5]

"Well," he retorted, "*Grischa* is a war book. It's not hard to interpret war. When a man goes to war it burns itself into his consciousness. He can't forget it, and in most instances he can't help expressing some of it. I can remember fifteen war books—all of them good. The real determinant of ability is to interpret life generally. In that some of your other Jewish writers have succeeded admirably."

By way of answer to another interrogation, he flung back at me— "Lewisohn? Like most Jews he's neurotically self conscious of antagonisms. As I remember, his first short stories were the most beautiful of his writing. They were glorious. Then he was sidetracked—went off into the Middle West or some place and started teaching. He was dormant for a while. After that the first thing he did was *Upstream*. Somehow he'd lost his graceful short stories in an effort to interpret something. . . . Maybe I'd better not say that," mused Dreiser, "I'd rather not hurt his feelings—and that might!"[6]

---

against local securities, they played little role in the development of the letter of credit and similar potentially international transactions.

2. The Montefiore family, which had immigrated from Italy to England during the eighteenth century, were wealthy London bankers and brokers; the Rothschilds, originally a German banking family, had major branches in London, Paris, and other European capitals.

3. The Swiss-born Bloch (1880–1959) had immigrated to America in 1916; he often wrote music on Jewish subjects.

4. Dreiser's prose-poem was published in a limited edition in 1929, with illustrations by Max Pollock (1886–1970).

5. The reference is to Arnold Zweig (1887–1968), a German Jewish novelist, and Stefan Zweig (1881–1942), an Austrian Jewish novelist; Arnold Zweig's *Case of Sergeant Grischa*, which appeared in English in 1928, contains a negative dramatization of German military justice.

6. Ludwig Lewisohn (1882–1955) was raised in Charleston, South Carolina. Initially hindered by anti-Semitism in his efforts to pursue a scholarly career, he turned to writing. With

The Maurizius Case he professed not to have read.[7] I had spoken of it in connection with Mooney, whom, the day before, Dreiser had visited at San Quentin prison.[8] I mentioned that Count Karolyi[9] had sent *The Maurizius Case* to Mooney, thinking of the analogy in their two experiences. Then I briefly outlined the plot, emphasizing that although the machinery of Justice had finally relinquished an unguilty and unwilling victim, Maurizius had lost entire touch with life and with mankind; and how poor Maurizius finally found escape by leaping from a fast train into an abyss, and death.

Berkman's Similar Fate

"That's it. That's it," whispered Dreiser. "That's what happened to Berkman when they released him from prison. The years of solitude had turned the fiery, idealistic anarchist into a man who walks with bent head, muttering between pursed lips, quietly, of the world's injustices. That's it. Yes!" he said softly, "You remember the case of Emma Goldman and Berkman?"[10]

Dreiser has distinct mannerisms. He is a large man. Tall. Heavy. He has a big nose, and a beetling lip. His face was tanned. His lips were cracked from the sun. He wore a grey suit with dark penciled stripes intersecting in squares. His cap was brown, and the crown was unbuttoned from the visor. It gave the novelist a querulous-half-tourist look. He refused a good cigarette, so I suppose he doesn't smoke.

Dreiser's aid Lewisohn published his first novel in 1908, but in 1910 he moved to the University of Wisconsin (and later Ohio State University), where he taught German. He returned to New York and writing in 1917. *Up Stream: An American Chronicle* (1922), his best-known work, is an autobiographically based account of the difficulties facing Jews in America.

7. This is a novel written by the German Jewish writer Jakob Wassermann (1873–1934) and published in English in 1929 by Dreiser's publisher, Horace Liveright. The novel, an indictment of the German criminal justice system, centers on the imprisonment of a man for a murder he did not commit.

8. A radical leftist, Tom Mooney (1882–1942) was convicted and sentenced to death in 1916 for planting a bomb that killed ten people at a San Francisco prowar rally. After evidence of an unfair trial surfaced, his sentence was commuted to life imprisonment in 1918. Until his pardon in 1939, left-wing groups throughout the world were active in efforts to free him.

9. Count Mihály Károlyi (1875–1955), the antimilitarist president of Hungary during 1919, lived in exile during the 1920s and 1930s.

10. In 1892, while the anarchists Alexander Berkman (1870–1936) and Goldman (1869–1940) were lovers, Berkman shot and wounded Henry Clay Frick, head of Carnegie Steel. He spent fourteen years in prison; both he and Goldman were deported in 1919.

Dreiser, Big Farmer

Dreiser is a big farmer with white hair, and heavy sun-burned-black hands.

He returned again to the themes of Zionism and intermarriage. "It's an odd thing that though Jewish self-consciousness is so strong, that although you all are moved to such fervor by racial causes, and the sense of your own heritage of indignities and glory—that you should not wish to be a nation. I'm quite sure from talking to a variety of Jews from the assertive ultra-Jewish ones like Konrad Bercovici to the opposite genre, that in the main you don't want a country of your own.[11] But it's an odd thing, in view of your strong self-consciousness—your fervent belief in yourselves and in your abilities. It's very odd"—he shook his head.

I thought of an odd thing. Of five persons recently interviewed, each, including Dreiser, struck an analogy between the Jew and the Negro—touching upon his problems—his internal conflicts, and his clashes with his environment. None went so far, or even in the direction of California chauvinist Chester Rowell, who not long ago wrote in a great Western newspaper words to the effect that the United States has two castes—Negro and the Jew, and *we don't want to add a third.*[12]

Solution of Miscegenation

Dreiser has remarked that many saw the only solution to the "Jewish problem" as a blending of Jews and non-Jews in line with the advocated miscegenation of whites, yellows and blacks.

He grimaced, "Some little squeak is always interpreting the law, to get some poor devil into jail—and to keep him there without rhyme or reason. It's a G . . . d . . . shame to seize any man and toss him into gaol. We're always yelling about the Constitution. But the ones who make the loudest noise are usually those who misinterpret the Constitution for their own ends. The American people have lost interest. Seeking for power, for individual glory and hyper-comfort they neglect the things for which the great idealists who made this country paid so dearly. And Jews, the lawgivers, Jews, vehicle of the law, are found, nearly every man-Jack of them, among this

11. Bercovici (1882–1961) was a Romanian-born writer of novels about American Jewish life. During the 1920s and 1930s Zionism was far more popular among European Jews than it was among American Jews. Dreiser himself supported Zionism during this period.

12. Chester H. Rowell (1867–1948), a well-known Progressive Party figure in California politics early in his career, had strong sentiments against further Asian immigration into the state. He was at this time a widely read columnist for the *San Francisco Chronicle*.

indifferent, careless mob. That's a great shame. You ought to change it. What this country needs is a change of heart, a change of ideals, and not puff.

Ignoring Happiness Principle

"We're ignoring the great principles which make happiness in life assured and possible. For one thing we're each seeking a justice which is for the *one*, as against the *all*. It's a pitiful thing! Organized society isn't functioning and organized society means everybody. Organized society implies that every man should get a *break* and not one or just a few.

"Organized religion is in the way of progress. Dogmatic ideas, sectarianism are a square impassable barrier upon the road of human progress. I hope to H . . . that dogmatic religion is breaking down.

"*Reform Judaism is good!* If it is necessary for men to meet and declare their collective reverence for the great forces of nature with which they are poetically impressed, it is well that they should meet upon the platform of a creed which is integral with actuality, which is not in the way of progress, but beyond and an index to progress!

"Personally it appeals to me to do these things privately."

Dreiser Asserts His Books Never Will Sell for $1.50
Novelist on Trip to Verify Belief of Unhappiness of Americans; Popular Uprising against Trust Predicted

By David W. Hazen

*

Portland Morning Oregonian, 13 June 1930, p. 9.

Dreiser and Helen had driven from San Francisco to Portland to visit Helen's mother and sister.

"They won't sell any of my novels for $1.50, what do you know about that?" and Theodore Dreiser's cane hit a rousing smack on the hardwood floor. This famous American novelist was talking about the recent announcement of a New York publishing house that hereafter its novels will retail for $1 and $1.50.[1]

"I don't have to give any of these publishers my books," he continued. "In fact, I never had to do anything. Sometimes I went hungry, but I didn't let them dictate to me."

The author of "The 'Genius'" and "An American Tragedy" now publishes first editions in very limited numbers, and rich collectors gobble them up at $35 and $50 each. Thus does the Indianan who now dwells in New York beat the publishers.[2]

He is touring America in an automobile to learn if the people are happy. He's getting an earful everywhere he goes. Talks to bankers, butchers, ex-bartenders, barbers, barristers, bums, all classes come within his range of questioning.

1. Earlier in June a number of New York publishers announced that they were reducing the price of a novel to $1.00. Dreiser's publisher, Horace Liveright, refused to accept the reduction and continued to charge from $2.50 to $5.00.
2. During 1929 and 1930 Dreiser published four limited editions of minor works: *The Aspirant, My City, Epitaph,* and *Fine Furniture*.

"We can stand a lot, we Americans," Mr. Dreiser said, "and we are now letting the country be run by trusts and corporations. They have the little fellow scared to death. They've got a gun to his belly, and he can't do a thing.

"On my way out here I've talked to everybody, high and low. I want to find out if it is true that the reports regarding the unhappiness and unrest of the people are overstated. Let me tell you, the country is unhappy!"

He pointed out that the American Telephone & Telegraph company is the outstanding trust of the nation. He asked a few questions about the local situation, answering them himself, then explained his troubles back in New York.

"I used to have a little studio in Greenwich village," he said, swinging the cane around, "and there I had a phone that I could use as often as I wanted to, and my friends could call me when they pleased, all for $4 a month. But I needed a little larger studio, and my telephoning became more frequent, so what do you think they do to me now?

"Well, I am allowed two calls a day for $4 a month, and all over that are five cents apiece. And they've sprung a new one—you have to pay by distance. Say I call a number on Fifty-third street, it would be five cents, but if my call is on Ninety-seventh street it might be ten cents, and out a few blocks farther it would be 15 cents.

"Don't get surprised. You'll get it the same way before long."

Mr. Dreiser declares the railroads now function as government. He states that the interstate commerce commission allows the companies to say what the rules shall be.

"The commission has said that the railroads shall be allowed to make 7 per cent on their investments. God only knows who gave them this right," the novelist said. "When the people, through some legal action, get after the railroads they run to mamma back there in Washington, and Mamma Commission says:

"'Don't you do anything to these poor children, they are part of the government now.'

"So it goes. The telephone company says the bigger the city the more money it loses. They have reached such a tearful stage in saying this that I can't understand how they operate at all.

"The American people stand for this, and a lot more. They are long-suffering. But listen—they can do more damage in a little while when they once get angry than any other people in the world. Look at those times in Herrin, Ill., when they met the strike-breakers coming out of town. Look at Sherman, Tex., where they burned down the entire courthouse and court records to get a negro killer.[3]

3. In June 1922 a mob of striking coal miners killed twenty strikebreakers near Herrin,

"When 60 per cent of the people are going hungry, when the kid dies because proper care cannot be paid for, then watch out. There will be plenty done then, and the people will be the power that will rule, don't forget that."

Mr. and Mrs. Dreiser[4] left Portland yesterday to continue the study of unhappy Americanism to the northward.

Illinois, in an incident that became known as the Herrin Massacre; in early May 1930 a Sherman, Texas, mob lynched a black man alledged to have attacked a white woman.

4. Helen and Dreiser did not marry until 1944.

Dreiser Brings Pessimism Back from U.S. Tour
Constitutional Government Has Abdicated
and Trusts Control, Novelist Declares
Literature Practically Dead
Country Is Headed for Great Social Changes, He Says

By James Flexner

*

New York Herald Tribune, 8 July 1930, p. 14.

Theodore Dreiser has returned from his voyage of exploration through the
United States more than ever a pessimist. Yesterday he fumbled silently with
the papers on his desk for ten minutes before he suddenly rose, drew himself to his full height and exclaimed, "All newspaper interviews are stupid.
For years I have not seen one that is worth anything. I will bet you $10 that
you cannot get into your paper the things that I am going to say."

The wager was taken up and the novelist enthusiastically discussed the
ills of the universe for an hour and a half. Since modern business and
financial developments have made American citizens into nothing but
"trudging asses," there is no great contemporary American literature, he said.
If there is to be any in the future, it will have to take the form of satire or
expressions of despair.

Hardly an Individual Remains

"The constitutional government of America is abdicated. In every state in
the Union there is no such thing as representative government," Mr. Dreiser complained. "America is controlled by trusts that function as government. They have the power to tax, which is the power to destroy.

"The mental capacity of our school teachers is practically nullified by
business authorities dictating what they may teach. They must denounce
bolshevism and keep their mouths shut on Darwinism. The great educational
thing, they are told, is the flag, and it is the duty of every citizen to be 100
per cent American—in other words, a damn fool."

He said that big business movements are making it impossible for men to express themselves as individuals. Because they cannot hope to succeed in small, private enterprises, American citizens have lost their initiative and their power to think. There is hardly any such thing as an individual left in America, he said.

Literature Practically Killed

When asked if these things would kill American literature, he rose from his chair in excitement. "They have already practically done so," he exclaimed. "Just name me a single great writer. And supposing there were one, what chance would he have of being popular?

"What do the books concern themselves with nowadays? Why, with a little love affair, perhaps, or people's marital experiences for twenty years, or the adventures of some dub in the detective world, or how terrible the world looks to some dub who has never looked at it at all."

Mr. Dreiser attacked introspective novelists who "cannot step out into the world and survey it as it is." They were not writers at all, but merely autobiographers. He had hopes, however, that despite all modern handicaps, American literature would become great.

Life Here Invites Satire

"Life is life. It may be a lolling, fat, disgusting thing, but in the hand of a master it would become a very sardonic thing. The life of America today, fast verging as it is on social tragedy, should lend itself to satire and irony. Or, perhaps, we might have a literature of despair like that of Dostoievsky. That might be a good thing. Conditions here are in many ways similar to those in Russia before the revolution."

As Mr. Dreiser talked a silky wolfhound, three feet tall, lay curled at his feet. The big sitting room in his duplex apartment at 200 West Fifty-seventh Street was decorated with several modernistic pictures, large as barn doors, and on one side was a painting of Mr. Dreiser when he was younger. Lolling in a straight, uncomfortable chair, the novelist kept rolling and unrolling his handkerchief. He spoke with great intensity, never taking his eyes off his interviewer.

"I have returned from a tour which I took to revive my understanding of America," he said. "I am more convinced than ever that the country is headed for great social changes that will frustrate the life of the ordinary individual unless they can be checked by a really important stand on the part of the intellectuals."

Traces Rise of Rackets

He said that everywhere he went he found that corporations were functioning as government. Indiana had established the doctrine that it was illegal
to enter "unfair competition" with anybody. This, he said, was used by chain
hotels to close their small competitors.[1]

Having attacked the telephone and railroad companies, he said that in
Minnesota a radical newspaper had been suppressed by big business interests on the ground that it was a public nuisance.[2] Graft and crookedness in
government was the principal topic of every newspaper he had seen during
his travels.

Small dealers cannot make a living unless they band themselves together
into racketeering groups that serve to shut out competition by illegal methods, Mr. Dreiser said. Because the "trusts" kept them from getting a profit
on their crops, farmers could not make a living.

"Nothing will be done until 50 or 60 per cent of the people of the United
States feel the pinch that follows the right of the corporations to tax them to
death," he said. "The only thing that will stir the people is misery. They are
not miserable enough yet, but they soon will be. Men could organize this land
so it could support three or four times its population without any misery.

"I have never seen a land more beautiful. It is self-sufficient, it could close
its borders and live without any contact with the outside world. It could live
beautifully."

Mr. Dreiser rose from his chair. "Be sure to mail me that $10," he said.

1. This incident, to which Dreiser again refers on p. 224, has not been identified.
2. "The Minnesota Gag Law Case" of 1927 involved a small antivice newspaper, the Minneapolis *Saturday Press*, which was shut down under the provisions of a state law permitting
the closing of newspapers printing "scandalous" material. The law was upheld by the state
supreme court but declared unconstitutional by the U.S. Supreme Court in 1931.

Dreiser Now Rediscovers America
Move Wall St. to Washington, So Corporations
Can Rule Us Openly, Author Suggests
Back from Tour of Country, He Finds Our
Scenery Superb, Our Citizens in Need of Revolt

BY FORREST DAVIS

*

New York Telegram, 9 July 1930, p. 9.

Theodore Dreiser discovered America and found it more than a little cock-eyed—beautiful but dumb.

Back from a 10,000-mile motor trip to the Bad Lands, Shasta, the Red Woods, Pueblo and Indianapolis, the republic's prime novelist found his fellow-citizens—dwelling on the most magnificent continent—preparing to rebel against shameless corporate rule of their government.

The corporations have taken over the country, the government and, now, the people. Power and utility trusts let Americans starve in the streets while they knock each other down in the market places.

Dreiser found garage men in Bismarck, N.D.; bankers in Tucson, Ariz.; druggists in California, diners in prairie hotels talking about the government taking over the railroads and the telephone trust. Without political leadership they are talking seriously of these things.

People Awaiting Leader

The common people are ready for a leader—a flaming, silver-shielded leader who will spring from the grass roots and free them of "financial Caesarism." The trouble is that no politician will do. The people have no more confidence in politicians than in "racketeers or gangsters."

The ideal leader must be a man who is devoid of the "money bug idea" with which Wall St. and the American people have been "doped" for the last five years.

Dreiser today is inarticulate over the country's physical beauty and inarticulate likewise when he contemplates the error, the fraud and corruption he located on his hurried and sentimental journey. He hates the way things are between the Atlantic and the Pacific. He hates what he perceives to be a cynical throttling of community life by corporations in Chicago, Minneapolis, Tucson, San Francisco and way stations.

Has he a remedy? Yes. Today, in his 57th St. apartment, he recommends that Wall Street move to Pennsylvania Ave.

Give Bankers Full Control

Give bankers and industrialists open, formal, official control of the government and see what happens.

"Make Mr. Rockefeller Secretary of Oil and Gas. Send Mr. Atterbury to Washington to be director of Railroads. Keep Mr. Mellon where he is.[1] Add all the banks and insurance companies, all institutions that deal in money, to the Treasury Department," said the author of "An American Tragedy" and other novels of naïve despair.

What Dreiser suggests is a communization of the land, with the high-powered, influential merchantmen and money lenders in frank command. He proposes that we adopt the scheme that in Russia sends chills up and down the capitalistic spine of the world. Being a practical people, he foresees that we would adapt it differently than Russia.

"Other peoples other ways," he said. "Why shouldn't we draft Mr. Ford and Mr. Rockefeller and make them serve the people? We couldn't pay them the big rewards they get now. We should have to pay them in honor, position."

Honor as Reward

The novelist was reminded that the Founding Fathers had such a system of rewards in mind when they fixed official salaries at modest sums.

"We ought to get back to those days," he said and instantly amended himself. "The old Yankee nutmeg individualism is dead."

"It is only an economic battle," he said. "They knock each other about in the markets or the world, seizing raw materials, suborning governments. The railroads and utility corporations function now as super-governments. Let them govern actually."

Let the corporations rule in fact instead of through dummies! If that be Communism make the most of it.

1. For Rockefeller, see p. 112, n. 11. William W. Atterbury (1886–1935) was the president of the Pennsylvania Railroad system, and the financier Andrew Mellon (1855–1937) served as secretary of the U.S. Treasury from 1921 to 1932.

No Leadership from Writers

Where will the leadership of the new day come from? Politicians are discredited. Literary men—

"Literary men—hell! With millions of people in the country experiencing great and sorrowful distress what do the literary men do? They sit in New York composing odes to spring. You can't count on them for leadership."

Perhaps the shrewd, disillusioned, fallible captains of industry themselves may point the way. But Dreiser has little enough respect for the average executive who occupies a West End Ave. or Park Ave. apartment.

"The heirs of the men who founded the corporations, like the railroads, the Commodore Vanderbilts, the James J. Hills, &c., today are getting the benefit of their originality.[2] The power has gone out of the railroads. Take seventy-five clerks fresh out of college and turn the Pennsylvania Railroad over to them. They would run it as well as or better than the present executives do. Running a big corporation is routine now. All the important things were learned long ago."

No Respect for Plutocrats

Nor does the Sage of Manhattan—the gray-haired, ruthless Hoosier who suffers from bronchitis and what he considers to be a crystal clear vision of the world round about—bend in respect to the plutocrats who hire the high-powered executives.

How do the money barons—those wise men who have "at last established a money standard"—spend their vast profits? For the benefit of man? No!

"In the first place," said Dreiser, "they send millions to China, Japan, Finland, Poland, Roumania and elsewhere to bolster the fight against Communism to protect their holdings here. They throw millions over there, but they don't see to it that the average small man is sure of a job.

"Then they build the most asinine buildings in the world, with marble, malachite and other semi-precious trimmings; buildings that the insurance companies won't insure because they have only sentimental value.

2. Cornelius Vanderbilt (1794–1877) founded the New York Central Railroad, and James J. Hill (1838–1916) was responsible for both the Great Northern Railroad and the Canadian Pacific Railroad.

Luxury Despite Jobless

"They can get the dough to pay for gold swimming pools at their country houses, they can buy thousand-acre tracts to keep off neighbors and indulge in all that swill, but they can't arrange things so a man can have a job."

The whole scheme is slightly insane, Dreiser holds, when "little Vincent Astor" can inherit $300,000,000 and turn it over to the Guaranty Trust to manage. The bank, he says, then holds the estate because it manages it.[3]

"By what right does Vincent Astor, a nice man, own those ancient franchises or freeholds? If that's a sane system, then I'm the damnedest fool in the town.

"What have we come to? We can't get banks big enough. I read in the papers that the Chase National has so many billions that you and I can't even imagine what it would be like to have them.

Is Wall Street for Welfare?

"What is the use of larger assets? Merely to finance governments and broad-scale operations. But what is the use of large scale operations? Surely not to add to the wealth of a little group in Wall Street. Their only use is to add to the welfare of the people. Do they do it? I leave the answer to you."

The gospel, according to St. Theodore, is austere. He scolds as any Isaiah, although, the Lord knows, he himself is well heeled with a millionaire's town place, a broad farm in the Croton neighborhood, motor cars and bonds in the safe deposit box.

He detests the new dogma that competition is "unfair." He rages and storms because out in Anderson, Ind., he found a chain hotel suing in the courts to restrain the building of a competitive inn.[4] The whole era of business co-operation, with its luncheon club philosophy, exemplified by admirers of President Hoover's engineering efficiency, the eminent novelist finds unpleasant and more than a little crackpot.

"We Need a Statesman"

"We need a statesman, not an engineer, in the White House," he said.

The country has gone dopey over money.

"The fellow who gets $5,000 more than you a year says 'who the hell are

3. Vincent Astor (1891–1959) was the son and heir of John Jacob Astor IV, who went down on the *Titanic* in 1912. Vincent thus inherited the vast Astor real estate holdings at the age of twenty-one.

4. See p. 220, n. 1.

you?' That goes all through the scale," Dreiser fumed. "At last they've got money as the standard."

Dreiser the Discover, back from his first continental voyage, reports things going badly in Chicago, where the Illinois Central still preempts the lake front; in Minneapolis, where all the State courts permitted a critical newspaper to be suppressed as a public nuisance;[5] in California, where the Southern Pacific still blocks other railways out of San Francisco; in Tucson, Ariz., where the same railroad arrogantly bisects the lovely town and condescends at long intervals to permit the people to burrow tunnels under its right of way so one-half may communicate with the other.

Dreiser is disgusted, outraged and thoroughly mad at the way he believes the corporations have taken the country by the throat.

Scores A.T.&T. in Oregon

It makes Dreiser boil to think that the A.T.&T. out in Oregon has thumbed its nose at Portland, a city of 300,000 souls, for three years. The telephone company, having raised its rates, as did the New York subsidiary recently, was penalized with a franchise tax. The State Utilities Commission, made up of four men drawing only $4,000 a year each, countersigned the "rate grab."

"The city government," said Dreiser, "held that as the phone company was taxing the people through the higher rate, they would tax the phone company. The franchise tax was legal—that is to say, constitutional.

"Did the company pay it? They haven't, for three years."

The author, proceeding on his leisurely, perplexed two-months tour of the continent, was tempted to mount the soap box in Portland, without a license or franchise, and expose the fact that the phone company, equally without a license or franchise, daily did business in the northwestern metropolis. Leading citizens advised him against such a step.

"An Economic Joke"

Dreiser thinks his findings lead inescapably to the view that there should be only one, not two, governments in the land. He thinks that the United States under the present arrangement, with the corporations ruling alongside the constituted government, is "slowly, but surely, dwindling into a kind of economic joke."

He is no minion of Moscow. When he was there a couple of years ago the Communists called him an American spy and a reactionary. He does

5. See p. 220, n. 2.

not advocate the Russian kind of Communism for this country. Merely the Wall Street kind.

Nor does the philosopher of 57th St. desire a dictator to bestraddle the country he loves with a warm, but sardonic, passion.

"In a low stage of society," he conceded, "the value of an individual with a highly developed organic sense might have been appreciated. He might have been very useful then. But now there are far too many people who understand governmental organization to permit a few to tell all the rest what they can or cannot have."

Calls Americans Fatuous

The reason the country has got into such a state, with chain stores, co-operation and corporate control, is that the native-born, Gentile American is somewhat of a fatuous citizen who believes that once you start a good government going, equipped with a constitution and high ideals, it will stay on the rails forever without further attention.

But every government needs frequent checkups, as does every business.

"The Gentile American," said Dreiser, "is a very simple and idealistic person who wants to have faith in the good intentions of his fellow citizen. He actually feels that. Consequently, he is very hurt and sore and gets very bitter and critical when he sees it doesn't work.

"But the failure of the system to protect him doesn't kill his desire to see a modicum of fair play in public relationships."

Enthused Over Our Scenery

If Dreiser has[n't] a kind word for his fellow citizen, he is ecstatic about the environment in which the American human has his being. If the American doesn't "fight in the streets," as Dreiser thinks he well might if he realized his manhood against all sorts of injustices and perversions, he, at least, dwells in a splendid paradise.

"This country has got Europe backed off the boards for scenery," he said. "I've been everywhere in Europe, from the Urals to the Channel, clean down to the Afghan border, and I never saw anything to touch fifty, yes, one hundred, beauty spots that we visited on this trip."

The somber novelist, the tragic, brooding Dreiser of "Sister Carrie" and "The Genius," is a lyrical, 100 per cent booster for the glories of the Redwood forests, of the painted buttes, the towers of the Rockies, the purple hills of Montana.

Blame the money madness of the Americano for his plight, fix him up with a government by financiers in Washington, under a statesman—that he yields to sentiment—but admire the yokel's scenery. That is the wisdom of Dreiser.

Sees Changes in West

And he sees a change coming on the dusty roads of the West.

"The hour has struck," he said. Out in the grain and cattle States, in the Hood River Valley, in California's coastal cities, throughout the sunburned Southwest, people are talking about ridding themselves of the railroad and utility octopi.

"It was the same in France and Germany before the war," he said. "People in cafes and on trains were talking about how inevitable a war was. They sensed it. The people out West are sensing this change now. It is sure to come and the politicians may not know about the change until it hits."

Dreiser returned with a new slant on New York. It still is his spiritual home, but he isn't sure he won't buy a ranch on the road from Albuquerque to El Paso and go Western himself.

Theodore Dreiser at Home

By Karl Sebestyén

*

Living Age 339 (Dec. 1930): 375–78. Translated from *Pester Lloyd*, a Budapest German-language daily.

Through the good offices of a friend and pupil of mine, I made the acquaintance of Theodore Dreiser, the most distinguished American author now living and one of the most important contemporary novelists in world literature. We found him at his home on Fifty-Seventh Street, New York City, where we spent an hour and a half in his company. In appearance Dreiser is a giant, a veritable Titan, tall, upright, strongly built, with a tremendous great head and a shock of pure white hair (he is fifty-nine years old) and strangely blazing steel-gray eyes. He is a thorough German. His father, a German born and bred, was a peasant who lived near the Moselle and emigrated to the United States in 1848. He gave his son a strict Roman Catholic education.

After the first introductory formalities our conversation soon flowed rapidly. Dreiser speaks well and gladly and makes no secret of his opinions. Politically, he is a radical or what we should call an adherent of the extreme left. After his journey to Russia he wrote a book describing his experiences and in doing so he found himself quite at odds with the Soviet potentates. Now, however, his opinions of Lenin and the Bolsheviks are much more lenient, although he is fully convinced that Russian methods cannot be transplanted either to Europe or to America. His partiality for Russia arises from a deep dissatisfaction with the existing order, especially in his own country.

"Our chief trouble here," he said, "is that we produce too much. We made too many goods in the prosperous post-war period. The result was that we had to slow down production, and as a logical consequence thousands of workers were thrown out of employment. Furthermore, something even more unthinkable in America happened. We not only had to institute soup kitchens, bread lines, and all the other insupportable creations of philanthropy, but we also witnessed demonstrations of the unemployed as well as interminable, fruitless, tiresome conferences on ways and means of overcoming the difficulty. In this finest and best of all possible worlds only those who make a great amount of money are happy and they naturally do not want any changes. The great masses of the people must keep their mouths shut. In this land of freedom the powers that be do not relish the publication of any new political or social creed and any such activity is forbidden and is strictly suppressed. I could cite a whole list of such cases, including among them the arrest of a leader of a parade down Broadway, the arrest of two girls in Ohio, of a hundred and thirty-seven men and women in Chicago, and of nine hundred people in California, all of whom were accused of participating in forbidden demonstrations and were given long jail sentences.[1]

"I see the last hour coming when some remedy can and must be found. Above all else, freedom to express political and economic opinions must be returned to us. In America, and from what I know, in many European countries too, what is happening now offends not only the laws and constitutions but also human understanding and can only lead the great masses of the people to catastrophic revolution. The great minds everywhere must unite and devise some way out of the crisis humanity is now facing. For as long as America allows the ignorant, the weak, the despairing, and the outcast to be shot down humanity's problem has not been solved. Every man and woman with courage should step forward, bravely and freely demanding that intellect and not brute force should take over the conduct of the world."

"You are not thinking of a republic in Plato's sense, a state where leadership is trusted to philosophers or writers?"

"No, no. You must have quite misunderstood me. They are the last people I should think of. What are my honorable colleagues in the writing profession doing? Unconcerned with the desperate plight of a world that is on the brink of ruin, they sit in New York writing odes to Spring and continually demanding higher prices for their work. No, literature is the last thing I want to hear and know about. Here on my table is a pile of the latest works of the fellow members of my profession. Carried away by an irresistible impulse, I have read nearly half of them, but there is not a trace of greatness or monumentality anywhere. Can you find among them a single book that might be compared to Thackeray's *Vanity Fair* or to any novel by Dickens, Dostoievski, Balzac, or Tolstoi? You will find some good routine writers but never a great artist. Take, for instance, my colleague, Sinclair Lewis, who has caused such a stir in Europe. I gladly acknowledge that once, in *Arrowsmith*, he succeeded in executing a brave task and portrayed the tragedy of a great scientist. But what else has he written? Nothing but popu-

1. Dreiser refers to the common response by local officials throughout the country to public demonstrations by Communist organizations. Early in 1931 he accepted the chairmanship of the National Committee for the Defense of Political Prisoners, a Communist-sponsored organization that sought to protect the civil rights of left-wing groups and figures.

lar novels suited to the taste of the average American audience, and when he dares to become sarcastic and throw bitter truths in the face of his fellow countrymen he recalls that the loose-tongued audacity of *Dodsworth* is still shocking his middle-class audience."[2]

"Your prejudice against American writers sounds as if you had consciously taken the opposite direction and had chosen to follow systematically a solitary path of unpopularity."

"No, that is a mistake. Of course, I go my own way and I am proud to know that I am un-American in that respect, although I am a Yankee body and soul. I never went after success and success took vengeance on me mightily by staying out of my way for decades. Now I have arrived." At this point Dreiser sighed. "My *American Tragedy* was made into a silent and then into a talking film and I keep receiving lavish offers for writing short stories."[3]

"Do you fill these orders?"

"Certainly, why not? One is very well paid and, what is much more important to me, these stories do not have to be too short. You know that it is a habit of mine to paint on a broad canvas, to explain at length, and to spend a long time expounding a philosophic thought or a social idea. Previously this prolixity was a handicap to my progress, but now the publishers accept it with happy, cheerful smiles. These gentlemen are very nice to me and I must especially praise my German publisher, Paul Zsolnay, who, I believe, is a fellow countryman of yours and whom I got to know well during my visit to Europe three years ago."[4]

"I am bringing you warm greetings from another of your friends in Europe, Professor Bruno Walter."

"Ah, Bruno Walter!" Dreiser's eyes lit up with joy. "Those were grand days and nights I spent in Salzburg talking with that artistic genius and utterly great man.[5] To be with such men is the greatest and purest pleasure we can enjoy. When you see him, give him my heartiest good wishes.

2. Dreiser held various grudges against Lewis (1893–1961). In late 1928 Lewis supported his wife, Dorothy Thompson, when she accused Dreiser of plagiarizing material in *Dreiser Looks at Russia* from her book *The New Russia*. The "stir in Europe" to which Dreiser refers may be either Lewis's rivalry with Dreiser for the 1930 Nobel Prize in Literature or the actual awarding of the prize to Lewis, which was announced on 5 November 1930. In a much-reported incident that occurred not long after this interview, in March 1931, the two men had words at a public social occasion and Dreiser slapped Lewis.

3. An error by either Dreiser or the reporter. There was no silent-film version of *An American Tragedy*, and although Dreiser signed a contract for a sound version in early January 1931, it had not been made at the time of this interview.

4. Dreiser met the Hungarian-born Zsolnay (1895–1961) in Berlin during the summer of 1926 while touring Europe with Helen.

5. In 1926 Dreiser also met Walter (1876–1962), the great German Jewish conductor who later immigrated to America (see the previous note).

"Outstanding artistic personalities still exist, especially in Europe, but our own are mostly imported goods. Yet in the field of exact science America can well be proud and take satisfaction in the steady progress her great inventors have made and in their incontestably important discoveries and in the splendidly organized and handsomely endowed institutions in which they work. There is a long roll of honor of American physicists, doctors, and technicians who have led the way in human progress. But we are more in need of leading statesmen to bring us back to some endurable national policy. We want a statesman in the White House, not a technician. Since Hoover has been in Washington everything has run downhill."

"Were you more contented with Wilson or Coolidge?" I inquired, very curious to see what answer my question would bring.

"Wilson was an idealist and an idealogue,[6] and a great statesman is neither the one nor the other. Coolidge revealed himself as a harmless man who kept silent because he had nothing to say. Under his presidency things went well and he was therefore known as a good president. Now things are going badly and Hoover has to bear the responsibility.

"Wherever you look you see demoralization. Plutocrats are squandering their money on anti-Socialist propaganda in Europe instead of spending it here in their own country to decrease the number of the unemployed. They are building asinine palaces of marble and malachite and other semiprecious stones, palaces that insurance companies do not wish to insure since they possess only a sentimental value. Little Vincent Astor inherits three hundred million dollars,[7] while hundreds of thousands of people go destitute. For my own part, I believe that there is only one cure for the poverty in our big cities—a concentrated, thorough relief programme.

"Out into the open air, out into the strong living air of nature. I have just returned from the West by motor, but as soon as I have finished the work on which I am now engaged I shall go West again. In Europe people are attaching importance to the motto, "*Ex Oriente lux.*" We in America are beginning to feel that "*Ex Occidente lux*" is the order of the day and that the West will give us light and warmth as well as a new, healthy, active humanity."[8]

He raised his voice. Its metallic sound and the excited face and glowing eyes of the speaker reminded me of one of the Old Testament prophets. The whole man had suddenly changed. He had become simple, kind, and friendly. He whom his critics accuse of lacking humor actually glowed with

6. Both the context and the fact that *idealogue* is not accepted English usage suggest that Dreiser's intended *ideologue* was either misheard or mistranslated.

7. See p. 224, n. 3.

8. "Out of the East comes light" and "Out of the West comes light."

it warmly and deeply. Theodore Dreiser, the dark, doubting pessimist, became a laughing child. I grasped his right hand in mine and as I took leave of him I had the stimulating sensation that I had met a man who is one of the spiritual leaders of our time.

"Hooeyland" Says Dreiser, back from Film Capital

*

New York American, 12 April 1931, p. 22-L.

Although Dreiser and his publisher Horace Liveright sold the film rights of *An American Tragedy* to Famous Players (a precursor of Paramount) in 1926, the film was never made. Early in 1931 Dreiser renegotiated with Paramount over the rights to a sound version of the novel, and the studio quickly put the film into production. He was appalled by the script, however, and in March he and his own scriptwriter went to Hollywood in an attempt to persuade Paramount to revise its version. The company refused, and in June Dreiser invited a committee of writers and critics to view the just-completed Paramount version and decide whether it was true to the novel. Armed with their negative judgment, he unsuccessfully sought an injunction to prevent the distribution of the film. (See also Dreiser's 12 April 1931 interview in the *New York Herald Tribune* on the same topic.)

The ordinarily sedate and composed Theodore Dreiser momentarily threw off his poise yesterday as he touched a verbal match to Hollywood and watched it devastated in the flames of his wrath.

And the famous author of "An American Tragedy" was a trifle burned up himself. He had just flown back from the Coast, and although he was not in Hollywood very long, he was there long enough to gather sizzling impressions of what's wrong with the movie colony, to which he gave vigorous utterance. Dreiser said Hollywood should be renamed "Hooeyland."

Brains? None!

Shifting about in a comfortable armchair in his apartment at 200 W. 57th St. from the very fervor of his rage, the distinguished writer cynically averred that the cranial density by volume of Hollywood producers will never violate the next amendment to the Constitution, which, he said, will prohibit people from thinking. He cried:

"When we get a Volstead, who will put through Congress a bill prohibiting free thought, it will be a great boon to Hollywood.[1] But it won't cramp their style any. I don't recall contacting any producing brains that assayed more than one-half of one per cent."

Dreiser's "An American Tragedy," recently purchased by Paramount for $150,000, has just been produced at the West coast studios of that organization. "Traduced," the author says, would be a better word. According to Dreiser his contract provided that the script was to be shown to him, and the high moguls of the talkies were to consider any changes he recommended. But when he saw the script, he left town by the next plane. It was, in his own language, "unbelievable."

The author plans to see the finished picture here in New York within the next few weeks with several of his friends. And if it does not meet with his approval . . . Dreiser almost surged out of his armchair with rage and announced:

"I'll get a lawyer and take them to court. I'll see whether a writer cannot prevent himself from being misrepresented before the public."

Dreiser contends he has an "equity" in his own characters, and that if "An American Tragedy" should turn out to be something more properly to be titled "A Mexican Comedy" he is going to take the matter to the highest court in the land, if necessary. He said:

"They discarded the first third of the book, which established the psychology of poverty and the background which would cause the boy to want something he had never had. Then they suddenly conceived the great notion that a death house scene was too gruesome to show to the American public, though the play has been packing them in, with that scene intact, for three years.[2]

"My contract for the stage rights provides that if they don't play to seventy-five successful performances a year the rights revert to me—and I've never been able to catch up with them.[3] I'd certainly like to do it, too."

---

1. Andrew J. Volstead (1860–1947), a congressman from Minnesota, sponsored the Volstead Act of 1919, which provided for the enforcement of the Eighteenth Amendment prohibiting the sale of alcoholic beverages.

2. A dramatic adaptation of *An American Tragedy* by Patrick Kearney opened in New York on 11 October 1926 and played until mid-1927. By still "packing them in," Dreiser is referring to the road company productions.

3. The "seventy-five . . . performances" in Dreiser's contract with Liveright referred to productions anywhere in the country.

Dreiser Wants Courts to Save "Tragedy" Film
Declares Hollywood Version of
Work Is False; Will Sue to Prevent Showing
Denounces Whole Industry
Says Right Length for a Kiss
Is All of Life to Producers

BY ELENORE KELLOGG

*

New York Herald Tribune, 12 April 1931, p. 4.

For the general background of this interview, see the headnote to the previous interview, p. 233. Portions of the *Herald Tribune* interview were republished as "Dreiser on the Sins of Hollywood" in *Literary Digest* 109 (2 May 1931): 21.

Theodore Dreiser returned from Hollywood yesterday full of smoldering anger over what the films have done to his book, "An American Tragedy," and announced that he was going to "fight for my literary character if it takes years."

He told why: because in a land torn with serious problems he thinks the films are feeding the people "hokum, insincere sexy stuff, crazy and expensive, but just make believe." He believes this "opiate" is not only blinding America to social problems, but is lowering this country in the eyes of the world. Also, because what the films are doing now is "damned economic nonsense," he foresees that bankers will supplant pants pressers as the heads of the industry,[1] that more producing will be done in the East and abroad, and that Hollywood will be slowed up—Hollywood, which he characterizes as "that game out there."

---

1. This is a covert allusion to the fact that many Hollywood studios were controlled by Jews who, Dreiser assumes, had their roots in the New York garment industry.

Angry at "Generalissimos"

The pioneer American realist talked feelingly of his experience in Hollywood. He said he was "led through double doors to meet generalissimos who jumped around like monkeys and talked like children." He was told by Josef von Sternberg, who is directing the picturization of his book, that "America has nothing to learn from Europe." (Mr. Von Sternberg was born in Vienna.)[2] As for the picture itself, he declared that they had left out all the first part showing the boy's development and had ended the film with the boy, now grown up, receiving his death sentence. The death house scenes, with their deeply moving psychological probing, also were left out as "too drastic," though Mr. Dreiser pointed out that the play with the death house part in it ran here to packed houses.

"I am going to fight," declared the author, referring to his announced intention of bringing suit to restrain the producing company from showing the picture. "I have a literary character to maintain, and I contend that I have a mental equity in my product and the character of my product. Even though they buy the right of reproduction, they don't buy the right to change it into anything they please. The word reproduction means about what it says.

"They can't take a piece of work that is inimical to my standards and picture me as writing something I never in the world could have written. Law or no law, I believe I can go before the courts of equity, and the Federal court, and get a decision, and I will get it if it takes years."

He is "not necessarily" through selling film rights to his work, "but when they're sold, they will be sold as they are." "I don't want to compel them to lose money," he continued, "but I don't want to be injured either. And I don't think they would lose money if they made the picture nearer reality."

Mr. Dreiser, who has made money from realism, spoke his mind on the films in his vast Gothic studio, high-ceilinged and expensive, lined with books and hung with modern paintings, and with a supercilious colored servant on guard outside. He sat in his shirtsleeves at a desk piled with mail, and even so managed to look remote and unapproachable. No matter how bitter the words, his voice never lost its level, impersonal tone.

2. Von Sternberg (1894–1969) made his reputation directing Marlene Dietrich (1901–92) in *Der Blaue Engel* (1930), released in the United States as *The Blue Angel*. He and Samuel Hoffenstein collaborated on the adaptation of *An American Tragedy* for Paramount's version of the novel, which premiered on 22 August 1931.

Length of Kiss Chief Concern

"If an earthquake or any other catastrophe happened, much less an economic depression, they would still be employing their magnificent brains out there on the right length of a kiss, or on 'the impatient virgin,'" he asserted.

"They think they can evade problems if they make everything conform to the lowest grade minds in the country, these little state reformers. If you mention a problem they throw up their hands and say, 'My God, what would we do with a problem?' Sex and love, love and sex, that's the American interest. They get a telegram from the manager of some little theater in Hocus, S.D., saying his audience can't understand problems, give them love.

"These enormous studios extending over blocks, with 10,000 cars standing outside, look as though the world could be made over in them. They have conferences every day, they talk about what they will do, but it always comes back to the same thing, the right to kiss.

"They are dealing with the total average mind of the United States, these movies, and what they're doing to it is fantastic. They're making the average housewife or clerk believe that all that's important is this junk, that this is the way life is to be dealt with.

"There is danger in New York right now of two or three of the greatest financial institutions in the world tumbling, and if they did the condition of the country would be much worse. It doesn't occur to them that economic or social or educational problems are subjects for movies. They have to get back to the kiss stuff. For purely commercial reasons they try to find what pleases the dub at his lowest, because he is the most numerous.

"That's what's the matter with the mind of America today. John Dewey and other radicals say you can't interest Americans in any serious problems.[3] Why? It's the damned movies, like bread and circuses in the old Roman days. Here they fill 'em up with kissing scenes. It's a low mental condition for a country to be in and a low comment on the United States that an enormous industry should flourish on that basis."

Mr. Dreiser glanced at the fresh-faced young woman secretary who was sitting beside him, drinking in these bitter words, and went on to talk about what Hollywood does to it stars.[4]

"One moment they will tell you these people are worth millions," he said, "and the next they waste that talent. One fellow told me the great thing to

---

3. Although hardly a "radical," John Dewey (1859–1952), a philosopher and an educational theorist, did deplore the disappearance of an informed public in his widely discussed book *The Public and Its Problems* (1927).

4. Evelyn Light had become Dreiser's secretary in February 1931.

do is to get it while you can, show a star in three or four things that get the public attention, and then they can put over nine or ten more and make their money. A shrewd person would say they should get really important vehicles so the public would build up that sort of association with the name of a star. Instead they use them up, wipe up the floor with them, then pitch them out and look for some one else.

"Ruth Chatterton, for instance, has done very sympathetic work in one or two things, but along comes Marlene Dietrich or some one wearing a high hat and tights, and so they compel this serious actress to imitate that sort of thing, to wear a silk hat and tights, and she can't do it.[5] Instead of finding vehicles for Greta Garbo, they put her in things that any little squeak could play.[6]

Sees Contract Slipping

"You'd think a person with any sense would say, 'I won't play this,' but that is called breaking their contract and would bar them from the movies. That's in the class with what I've done. I wouldn't be surprised if I were barred from every studio, which"—Mr. Dreiser's heavy, angry glance was as emphatic as a blow of the fist—"would give me cramps, NOT!"

But Mr. Dreiser foresees an end to all this. "I have a feeling," he said, "that the whole situation is going to change in Hollywood. The financial situation may force a change. Bankers will get control of the industry and force them to give up selling sex for so much a seat. Nobody objects to sex, not even I, but there are other things in life.

"They are building studios in France now because they have to, and because fine things are being produced there with their own money they have to let them in. People will demand more good pictures and there will be less for Hollywood to do. I just read in a trade publication that 40 per cent of one studio's productions were going to be made in New York. I sincerely believe that the handwriting is on the wall."

For the rest, Mr. Dreiser thinks Hollywood is a "charming little place," full of climate, oranges and cheap bungalows, despite its million population, "a small town with mistaken notions about life."

5. Ruth Chatterton (1893–1961), a Broadway star, was twice nominated for an Academy Award during her Hollywood years of 1928–31. Marlene Dietrich became an international film star following her performance as a cabaret performer (in tights and a top hat) in *The Blue Angel*.

6. Greta Garbo (1905–90) came to America in 1925, and though her films up to the time of this interview had met with great popular success, almost all were undistinguished.

Dreiser, 60, Glad He's Rich, but Doubts He's Happier
Writer Recalls Days of 1922, When He Was
One Jump ahead of Landlord

*

New York World-Telegram, 27 August 1931, p. 3.

From 1931 until his death, newspapers frequently sought out Dreiser for a birthday interview, an opportunity he usually seized upon both to reminisce about the past and to attack present conditions.

Theodore Dreiser turned 60 today.

He observed his birthday by doing his customary stint of work while servants rushed about the place doing final bits of packing preparatory to a move.

Dreiser is giving up his big studio apartment at 200 W. 57th St., which for five years has been the outward expression of the prosperity that came to him so belatedly in 1926. He is moving out to his country place at Mount Kisco and may never again live in New York City.[1] He will keep only a small writing hideaway in town.

The Problems of Wealth

He sat today at his big piano desk in the nearly bare studio and discussed the benefits and troubles of wealth.

"Six years ago," he said in his shy, brooding way, "I was living in a $70-a-month apartment over in Brooklyn.[2] In 1922 the most I could get out of a publisher was a drawing account of $125 a month.

1. In 1926, flush with the profits from *An American Tragedy* in both its novel and dramatic forms, Dreiser purchased a large tract near Mount Kisco, New York (about twenty-five miles north of Manhattan), overlooking Croton Lake. He had built there, with the aid of a number of artist and architect friends, a summer home of rather bizarre appearance that he called "Iroki," the Japanese word for "beauty." From 1935 to 1938, when he moved to Los Angeles, he often lived there during the winter as well.

2. For much of 1925 Dreiser and Helen lived in Brooklyn in a flat on Bedford Avenue while he completed *An American Tragedy*.

"But that was all I needed. I could live on that.

"Then suddenly a book caught on and I was prosperous. I'm glad it happened. I'm glad I know how it feels to have anything you want. But it hasn't made me any happier.

"I haven't been any happier with plenty of money than I was when I didn't know where the next month's rent was coming from. It was always a race between me and the landlord and sometimes even eating was a problem.

"But a writer doesn't need anything more than that. Money won't help him."

He brooded for a moment, fumbling with a manuscript on his unkempt desk.

"What do they do with it all—these people who have enough of it. They want more and more, but it doesn't make them happy.

When Riches Increase

"I remember when Thomas F. Ryan bought the old Yerkes house on Fifth Ave., a beautiful place. I wondered what he wanted with it. I went over to ask him. I thought maybe he had some plan for it. But, no, he had bought it just because he wanted it. He was like an old tiger. I don't think his wealth made him happy.[3]

"There is a passage in the Bible that says it all:—

"'When riches are increased, they are increased that eat them.'[4]

"It seems to me a balancing process. When you get money you get encumbrances. You are weighted down. You find things to worry about that never entered your mind before. If you get, you've got to give. There's no way out but that."

So Dreiser sat there in the nearly bare studio, the place that cost more per year than Dreiser had ever made in three years of labor before 1926, and discussed why a writer writes.

"A writer wants only to feel internally that he has achieved something," said Dreiser. He seemed to gesture his luxurious apartment away almost in dislike, seemed to blink it away into the limbo of things that have never existed.

3. Ryan (1851–1928), a flamboyant financier and self-made multimillionaire, owned the house adjacent to the house and art gallery of Charles T. Yerkes on upper Fifth Avenue. In 1910, some years after Yerkes' death, Ryan purchased Yerkes' art gallery (not his house) in order to pull it down to make a garden. Dreiser of course would have been especially interested in Yerkes' house since he had based the figure of Frank Cowperwood in the Cowperwood trilogy on Yerkes, but the house Ryan owned was not that built and owned by Yerkes.

4. Dreiser is slightly misquoting Ecclesiastes 5:11: "When goods increase / They increase who eat them."

"It was a beautiful place," he said softly. "I'm glad I was able to have it. But a writer doesn't strive for material things."

Did he believe that the average human being would ever desire anything but material success?

Masses Are Imitative

"The vast masses have always been imitative," he answered. "They have always wanted what it happened to be the fashion to want. Everybody wants his name on some trashy little corporation today. If they rig up some lousy little business and become president or vice president they are satisfied.

"But the world will be better when we put the corporations in the hands of the people. That will happen some day."

On the table in the reception hall was a pile of toys.

"They send them to me every year, for my birthday and Christmas," smiled Dreiser, the man painted to the public as the sad brooder of America. "Those came last Christmas. This morning I got a toy electric train. Why do they send them? Don't ask me. I don't know why people do things."

Dreiser Carries His Pessimism Lightly at Sixty
First American Realist, in Birthday Interview,
Says He Was Gloomier at 20
Denies Life Is Miserable
Easily Diverted and Thinks Speakeasies "Charming"

By Elenore Kellogg

*

New York Herald Tribune, 28 August 1931, p. 11.

Theodore Dreiser was sixty years old yesterday and full of sardonic good humor about it. His message in a birthday interview was: "Tell the waiting world that I'm not as bad off as they think."

Sitting in his dismantled studio in his shirtsleeves—for the first American realist is moving—he observed with more chuckles that he was less pessimistic than when he was twenty. Not that he thinks the world is any better: he is just about to publish a blast against these capitalistic United States,[1] "after which I suppose I'll have to move to Kamchatka," he said. But he has learned that one can be diverted, that the "contemplative mind can be put aside like a book," and that "one doesn't have to wear one's deepest suspicions of life on one's sleeve all the time."

Carries Pessimism Easily

"I can look reality in the face and describe it, and that makes everybody think I must be miserable," he said. "If anything, I was more pessimistic at eighteen or twenty. My viewpoint was darker than now. But my pessimism doesn't cause me any aches or pains.

"Reality makes most people sick at the stomach. They can't contemplate it without losing their minds or screaming or making asses of themselves. I could always face reality and look my own shortcomings in the eye as well as other people's.

"A critic of one of my recent books said I must be a miserable man with-

---

1. Dreiser's "blast," *Tragic America*, appeared, after much delay, in December 1931.

out any friends, and all that sort of thing. I've never wanted friends and have never been in a position where I didn't have to fence myself in. Having a realistic mind hasn't debarred me from thinking I can live the same as anybody else. Some people believe anybody who thinks must be pessimistic.

"As a matter of fact, I'm easily diverted, particularly by liquor. If I can get into one of these charming speakeasies where they have everything we had before the war, I can forget my troubles and be so foolish I am ridiculous. And nothing has been so diverting as the musical revues and the popular comedians. God knows how much I owe to Joe Cook and Ed Wynn and the others. Comedians have saved my life ever since I used to watch Frank Bush in 10-cent vaudeville in the Middle West."[2]

How does he feel at sixty?

"It hadn't occurred to me to feel anything," replied the realistic Dreiser. "I feel just the same as before." Then with another sardonic laugh, he said "It's a damn good thing people get old and die. It keeps things rather interesting. It provides a new deal every fifteen minutes. The president of a corporation kicks off, and little Willie gets the job. It makes him think life is all right whether it is or not.

"I've seen people die like flies. Fully 70 per cent of the people who started out with me—better people than I am—have passed out long ago. When I think of all the charming spirits that have passed on, I'd just as soon join them. The nothingness that holds them is good enough for me. If I thought I was going to walk in the same vale as Shelley or Shakespeare, I'd depart this morning."

Does he think a man's best work is behind him at sixty?

"I think I'm hopeless, all through," said Mr. Dreiser, his eyes positively twinkling. The interviewer suggested that he didn't look as though he meant that, and Dreiser added: "I like to think that, because if I do anything more I'll surprise myself."

It appears that Mr. Dreiser will be surprised for some time to come. He is working on the third volume of his financial trilogy, the first two being "The Financier" and "The Titan." The third volume, to be called "The Stoic," will be out next year.[3]

Then, he is also doing a book on the "economic, social and mental processes of this country since the Civil War." It brings things up to the present,

---

2. Cook (1890–1959), Wynn (see p. 192, n. 7), and Bush (1856–1927) were well-known vaudeville comedians.

3. After putting aside *The Stoic* on publication of *The Titan* in 1914, Dreiser worked intensively on the novel during much of 1932 but nevertheless failed to complete it. He did so at last in late 1945, shortly before his death.

where "no one knows anything at all about anything," and the remedies proposed are all a "variety of nonsense."[4]

Mr. Dreiser, who has grown comparatively wealthy under it, arraigned "the whole business of capitalism" as "lousy."

"That 3 or 5 per cent of the people should possess all the money and the power, with their insulting contempt for the source of their power, is insane," he asserted.

Objects to Radio City

"Take Rockefeller City," he went on, referring obviously to Radio City. "Who wants Rockefeller City?[5] They can't rent all the buildings they have now. It's all right for personal vanity, but so far as the national organization is concerned, it's the height of asininity. Why should the resources of the country be in the hands of a few people to slash around with, when most of their ideas run counter not only to welfare and peace but to the welfare of the individual? Mr. Rockefeller isn't an economist. He can organize for cash results.

"Some fellow from Bessarabia or Galicia comes here and in ten or twenty years is worth $30,000,000—somebody who hasn't anything to do with the country and hasn't even any sympathy with it—while the natives who are the bone of the country walk around not knowing where to turn.[6] You can't say, 'Let them die if they have no brains,' because that means you have no regard for the country or its people."

Meanwhile Mr. Dreiser is retiring to his country place at Mount Kisco for a while. He will be back in the fall.

4. This may be a further reference to *Tragic America*, since there is no evidence of another book of this kind in progress.

5. During 1931 the Rockefeller interests began the construction of Rockefeller Center, a complex of modernistic buildings in central Manhattan that would include such New York landmarks as the RCA Building and Radio City Music Hall.

6. An ethnically charged remark, since immigrants from these Romanian and Polish provinces, largely Jewish at the time, are contrasted unfavorably with "natives" of America.

Writers Are to Test Harlan "Free Speech" for Miners on Nov. 8
Theodore Dreiser's Committee Will Leave Tuesday to Investigate Charges of Terrorism in Mining Section

*

Knoxville News-Sentinel, 3 November 1931, p. 3.

Dreiser's most extensive personal foray into social activism occurred in November 1931, when he chaired a committee of the National Committee for the Defense of Political Prisoners (NCDPP) that visited Harlan County, Kentucky, to investigate the suppression of efforts by the Communist-controlled National Miners Union to organize the miners of the region. When Dreiser's initial attempt to enlist a number of nationally known liberal figures as members of the committee failed, he asked for volunteers from the NCDPP itself, and it was this group, consisting largely of left-wing writers, that arrived in Pineville, Bell County (adjoining Harlan County), on 5 November. The *Knoxville News-Sentinel* was one of the few newspapers of the area to report the committee's activities fully and without bias.

New York—Theodore Dreiser announced today that the committee of writers which he will head on a trip to Harlan, Ky., to investigate charges of official terrorism and gunman rule, will stage a free speech test for the miners' union in Harlan County, Nov. 8. Committee members will leave Tuesday for Pineville, Ky., where they will meet Nov. 5 and proceed in a body to Harlan the following day. The investigation is being conducted by the National Committee for the Defense of Political Prisoners.

The committee will consist of Dreiser, author of "An American Tragedy"; John Dos Passos, author of "Manhattan Transfer" and "The 42nd Parallel"; Bruce Crawford, editor of Crawford's Weekly, Norton, Va.; Charles Rumford Walker, author of "Steel" and "Bread of Fire"; Josephine Herbst, author of "Money for Love" and "Nothing is Sacred"; Lester Cohen, author of "Sweepings"; Samuel Ornitz, author of "Haunch, Paunch and Jowl," now connected with the Metro-Mayer-Goldwyn studios; and Anna Rochester, coal expert and author of "Labor and Coal."[1]

In Pineville, the committee will be greeted by a mass meeting of the National Miners Union, and the International Labor Defense.[2] The miners charge that armed deputies have broken up every meeting they have tried to hold, even raking them with machine gun fire.

Inquire Into Charges

Dreiser, who is chairman of the National Committee for the Defense of Political Prisoners, said that the delegation will hold an open inquiry into the following charges:

1. The denial of all constitutional and civil rights, as well as ordinary human rights to 18,000 Harlan county miners and their families. This includes the driving of miners out of post offices and withholding of their mail; compulsion to buy from company stores at high prices; invasion of homes without search warrants; arrests for possessing newspapers and magazines attacking the mine owners.

2. The kidnapping of union organizers and local miners active in the union; the shooting of newspaper reporters; the arrest of theological students and defense representatives bringing aid to imprisoned miners' children, the dynamiting of relief cars and soup kitchens.

3. The eviction of miners from their homes and the death of miners' families from a hunger disease known locally as flux.

4. The indictment of 34 miners for murder on "flimsy evidence." Trials have been set in counties 200 miles away so that the miners, who are penniless, cannot afford to transport witnesses.

5. The murder of two miners operating a relief soup kitchen, both shot in the back. One man is said to have been brought from Chicago to teach the newly sworn-in deputies the use of tear gas bombs and machine guns.

---

1. Dos Passos (1896–1970), Herbst (1897–1969), Cohen (1901–63), and Ornitz (1890–1957)—all at this time well-known writers with communist or leftish sympathies—were members of the NCDPP. Crawford's *Crawford's Weekly* frequently attacked the Harlan mine owners, and Crawford himself had been shot in the leg in July 1928 while reporting a story in the area. Walker (1893–1974) wrote novels about and reports on the American steel industry (his novel is *Bread and* [not *of*] *Fire*); he was accompanied by his wife, Adelaide Walker. Rochester (1880–1966) was a Marxist economist and historian. In fact, neither Herbst nor Rochester made the trip to Harlan. The party did contain, however, a number of minor Communist Party functionaries: Melvin P. Levy, secretary of the NCDPP; Harry Gannes, a *Daily Worker* editor; George Maurer, a representative of International Labor Defense; and a stenographer. Also accompanying the group was Marie Pergain (probably a fictitious name), Dreiser's "companion."

2. Founded in 1925, International Labor Defense was a communist-controlled legal-action organization that represented jailed union and political activists.

"Still Armed Camp"

"Sheriff Blair has announced since the formation of this committee that there is no terror in Harlan and he will welcome an investigation," declares Dreiser's statement.[3] "We hear from authentic sources in Harlan, however, that the county is still as much an 'armed camp' as it was a month ago when Louis Stark of the New York Times fled to Chicago before feeling safe enough to release his news.

"We are informed that the miners, despite Sheriff Blair's denial, are still not allowed to hold union meetings; that as the strike spreads in Straight Creek there are more arrests for 'criminal syndicalism' almost daily;[4] and that even relief kitchens cannot function without an outpost miner on guard against the coming of the 'law.' These are the charges our committee wants to examine and make public report on."

Senator Couzens of Michigan has endorsed the investigating committee in a telegram expressing "entire sympathy with and interest in your proposal," Dreiser declares. Ill health, the senator wired, prevented him from joining the delegation, as it did William Allen White, of Emporia, Kans.

Senator Norris wired Dreiser that he was "interested in the subject." Arthur Braden, president of Transylvania College, Lexington, Ky., declared in his telegram that he is "convinced a terrible situation exists in Harlan." Edward J. Meeman, editor of The Knoxville News-Sentinel, wired he "hoped efforts to obtain a senatorial investigation will be successful."[5]

Dreiser declared that the hunger and need of the miners, he had learned, was so intense that the writers' committee planned to bring relief. A public appeal was being made to provide the families of strike prisoners with funds for milk, bread and clothes. Money should be sent to Lincoln Steffens,[6] treasurer of the National Committee for the Defense of Political Prisoners, Room 430, 80 East 11th Street, New York City.

Telegrams endorsing the investigation committee have been received by

---

3. John H. Blair, the sheriff of Harlan County at this time, was allied with the mine operators and responsible for much of the violence in Harlan through his practice of deputizing the thugs whom the operators hired.

4. For criminal syndicalism, see p. 256, headnote.

5. James Couzens (1872–1936) was a Republican senator from Michigan; White (1868–1944) was the editor of the nationally known *Emporia Gazette*; and George W. Norris (1861–1944) was a Republican senator from Nebraska. These figures, along with Braden (1881–1944), Meeman (1889–1966), and a number of others who also refused Dreiser's invitation (e.g., Felix Frankfurter, Senator Robert La Follette, and Roy Howard), were not associated with the left but rather had in common both public prominence and a reputation for independent thinking.

6. Steffens (1866–1934) was the author of *The Shame of the Cities* (1904), an exposé of American urban political corruption; he was also famous for a remark he made on returning from a visit to the Soviet Union: "I have seen the future and it works."

Dreiser, chairman of the committee, from the John Reed Club of the University of North Carolina[7] and from Charlotte, N.C., where a mass meeting to express sympathy and raise funds is being arranged.

Replies [have been] received from Senator James Couzens and Senator William E. Borah[8] to Dreiser's request for a senatorial investigation of official terrorism and blackjack suppression of miners in Harlan County, Ky., showing a "complete breakdown of the American government's ability to protect the worker in his fight for ordinary human rights," Dreiser declared.

"Senator Couzens writes me that evidence collected by our committee may be used by the U.S. Senate to instigate a senatorial investigation," declared Dreiser. "He is, however, very skeptical as to just how much good a senatorial investigation would prove toward relieving the distress of the miners. He writes that [although] the 'records are clear on the deplorable conditions in the bituminous coal fields in Pennsylvania and West Virginia,' his committee was 'unable to find any legislative way to relieve the conditions in the bituminous coal fields.'[9]

"Senator Borah is equally frank when he answers that he is 'not clear just what beneficial result would follow from such an investigation.' What both Senator Couzens and Senator Borah admit then, is that the United States government cannot—or more likely will not—interfere with owners of industry when they find it expedient to terrorize and kill workers.

"In the case of the Harlan miners it means that the United States government is either unwilling or unable to protect the worker in his struggle against such mammoth exploiters of labor as the Ford Motor Co., Insull interests, J. P. Morgan's U. S. Steel Corporation, the Mellon, and Rockefeller interests to whom these Kentucky coal companies are subsidiary.[10] That is why such an investigating committee as ours is necessary."

7. John Reed Clubs (named after the Harvard-educated radical writer) were established by the Communist Party for the encouragement and political education of left-leaning writers and intellectuals.

8. Borah (1865–1940), a Republican from Idaho, was yet another independent-minded prominent figure.

9. A Senate committee held hearings on Harlan in 1932 but decided not to conduct an investigation on conditions there; in 1937 Senator Robert La Follette finally did lead such a Senate investigation.

10. The Ford Motor Company, the United States Steel Company, and companies controlled by Samuel Insull (1859–1938), a electric power magnate, owned mines in the area; the Mellon and Rockefeller financial empires did not directly own mines but had an interest in several.

Dreiser Demands Witnesses' Safety
Opens Hearings at Harlan and Promises New Evidence if Immunity Is Assured Will Hear Anyone's Story and All Meetings Will Be Open, Says Dreiser of Probe In Harlan to Find Out about Reports That Constitutional Rights Are Denied to Miners; Invites Everybody to Speak Out

By Edward B. Smith

*

Knoxville News-Sentinel, 6 November 1931, pp. 1, 12.

Harlan, Ky.—A dozen or more men identified as discharged miners and victims of official terrorism in the mine labor war here waited to testify as the Theodore Dreiser committee arrived here and went into action.

Headquarters for the committee, representing the National Committee for the Defense of Political Prisoners, was established in the Lewallen Hotel and open hearings were started in a room on the second floor. Dreiser, chairman of the committee and known best as author of "An American Tragedy," acted as examiner while a court stenographer took down questions and answers.

Promises New Evidence

Hitherto unpublished evidence of gunman rule and suppression of constitutional rights were promised by Dreiser if Governor Sampson[1] and local civil authorities will guarantee protection of witnesses. Telegrams requesting this protection were sent last night from Pineville, but were still unanswered early today.

The first witness to testify here was Henry Thornton, negro who said he

---

1. As did most civil authorities, Flem Sampson (1875–1967) resented the presence of "outside radicals" in Kentucky.

was dismissed by the Harlan Gas & Coke Co. for alleged attendance at union meetings.[2] The meetings were held by the United Mine Workers, Thornton said, but he did not actually attend them. Subsequently, he said, he was arrested by Harlan police on a charge of drunkenness, which he denied, beat over the head and jailed for 14 days. Since liberation, he said he has been active in National Miners Union, a radical organization.

Included in the small group of onlookers at the hearing are three National Guard officers, acting as "observers" for Governor Sampson. They are Major George Chescheir and Capt. Frank McAuliffe of Louisville, and Major John Polin of Springfield. The three were sent here after Governor Sampson canceled previous orders for a detachment of state troops to Harlan.

To Invite Operators

Dreiser said several mine operators and civil authorities will be invited to appear before the committee here today.

"If they decline to appear at the public hearing in the hotel, members of the committee will probably call on them at their offices," Dreiser said. "We are going to make every effort to get a complete picture of the situation."

Greeted at Pineville

A small group of public officials and representatives of labor organizations met the committee on its arrival at Pineville yesterday. At the same time, however, agents of the General Defense Council, legal arm of the I. W. W. which is conducting the regular defense for miners accused of murder in riots of last spring,[3] characterized Dreiser's visit as "an important gesture" since the group had no power to summon witnesses.

A public meeting will be held Saturday at 5 P.M., at a church at Straight Creek and Sunday at 2 P.M., in a school building at Wallins Creek, both avowedly for the purpose of testing for freedom of speech in connection with the writers' charge that miners are being denied constitutional rights.

---

2. The testimony of witnesses appearing before the committee and a good deal of other material deriving from the committee's Harlan experience appear in *Harlan Miners Speak* (New York: Harcourt, Brace, 1932).

3. During April and May 1931 armed clashes between miners and deputies had occurred near Evarts, in Bell County, and resulted in several deaths. The General Defense Council of the I.W.W. (Industrial Workers of the World) was established to defend workers imprisoned while seeking to establish a union.

To Pass Facts On

"Facts we uncover here in open hearings we will pass on to the public thru the press," said Dreiser in an interview after his arrival in Pineville yesterday. "Then the public may be the judge. In New York we hear and read reports of official terrorism and the denial of constitutional rights to miners. We are here to find out what truth there is in such reports, and, if possible, the reasons back of armed clashes between the workers and mine operators.

"We will hear anyone's story. There will be no secret sessions, and we will do our best to get a view of the picture from every perspective. Just how true and complete the picture will be is entirely up to all interests involved. We invite them to speak out."

Denies Affiliation

Dreiser denied reports that his committee is affiliated with either organized labor or communist organizations.[4]

"It (National Committee for the Defense of Political Prisoners) was organized a year ago for other purposes," Dreiser said. "But it so happens that our objectives are broad enough to include the situation here. It is made up of men and women who are free thinkers and are sincerely interested in social conditions. That most of us happen to be authors may be due to the fact that in our researches we have come into contact with social conditions which have aroused a deep interest.

"If America is becoming capitalistic and is satisfied with that condition, now is the time to find it out."

Dreiser said a stenographic report of testimony would "undoubtedly be turned over" to Senators Borah and Norris and that "if there is justification we will ask for a Senate inquiry."[5]

Hold Meetings Any Time

"We will hold any meeting at any time anyone has anything to say," said the author.

---

4. Dreiser was technically correct, since neither the NCDPP nor International Labor Defense was "affiliated" with the Communist Party. Both groups had been established, however, with party support and were dominated by party members. The greatest weakness of the National Miners Union and its supporters in their efforts to organize the Harlan mines was the deep suspicion toward communism by not only the mine operators and their allies but by the miners themselves.

5. See p. 248, n. 9.

Dreiser; John Dos Passos, author of "Manhattan Transfer" and "The 42nd Parallel"; Charles Rumford Walker, author of "Steel"; and Mrs. Walker formed the vanguard of the committee, arriving by train from Cincinnati yesterday afternoon.[6] Others came in by car and train last night.

Pineville, immersed in politics after a city and state election, gave little attention to the approaching visit of the eminent writers. Mayor J. M. Brooks headed a small delegation of officials who met the group at the station.

Greeting by Viola Grace

But as the train pulled in, suddenly there appeared diminutive Viola Grace, National Miners Union agent at Wallins Creek.[7] Apparently she knew the writers personally for she greeted each with enthusiasm as the railway coach disgorged its passengers. She had taxis waiting, and hotel reservations made, and whisked the whole party away before the mayor and his reception committee could get into action.

Mrs. Grace made arrangements for two public mass meetings under auspices of the National Labor Union[8] and International Labor Defense. One will be at 5 P.M. Saturday at Glendon Baptist Church in Straight Creek, Bell County; and the other at 2 P.M. Sunday in the school gymnasium at Wallins Creek, also in Bell County.

Neal on Hand

Among those who conferred with Dreiser and his committee last night were Dr. John R. Neal of Knoxville, who said he was here to watch developments from a purely legal angle; Circuit Judge D. C. Jones of Harlan, who heard all the cases growing out of the Evarts and Harlan disorders;[9] and William Turnblazer of Jellico, president of United Mine Workers of America, District 19.

Altho it is generally believed that many of the authors here will gather local color and information for future literary efforts,[10] discussions of art and literature were "absolutely out," according to Dreiser and Dos Passos, spokesmen for the committee.

6. See p. 246, n. 1.

7. Both Viola Grace and her husband, Jim Grace, were organizing agents of the National Miners Union. Mrs. Grace arranged for the appearance of most of the miners offering testimony at the hearings.

8. No doubt an error for the National Miners Union.

9. See n. 3 to this interview.

10. Two such efforts are Dos Passos's "Camera Eye (51)," in *The Big Money* (1936), the third volume in his *U.S.A.* trilogy, and Samuel Ornitz's play *In New Kentucky*, which was never produced but which appeared in the *New Masses* in 1934.

Dreiser Speaks His Mind Here
Asserts That He Was Victim of Kentucky Frame-up
To Ask Officials' Removal
Reports 18,000 Miners in Straits, with 3,000 Blacklisted

*

New York Sun, 12 November 1931, p. 9

Although Dreiser dismissed as petty persecution the adultery charge brought against him by the Kentucky authorities, he was disturbed that it (and his burlesque refutation of the possibility of his guilt) received far more attention in the national press than did the findings of the investigating committee. Marie Pergain has never been identified; the name was probably adopted for the occasion.

Theodore Dreiser, the author, and other members of the committee which has been investigating conditions in the Kentucky coal mines, returned here today and said that they found them pitiful.

Mr. Dreiser declared that the indictment charging him with adultery which a Grand Jury returned in Pineville was necessarily without foundation.

"I would like to go on record now in such a manner as to settle all such charges in the future as well as this one," he said. "I want this matter of my sex life settled from now until I die. I am thoroughly impotent. I am too old."

Mr. Dreiser received reporters at the Hotel Ansonia,[1] where he, John Dos Passos and other committeemen arrived at 5 A.M. He said the charge against him was obviously a frame-up to becloud the real issue, and asserted that before he left Kentucky two lawyers warned him that he would be the victim of a frame-up. He said that the charge doesn't worry him. He is liable

1. In September 1931 Dreiser had moved from his Fifty-seventh Street apartment to a small suite at the Hotel Ansonia, at Broadway and Seventy-third Street. This was to be his New York base until February 1935.

to a fine of from $20 to $50 if convicted. He doesn't know whether it is an extraditable offense.

Unaware of Toothpick Test

About the "toothpick trap" he said he knew nothing. It was reported that toothpicks were set against the floor of a room to show whether or not he left there during the night. "There are strange people down there," he said, "and they divine things in a strange manner. I suppose if the toothpicks are up I'm guilty; down, I'm not guilty.[2] At that, that's as fair as the means they are using against the miners."

The committee's report, he said, will be ready in five or six days, and will be sent to the Kentucky Legislature and Bar Association, and to others, including Senator Norris,[3] who said that if the report warranted, he would seek a Congressional investigation. The report will ask for the removal of Judge D. C. Jones, Commonwealth Attorney W. A. Brock and Sheriff John H. Blair, all of whom have jurisdiction in the mine territory.[4]

These officials, said Mr. Dreiser, seem to have three principal aims in life—to prevent the miners from joining unions, to keep them from reading the Daily Worker,[5] and to prevent meetings at which men may speak their minds.

He said that there are 18,000 miners in the territory, the average wage being $30 a month, from which there are medical and burial deductions totaling $2.50, after which the remainder is paid in scrip, good only at company stores, where, Mr. Dreiser said, prices are about 50 per cent too high.

Fearful of Bloodshed

He predicted bloodshed if there is not a change in conditions, and said that 3,000 miners on the blacklist are in particularly desperate straits, as they cannot obtain work, haven't money to get away and are unable to obtain the necessaries of life.

2. Observers at Dreiser's hotel, noting that Miss Pergain entered his hotel room late in the evening, placed upright toothpicks against its outside door. When in the morning the toothpicks were found to be still in place, it was assumed that an illegal sexual act had taken place.

3. See p. 248, n. 9.

4. The mine workers held that these three public officials functioned as the civil power of the mine operators: Blair deputized thugs hired by the operators; Brock indicted for criminal syndicalism any miner named by the deputies as actively supporting unionization; and Jones ensured that they would then be jailed awaiting trial. In fact, this was a process of intimidation, since few men were tried.

5. Published in New York, this was the national organ of the Communist Party.

He said that miners have been threatened with suspension of Red Cross assistance if they join unions and ex-soldiers have been told that to do so would mean losing their bonuses.

Possession of a copy of the Daily Worker, he said, may mean that a man will be held in jail without a hearing for more than a month, then released without trial, warned not to read it again, not to join a union and to get out of town.

The trouble, he said, arises from the desire of the owners to make the mines pay even during the depression; as they can't do this and pay wages they are resorting, according to Mr. Dreiser, to terrorism and no wages.

Mr. Dreiser was rather hot about the way he has been treated by the Kentucky newspapers and the news associations, which he said have deleted information.

The name of the young Communist named in the indictment with him, Mr. Dreiser said, is Marie Bergain—not Pergain.[6]

"Of course," he remarked, "I'm a most immoral man because my public opinions are exactly those which are most American men's private opinions on the question of sex."

6. It is not clear whether Dreiser is correcting previous reports of the name of the woman who accompanied him to Harlan or is rather seeking to confuse anyone attempting to identify her.

Dreiser Case May Be Fight to Finish as John W. Davis Takes Writer's Defense
Dreiser Ready to See Harlan Battle Thru, to Fight Extradition for Principle but May Stand Trial Later

By Dexter H. Teed

*

Knoxville News-Sentinel, 23 November 1931, p. 2.

During and shortly after World War I many states adopted "criminal syndicalism" laws, which made it a crime to advocate violence for the achievement of political or economic change. In the 1920s and 1930s the laws were used primarily in the West and South to combat unionization efforts. This NEA Syndicate interview also appeared in the *Kentucky Post* of 22 November 1931.

NEW YORK—The indictment of Theodore Dreiser, one of America's foremost novelists, and other members of the committee that investigated conditions in the Kentucky coal fields, on a charge of criminal syndicalism has developed into a critical situation that may result in a show-down on such laws in particular and free speech in general.

The case assumed a national and even an international aspect when John W. Davis, Democratic candidate for president in 1924 and former president of the American Bar Association, agreed to act as counsel for the accused men in the fight to prevent them from being extradited.[1]

When formal request is made by Bell County authorities for extradition of Dreiser and the others, the decision will be up to Governor Roosevelt, himself a potential presidential candidate.[2]

1. Davis (1873–1955), a West Virginian, had been the Democratic nominee for president in 1924. Although at this point a Wall Street lawyer, he was still noted for his espousal of liberal causes.

2. Franklin Delano Roosevelt (1882–1945), at this time governor of New York, was indeed preparing to run for the presidency. The Kentucky authorities did not petition for extradition, and the charges were eventually dropped.

No one can foretell what Roosevelt will do in this unquestionably ticklish situation. Three years ago he refused extradition of Fred G. Biedenkapp and Paul Crouch to Massachusetts.[3] These men were wanted in Massachusetts on somewhat similar charges to those now facing Dreiser.

Governor Roosevelt refused on the ground that the accused had not been molested while in Massachusetts, and had been sought only after they had left the state; therefore they were not fugitives from justice in the Federal sense. Whether the circumstances of the Dreiser case, externally similar, are really so, will be up to Roosevelt.

Dreiser is so incensed over what he terms being "framed" in the syndicalism and misconduct cases that he is determined to battle thru to the bitter end, regardless of personal comfort or safety.

Considers Cell An Honor

"I am not afraid to got to a penitentiary for my ideals," is his fiery challenge. "If I could do away with the abuses which I see I would consider it an honor to sit in a cell."

The indictments charge that Dreiser and his associates unlawfully banded together "to commit criminal syndicalism and to promulgate a reign of terror" in the coal fields; and that, further, the Dreiser group had suggested disorder and resistance to the government of the United States and of Kentucky.

Those indicted besides Dreiser are nine members of the investigating party, including John Dos Passos, author; George Maurer, representative of the International Labor Defense; Charles Rumford Walker, Adelaide Walker, Samuel Ornitz, Celia Kuhn, M. P. Levy, Marie Pergain and A. Gannes.[4]

Dreiser hotly avers that the charges are groundless, and that both the syndicalism indictments and the charge of violation of the Kentucky morality laws are a smoke screen to hide possible exposure of intolerable conditions in the coal fields.

"Never Made a Speech"

Of the charge that he tried to inflame the miners by addressing them, he says this:

"I never made a speech in my life."

3. The labor leaders Biedenkapp and Crouch had been indicted for conspiracy in Massachusetts while participating in a strike at a New Bedford textile factory. On 18 February 1929 Roosevelt refused an application for extradition by the Massachusetts authorities.

4. See p. 246, n. 1. Celia Kuhn was the secretary who accompanied the group. "A. Gannes" is correctly "Harry Gannes."

Just that, and in New York it is recalled that he would never make a speech at any of the literary events which he attended.

Even if he is successful in fighting extradition he may go back and face trial. Now, he is primarily interested in winning the extradition fight because he wants to discredit the Harlan County officials.

"Why didn't they arrest me when I was there?" he demands. "If the crimes they accuse me of were committed, why didn't they arrest me then, as has happened in other cases?"

Explains Charity Donation

His answer to these questions is that they merely sought to discredit the committee investigation and prevent the true facts of horrible distress among the miners from being published.

He claims, further, that unfair news dispatches were sent out of the Kentucky area when he was there. One which especially roused his ire was about his income of $35,000 a year, none of which was given to charity, the dispatch said.[5]

"Every year 20 per cent of my income is given to help other people and organizations, but I do not and will not give to organized charities," he says. "Among those I support or help are seven relatives—but I believe large-scale charity is properly a function of government."

If the extradition fight is won he will have time to complete and publish his report on conditions in the Harlan County area and call a mass meeting in New York to discuss what may be done to help the unfortunates, who he says are near death from hunger and living on nothing or starvation wages.[6]

"The time has come for equity,"[7] he asserts with a flaming spirit that belies his almost shy nature. "This country has flirted with democracy, and now we must see that the poor people have a chance."

And what will happen if he goes back to be tried? He isn't worrying about that. He isn't afraid of jail or violence, for, as he explains it, if reasons for going back outweigh those for remaining here and fighting while at liberty, he doesn't care about personal danger.

---

5. Harlan Evans, the editor of the *Pineville Sun*, had asked Dreiser his income for the previous year; when told it was $35,000, he had then asked how much the writer gave to charity, and Dreiser had replied, "Nothing." The exchange, like the toothpick incident to come, was widely reported.

6. Dreiser's "report," *Harlan Miners Speak*, appeared in late December 1931. Although the "mass meeting," which occurred on 6 December, drew three thousand, Dreiser did not attend.

7. During the 1930s Dreiser frequently used the term *equity* to represent his social beliefs.

"Let this be clearly understood," he says. "The committee did not run away. None of us is a fugitive from justice. The officials made no attempt to hold us there and Governor Sampson even gave us an escort."

If he does eventually return to fight the case will John W. Davis defend him in court as he plans to do in the extradition hearing? That hasn't been decided yet. It won't be decided until the extradition matter is settled.

Ready for Show-down

But Dreiser, vigorous despite his 60 years, is making plans now for anything that may happen. The International Labor Defense, under whose sponsorship he went to Kentucky, is ready to take any necessary action.

That is the situation. With the distinguished Davis in the case, every lawyer, legislator, and voter, will watch to see what happens. Europe will look towards America.

"America must be awakened," is Dreiser's final challenge. "As long as conditions like those in Harlan County exist, we must meet them with fairness and justice. I'm going to see this thru to the bitter end."

Dreiser Holds Mooney Bomb Sympathy Act
Noted Novelist Expresses Contempt
for Critics in Visit Here

By Zilfa Estcourt

*

San Francisco Chronicle, 6 November 1932, p. 4.

Theodore Dreiser came to town yesterday morning to champion Tom Mooney and express contempt for a great many other people.[1]

He called me a "damn fool." I felt quite honored. It put me in such good company. He slapped Sinclair Lewis for disagreeing with him a few months ago.[2] Newspaper reporters as a class he characterized as "intellectual racketeers." He used to be one.

Compassion for Oppressed

"Tom Mooney did what he did, if he did it (I do not know whether he did it or not), to show his sympathy, his compassion for the helpless oppressed," orated the venerable author to a group of newspaper representatives and others in his best platform manner. The welcoming reception was over and the author was relaxing as he leaned against the highboy in his room at the exclusive and expensive Hotel Mark Hopkins. In his hand he held a glass of Scotch whisky, which every now and then he replenished without inviting his companions to join him.

"It was sympathy that prompted Mooney," he began again after tossing off his drink.

"Oh," said I. "So that's the reason he left a bomb to kill fifteen or twenty of them? What a curious way to express sympathy."

1. Dreiser was in San Francisco to speak at a rally for the imprisoned Mooney on 6 November (for Mooney, see p. 212, n. 8). He also spoke personally both to the local district attorney and to the judge hearing Mooney's appeal.

2. For Dreiser and Lewis, including the slapping incident, see p. 230, n. 2. The incident occurred in March 1931, not "a few months ago."

Expresses Wrath

The leonine head went up. The stern face registered amazement. The eyes flashed lightnings of wrath.

"That," he said in thunderous tones, "is the remark of a damn fool."

Dreiser was in vituperative and vitriolic mood. The forthcoming presidential election "does not amount to a damn, either way it comes out," he declared.[3]

"The majority have not had to suffer or to think until recently. A new kind of people are now feeling the knife. As they feel the prick they begin to move. More people are thinking economically now than ever before. The ones who have had the worst deal are not the labor union men. They are the hardworking, willing, honest men ready to give fourteen hours' labor a day. They are the ones who get the rotten deal."

Talks of Kentucky

Reference to his experiences in Harlan, Ky., where he and his aids were arrested for criminal syndicalism during their investigation of the conditions in the coal fields,[4] brought bitter laughter from the "bad boy" novelist. He was indicted while there on a morals charge involving a blonde girl secretary.

"Any repercussions from that experience?" he was asked.

"What repercussion would there be?" he countered. "If I went back there they would arrest me for criminal syndicalism and send me to jail for twenty-five years. Or perhaps fifty years, or eighty, if I lived long enough. The Sheriff down there is a ———. The miners down there are underpaid and abused. Scores of them have been arrested merely to intimidate them.

Fought Oppression

"It was to fight against the same kind of oppression that Tom Mooney took action here. It was rebellion, war, as much as was the Civil war. We honor the Confederate Generals, but we have let Tom Mooney rot in jail.

"We feed the starving in China and we send hundreds of thousands of dollars for missionary work in India while Americans starve and our own wage slaves sweat."

---

3. Franklin Delano Roosevelt (Democrat) and Herbert Hoover (Republican) were the major party candidates. Dreiser supported William Z. Foster, the Communist Party candidate.

4. Although Dreiser and his companions were threatened with prosecution for criminal syndicalism for their actions at Harlan, no arrests were in fact made either at that time or afterward.

Dreiser at first banned literary talk, but disdainfully flung a few words of advice to young authors into the closing moments of the interview.

"No writer should start out looking at life with preconceived notions," he said. "He should find out first what he is dealing with. With the lone exception of Edgar Allan Poe, bless his memory, American writers deal with the surface health of man as he goes about his affairs in business, society and riding about in his automobile. We ignore the other side, the disarranged, abnormal, emotionally defeated and frustrated. Until the literary workers of America see life in its entirety and write of it as it is, the abnormal as well as the normal, we will never attain a really high literary plane in this country."

Dreiser Overlooks His Former Experiences with Hollywood, for Things Will Be Different in the Filming of "Jennie Gerhardt"
Back from the Coast, Novelist Says That He Has Gone Over Everything with Director— Appealed Again for the Release of Tom Mooney World Is Crazy, He Insists, and Is Producing a Race of Stoics

By George Britt

*

New York World-Telegram, 15 December 1932, p. 15.

After speaking at the San Francisco Tom Mooney rally, Dreiser went to Los Angeles, where he sold Paramount the film rights to *Jennie Gerhardt*. Since he had quarreled bitterly with Paramount early in 1931 and then sued the company in July 1931 over its adaptation of *An American Tragedy*, there was interest in this apparent change of heart. Although Dreiser had doubts about the film version of *Jennie Gerhardt* while it was in production, he was in the end pleased with it.

"The world," said Theodore Dreiser today, "is crazy—absolutely crazy."

He was not in one of his moods. He wasn't preaching, denouncing or criticizing. Back in New York, from Hollywood, he was, in fact, feeling very good. For he had just sold "Jennie Gerhardt" to the movies, and he was getting along well on his new novel, "The Stoic," which will fall into line after "The Financier" and "The Titan," completing that trilogy of the life of Frank Cowperwood which he began twenty years ago.

"The world has been just as crazy for 100 years past, or 150 years, as it was a thousand years ago under the compulsion of the medieval church. Is there chance now for it to recover? I hope not. By that I mean I hope it never gets back to the insanity it was experiencing up to 1929.

"And it will not. The handwriting is plain on the wall, in letters just as big as at Belshazzar's feast."[1]

Subscription Price—One Ham

The new, saner world which he foresees will permit a simpler life, including a lot of barter. The bankers have been arrogating to themselves the dignity of popes, as he observes them, and the railroads have been kidding the government when they said they were essential.

"If a man comes in and gives us a ham as his subscription price to the American Spectator,"[2] said the novelist, "it's just as good as his check, and better. For we meet together on the ground in a friendly human way, and I remember him as the man who makes good hams, and he has a personal contact with me."

He isn't dogmatic about communism, Dreiser explained. He doesn't think the system that works in Russia is likely to fit here. He wouldn't cut out the lives of the Eskimos and the natives of Tahiti by the same pattern.

"98–2 Justice"

"They wouldn't take me in the Communist party, you know," he said.[3] "I don't take my communism orthodox, any more than I take anything else. But a system can be worked out here, perhaps, not to give justice 50–50 to everybody, but to break up this old ratio of 98–2—and our American folks will like it."

Dreiser was out in California last month to urge again the release of Tom Mooney from San Quentin Prison, and he went to Los Angeles to take some verbal cracks at the notorious Captain William F. Hynes, head of the police "red squad."[4] He may go back next spring to make a real fight on Hynes.

1. Daniel 5–6 says that during a feast Belshazzar, king of Babylon, saw handwriting on the wall prophesying the loss of his kingdom; Babylon was conquered that night.

2. During the summer of 1932 Dreiser had agreed to become a principal editor of a new literary journal, the *American Spectator;* its first issue appeared in November 1932.

3. Early in 1932 Dreiser had spoken with Earl Browder, head of the Communist Party in America, about joining the party. Browder believed that Dreiser was too unreliable and refused the request.

4. During the 1930s several major American cities formed special police units to break up, often violently, demonstrations and meetings by far-left groups. The Los Angeles unit, known informally as the "Red Squad," was headed by Hynes (1896–1952); on his arrival in Los Angeles soon after addressing the Mooney rally in San Francisco, Dreiser was quoted as saying that he would defy Hynes and speak publicly if he wished to.

But while he was there he sold "Jennie Gerhardt" to be produced by B. P. Schulberg as a film for Paramount release.[5]

But how about all his trouble over the movie of "An American Tragedy" and the harsh things he said about Hollywood then?

"But this is going to be different," said the optimist. "My attitude is unchanged. I am not selling them 'Jennie Gerhardt' with the idea that it will be their property to do with as they please. I have gone over it with the director, and I am convinced it will be done as it should."

The picture will have Sylvia Sidney as the leading woman, Marion Gering as director.[6] Dreiser likes them both very much.

He has fifty-five chapters written of "The Stoic." It will take fifty more to complete. Then he'll cut it down a great deal. He's pleased with it, but he wouldn't hazard a guess as to its quality.

All Are Stoics

"I think maybe 'Twelve Men' or 'Chains,' you know, just short stories, are as good as anything I ever wrote," he said.

He didn't intend to complete his trilogy of American business immediately after "The Titan." He's been thinking about it, observing events. The new novel will round out a historical period such as will never come again. The title, of course, was inevitable.

"Everybody becomes a stoic," he said, "if he lives long enough."

5. Schulberg (1892–1957) was head of West Coast productions for Paramount during this period.

6. Sidney (1910–95) had recently become a star; she often played downtrodden working-class women, as in her role as Roberta Alden in Paramount's 1931 adaptation of *An American Tragedy*. The Russian-born Gering (1901–77) frequently directed Sidney for Paramount during the 1930s.

Dreiser Says NRA Is Training Public
Promises on 62nd Birthday to
Spend 40 Hours a Week Defending It
Scores Novel Patterns
Holds Chances of a Significant Book
Are Hindered by Too Much Second-Rate Work

*

New York Times, 28 August 1933, p. 19.

The National Recovery Act, proposed by President Roosevelt in May 1933 as an emergency economic measure and quickly passed by Congress, established a process by which the government could set up codes of employment, including wages and hours, for all industrial activity in America. The act was declared unconstitutional in 1935.

Firmly convinced that the NRA codes were "stolen direct from Russia," but also firmly convinced that it "was an excellent move," Theodore Dreiser pledged himself yesterday to "defend President Roosevelt forty hours a week at a minimum of 40 cents an hour." The occasion of the interview was Mr. Dreiser's sixty-second birthday, which fell yesterday, but Mr. Dreiser was supremely uninterested in that. He talked of literature, economics and motion pictures.

"The NRA is all right," he said, "but the great thing, accidental rather than intentional, is that the American public is actually being schooled in economics and government, in the significance of government.

"Before, government was just something that happened. Government jobs were just jobs, with much backslapping if you got one.

Noses Rubbed in Economics

"Now the nose of the public is being rubbed in economics. We are going down to the humblest factors. We are acknowledging, publicly and in ways plain to the feeblest intellects, that child labor is unnecessary, that forty hours a week are enough to work, that there should be such a thing as a minimum wage. These are amazing facts to have publicly admitted, to have the mass of people actually thinking about."

A further step he would like to see taken is the marking of maximum salaries or incomes, of maximum fortunes.

"Let's get the loafers out of the too comfortable places, do something about the heirs," said Mr. Dreiser. "But we are a long way from that yet. There is no use discussing equity. We are not handing that out yet. But what is being done is marvelous."

Socially optimistic, he finds no exaltation in the present state of literature in America.

"There are all these thousands of little novels of love and trouble. A man marries and loses his job. He has trouble finding another.

"Patterns! There are so few books containing the temperamental elements that distinguish.

"Critics' Standards Down"

"The chance of a really significant book is hindered by all these books that are pouring out all the time. There is being created a second-rate reading man, so used to junk he doesn't know the good when he sees it. Critics see so much junk, so little really important matter, that their standards are down. It is lunatic to pay attention to critical applause when tenth-rate things are applauded so much. We are champion buyers of mediocre stuff."

He said that he thought a good "movie job" had been done with "Jennie Gerhardt," but that only a novel with a very thin story could be really put on the screen and that his estimate of the screen worth of "Jennie Gerhardt" was comparative.[1]

"They make them from patterns," he said. "Movie audiences are so trained to a low level of stuff that they are frozen out of the theatre by anything else."

Going back to books, he said that a good many modern novels include "five cents worth of realism, which is written as though it was $17,000.50 worth.

"But when you come to the end," he concluded, "it is only worth five cents."

1. For the film version *Jennie Gerhardt*, see pp. 263.

Interview by Allan Chase
for Central Press, December 1933

An unpublished interview, extant in typescript in the Theodore Dreiser Papers of the University of Pennsylvania Library and headed "Interview by Allan Chase for Central Press. Without editorial cuts, or
revisions." In a 28 December 1933 letter to Dreiser (also in the Dreiser Papers), Chase, a reporter for the Central Press newspaper syndicate, explained that the syndicate had decided not to run the interview
because his editors had found several portions "unacceptable." These
objectionable sections may have included Dreiser's remarks on the
Catholic Church and on the possibility of revolution in America. The
interview concludes with Dreiser's acknowledgment—one he frequently made during this period of his career—that he is a communist,
though not of the Russian variety.

"Forecast what is in store for us in 1934? Lord! No one man can. . . ."
Theodore Dreiser leaned against the wall of his apartment and fidgeted with
his pocket handkerchief. Tall, grey, and sixty, Dreiser groped for words in
the manner characteristic of the inarticulate Americans in many of his
novels. Or perhaps it was that, called upon to be an oracle, Dreiser groped
for ideas just as in his novels he has always groped for the truth. "It looks to
me as if 1934 will be a hard year. A very hard year, I might say."

Dreiser today stands over the field of contemporary writers like the
Empire State building set in the middle of a block of apartment buildings.
He is, perhaps, the one American writer who has succeeded in recording
the broad panorama of America—and is hailed as such in Tokio, and Moscow, and Paris, and London, as well as in his own country. Yet, despite his
deep understanding of Modern America and its background, Dreiser spoke
slowly, haltingly, almost reluctantly when he touched on the prospect for
the coming year.

"Roosevelt has aggravated the problem for thinking people," Dreiser said
in response to a question about the value of the NRA program.[1] "The codes

---

1. For Dreiser and the NRA, see pp. 266–67.

haven't solved things. Far from it. I don't think any system that leaves untouched the swollen fortunes of the big millionaires is going to bring any benefits to the rank and file American. The big money crowd is just about where it was before Roosevelt was elected. Well, we have a new banking law, it's true, but it doesn't mean too much. The NRA is leaving the American public in the same frame of mind as it was before—with the idea of individualism in the foreground.[2]

"Maybe the eight hour day and 40 cents an hour minimum wage has made over the American people," Dreiser continued, "but I don't believe it. Look how the Bell Telephone dictatorship is trying to shake off regulation on the grounds that it is not a competitive industry. What's to stop the power trust from saying the same thing? What's to stop the various railroads, or the few giant auto concerns from uniting and saying the same thing?

"Under the NRA we find the Catholic Church with eight billions in untaxable property. The American Express gets away without taxation. The telegraph taxes are passed on to the fellow who sends a telegram so that dividends may be protected."

Dreiser folded his handkerchief into a neat square. "Well," he said, "if all this spells a happy 1934, then Okeh. I can't see it though."

The author of "An American Tragedy" may have spoken slowly, but he minced no words. "I don't believe that the rank and file are going to sit by and tolerate peacefully the ownership of millions by people who never really earned them," he said. "Either this program," Dreiser said of the NRA, "will prohibit inheritances, limit fortunes, and otherwise introduce some forms of economic equity, or we'll have another terrific row. There is no way of telling how this row would turn out. It might lead to the most brutal money autocracy, and it might result in the people taking over the government for themselves."

Dreiser's touching the prospect of a money autocracy led the interviewer to mention Roger Babson's forecast of Fascism for the United States at the recent Annual National Business Conference. Dreiser exploded. "Babson," he retorted, "is a loud mouthed ass who is always predicting things that don't come true—and if we are going to have Fascism, then Babson doesn't know it. According to Babson, the depression was going to end in November, 1931."[3]

2. Dreiser uses the term *individualism* in this passage and elsewhere in his social writing of the 1930s to express his belief that the term has been warped in meaning from its original notion of a belief in individual freedom to a defense of an oppressive corporate freedom. See his "Individualism and the Jungle," *New Masses* 7 (Jan. 1932): 1–2.

3. Roger W. Babson (1875–1967) had already made a fortune as an investment advisor when he founded the Babson Institute (an early business college) in 1919. On 8 September 1933,

A moment later, in discussing the wide student activity encouraged by the American League Against War and Fascism, Dreiser declared, "fascism— and war, are very likely to be with us before the students can do a thing."[4]

In view of the feverish war preparations going on in Europe and the United States, did Dreiser think that the prospects of peace for 1934 were very good?

"Anybody that sits up with a wise look in his eyes and tries to answer that," Dreiser declared, "is just bluffing. Mussolini, Hitler and the French are absolutely satisfied that we're headed for war. Hell is about to break loose. There are all these little intrigues . . . all these alliances against Russia. Maybe because every country in Europe is armed to the teeth they may not fight. But the situation is like a dozen glasses perched in a tray on the palm of a waiter. If it wobbles, the whole business goes off.

"The recognition of Russia," he continued, "is likely to prolong peace by stopping Japan.[5] With a little support, I believe the Red Army can whip Japan. But no statesman has the war menace in hand. Roosevelt, and Litvinoff,[6] and all the rest, are in the position of holding a team of wild horses by a shoe string."

"What," the interviewer asked, "do you propose in place of the NRA?"

"It's not so easy to reach a state of real equity," Dreiser replied. "It may take brutal domination by an honest and determined set—but that's alright. In the Soviet Union there are plenty of people who want the old regime back, but they stand in the way of progress, and are treated ruthlessly.

"Now don't make any mistake," Dreiser added quickly. "I'm a communist. But I'm an intellect, too. To be opposed to a brutal capitalistic system, and then to get a working plan to replace it, are two different things. I don't believe we can take over the Russian scheme as it stands for America. Communism has got to be modified to fit American ways."

---

in a speech at the institute, he warned that the struggle between labor and capital in America might lead the middle classes to embrace fascism.

4. The league was founded in the fall of 1933 in response to a call for its formation by Dreiser, Sherwood Anderson, and Upton Sinclair. (There were similar groups in several European countries.) Although communists played an active role in its affairs, the league attracted a broader spectrum of political belief than most 1930s peace-oriented groups.

5. On assuming the presidency in early 1933, Franklin D. Roosevelt established formal diplomatic relations with the Soviet Union, signaling—some sixteen years after the Bolshevik Revolution—U.S. acceptance of the Soviet government's legitimacy and thus implying that an effort to overthrow it by an outside power would constitute an act of aggression.

6. For Litvinov, see p. 173, n. 2.

Dreiser, at 63, Believes His Best Book Is to Come
Famous U.S. Novelist Looks More Like 40 on His Birthday

By Henry Paynter

*

New York Post, 27 August 1934, p. 12.

Theodore Dreiser celebrated his sixty-third birthday today, quietly happy in the conviction that his greatest literary work lies ahead of him.

The novelist who is generally credited with having changed the whole course of American writing spent the day in his suite at the Hotel Ansonia.

His schedule for the day: a light breakfast, a little work, no lunch, a little drinking and loafing, and dinner with a few old friends in his rooms.

Dreiser looks more like a vigorous man of forty than his true age.

Tall and bulky, he moves with the grace that comes of perfect muscular co-ordination, especially noticeable in his big but gracefully expressive hands.

His white hair is brushed straight back from a pink, healthy unwrinkled face (except for heavy lines around the mouth) and his gray eyes are lively.

Physically he feels fine, he said, and by moderate eating, moderate drinking and careful use of his body intends to remain that way.

"Does he feel that as the years go on a writer has greater or less use of his talent?"

Dreiser wasn't at all in doubt.

Man's Power Increases

"I feel that, if anything, the intelligent man's powers increase. Observation is more acute and a deeper understanding grows slowly with time.

"Remember, I wrote the 'American Tragedy' when I was fifty-seven. Du Maurier's entire literary reputation rested on what he did between the ages of sixty-seven and seventy-two. Schopenhauer did his important work when he was well along, and so it goes.[1]

---

1. George du Maurier (1834–96), who spent most of his career as an artist and illustrator, did not publish his first novel until 1891 at the age of fifty-seven (not sixty-seven). He later

"Any man who reads Shakespeare carefully knows he was no youth. And no actor, either. Especially the sonnets. It was a man well along that wrote them.[2]

Life Changes at Forty

"I think a man goes through two phases, with important chemical changes, very profound changes, when he reaches forty.[3]

"When he is young, he is affectionate, emotional, temperamental; he acts upon impulse rather than upon reason. If he don't we wouldn't have any economic problems to worry about.

"When a man passes forty he no longer acts on impulse; he no longer feels those irresponsible promptings.

"Then he begins to act from the intellect. Everything is reasoned out and his behavior is rational.

He Understands Now

"I find that, as time goes on, I have a profound understanding of underlying things that I only guessed at before. I believe that my best work is ahead of me."

He was asked whether he found his interests, his fundamental point of view, changed much with time.

"No," he said. "I am interested in the same thing I have been interested in since I was a small boy—the American economic scene. I think it is the most absorbing thing in the world.

"When I was still a small boy I began wondering about things—why some people lived in big fine houses and others lived in hovels.

"I followed these questions up, step by step, as they occurred to me, as I grew older.

"I am still fascinated.

"The illusion of freedom and liberty in America, for example. I believe

---

wrote the best-selling novel *Trilby* (1894). Dreiser is mistaken about the philosopher Arthur Schopenhauer (1788–1860), most of whose major work appeared during his twenties. Schopenhauer did not become well known, however, until the last decade of his life.

2. While working as a reporter in Chicago in 1892, Dreiser met the journalist John Maxwell, who later wrote a book supporting the belief that Shakespeare's works were written by Robert Cecil, the earl of Salisbury. Dreiser became a strong supporter of Maxwell's theory and for many years attempted, unsuccessfully, to interest a publisher in the book.

3. Dreiser's account of Hurstwood at the opening of chapter 30 of *Sister Carrie* is an early expression of his belief (apparently derived from the amateur psychologist Elmer Gates) that important changes in character are linked to internal chemical changes occurring at forty.

it was merely due to the pioneer development of a rich new land. When things went bad, there was always somewhere else for people to go and try again.

"Actually, I believe, there is little difference between the present and other periods so far as most of the people are concerned.

Few Own All Wealth

"A few people, a few hundred, own all the real wealth in America. They own more now than they did before the depression. The small stockholders are wiped out—I lost $300,000 in a few days[4]—and the real assets remain in the hands of a few men."

"What would you do to correct the situation if you had the power?"

"It would be very simple," he said. "I would take all their holdings from them—the railroads, the electric power lines and plants, the factories, the real estate. . . .

Would Give Jobs

"Pay them for it if necessary, but remove them from any control—those things now are operated by able salaried technicians, anyway—and run them for the benefit of the whole people, giving employment to everybody. They could find something else to absorb their attention without doing such great harm to the nation."

"Do you think there is much likelihood of a revolt of the unemployed?"

"Practically none now," he said. "Unemployment's worst result is the destruction of character. A man who has been down and out and taking charity for years no longer has the spirit in him to revolt. He is cowed and docile."

"As the result of your long experience as an editor and as a writer, what would be, in a nutshell, your present advice to a young writer?"

"If he wants to make money, let him write for the movies. If he wants to write for the love of writing, let him find some other means of earning a living."

4. Reliable estimates (e.g., W. A. Swanberg in his *Dreiser* [see p. 88, headnote]) place Dreiser's 1929 stock-market losses closer to about a quarter of the sum he here cites.

Dreiser to Commit Suicide if Bored, He Insists at 63
Why Stick Around When Life Becomes Uninteresting? Novelist Asks as He Enlivens Interview with Digs at the Elder Morgan and Millionaires

By Earl Sparling

*

New York World-Telegram, 27 August 1934, pp. 1, 8.

"Come in," said Theodore Dreiser in his gruff, diffident way. "Sit down," he ordered.

"Yes, I'm 63 today," he admitted in a detached, what-of-it tone.

"Does life begin at 63?"

"I find life still interesting," answered the gray, glum novelist, the grim realist who shocked pre-war America with "Sister Carrie" and changed the national literature.

"When I get to the point where I don't find it interesting," he added, "I'll get out of it."

"That sounds—do you mean suicide?"

"Of course," he replied. "Why not, if I ever find life uninteresting? Why stick around?"

"F. Scott Fitzgerald once promised to commit suicide when he had reached 35."

"Who?" he rumbled.

"Fitzgerald."

"Humph," he said with no sparkle of recognition.[1] "I knew Chauncey M. Depew when he was in his 90's. He was more alive than anyone I knew."[2] He snapped his fingers a couple of times in invocation.

1. The only known contact between Dreiser and Fitzgerald occurred in early 1923, when Fitzgerald attended a large party at Dreiser's Greenwich Village apartment. Fitzgerald had at that time published two novels but was not as well known as he was to become after the appearance of The Great Gatsby in 1925.

2. Dreiser always admired Depew, the long-time head of the New York Central Railroad.

"Do you want to live to 90?"

"Not unless it's interesting," said Mr. Dreiser. "When it gets dull I'll quit," he repeated.

But today at 63, lounging comfortably in his Hotel Ansonia apartment, he did not seem in any imminent danger of melancholia. A tidy, massive chap, he was dressed carefully in gray—gray shirt, gray slacks, white belt, white shoes, a neat black bow of a tie. His ponderous pink face was in repose until he started frowning, which he did the moment the talk shifted to economics.

"We don't have any first class millionaires," he rumbled. "They don't have first class minds. All any of them has is a superiority complex. They are a bunch of Chinese generals. Take old Morgan senior. I interviewed the old bandit once. All he was ever interested in was selling this country out to England.[3] What his firm has done all came out in the recent Senate investigations.[4] But what does America do about it? Nothing. In Greece or Rome men like Morgan would have been exiled, if nothing worse happened to them."

He gave a growl that started down under the white belt and waved his short spare white hair as it emerged.

"I was at a party one night," he said. "One of Morgan's young partners had just got back from Russia. He started shooting off his mouth. He said Russia was nothing but mud and dirt. I told him I had been in Russia and thought it was the greatest and finest human experiment in all history. He said, 'You're a Communist.' I said, 'You're a fool banker and a brigand at that.' He squared off and said, 'I don't care for your language.' I said, 'I like yours less than that.'"

"Hostesses must have a bit of time with you?" ventured the birthday interviewer.

He had interviewed Depew in 1898 ("Life Stories of Successful Men—No. 11, Chauncey Mitchell Depew," *Success* 1 [Nov. 1898]: 3–4) and in 1903, when Dreiser was mentally exhausted and needed a recuperative job involving physical labor, Depew came to his aid. The meeting with Depew at ninety to which Dreiser refers no doubt occurred in connection with his second article on him in 1925 (see p. 109, n. 3).

3. Dreiser may have interviewed J. P. Morgan during his freelance reporting years of 1898–1900, when he interviewed many successful business figures, but if so, the interview was never published. Aside from his antagonism toward Morgan as a multimillionaire Anglophile, Dreiser also may have held him responsible for Harper's refusal to publish *The Titan* in 1912, even though the book had been printed. The Morgan interests, which had a large stake in Harper's, were concerned both about the negative portrait of an American financier and about the possible appearance of J. P. Morgan as a figure in the last volume of the trilogy.

4. During May and June 1933 the Senate Banking and Currency subcommittee held a widely reported series of hearings on the failure of J. P. Morgan and Company and many of its partners to pay U.S. income taxes.

Won't Stand For "Hooey"

"Oh, sometimes they ask me to be careful. They know I won't stand for any hooey. A few nights ago I was at a party and this attorney—well, I won't mention him in print. He is one of the biggest international lawyers in the county. I told him what I thought of him and his gang. I told him the chief international law work he had ever done was selling out his own country. Sure, I tell them, unless they keep their mouths shut."

"And do you get invited around much?"

"I get invited more than I can accept," he said. "Heywood Broun once wrote a whole column about what a friendless fellow I was, all alone and unliked.[5] He must have had a bad night and was short for copy. We started speaking again just a few months ago. Let's see, 1915, 1918, 1919. For eight years when I lived in the village I kept open house.[6] I used to be afraid the floor would cave in. They would tap on my window in the middle of the night and ask for a $10 loan. Friends! I had my fill of the literary set."

Her Four Days in Russia

Speaking of literary people reminded him of Mary Roberts Rinehart. He pulled out a newspaper clipping in which Mrs. Rinehart, returning from a European trip which included four days in Russia, stated that everywhere in Russia there was callousness and indifference to life.[7]

"She learned that in four days," he growled.

"I suppose she inspected all of the three and a half million people in Moscow and learned all about the rest of the country in four days."

"Where is a person's brain?" he asked, rhetorically, "Where is a person's decency?"

The interviewer changed the subject by asking what he had been reading lately.

He said:—"I read 'The Robber Barons,' a good book. I've forgotten who wrote it. I read two books by Stuart Chase and liked them. I've forgotten their titles. I read 'The Power Age,' by some one. I read 'I, Claudius' and a

5. Broun (1888–1939), an acknowledged socialist and one of the founders of the Newspaper Guild (the journalists' union), was a widely read columnist for various New York newspapers during the 1920s and 1930s. The specific column to which Dreiser refers is Broun's "It Seems to Me," *New York Telegram*, 1 July 1931, p. 25.

6. Dreiser lived in the Village from July 1914 to October 1919 and again from October 1922 to January 1925.

7. Rinehart (1876–1958) was a prolific writer of best-seller mystery stories. Dreiser's clipping was perhaps "Mrs. Rinehart Returns," *New York Times*, 25 August 1934, p. 1, since it includes Mrs. Rinehart's use of the terms "indifference to life" and "callousness."

book about Hadrian and a book about Ghengis Khan. I read 'The Insolence of Office,' by this fellow who investigated Tammany Hall—what's his name? An astounding book! I suppose it sold about 500 copies. You can't get Americans to read real books like that."

The books to which Mr. Dreiser evidently referred were:—"The Robber Barons," by Matthew Josephson; "The Economy of Abundance" and "The Promise of Power," by Stuart Chase; "The Power Age," by W. N. Polakov; "I, Claudius," by Robert Graves; "Ghengis Khan," by Harold Lamb; "Hadrian, the Seventh," by F. Corvo, and "The Insolence of Office," by William B. and John B. Northrop.[8]

8. The interviewer correctly identifies the works cited by Dreiser, except that "a book about Hadrian" may refer not to Baron Corvo's work but to *Magnificent Hadrian*, a study by Sulamith Ish-Kishor, which Dreiser had read in manuscript form in the spring of 1934 and for which he wrote an introduction on its publication in 1935.

Dreiser, at 63, Clings to Hope of Better World
Novelist at Work on Third Book
of Financial Trilogy, Thinks about War
Feels It's in the Offing
Says Russia Ought to Take
a Good Poke at Japan

*

New York Herald Tribune, 28 August 1934.

This interview is extant in the form of a clipping in the Theodore Dreiser Papers of the University of Pennsylvania. Although the clipping includes the page header "Herald Tribune, Tuesday, August 28, 1934," the article itself has not been found in preserved microfilm runs of the *Herald Tribune* for this date. Its absence is probably attributable to the appearance of the interview in an early edition of the *Herald Tribune* for 28 August 1934, whereas the "Late City Edition" was photographed for preservation purposes.

Theodore Dreiser was sixty-three years old yesterday, and still waiting for "the Parliament of Man, the Federation of the World."[1] The author of "Jennie Gerhardt" and "Sister Carrie" is not one of those to whom age brings a contracting and hardening of the human sympathies. His principal celebration of the anniversary was an outpouring of the ponderous, limitless, half-articulate sympathy with his fellow beings and their various plights which has led not a few to proclaim him one of America's great writers.

A hope for one small war also was expressed by Mr. Dreiser as an obiter dictum. Russia has permitted herself to be kicked around by Japan, in his opinion, and he would like to see the Soviets "get up enough courage to manhandle" their opponent a bit and teach them a lesson.

1. Alfred Tennyson (1809–92), "Locksley Hall" (1842), line 128; this portion of the poem portrays an ideal future world.

Birthday Present Falls Through

Except for his announcement of the present state of his opinions and hopes Mr. Dreiser worked as usual in his apartment at the Hotel Ansonia, Broadway and Seventy-third Street, where he maintains his city headquarters in a small room chiefly remarkable for its dark, heavily carved Victorian furniture. He was waiting not only for the Federation of the World, but also for the settlement of his legal difficulties with his publishers, Liveright & Co., with whom he has been trying to sever relations for two years. The settlement was to have been his chief birthday present but the decision of the arbitrators, headed by former Justice Robert McC. Marsh, was not handed down yesterday.[2]

Mr. Dreiser was working on a short story when a caller discovered him, his heavy shoulders hunched and his large, foreshortened head bent over his desk. He explained what he was doing. Yes, he said, he would soon publish another novel, to be called "The Stoic." It would complete the financial trilogy begun with "The Financier" and "The Titan." It would come out as soon as his publishing affairs could be settled.

"But don't let us talk about books and literature," he added. "Good God, there are thousands of things to talk about. Writers and their books, and a whole world in turmoil. You ask me what I think of it. Well, I would like to see the Russians get up the courage to manhandle Japan a bit. I don't want any more war, but they have let themselves be kicked around too much. Perhaps it would be better for them to fight and have done."

War and the Possibilities

He rose from the desk and moved to a stiff sofa along the wall, where he curled himself into an uncomfortable looking posture and plunged into a discussion of war and the possibility of it. War is not far off, he believes, and not merely a war between Japan and Russia but a world conflict. He talked of it sadly, clenching and unclenching his hand over a handkerchief with each sentence. It would be like casting the dice, he said. None could predict the outcome. But it could scarcely be avoided, since Europe was such a miserable tangle. He digressed for a while into the penalties of European travel, the bitterness of the atmosphere and the small inconveniences to the traveler.

2. After his monthly drawing account was canceled by Horace Liveright, Inc., in 1932, Dreiser sought to end his relationship with the firm by purchasing the unbound sheets, plates, and copyrights of his books that they held. The cost of this transaction was in arbitration for much of 1934; the case was finally settled in September 1934.

"Europeans must straighten themselves out, or they'll be fighting directly, before they know it," he said. "And then what'll happen to us?

"I don't see how we can keep out, for we can't keep out if we trade with the combatants, and if you don't let people trade with the combatants, there would be enough people just bleeding at the nose with passion to sell their goods to ruin things anyway. What will happen to us and the world in any case? Heaven knows, but something must. We must establish an equitable democracy. In Russia they are trying to. I am a convinced Communist, you know. In this country I think Roosevelt is trying to, but he can't do it until he forgets his mild liberal training. He is hoping that the owners of this country can be persuaded to give up some of their profits, to pay decent wages and work men shorter hours. They can't, and as he's dealing with them they'll catch him somehow or other."

Complete Transfer of Power

Again Mr. Dreiser digressed into a description of all the misery he had seen in America, of the miners shot before his own eyes by mine owners' deputies, of the horrors of the factory towns and the uglinesses of the dark corners of industrial capitalism. His hand opened and shut ever more rapidly over the handkerchief as he voiced his conviction that no wrongs could be righted without a compete transfer of power and ownership from the capitalists to the workingmen. His voice took on a bitter scorn as he denounced those who feared an upheaval because it would bring in a "less comfortable society," and he told a satiric story of parlor radicals and their conversion to conservatism by bad Russian hotels.

"We must have a leader," he said. "There must be a man who can handle the American mind as it is, who can make Americans understand that their mild, personal individualism is no match for the individualism of the United States Steel Company."[3]

He paused for a second and thought.

"And it must come for writers, too," he went on again. "You see every one is brought up with certain material around which his imaginings are expected to cling. It must be common material, general material, widely believed. If the writer himself can't believe in the world around him—that material—he is lost.

"I don't believe in literature written for propaganda purposes. If you see a tragic condition and describe it, it may be propaganda. It may not. Edith Wharton's 'House of Mirth,' a very fine book, is based on the tragedy of lost

3. For Dreiser's distinctive sense of the term *individualism*, see p. 269, n. 2.

social position.[4] There can be tragedy in anything, even the loss of the society of millionaires, but writers cannot dig it out, cannot write, if they cannot be sure of what they write of. They must have a secure world. And it isn't only writers who need a secure and equitable world."

He paused again, put down the handkerchief, and rose.

"I've been going on and on, I see," he said. "But I can't help it, for these things are the only things that interest me any more, and I can't get them out of my head."

4. *The House of Mirth* (1905), by Edith Wharton (1863–1937), deals with the tragic failure of a young New York society woman to overcome the habits of mind and taste that her early social environment had imposed on her.

A Day with Theodore Dreiser
At Home with America's Literary Mastodon

By Bruce Crawford

*

Real America 6 (Nov. 1935): 49, 68–69.

Crawford, the editor of the radical newspaper *Crawford's Weekly* (Norton, Virginia) from 1919 to 1935, had played an active role in Dreiser's November 1931 investigation of the conditions of the Harlan miners (see p. 245). They continued to correspond and occasionally meet throughout the early 1930s. Crawford reprinted this interview, under the title "Ere the Sun Sets," in the *Sunset News* (Bluefield, West Virginia), 18 April 1938, pp. 1, 10.

On the left a sign, a large blue arrow, pointed down a side road that turned from the woodland highway into a clearing.

"Turn at that arrow." It was Theodore Dreiser directing. He had been talking about artists, European nobles, bankers, people of wealth from everywhere, who "have summer homes in these woods." We were in the Mt. Kisco section, forty miles up the Hudson River from New York.

I was driving his maroon roadster. Before leaving his hotel he had said, "You take the wheel." (Once, when at the wheel himself, he had run through a stone wall and landed in a fastidious lady's flower garden!)[1]

We had become acquainted on Kentucky's "Harlan front," where I, a Virginia country editor, had been shot in the leg for writing about coal barons and he had been insulted and framed for conducting an unwelcome investigation. And here we were now, turning in at the summer home of the author of "An American Tragedy."

Down on a broomsedged slope was his country house, an oddly rustic structure, the first story of stone, the second of boards, with a steep slab roof. Planks in the eaves were each painted a different color, suggesting a tropi-

---

1. Crawford may be referring to an incident in July 1932, when Dreiser did considerable damage to a garden in Somerville, N.J., while driving.

cal bird's wing, blue predominating. An outside chimney of rough field stones, picked up on the place, was Dreiserian both in style and, I later learned, in history. Landscaping was in progress, with fresh dirt pulverized in flower beds and warmed by the sun of this last day in April. Leaves were putting out and insects were astir. A door opened and quietly therefrom came a lady with a summery smile, auburn hair, and bluish eyes—again his favorite color. "This is Helen," he said.

Mrs. Dreiser made you think instantly of fascinating screen personalities. (She was in Hollywood, in fact, when he found her.)[2] She showed him the landscaping she had been having done. "And today," she announced with a soft, musical laugh, "we're to have a fish dinner and everything to go with it." She then went into the house to give the Negro cook his instructions, while Dreiser and I stood around in the sunny yard talking about his house.

"That chimney I had difficulty getting built the way I wanted it," he said. "You will notice some of the stones near the ground are smooth and laid with regularity. Well, the masons were too conventional. They couldn't get the idea that I wanted the stones picked up and used just as they were, you understand, with no hewing and no placing with smooth surfaces out. I would go to town and return to find they had tried to be too exact—as right there, you see. Finally, after much fuss on my part, they got the idea, as you can see from there on up."

The chimney suggested Dreiser himself, the smooth, regular places representing early attempts to conventionalize his life. And it was suggestive of his writing. "The masons," I observed, "were like those writers turned out by colleges to write just so."

"Exactly," he agreed. "Standardized writing. Why, that's the trouble with most writing. It doesn't express individuality. It's as if one ghost wrote all of it. What's more, too many editors have presumed to refine individual writing, and the result is not always recognizable as any particular man's work. A college graduate once was hired to correct a job of mine. Well, it was just all correctness, don't you know, with nothing of myself left in it. The publisher saw the mistake and abandoned the idea."[3]

So that chimney is like Dreiser's prose, his books, his body, his personality—individualistic, rough, strong, plentiful, of the earth, without the exactitude of orthodoxy.

Joined to his house by a short bridge is the "annex," a separate home for guests. On top of it is a square tower, or lookout, with a railing. We climbed

2. Dreiser met Helen in New York in September 1919; soon afterward they moved to Los Angeles so that Helen could pursue a film career.
3. This incident has not been identified.

up there by means of a ladder built against the wall and sat in the sun. He talked as he looked at the distant hills beyond Croton Lake and, with what seemed a hostile gray eye, to faraway things in his imagination or memory. He was a king of beasts, safe in his retreat, yet challenged by a world that too often ruffled him. His mouth hung open in a sort of snarl, until he flashed his teeth in a husky chuckle. The rectitudinarians of Kentucky amused him.

Wasps from the slab roof whizzed over to us. He cast a quick eye at one, but watched it tolerantly as it flew back to the roof. He is a man who must know intentions at once.

Intimate details in the lives of insects, little animals and snakes—their struggles, wars and tragedies—stirred his imagination as he related personal observations that were reminiscent of Fabre and W. H. Hudson and John Burroughs, whom he had known.[4] I remember he had said, "There's neither good nor bad, but only the triumph of the strong over the weak." Lately, of course, his views had changed somewhat. There *is* good and bad. There are the inventors and artists who create things, and "flies and locusts"[5] who prevent society from benefiting as it should by the works of its creators.

Down below the house a proletarian hound, scenting a rabbit, was wiggling among the broomsedge, his tail indicating he was hot on the trail. Suddenly he lifted his head and, with a leap high above the grass, yelped an ecstatic note.

"Good!" hurrahed Dreiser, "he jumped it."

At that instant his aristocratic Russian wolfhound, which had been watching comfortably from a sunny porch, barked audibly and went to look into things.

"Now, there you are," Dreiser commented, with a laugh that was part snarl. "Just like a certain parasitic class—letting the common dog do all the work, make the discovery, produce the goods, and then jumping in to take the benefits."

He motioned to a pool under tall willows and hickories below the house. "How about a plunge before we eat?" he suggested. The day was warm, but too early in the year for a Southerner to go into water outdoors. Dreiser himself was going in, however.

"Helen," he called, "throw me a towel."

Bringing a towel out, Mrs. Dreiser asked if he wanted a bathing suit too.

4. Jean Henri Fabre (1823–1915) was a French entomologist and author noted for his studies of insect behavior; W. H. Hudson (1837–1921) was an American-born British naturalist and novelist; and John Burroughs (1837–1921) was an American naturalist and early conservationist. Dreiser interviewed Burroughs in 1898: "Fame Found in Quiet Nooks," *Success* 1 (Sept. 1898): 5–6.

5. The conventional term for a plague on a society, drawn from Psalms 105:31, 35. Crawford may also be alluding to Dreiser's own use of the phrase as the title of an anticapitalistic article, "Flies and Locusts," *New York Daily Mirror*, 1 August 1933, pp. 19, 31.

"Naw," was his disdainful reply as he took the towel. The three of us went down to the pool. Mrs. Dreiser and I sat on a rustic seat beside the pond, chatting rather furiously—I was, at least—to ignore his stripping for the plunge. Yes, she had been in Hollywood, she said, and to Charleston, among other places in the South, and. . . .

"Woof! It's plenty cold," Dreiser shuddered. We looked. He was standing on a stone step, sampling the water with a foot. A large torso, thick, tapering thighs and slim legs—not an Apollo, but a bearish he-man there in the nude. Bravely he stalked into the cold water and then splashed as he spread for a swim. He blew and lunged and snorted like a hippopotamus.

These swims, from early spring till late fall, keep him fit for work. No mollycoddle could take to cold water like that.

On the bank again presently, he was inspecting some small trees he had planted in the fall. He called out attention to this and that sapling. The sun glistened on his wet body.

Finally, his clothes on, he joined us, fresh and energized, radiating well-being, proud of himself. "How warm the sun . . . what a gorgeous day!"

The fish dinner was ready, the cook announced.

"You two would have keener appetites for that fish," Dreiser said, "if you had joined me in a swim."

He loves eating where there is company and argument. Notables and common folk dine with him at the same time and he enjoys the interplay of instincts. He may ask somebody, "What do you think of spiritualism?" in order to start an argument. If he becomes excited in defense of a pet theory, he mops his mouth with a quick dab of the napkin and gesticulates with knife or fork. Lustily he eats and lustily he laughs, telling stories or uproaring at those told by others. He will repeat a big, hoarse laugh with a gusty "Oh, gad, that's good!" The prevailing impression that Dreiser never breaks his brooding stare with mirth is erroneous.

When we got on the subject of writing, he confessed a keen appetite for John Cowper Powys and his brother, Llewelyn Powys.[6] He expressed great admiration for Pearl Buck's "The Good Earth," which he described as a "simple, masterly portrayal."[7]

He talked little about any writing he was busy at. It was generally understood he was at work on another novel, but he didn't refer to it.

He did mention foreign rights to "An American Tragedy"[8] and incidents in his career. You wondered if this Titan of American literature would sur-

6. For Dreiser's relationships to John Cowper and Llewelyn Powys, see p. 189, n. 1.
7. *The Good Earth* (1931), a novel of Chinese peasant life by Pearl Buck (1892–1973), won the Pulitzer Prize for fiction in 1931; Buck herself won the Nobel Prize in 1938.
8. Dreiser expended much effort during the 1920s and 1930s in attempts to secure the royalties due him on the many foreign translations of his works.

pass himself. He was about sixty-five now, with an impressive list of works to his credit. Some left-wing critics think his writings in future will be of less importance. They say he doesn't measure present world-shaking changes by the correct—the Marxian—yardstick. Others believe he may become the American Gorki. Was not the Russian far past middle age when he proved he was still green enough to grow, to catch the new spirit, to remain, under profound revolutionary change, a passionate, sympathetic interpreter of his people?[9] Honest Dreiser has unimpaired intellectual awareness and virility.

At any rate, Dreiser though denied a place in his Hoosier State's literary Who's Who, stands and will continue to stand as a figure representing a period.[10] He is, like most creative artists, an individualist, but an individualist in the highest sense. He approves of collectivism as enabling the *individual* to seek his own welfare through cooperation with *individuals*. Yes, he is a dinosaur of his period, or a literary mastodon—it's so easy to apply terms of vastness to him—whose bones will be something for coming generations to marvel at. Indeed, future historians, when they dig into the debris of American civilization of the early twentieth century, doubtless will unearth great hunks of Dreiser.

We were now in the sun again after the meal. "More leaves have opened already," he noted eagerly. Birds were calling from distant woods. The dogs capered in the broomsedge. And Dreiser, away from the jam and noise of Manhattan, was basking in this spring day with dreamy contemplation. Was he thinking, like the caged lion, of a lost glory? Or was he envisioning a society in which individualism would be, not for a parasitic few as under capitalism, but for all who worked and added to the abundance and quality of living?

"You know," he was saying meditatively, as he breathed in the spring life about him, "we humans have gotten too far away from the earth. With all our learning, we have lost something the other creatures possess—something, you know, that would make us happier. Maybe it's the frankness of honest contact with our fellows, all of the earth elemental. A kind of humanistic naturalism, if that isn't a paradox. Rousseau saw it. Walt Whitman sang it when he rhapsodized democracy."

9. Maxim Gorki (or Gorky), the Russian social realist, produced his best plays and fiction in his thirties, when such works of social realism as *The Lower Depths* (1902) and *Mother* (1906) made him world famous. By "far past middle age," Crawford is referring to Gorky's enthusiastic endorsement of the postrevolutionary Soviet Union in his later work.

10. Crawford appears to be referring not to a specific *Who's Who* volume but to the hostility toward Dreiser's work often expressed by the almost uniformly conservative Indiana press.

Will the Movies Kill the Novel?
A Visit with Theodore Dreiser
American Novelist

By Vladimir Pozner

*

Les Nouvelles Littéraires, 29 August 1936, p. 6.
Translated from the French by Carol Pizer.

For a European, any American location looks like a movie set. Thus this little railway station in Mount Kisco, near New York, with its employee in a peaked cap, its Negro shoe-shine boy, its small group of gum-chewing bystanders.[1]

The taxi sets me down in front of a barrier whose presence in the middle of nowhere has no explanation. I follow a path, and suddenly, behind a knoll, appears a gingerbread house reminiscent of a Swiss chalet and the fairytales of Grimm.

Theodore Dreiser is there waiting for me. He is tall, portly, graying. Big lips, a fleshy nose, little eyes. He speaks as he writes, going into all the details.

"You see," he says," I don't think that the roman-fleuve has lived out its life, any more than the short novel or the novella.[2] But new means of expression have appeared that tend to replace the novel. Movies have weakened and devalued the literary form in the United States. For example, it is certain that any best-selling novel will immediately be bought by a film company. At the same time, if an interesting item appears in the newspapers, it can serve the same purpose. The story of Al Capone was filmed without literature serving as an intermediary.[3] Research in the area of news or history is enough for the cinema. I have the feeling that the film producer

---

1. For Dreiser and Mount Kisco, see p. 239, n. 1.

2. Although Pozner uses *roman-fleuve* in the original French, Dreiser apparently means simply the long novel. *Roman-fleuve* is usually restricted to a series of novels dealing with a similar set of characters, often members of the same family, as in John Galsworthy's *Forsythe Saga*.

3. There had been several films based on the life of Al Capone (1899–1947), the famous American gangster, but Dreiser is probably referring to the most popular of these, *Scarface* (1932), starring Paul Muni.

is encroaching on the written work. If he is an authentic creator, he is as interested in the drama of life as the writer. And that's as it should be, as you know yourself. We are approaching a period when a new Shakespeare will be able to take some cheap drama and turn it into a *Macbeth*. Yes, I have the feeling that the cinema is in the process of building something that could eventually replace literature. Best-sellers used to easily sell a hundred or two hundred thousand copies. Now an edition of 7,000 constitutes a major success. Whereas for the cinema, 70 million Americans go every week. In two weeks, you can show a film to more people than the number of readers a book will ever have. A new Shaw could appear, in the movies, who would have the same world-wide audience, the same influence, who would convey a message, a philosophy in his films. Balzac would have been a great film director. We must look forward, not backward."

"Do you think that the cinema is going to kill literature?"

"It is not going to eliminate those who are determined to keep literature as their means of expression. There was a period when there were very few novelists. They were created by the vogue of a genre that has existed only since Richardson. Today they number in the thousands. Why? Because of the success of the novel. This was, for many people, a perfect means of expression. Then the cinema appeared. Little by little, we will see the development of original films. They will offer the same possibilities that the novel offered 150 years ago. And newcomers, seeking a means of expression, will prefer to turn to the cinema. I don't think that films will completely kill literature. And yet. . . . Look at what is going on—but you must know this yourself—as soon as a novel is successful, Hollywood grabs its author right away and says to him, 'Write for us.' The novelist had earned a few thousand dollars, the scriptwriter will collect tens of thousands.

"The newspapers must also be considered. For millions of men, they replace serial novels. Take the Hauptmann case.[4] Americans have followed the twists and turns of the story in the press from day to day. That's the way people used to read Dickens's novels, published in installments. Only, instead of one writer, there are many that collaborate on the same subject. There are, let's say, five hundred who assemble the documentation, another five hundred who write the text, another five hundred who edit the copy. And this drama is read, understood, loved by millions of people. *Vanity Fair* never had more readers than that.

"Life is constantly changing. There is no constant in art, as you know yourself."

4. The child of the world-famous aviator Charles Lindbergh had been kidnapped and murdered in 1932; Bruno Hauptmann (1899–1936) was charged with the crime and executed on 3 April 1936. The story preoccupied the country for over four years.

"Isn't it possible to use in literature the new techniques of cinema and journalism?"

"I don't write only for you. The writer works for his time, for the turbulence of life. And he hopes that his work will not founder. He wants millions of people to read him and be touched. Imitate the cinema—an art that has an impact—in books that will not sell? What good is that? You have to get something back. Not money, I'm not talking about money. But encouragement. Because the novel has been successful in the course of recent centuries, we have believed it to be immortal. The Romans who wrote on wax tablets must have believed that this was the best way to make thought permanent."

"But only the technology has changed. The printing press replaced the stylus, that's all."

"Yes, but people listened to Demosthenes: he spoke. Today, making speeches wouldn't be enough to combat Philip of Macedonia.[5] People would use the printing press, the radio, the cinema."

And Dreiser said, a bit timidly, "I would like the novel and the short story to continue to exist; they are beautiful genres. But, you know, I'm not sure. Previously, in the Orient, stories were not printed; people assembled on street corners to hear them being told. And that lasted for centuries.

"Now, television is coming on the heels of the cinema and the radio.[6] I went to a demonstration. And I had the clear impression that the screen could be placed at the foot of my bed and that I could see and hear Mussolini, or Roosevelt, or Toscanini conducting a concert, or a film, or a comedian on a stage. And I would be there, stretched out comfortably in my bed. It is possible, perfectly possible, that the variety offered to me by television would prevent me, that day, from opening a book."

"What chance does a writer have today to communicate with his readers?"

"First—you must know this yourself—most books that are published these days are standardized. Take from my library a book that just came out and a ten- or fifteen-year-old volume; they are very similar. A young man tells how unhappy he was growing up in the bosom of his family, and he doesn't realize that it's the same in all families. There are attempts to formulate things in a new way, but great novels are rare, as they have always been. Balzac was successful."

5. In a series of orations known as the "Philipics," the great Greek orator Demosthenes (384?–322 B.C.) opposed the efforts of Philip of Macedon to overthrow the freedoms of Greek democracy.

6. Although television was under development throughout the 1930s, it was not then available to the general public.

Dreiser searches through the centuries.

"Hugo also, in *Les Misérables* and *Nôtre-Dame de Paris*. There are one or two novels by Thackeray that count. Three or four by Dickens, the rest. . . . By Tolstoy, *War and Peace*, *Anna Karenina*, and the short stories. Almost all of Dostoyevsky has survived, because it is always himself that he is describing. In the United States, we have a very good literary tradition: Poe, Hawthorne, Mark Twain, a great writer. But here true realism was most often a failure: it was simply rejected. Writers were terrorized in a way. There are many who started with an excellent novel, a realistic novel, and ended with *The Saturday Evening Post*."[7]

"And those who didn't let themselves be terrorized?"

"I carried on the struggle until 1932. I'm still doing it. I've written, I've spoken. I went to Kentucky during the miners' strike. Because I wanted to ask a witness a simple question, a bully boy pushed his gun into my belly and ordered me to leave. And he would have pulled the trigger! Who could I complain to? It's ridiculous. The press, the law, everything belongs to the trusts. I wrote a book: *Tragic America*. It was practically suppressed. Terrible country where mysterious things happen. Where a group from Wall Street controls the cinema. Where it is impossible to talk about politics or social questions on the radio. I was asked one day to speak before the microphone. I could have prepared a series of lectures on subjects that I care about. I asked if I would be free to say anything I wanted. The answer was that my lectures would be reviewed beforehand. 'It's like that?' I answered. 'Then goodbye.'

"I've given a multitude of interviews to the *New York Times*, to the *Herald Tribune*, to other newspapers; every time I happened to say anything significant, it was glossed over.

"I wish, certainly, that communism would assure us an era of peace. Personally, you see, I have gone from nothing to too much. But if I were sure that once communism was installed in the United States, I would have a room and the opportunity to work and to make a living from the product of my work, I would say, Go ahead, right away. As long as everyone has the same possibilities. Today, I have nothing more than what I had when I was living in one room and writing my first short stories. If it is sure that the communist system won't produce more bureaucracy, let it be established. In any case we need to try it. It couldn't be worse than the current system, and it might well be better. There are so many people who are suffering, who have nothing, who are in despair, and others who live so well. Luxury, games,

7. An extremely popular magazine during the 1920s and 1930s, its fiction was known for formulaic fulfillment of conventional expectation.

amusements ought to exist, but they shouldn't be reserved for the exclusive use of a few people. It's unjust and useless.

"I would like to witness the change that is being prepared and see if it will bring with it, as some claim, the death of adventure, the death of tragedy."

"Tragedy? And the shipwreck of the Tcheliouskine?"[8]

"Yes. There will always be tragedy. But its nature will change. So much the better. Look at what is happening here. American financiers are rapidly learning the practice of fascism. They want to replace the liberal oligarchy with a tyrannical oligarchy. They already control the press, the radio, the cinema. They want to take over education, to condition people. Teach only slogans in order to keep people in servitude. Personally, I would like to see a more varied, a freer world. Fascism is deadly. They manufacture ten thousand wooden soldiers. And then? They are like toy manufacturers. They are looking for peace. Wooden soldiers are safer than men."

"But the raw material they use is flesh, not wood. Can people fool their stomachs?"

"It is possible. My father did it for years, for almost all his life. A devout Catholic, he deprived himself of necessities in order to give to the Church. The power to implant illusions in the mechanical creatures that we are is very dangerous.

"Myself, I have always fought against fascism, and if it were to triumph, I would doubtless have to flee to Mexico. And there I wouldn't be alone. You know, my books are forbidden in Germany.[9] Today, money is the only force that directs the world. Oh! Don't believe that I am without hope. But I look things in the face. It's like a cancer that kills millions of people. We try to discover the microbe, to combat it, but in the meantime cancer kills."

"And what will bring on the discovery that puts an end to cancer?"

"Fear. . . . I believe that life is a mechanical phenomenon, that men are mechanical beings. I don't think of myself as an individual, not more than anyone else. This has always amused me: how did men manage to set themselves up as individuals? I am part of a flock of birds. No flock, no birds. . . . I, Theodore Dreiser, writer, I attract people who are realist, sensible. Those who read me are against the injustices of life. I have never had any other readers. I will never write for the partisans of the established order. Life is essentially a changing thing, sad, tragic, and beautiful. And I love it."

8. In February 1934 the *Chelyuskin*, a Russian ice-breaker, was trapped and then partly broke up in the Bering Sea. A dramatic rescue effort by Russian aircraft that lasted almost two months and attracted worldwide attention succeeded in rescuing all those involved.

9. On several occasions during the 1930s Dreiser expressed his conviction that his books were banned in Germany because the Nazi authorities believed he was Jewish.

Author! Author!
Theodore Dreiser, Cheerful at Sixty-Six
Still Thinks Life's a Tough Business

By May Cameron

*

New York Post, 5 February 1938, p. 7.

During the late 1930s Dreiser's attention centered on the completion of his massive philosophical study—published posthumously as *Notes on Life* (1974)—in which he sought to substantiate his long-held belief in a physical universe both mechanistic in operation and spiritual in essence. This preoccupation led him to visit several marine biological research centers, including those at Cold Spring Harbor, on Long Island, and Woods Hole, near Cape Cod. May Cameron reviewed books and interviewed authors for the *New York Post* for many years.

Life is still pretty tough, according to Theodore Dreiser, back in New York for the winter after several months in a science colony on Long Island.[1] The author of "Sister Carrie" and others of the most controversial—and important—books of the century has returned to the old Rhinelander Gardens on Eleventh Street.

Twenty years ago he lived in the same building,[2] and considerably more than twenty years ago "Sister Carrie" was beginning a difficult climb into recognition. Soon a lavishly illustrated edition of Dreiser's first novel will find a place on the shelves of the wealthy—along with other timeless classics—a literary treasure offered to members of the Limited Editions Club.[3]

To those readers who have followed the long progress of Dreiser's thought, his scientific summer and studies will seem the logical culmina-

1. Dreiser spent three months during the summer of 1937 at the Carnegie Biological Laboratory, Cold Spring Harbor, Long Island.

2. Dreiser was living in at apartment at 118 West Eleventh Street in a row of buildings known as the Rhinelander Gardens. He had lived there earlier as well, from September 1923 to January 1925.

3. The Limited Editions Club edition of *Sister Carrie*, illustrated by Reginald Marsh, appeared in 1939.

tion of feelings and ideas that germinated back at the turn of the century. His present concern with "speculative biology" is of a piece with his earlier speculation upon "chemic compulsion." As with Jennie Gerhardt and Clyde Griffiths, so with all of us: the focus of blind, malevolent forces.

Alert and vital at sixty-six, and surprisingly gay in spite of his philosophy, Theodore Dreiser hooted down rumors that he was concocting some new American tragedy among test tubes and microscopes.

Where Humanity Is Going

"There's nothing mysterious about the science colony," he said. "I spent several months at Cold Spring Harbor because I have friends there, and because I have always been interested in biology, chemistry, physics and philosophy. Particularly, speculative biology. That term may enrage some of them out there, but there are others who feel just the way I do.

"I noticed many a fellow who could have run off to amuse himself working late at night in his laboratory. One man got so close to a cure for hay fever that what must have been the virus would, merely rubbed on the skin, produce a swelling and fever in the part touched. A definite cure would be a world-wide blessing, yet all his findings were handed out to the scientific world—to anybody. They get a personal satisfaction and a mental profit, but it sort of throws a new light on what is an ideal profit motive. If there is any, this sort of looks to me to be one.

"The older scientists seem strangely meditative and anxious to do something about what they call the progress of humanity. But I swear I don't see where humanity is going to progress except to make each more comfortable at the expense of the other fellow. It seems to be a case of the strongest fellow getting the best of the rest of them—and turning the guns on his associates. Look at Mr. Girdler and at our own capital and labor. Look at how they shot them down out in Chicago.[4]

"Some scientists, Millikan, Eddington and Compton,[5] among others, seem to consider man really joined with God in some great purpose, leading mankind onward and upward to some noble level. But I can't have any conception of a deity that would create and okay and sustain what's going on in the world today. Now birds are fairly respectable creatures, except that

4. Tom Mercer Girdler (1877–1965) was the president of the Republic Steel Corporation, a company with a strong antiunion position; several strikers were killed in a riot at the company's strike-bound Chicago plant in late May 1937.

5. Robert A. Millikan (1868–1953), Sir Arthur S. Eddington (1882–1944), and Arthur H. Compton (1892–1962) were renowned physicists who were, in varying ways, attempting to relate philosophical and religious ideas to natural phenomena.

they murder each other like common holdup men. A crow will grab a duck-
ling trotting behind a duck. A bluejay will kill its young and eat them, and
certainly the kingbird, little as he is, will peck out a crow's eyes just as fast
as he can get to him.

As Old as Philosophy

"That's old stuff, old as philosophy, but I doubt that anybody can go through
my books and not fail to see there has always been a philosophy there.[6] My
earliest suspicion was that there was something crooked about the whole
business. I haven't as yet been able to prove that what I suspected then isn't
so, pleased as I would be to do it. I haven't been able to change my attitude
one penny's worth, for I can't escape the sense that we're just out for the ride.

"Some of the people you and I know are spinning around gayly, interested in polo and the stock market, good clothes, a new girl or restaurant,
the right trip at the right time—and not an idea in their heads. But for
millions and millions that isn't so, unless it goes for the lack of ideas. As to
that, we're all more or less afflicted. You see trouble in their eyes, hear it in
their voices. There are too many asylums and penitentiaries and slums, and
here in America—the world's great economic success, as I hear—there are
30,000,000 people dependent upon other people. And look at Europe!

"If there is a criminal in all this, it is nature. Life is the crook, if there is
one. For life is the author of every drama, tragedy, dream or eulogy that has
ever appeared. There is no other author; we are fountain pens in some big
hand. Remember Dillinger and consider his social history; life, and no one
else, was shooting through Mr. Dillinger.[7]

"Most people seem to be puzzled about life. The variants of philosophy
won't solve anything, and there is no use turning to religion, because it can't
do a damn thing for you. You take it, if you can; if you can't, you jump out
the window.

"But don't think I am miserable. I have my work, interesting connec-
tions and lots of friends. I don't sit around and hang my head."

The next book? Mr. Dreiser very carefully had nothing to say.

6. Dreiser clearly intends "fail" rather than "not fail" in this sentence.

7. John Dillinger (1903–34), a notorious bank robber, eluded the police for several years
until killed by FBI agents in 1934. He did not, however, come from an impoverished background.

Theodore Dreiser Discusses Dallas and His Next Novel

By Lon Tinkle

*

Dallas Morning News,
14 August 1938, sect. 2, p. 8.

Tinkle's interview was conducted in Paris in late July during Dreiser's visit to the city to address the International Association of Writers for the Defense of Culture. The *Dallas Morning News* prefaced the interview by reprinting a headline from a Paris newspaper announcing the address, with the following explanation:

> The eminent Parisian daily, Ce Soir, was quite excited over the presence in the French capital of the dean of American novelists, Theodore Dreiser, as can be seen from the above headlines which it displayed July 25, when Mr. Dreiser opened "la conference extraordinaire" of the International Association of Writers for the Defense of Culture. The noteworthy list of speakers was supplemented by messages from Romain Rolland, Thomas Mann, Heinrich Mann and Upton Sinclair, among others. Lon Tinkle of Dallas, visiting in Paris, ran across Mr. Dreiser, whom he knew from the latter's visit here a few years back, and elicited from him the exceedingly interesting comments set forth below.

> Tinkle was no doubt the anonymous reporter who interviewed Dreiser for the *Dallas Morning News* in May 1930 when Dreiser was passing through the city.

"I love Paris," said Theodore Dreiser as he sat beside me at the Lutetia's sidewalk cafe,[1] "but I do wish the French knew how to mix American drinks. If you want a decent drink before dinner, you have to order the proper ingredients and do the mixing yourself. I don't like the sugared French aperitifs

1. Dreiser was staying on the Left Bank at the Hotel Lutétia on the Boulevard Raspail.

and if you ask the waiter for a gin fizz, he'll inevitably spoil it for you with sugar or too much lemon."

Somehow it didn't seem suitable to tell Mr. Dreiser just then that the chocolate I was drinking was the best in the world, so I called the waiter to bring the great novelist the "proper ingredients." The garcon instinctively recoiled and it was plain he didn't intend to let barbaric Americans have complete freedom in their savagery. He insisted on crushing a whole lemon into Mr. Dreiser's glass. Wearily the novelist yielded to the display of national pride.

Preoccupied with Philosophy

"I'm thinking of writing a book on philosophy," he remarked, as I praised his resignation. "For the last seven years I have been perhaps more preoccupied with that than with anything else. I have all my life had 'hunches,' which I like to submit later to scientific verification. My hunches have nearly always been right and the wish to verify them perhaps explains my interest in biology, physics and chemistry, fields with which I've been keeping in touch for a number of years."

"Are you getting away from fiction?" I asked.

"Oh, no, certainly not. I'm working on a novel now that's approximately a third finished, one that I like very much. This time I'm doing a portrait of one of those numerous souls whom everybody refers to as "a good man" and whose life turns out pathetically, a life that does more harm than good, despite good intention.[2] This seems to me an eternally recurring phenomenon; but I don't know too well how to explain why these 'good' people, who are so rigid and ethical in their personal life, turn out really to be asses. I suppose it's because in one sense, though not practically, they're just simply stupid. They mean well, but they're so sure they're right, that they can't see the lack of humanness in their morality. I could point to many famous men who represent in some aspects the type I mean, though no one completely. Henry Ford has some of the elements, for instance. Colonel House is another example.[3] The important thing is that despite the damage such lives often cause to others, there is a pathetic beauty about them, the authentic beauty of tragedy."

2. Dreiser is summarizing the principal theme of *The Bulwark*.

3. The mechanical and organizational genius of Henry Ford (1863–1947) was widely accepted, whereas his reactionary social and political views were often derided or deplored. Colonel Edward M. House (1858–1938), Woodrow Wilson's closest adviser, was credited with great political acumen but was also frequently blamed for many of Wilson's blunders at the Versailles Peace Treaty conference.

"For you, yes," I replied, "but it's too bad they themselves never have that awareness."

Everybody Feels Tragedy

"Well," said Dreiser, "I think they do. If you think it's only those of us who are articulate that realize the presence of a certain noble beauty in sorrow and frustration, you're guessing wrong. I hold the belief that nearly everybody has his lucid moments of perceiving that we are all dismayed; of perceiving at the same time the sense of tragedy which makes us accept that dismay with a strange repose. Some of those who feel this most are among those who never think of fitting words to the feeling. That is one of the great traits of my masters, Balzac and Zola. They knew the average, run-of-the-mill soul at first hand and they didn't undervalue it. When I first read these great masters I found much in their books that I disbelieved, either because it was too realistic or too penetrating in its psychology. It was only later when I had had more experience of life that I appreciated their greatness, and was able thereby to measure my own growth. It's a good experience to have, to go back and read books that stirred up a violent reaction in you when you were young."

He lapsed into meditation. Then presently, "—But enough about myself. You know, I still have a vivid recollection of Dallas and of some of the people I met there. And I remember seeing a very fine play about a Negress—a play which would have been done on Broadway if we had a decent theater tradition in America. What was the name of that play? It was by a teacher in the Dallas schools."

"You must mean Kathleen Witherspoon's 'Jute,'" I answered.[4] "Any other Dallas memories?"

Wants to Come Back

"Yes," he replied, "a good many. I want to go back there some day. But right now I've a world of things to do. Tomorrow I have to preside at the second annual meeting of the International Association of Writers for the Defense of Culture—"

The next day, thanks to Mr. Dreiser, I was present at this "private" conference and heard him make a sterling defense of the liberty of the writer before a congress that included Ernst Toller, La Pasionaria, Rosamond Leh-

---

4. In April 1930 Dreiser saw this play, set in a Georgia mill town, in a production by the Dallas Little Theatre.

mann, Stephen Spender, Louis Aragon, Jose Bergamin, Ugolini and many other internationally known figures.[5] Dreiser was furiously applauded and warmly appreciated, as indeed he deserves to be.

5. Toller (1893–1939) was a German expressionist dramatist and communist activist; La Pasionaria—that is, Dolores Ibarruri (1895–1989)—was a Spanish communist who reached legendary status as an orator during the Spanish Civil War; Lehmann (1901–90) was a British novelist and supporter of the Loyalist cause during the Spanish Civil War; Spender (1909–95) was a left-wing British poet; Aragon (1897–1982) was a French surrealist and communist; José Bergamín (1894–1983) was a Spanish pro-Loyalist critic and dramatist; and Amedeo Ugolini (1896–?) was an Italian novelist.

Flirting Powers Held in Danger
Roosevelt's Hand Holding Deplored by Dreiser

*

Portland Oregonian, 16 February 1939, p. 1.

During February 1939 Dreiser undertook a lecture tour of the Far West, appearing in Portland, San Francisco, and Salt Lake City, among other cities. These lectures often incorporated the then-current Communist Party position that European capitalistic societies constituted a greater danger to America than did Nazi Germany.

If President Roosevelt doesn't stop holding hands with "dear old fascist France and dear old imperialist England" they will ruin us, in the opinion of Theodore Dreiser.

The famous American author, who will lecture on the Town Hall program tonight, said at Benson hotel Wednesday that Roosevelt "is better than any president in my lifetime," but that he didn't like the chief executive's foreign policy.

The "gang of highbinders" in control of France and England are sure to lead us into a war that will be ruinous to the United States if this policy continues, said Dreiser.

Democracy Rates Razz

He scorned the popular conception that those two countries operate under a democratic form of government and raised questions as to the purity of American democracy.

Those in control of Britain's government "chased out" Edward and Wally because the king "kept going around, talking to workers and finding out what the true conditions were," said Dreiser.[1]

---

1. Edward VIII (1894–1972) had abdicated the throne in December 1936 to free himself to marry a twice-divorced American, Mrs. Wallis Warfield Simpson (1896–1986). During his years as prince of Wales Edward had expressed liberal ideas at odds with those of the Conservative Party and Stanley Baldwin, the Conservative prime minister at the time of the abdication crisis.

"Germany and Italy are going to eat up France and England unless we do it first," he said.

Soviets Come a Cropper

The author admitted that although he had been "very strong for Russia" at one time, he realized now that communism won't work there—because of poor management.

"If Germany had it, it would be the greatest social experiment in history," he said.

"But I'm down on Hitler for monkeying with Spain," the writer added. He said Spain had a working democracy before the revolt.[2]

2. During the Spanish Civil War (1936–39) the fascist forces led by General Franco eventually gained superiority over the democratically elected Loyalist government, in large part because of aid supplied by Nazi Germany and Fascist Italy. Barcelona had fallen to the fascists in January 1939, and the war was now in its closing stage.

Dreiser, Here to Talk, Asks U.S. to Awake
Author Points Dangers of Fascism, Need for Preparation

*

Salt Lake City Deseret News, 20 February 1939, p. 1.

Wake up, America—or else.

This curt warning to the nation was expressed here today by cynical, white-haired Theodore Dreiser, author, lecturer and leading American crusader against mass exploitation and economic imperialism. He will lecture tonight in Kingsbury Hall.

The distinguished author of "An American Tragedy" said the tragedy of America as he sees it today is its people's indifference to the growing power of industrial overlords and politicians here and abroad.

Deplores U.S. Shortcomings

He likewise deplored refusal of the American public to face realities and live their own lives in terms of what life means to them, and their apparent willingness to let a true democracy slip from their grasp.

"America today," said the dynamic, ruddy-faced champion of the underprivileged, "is sound asleep, and if it doesn't wake up out of its dream that all is well, it will find itself paying dearly in the way of liberty and well being."

He belabored the typical American for paying too much attention to the other person's life and pursuits, refusing to make the most out of their own lives and allowing others to do likewise.

What the country needs, he said, is a clear, realistic view on the part of its citizens as to what life is and what can be, then fight to gain and hold what is for their best good.

Urges Defense

As to the best foreign policy for America to adopt in the world crisis, Dreiser's opinion is that the best the nation can do—and that, he thinks, is not much—is to prepare itself for defense, than go to the help of France and England if and when they scrap their imperialistic systems of government. First, however, he said, America must restore its own democracy, which he says exists nowhere in the world today.

England and France today, he said, are too weak to defend themselves alone, and democracy throughout the world is doomed to fascistic destruction unless supporters throughout the world work with open eyes to drive out its enemies at home and abroad and restore it to power in government.

Democracy, in the opinion of the writer, is a system which allows all men equal liberties and his proper share of the wealth of the land, according to what he contributes in brains and brawn, and a land free of political graft and industrial rule of the workers.

Dreiser will lecture here tonight under the sponsorship of the University of Utah extension division. The program will begin at 8:15 P.M.

Radio Interview with Theodore Dreiser

*

Interviewer: Edward Robbin
Station: KMTR, Hollywood
Time: Saturday, Feb. 1, 1941, 6:30 p.m.
Subject: His New Book, "America Is Worth Saving"

Dreiser relies in this interview on some of the evidence of America's social inequities he had used in his just published *America Is Worth Saving*. Several later reviewers of the book noted the suspect nature of much of this evidence. The interview exists in two forms: as a separately published brochure (in the Dreiser Papers of the University of Pennsylvania Library) and as "Theodore Dreiser Airs His Views," *People's World*, 6 March 1941, p. 5. The text in this volume is that of the brochure.

Good evening, friends. We have a real treat tonight. We have in the studio here as our guest, our great and good friend, Theodore Dreiser. Mr. Dreiser has just published a new book. It's called *America Is Worth Saving*, and I've asked Mr. Dreiser to come up here tonight so that we could ask him a few questions about his book.

DREISER: Go right ahead, Ed. I can't tell you very much about it in the short space of time we have. It's something you have to read.

ED: I'm going to do that in any case, Mr. Dreiser. In fact, I have my copy right here. I haven't had a chance to read the book yet, except in part. But I was particularly intrigued by the chapter headings. They tell a story in themselves, like *Scarcity and Plenty, Has America a Save-the-World Complex, Does England Love Us As We Love England.*

DREISER: Well, poverty in the midst of plenty, is as I said in my book. It reminds me of the song of the 20's, "Yes, We Have No Bananas."[1] It's nonsense. It's one of the great absurdities of our age.

ED: You have some very striking examples of that in the book.

DREISER: I think ten encyclopedias could be crammed with documents today showing how people starve and are without clothes and the materials

---

1. "Yes! We Have No Bananas" (1923) was written by Frank Silver and Irving Cohn.

they need to live, while millions of bushels of wheat are destroyed, human labor neglected and so on. Why, we have so much surplus food and clothing material that one of our main national problems is where to put it. Last May there were 615,000,000 pounds of surplus pork, more than one million pounds of surplus butter, sixty-two million pounds of surplus beef. . . .

ED: Better stop that, Mr. Dreiser. You're making a lot of people out there hungry.

DREISER: I'm sure of it, because a lot of them are hungry. And there's no person in this country that doesn't know it. They lie when they say they don't. Forty-one per cent of all our families live on an average of seven hundred and fifty-eight dollars a year. According to *our* government, eight million families continually face starvation, while another eleven million are fighting poverty. Those are *its* words. And yet we're rushing billions to save the richest empire in the world and the greediest.

ED: Well, what happens to this surplus?

DREISER: You know as well as I do. In the first place there is no surplus. It's just that the people who need it have no way of getting it. They destroy it; they plow it under; they kill the cattle; burn the oranges; sink shiploads of food in mid-ocean—anything to *produce artificial scarcity so they can make a profit.*

What knocks me out is that all through the ages mankind has been striving for the time when there would be plenty and now that that time is here, our corporations are fighting to maintain scarcity—our rich would-be money lords are. And yet this country alone could feed and clothe the whole world. But do we? We turn all our ingenuity (our corporations do) to the problem of how to get rid of the stuff the people need so badly, and finally, in the midst of this fantastic maladjustment of our own country, we are told that we should forget our troubles at home and go to Europe to help save British imperialism,—the very gang that is starving India at this hour. In truth I don't think we've ever seen such a fine bunch of patriots as we have in Washington today. The only trouble is they are British patriots instead of American—patriots in waiting to the king and queen of England and all the lords and ladies over there who hold hundreds of millions of people in the worst kind of subjection.

ED: Well, but what about Mr. Hitler? They say we've got to stop him.

DREISER: Dear! Dear! What do you know about that? Why, this war is nothing but a fight between Hitlerdum and Hitlerdee. Does anyone really think there is less Hitlerism in the British Empire than in Nazi Germany?[2] I've a chapter in my book that gives facts, figures and details on how Brit-

2. Dreiser's remarks about Nazi Germany and Great Britain are deeply colored by the Nazi-

ish capital and American capital too, for that matter, financed Nazism in Germany. Who created this Nazi regime? Big German capitalists, yes? You'll find a list of the various German corporations and how much they contributed to put Hitler into power in that book. But who was behind these capitalists? Beyond a doubt, their brother monopolists in France and Britain.

ED: But even so, Mr. Dreiser, a lot of people seem to think that British democracy, with all its faults, is better than Hitler's Nazism.

DREISER: Then I say they're people who don't know anything about it. I have studied these things a lifetime. I've been to Britain. I know the British lords and ladies because I've met a number of them and talked to them, and I know their contempt for the people. In my book I've described the horrible conditions of the British working class. Why, the British government has done nothing for its people; nothing to improve their conditions that hasn't been absolutely wrung from them. And as for the conditions of the hundreds of millions of people in England's colonies, in India for example, that makes Germany's cruelties look like a pipe-dream.

ED: Well, they tell me, Mr. Dreiser, that the British have brought sanitation and civilization to India.

DREISER: Don't make me laugh. In 1931 there was 92 per cent illiteracy in British ruled India. But I'm not going to talk about that—you have the book. Read the facts there. For an amazing picture of cruelty, inefficiency, and crass stupidity of that imperialist gang,—read the book. If Germany can beat England at the game of mass human torture and fabulous inefficiency it will have to go some.

ED: But, of course, Mr. Dreiser, the point you set out making in your book is something different.

DREISER: Yes, of course, the book is about America, Americanism, and what should be the objectives of the American people as opposed to those of our British patriots in Washington who are trying to get us into a war to save British Hitlerism, and who, in the process, by the way, are doing everything they can to put Hitlerism into operation right here.

ED: Well, Mr. Dreiser, what should be the true objectives of the American people?

DREISER: It's hard to tell you in a word, but I would say *peace and plenty*, and for that we need true Americanism. We need not only to talk about the Declaration of Independence and the Constitution, but to actually sit down and read and study them and guard them. We need to live by the Declara-

---

Soviet Nonaggression Pact of August 1939. The Soviet Union argued that this treaty, which angered many on the American left, was necessary to protect itself against those European capitalistic nations determined on its destruction. Dreiser reflects this position in the interview by portraying Britain as a greater threat to world democracy and peace than Germany.

tion of Independence and remember that no man in Washington, or any place else, is so big that he can set aside the fundamental rights and guarantees of the American people as set forth there. Americanism, as I understand it, with apologies to Mr. Dies,[3] means precisely giving equal chances to *all*, and nothing else.

ED: Well, I'm going to read the Declaration of Independence again myself.

DREISER: You don't tell me! Well do that, and tell your audience to do the same. Our newspapers today emphasize the idea that the Declaration of Independence and the Constitution were set up to guarantee the rights of capitalism and monopoly, but you'll find that monopoly and capitalism aren't even mentioned there. They were meant to protect the mass—make the mass happy—not the few, for instance—making medical care available to the sick, providing jobs at good pay and adequate pensions for those who can't work. That's working democracy! And above all, protecting the peace of America—not ploughing under every *fourth* boy. So I say, let us save America and democracy by not joining in this foreign blood bath, but rather by showing the world by our own example how democracy can work.

ED: And how can we do that now, do you think?

DREISER: Only by getting the mass to awake and getting it to act. No small group of a few thousand crusaders can do it. America will be on the road forward, solidly and unmovably on the road, when a great throng of people comes out into the streets of our cities with the Constitution and Declaration of Independence as their banners and where our un-American monopolists can and will see them and hear them. And then you will see a change. Their masters, the people, can and will tell them where they get off. This is 1941—A.D.—not B.C.

ED: Well I see our time is up. Thank you, Mr. Dreiser, for coming here to be interviewed.

DREISER: Thank you, Ed, for the opportunity. In these days, to get anything but pro-British ideas over is a privilege. Our corporations and their "Free Press" see to that.

---

3. Martin Dies Jr. (1901–71), a Texas Democratic congressman, was the first chairman of the House Un-American Activities Committee, which was created in 1938 to investigate communism in America. The committee was often accused of using methods that violated the civil rights of those being investigated.

An Interview with Theodore Dreiser
The Author of "An American Tragedy" Looks Back at the Struggles of His Youth

By Robert van Gelder

*

New York Times Book Review, 16 March 1941, pp. 2, 16.

Dreiser, who had moved permanently to Los Angeles in December 1938, visited New York and Philadelphia in late February and early March 1941 to address various pro-Soviet groups. Van Gelder reprinted this interview in his *Writers and Writing* (New York: Scribner's, 1946).

Theodore Dreiser has changed little during his years in California save that he now twists paper handkerchiefs while he talks rather than linen ones. He came to the interview with a fresh, thick bundle and rolled this bundle about in his hands, gently tugging at its ends and running his thumbnail over the paper surface while he described the "impossible" factors in America's economic life. "Imagine!" he'd exclaim. "Imagine trying to live on four or five dollars a week! But that's all the part-time girls who work in the big Los Angeles store where I buy my booze and coffee get on a Saturday night. What do you think of that? They work three or four hours a day—the busy hours— all week. For four or five dollars. And the full-time girls only get twelve dollars a week. I'll tell you, if we don't have a revolution here with America modeling itself on Russia, then Americans aren't Americans any more. I won't know what to think of them."

Mr. Dreiser visited Russia in 1927–28 as a guest of the Soviet Government and was feted there, extensively entertained. "When I stopped in England on my way back Winston Churchill asked me, he said, 'Well, what did you think of it?' I told him. I thought it was a wonderful country, a wonderful system. 'Nonsense,' he said. 'It won't last seven years.' That was in 1928.[1] Imagine! Churchill as mistaken as that. After those seven years were up he

---

1. Dreiser interviewed Churchill, then chancellor of the Exchequer in a Conservative government, in late January 1928. He noted the occasion on his return to New York (see p. 166).

changed his tune. A statement was issued over his name praising the Russian system as it works in Russia. Oh, you can't beat that system, you know. A whole country belonging to the people and run by and for the people."

"Don't you feel that Stalin's pact with Hit—?"

"Why shouldn't he have that pact? Don't you know your current history, darling? Hasn't any one ever bothered to tell you the facts of life? Don't you realize that France and England were all set to attack Russia? Oh, you don't. Well, you'll see what happens. Russia may not be the greatest military power in the world now. But it will be. Then you'll see."[2]

He had come East to speak under the auspices of a number of organizations many of the members of which hold similar views. He mentioned the difficulties that beset an outspoken man with beliefs such as his at this time. "Rows everywhere," said Mr. Dreiser. "Once in a while you'll find some one who agrees with you. More often the person you talk to won't agree at all. A conversation will start on a train and soon a row will start, some arguing on your side, some against. And intolerance. Some of them want to put you off the train."

"Any one try to have you put off a train, Mr. Dreiser?"

"They've talked about it."

He at first refused to talk of writing. "At a time like this, when a man can't afford even to sit down in peace, when the whole world is at a crisis— no, darling, that's not the time to discuss literature. That is a hell of a subject for you to be plugging at now. Why don't you try to catch up with the world? Do you think this system is so good it can't be better? Have you even seen Russia? No. And you want to talk about books"—

"What in Russian literature written under the Soviets do you feel is outstanding?" He mentioned "Quiet Flows the Don" as a book that he had greatly enjoyed.[3] "Are we doing anything worthy of comparison with that?" "That colored fellow," said Mr. Dreiser, referring to Richard Wright. "His was a good book, 'Native Son.'"[4] "And Steinbeck?" "Wonderful. Yes, yes. Of course, Steinbeck. You know; they hate him out in California. They blame all their troubles on him. They curse him instead of the devil. They get a heavy rain out there, it is Steinbeck's fault. They think he is a traitor to his State.[5] The smug people. They are so sure that they are right."

---

2. For the relationship of these views to the Nazi-Soviet Pact of 1939, see p. 304, n. 2.

3. *Quiet Flows the Don* (1934), by Mikail Sholokhov (1905–84), was one of Sholokhov's series of novels about life in the Cossack region. A devoted party member, he won the Nobel Prize in 1965.

4. *Native Son* was highly praised on its publication in 1940. At that time Wright (1908–60) was an active member of the Communist Party.

5. Since *The Grapes of Wrath* (1939), by John Steinbeck (1902–68), attacked the treatment of migrant agricultural workers by California state authorities and fruit growers, the novel received some adverse criticism in that state.

"When you were starting you were up against smugness. Was it in your opinion much the same?"

"Boy, were they smug! But they all came around. After Mrs. Doubleday had 'Sister Carrie' scrapped, kept out of circulation. Why, you'd have thought I was the devil. Nobody would have anything to do with me—none of the people in power. I took a copy around to the old Century Company to ask if they would take over the plates and republish my book. When I called to hear what they had decided the girl at the reception desk handed me the book. That was all. No one in the company would talk to me about it. The girl gave me the message that they didn't care to talk about it. That was all.[6]

"Later I finished the first chapters of Jennie Gerhardt and took it to John Phillips at what was then a big publishing house, McClures. He told me— he came out into the anteroom and told me—that if I wished to write such stories he supposed that there was no way in which I could be stopped, but he asked me not to come to him to discuss my writing.[7]

"Years later the man at the Century Company told me—when he was giving me an advance for some travel articles—that he regretted what he had done, that he no longer felt that way.[8] Years later also I met Phillips in downtown Fifth Avenue—at the corner of Twenty-second Street and Fifth Avenue—and he told me that he was sorry, that he didn't feel that way any more."

He pulled at his paper handkerchiefs and laughed. "Don't look so anxious. What are you worrying about? I got through it. I took a room over in Williamsburg—a cheap room, $1.50 a week.[9] It was out of the way, made a long walk to Manhattan. The Williamsburg Bridge wasn't finished and I had to walk down to the Brooklyn Bridge and then across to get here, to this island. I was sick, you see. Why? Because I could not feel that I had a place in the world.

"One day I went to a public charity organization in Twenty-second Street, near Fourth Avenue. They couldn't help me. You see, I had relatives who could have given me something, and they wanted the names and ad-

6. This is the only known account of Dreiser's attempt to have the Century Company publish *Sister Carrie*.

7. John S. Phillips (1861–1949) was a college classmate of S. S. McClure and a partner in the publishing firm of McClure, Phillips, and Company.

8. The figure mentioned is probably Robert Underwood Johnson (1853–1937), a long-time editor both at the Century Company publishing firm and at *Century* magazine. In late 1911 Dreiser contracted with *Century* to write several European travel articles that later were incorporated into *A Traveler at Forty* (1913).

9. The following account of this period in Dreiser's life, from moving to Brooklyn until becoming editor of *Broadway Magazine*, deals with events between February 1903 and the late spring of 1906. Dreiser covers some of the same ground in his posthumously published memoir *An Amateur Laborer* (1983).

dresses of these relatives so that they could go to them and beg for money to buy me food. I'd rather have dropped dead.

"Soon after that I told my landlady that I couldn't pay my rent any longer and gave up my room. I had 5 cents—no, 15 cents. But as I was putting on my clothes the morning that I was surrendering my room, I remembered my watch. I don't know why, but I hadn't thought of it before. I had paid $8 for that watch in St. Louis. I could pawn it.

"There was one of those State-controlled pawn shops next door,[10] or almost next door, to the charity where they had told me that they could not help. I went to that pawn shop. Well, I hadn't eaten for a long time and I was sick. The cold-eyed clerk in the pawn shop must have seen the shape I was in. Though he seemed hardly to look at me. He put the glass in his eye and examined my watch. I was thinking perhaps he would give a dollar. But I warned myself: 'Fifty cents; don't count on more than fifty cents.' After looking at the watch he asked for my name and an address at which I could be reached, not looking at me, looking at the paper, the chit, on which he was writing my name. The he pushed the chit over to me. It was marked $25. It was hard for me to speak. 'This,' I said, 'this is for $25.' 'I know it,' he said, 'come in and get your watch back when you can.'

"Imagine! I bought a pair of shoes for $2. The shoes I'd had were very far gone. And my hat had blown off in a subway. I bought a hat. A room at the Mills Hotel—25 cents a night.[11] I felt a slight return of confidence. Still I couldn't find a job—wasn't ready for one in my own line. I had heard of a fellow who had had a chance to quit newspaper work and take a job as a conductor on the New Haven Railroad and I had heard that this fellow Chauncey Depew at the New York Central would help newspaper men if they went to him.[12] I sent Mr. Depew a letter telling him what straits I was in and then went to see him. His secretary asked me what I wanted and I explained that I needed an outdoor job, a job as a laborer, anything that would give me a chance to work and be self-supporting. He told me that Depew couldn't see me, but he gave me one of Depew's cards with a message scribbled on the back, and that card got me a laborer's job at $15 a week—all I needed.

"I worked for that railroad for nine months. Working with those men,

10. By "State-controlled" Dreiser means regulated by the state, as was the custom at the time.

11. This was a well-known Greenwich Village hotel (on Bleecker Street) that catered to the down-and-out. Dreiser also stayed at the Mills Hotel in 1895, when he was out of a job after leaving the *New York World*.

12. Chauncey M. Depew was at that time both chairman of the board of the New York Central Railroad and a U.S. senator from New York. For Dreiser writings about Depew, see p. 109, n. 3, and p. 275, n. 2.

sharing their strength, learning their lives, seeing the wonderful goodness in the gang boss who could hearten a dozen men, healed me. At the end of nine months, with a few pennies saved, I went hunting a job at my own trade and found one with Street & Smith, the pulp-paper magazine outfit. I was editor of a magazine of theirs at $15 a week, and, boy, is there a story in that outfit? Men writing 40,000 to 60,000 words every week year in and year out for $50 or $60 a week. Imagine! I'm not kidding you.[13]

"It was while I was at Street & Smith's, Sixteenth Street and Seventh Avenue, that I started writing 'Jennie Gerhardt.'[14] I had the turn-down from Phillips, but it wasn't so bad, as at least I had a job. Then suddenly everything changed for the better. I moved up to a better editorial job on another magazine that paid me" (he kissed his fingertips) "$60 a week. Baby! And from there to the Butterick group, where I was general editorial director at $10,000 and up a year.[15]

"Of course I went back to writing, and then 'An American Tragedy' when I was 54 years old. . . . Now? I'll write a book of philosophy and then probably another novel. My autobiography? Listen, there's plenty of time for that. I've got it all in my head. It is all clear. I know just what I'll do with it. But now there's no time for private affairs, for matters of only personal importance. Son, don't you see the world is burning? In Russia"—

"The watch, did you redeem it?"

"The watch? Oh yes. I redeemed it after I got the job with Street & Smith."

"Was the same man there? Did he say"—

"No, no. It was another man. I never saw that first man again. . . . But what's the matter with Americans? They're not the people I think they are if they keep on being suckers to this system when in Russia"—

13. Dreiser's period at Street and Smith, a publisher of dime westerns and mysteries, is obscure. He began working at the firm's editorial office, apparently part-time, in the fall of 1904. In the spring of 1905 he was made editor of its new publication *Smith's Magazine*, which appeared initially in April 1905.

14. Dreiser means that he *again* attempted to work on *Jennie Gerhardt*, which he had put aside in mid-1902. He made little progress at this time and was not able to complete the novel until the winter of 1910–11.

15. In April 1906 Dreiser became the editor of *Broadway Magazine*, remaining in this position until he became the editor of Butterick's *Delineator* in June 1907.

Abuse for Britain Dreiser's Contribution
to Anglo-U.S. Amity
Second Fronter's Two Cents Worth
in "Democracy's Offensive"
Is to Wish Huns in England

*

Toronto Evening Telegram, 21 September 1942, p. 2.

Dreiser was invited by the Toronto Town Forum to lecture on September 22 on the need for a second front—that is, an Allied invasion of Western Europe to relieve the intense pressure on the Russian armies in the East. Despite the lengthy and difficult wartime train journey from Los Angeles to Toronto, he accepted the invitation, in part to have Hazel L. Godwin, who lived in Toronto and with whom he had been corresponding, join him there. On the morning of 21 September Dreiser was interviewed in his Toronto hotel room. Apparently irritated by the questions put to him by the reporter of the *Toronto Telegram,* a staunchly Conservative and pro-British paper, Dreiser responded with his characteristic anti-British beliefs of this period. When the *Telegram* became available that afternoon, the Toronto city council met in emergency session and canceled the talk. Dreiser was advised that it might be dangerous for him to remain in Canada, and he and Godwin left for the United States that same evening. The interview and Dreiser's abrupt departure were widely commented on in Canadian and American newspapers for several days.

Toronto citizens will be addressed by a man to-morrow night who stated to-day in an interview that he "would rather see the Germans in England than the damn snobs now there."

Theodore Dreiser, American author of German parentage, was the sponsor to these sentiments. He is in town to be guest speaker at the Town Forum series, Eaton Auditorium, to-morrow night and, after expressing himself as "lunatically for Russia," his subsequent words showed him to be similarly anti-English.

"Should Russia go down to defeat I hope the Germans invade England," he said. "I would rather see Germans in England than those damn, aristocratic, horse-riding snobs there now."

Mr. Dreiser went on to speak of the "unbelievable gall and brass of the English," who, he said, "had done nothing in this war thus far except borrow money, planes and men from the United States."

"Beg for Second Front"

"We saved the world for democracy once and now we're being asked to save it again," said Mr. Dreiser. "After the last war we were accused of being grafters, demanding our pay. This time we must go on our knees begging for a second front."

It was pointed out to Mr. Dreiser that President Roosevelt has considerable say regarding the second front, as well as the English, but the 71-year-old author disregarded the interruption.

"Churchill has no intention of opening a second front. He's afraid the Communists will rule the world. So he does nothing except send thousands of Canadians to be slaughtered at Dieppe. He didn't send any English. They stay at home and do nothing. Nothing."[1]

This reporter again interrupted the speaker's words to point out that thousands of Englishmen were fighting on the world battlefields including a major role in the Dieppe raid, but Mr. Dreiser doesn't bother with interruptions or corrections. He doesn't like the British. They are "lousy," he says. They have done nothing to make the world a better place and the only decent form of government in the history of the world may be found in Russia.

Admires Lindbergh

"Were you an isolationist before Pearl Harbor?" The Telegram asked.

"Isolationist? What is that?" Mr. Dreiser demanded belligerently.

"An isolationist is an American who didn't believe this to be their war."

"Yes," said the author in a quieter voice. "Yes, I didn't think we should get into this war. I'm a profound admirer of the flyer Lindbergh and his wife. I follow right along with their ideals."[2]

1. On 19 August 1942 an allied commando force consisting largely of Canadian troops assaulted the Normandy coastal city of Dieppe to test German defenses. Almost two-thirds of the men were either killed or wounded.

2. Charles Lindbergh (1902–74), the famous aviator, was a prominent member of the staunchly isolationist America First movement during the 1930s. In the following interview Dreiser qualifies his support of Lindbergh's isolationism.

Mr. Dreiser declared that his father was a typical German, "one who believed in action rather than talk," but the author himself was born in the United States. He went to Russia in 1928 and is an ardent Russophile. He also claims to hate Hitler—and most of his "hymn of hate" was directed against Hitler's most formidable enemy, Britain.

His subject to-morrow night will be "Democracy on the Offensive."

PM Interviews Dreiser to Learn
What He Said in *That* Interview

By George McIntyre

*

PM (New York), 22 September 1942, p. 13.

Before Dreiser left Toronto on the evening of 21 September, a reporter from the liberal New York newspaper PM interviewed him by telephone.

Theodore Dreiser, 71-year-old U. S. author who has been stirring up controversies all his life, was in the middle of a beauty in Toronto last night.

Following a demand by the Toronto City Council for his deportation, and another by Alderman John Innes for his arrest, Justice Minister St. Laurent issued an order enjoining Dreiser from making speeches in Canada and from making statements for publication. The order was issued under the Defense of Canada Act.[1]

Dreiser had gone to Toronto to lecture tonight at a Town Forum. Directors had cancelled the lecture before St. Laurent acted.

The Justice Dept. has not acted on another demand that the novelist be prosecuted.

All this, Dreiser told PM by telephone, was much ado about nothing—that is, nothing except an interview he gave a lady from the Toronto *Telegram*.

The published interview turned out to be a mixture of Dreiser's well-known views on England and some other things he said he didn't remember saying.

---

1. The Defense of Canada Act provided the Canadian government with special powers to curb any effort to undermine the war effort, including the prohibition of specific political parties and the restriction of subversive speech.

"PM Interviews Dreiser to Learn What He Said in *That* Interview," PM (New York), 22 September 1942, p. 13. The horseman is presumed to be a member of the Royal Canadian Mounted Police.

Language Colorful

The *Telegram* interview said, quoting Dreiser:

"Should Russia go down to defeat, I hope the Germans invade England. I would rather see Germans in England than those damn aristocratic horse-riding snobs there now."

Dreiser told PM he didn't remember the colorful language, but acknowledged he had said:

"I would be perfectly happy to see the Germans remove the 15 per cent that is holding down the English people."

The *Telegram* interview went on to quote Dreiser as commenting on "the unbelievable gall and brass of the English, who have done nothing in this war thus far except borrow money, planes and men from the United States."

Dreiser considered that paragraph, and then, repeating the old isolationist chestnut, told PM:

"Well, I can't see that they've done anything else. It has been three years since they told Poland they'd protect her and didn't. They wouldn't join Russia to save Poland. There has been a series of defeats which endanger the whole structure, including England.

"I don't think they've done much of anything, but maybe they have. If they'd care to publish a list of victories, I would applaud it."

Isolationist? Me?

Said the *Telegram* interview, quoting Dreiser again:

"We saved the world for Democracy once and now we're being asked to save it again. After the last war we were accused of being grafters, demanding our pay. This time we must go on our knees, begging for a second front."

Said Dreiser:

"Well?"

Said the interview:

"Churchill has no intention of opening a second front. He's afraid the Communists will rule the world. So he does nothing."

Said Dreiser to PM:

"I didn't say he does nothing. I said he gives no sign of intention to do anything."

Back to the *Telegram* interview:

"Were you an isolationist before Pearl Harbor?

"'Isolationist? What is that?' Mr. Dreiser demanded belligerently.

"'An isolationist is an American who didn't believe this to be our war.'

"'Yes,' said the author in a quieter voice. 'Yes, I didn't think we should get into this war. I'm a profound admirer of the flier Lindbergh and his wife. I follow right along with their ideals.'"

Dreiser told PM the lady missed the tense in that one.

"I said I *had been* an admirer of Lindbergh—before Pearl Harbor," he said. "Like a lot of other persons, including our Army and Navy leaders, I was deceived. They were telling us there was nothing to fear—that a Japanese war would be over in a week.

"So I thought: 'Why get into it if we're out and safe?'

"They were wrong and I was wrong. I'm no isolationist. In self-defense one cannot be."

He does, however, think the *Telegram* created a wrong impression.

"The impression around here is that I'm trying to break up the United Front against Hitler," he said.

"Nothing is farther from the truth. I want Germany defeated, in self-defense and to save the heroic Russian people. It is ridiculous to think I would wish otherwise."

Second American Tragedy
Novelist Dreiser Dodges Interview with Reporters

*

Port Huron Times Herald (Mich.), 24 September 1942, pp. 1–2.

From Toronto Dreiser and Hazel Godwin went west by train to Port Huron, a Michigan city about fifty miles northeast of Detroit and just across the St. Clair River from Canada. Since Dreiser was suffering from a bad cold, they registered (as Mr. and Mrs. Dreiser) in a Port Huron hotel and remained for several days before Miss Godwin was dropped off in Detroit. Dreiser then made his way to Indianapolis, where he rested for a week before returning to Los Angeles.

"I am the No. 1 victim of the four freedoms."[1]

Thus Theodore Dreiser, famed American novelist, explained his plight in a street-corner interview here this morning to climax a hound and hare episode rivaling Hollywood's version of how newspapermen get their story.

For 12 hours preceding Mr. Dreiser's "capture" in front of a Military Street business establishment, this same "No. 1 victim of the four freedoms" had successfully eluded a small battery of reporters in Hotel Harrington, where he and Mrs. Dreiser registered early Tuesday.

The "plot," as the world knows very well, began Monday in Toronto, where the eminent author of "The American Tragedy" and other best-sellers was barred from making public statements or speeches in Canada on a charge that he expressed anti-British views in an interview published by a Toronto newspaper.

The interview to which the much-harried author and lecturer finally yielded here was the first he had granted since his Toronto utterances, as a result of which a speech scheduled to be delivered at a Toronto Town Forum series Tuesday night was cancelled.

---

1. In a January 1941 message to Congress, President Roosevelt announced that the United States should commit itself to the world-wide establishment of four freedoms: freedom of speech and worship and freedom from fear and want. In an agreement reached off the Newfoundland coast in August 1941, Roosevelt and Prime Minister Churchill of England reaffirmed this goal as a postwar aim of their nations.

—Photo by Askar-Shain
Found standing in this dejected pose on a street corner here early today, Theodore Dreiser, noted novelist who authored "An American Tragedy" granted an interview after dodging reporters 12 hours. Dreiser's speeches were barred in Canada because of anti-British views. He thinks the United States is doing "fine" in the prosecution of its war effort.

"Second American Tragedy: Novelist Dreiser Dodges Interview with Reporters," *Port Huron Times Herald* (Michigan), 24 September 1942, pp. 1–2.

Left Toronto Monday

Dreiser was said by employees of a Toronto hotel to have checked out late Monday afternoon. From there on his movements were shrouded in mystery until he and Mrs. Dreiser were finally revealed to be in Port Huron.

Traveling "light," it was disclosed, "T. H. Dreiser and wife" checked in at the local hotel early Tuesday morning after being passed by customs and immigration authorities at the Tunnel depot.

Employees of the hotel saw little of the visiting celebrity and his companion, who were apparently determined to avoid the spotlight. Dreiser wore his incognito well and it was not until he had been in Port Huron nearly two days before his actual identity was learned.

Wednesday morning he was seen eating breakfast in a local restaurant and later in the day he was observed leaving the hotel to visit a nearby dairy bar. He and Mrs. Dreiser returned with a sack of popcorn or peanuts.

The Times Herald was informed Wednesday morning that Dreiser had entered Port Huron by train early Tuesday and that he had left town after a short stopover. Later The Times Herald learned he was registered in the hotel.

Didn't Know

A telephone call to his room on the fourth floor Wednesday afternoon was answered by a woman's voice.

"Mr. Dreiser, please?" asked the reporter.

"Mr. Dreiser!" answered the feminine voice.

"Please," the reporter.

"Why!" quoth the woman's voice. "Is Mr. Dreiser in town? . . . Where? . . . Say, I'd certainly like to meet him."

"Isn't this Mr. Dreiser's room?" came the next question.

"Oh, no, you must be mistaken," the woman's voice said. "Are you sure Mr. Dreiser is in town?"

"Oh, yes," quickly replied the reporter.

"Where did you see him?"

"On the street and eating in a restaurant."

"Well!" said the feminine voice, "there certainly must be some mistake. . . . Are you sure you have the right room? . . . I've never heard of Mr. Dreiser."

The second call brought the same sum and total.

Thereupon Times Herald reporters and a photographer took up their vigil in a room adjacent to the one occupied by "T. H. Dreiser and wife."

This morning Mrs. Dreiser "spoke" to the photographer and one of the reporters, expressing some concern about the presence of a camera.

Her indignation took a physical aspect when she suddenly slammed shut the door of reporter-photographer room and locked it with a key that was in the lock. The reporters were trapped.

While the reporters were waiting to be "rescued" by a bellhop with a pass key, Mr. Dreiser terminated his stay as a guest of the hotel.

The "rescued" reporter and photographer again took up the search.

He Is Found

A few minutes later they "found" a man standing alone at Military and Pine streets. It looked like Mr. Dreiser.

Another reporter also had arrived on the scene, so both approached the man in question.

One reporter extended his hand for the customary handshake upon greeting a prominent figure.

"Mr. Dreiser?"

The man in question kept both hands in his pockets.

"Yes," he replied. "What of it?"

"We learned you were in town," the reporter said. "It's been difficult to reach you for an interview."

"Well, why do you want to interview me?" Dreiser asked. "And why does it require more than one reporter? I used to be a newspaperman myself, you know."

"We wanted to be sure that we didn't miss you," the reporter replied. "You've been rather hard to locate since you left Canada the other day."

"Well, what do you want with me?" Dreiser asked.

"We'd like to have your comment on the treatment you received in Canada."

Says Britain Holding Back

"There isn't much I would comment," Dreiser said. "I stated I would rather see the Germans in England than to have England ruled by that aristocratic 15 per cent that are now ruling there."

"You feel that England and the United States are not contributing as much to Russia in this war as they should?" Dreiser was asked.

"I think the United States is doing very well," the author returned. "But I don't think Great Britain is doing a damned thing."

Dreiser expressed the view that England is not aiding Russia to the full extent of its ability because it wants Germany to win the war. He said he believes the ruling class of England is fearful that if Russia is victorious the Communist ideal will spread over the entire world. The Communist ideal, he said, is designed for the benefit of the greatest number of people.

"There have been some very uncomplimentary comments in the press on the remarks you made in Canada," the reporter said.

"O, I don't give a damn about those comments," Dreiser said. "I've been getting them all my life. They don't worry me a damned bit."

"What do you think about the Canadian ideal of freedom of speech, Mr. Dreiser?"

"I am the No. 1 victim of the four freedoms," Dreiser replied bitterly, referring to the freedoms listed in the famed Atlantic charter drawn up by President Roosevelt and Prime Minister Churchill of England.

The victim of the "second American tragedy" had little comment on the statement he made to the Toronto newspaper, in which he was quoted as saying:

"I would rather see the Germans in England than those damned aristocratic, horse-riding snobs there now. The English have done nothing in this war thus far except borrow money, planes and men from the United States. They stay at home and do nothing. They are lousy."

Dreiser asked a few questions about Port Huron, which, he said, he had not visited before.

"Is there a town there across the river?" he asked, nodding in the direction of Sarnia.

"Yes, Mr. Dreiser," the second reporter replied. "That's Sarnia—one of the Canadian towns that contributed a lot of men to the Dieppe attack."[2]

"Well," the 71-year-old writer said caustically, "those people over there must be proud of England, mustn't they?"

After posing for a photograph, Dreiser said he planned to leave Port Huron today for Detroit. He said he will remain in Detroit for a short time before going to Indianapolis, Ind., to "visit some friends." From Indianapolis he will go to his home in Los Angeles, he stated.

"Are you traveling alone?" Dreiser was asked.

"Yes," was the reply. "I'm alone."

Throughout his brilliant career as a writer, traveler and lecturer, Theodore Dreiser has been more or less of a "stormy petrel" in the world of letters. As a writer who has gained an international reputation, he is known as one of the first American realists of the present century. He gained his lofty perch in the literary world through a tempest of critical derision.

His newspaper career carried him from his birthplace in Terre Haute, Ind., to Chicago, St. Louis and New York.

It was in St. Louis where he first tried his hand at writing. In New York he completed his first recognized novel, "Sister Carrie," in the meantime working as a magazine writer and editor.

2. For the Dieppe raid, see p. 313, n. 1.

"An American Tragedy" Best

When his second novel, "Jennie Gerhardt," was published in 1911, Dreiser was considered by some as a menace to the moral standards of the country.

Probably his more famous work is "An American Tragedy" which was published in 1925. His latest book, "America is Worth Saving," was published last year.

Other Dreiser books include: "The Financier" and "The Titan," which with "The 'Genius'" form a trilogy; "A Traveler at Forty," "Plays of Natural and Supernatural," "A Hoosier Holiday," "Free and Other Stories," "Twelve Men," "The Hand of the Potter," "Hey Rub-a-Dub-Dub," "A Book about Myself," "The Color of a Great City," "Moods, Cadenced and Declaimed," "Chains," "Dreiser Looks at Russia," "A Gallery of Women," "My City," "Epitaph," "Dawn," "Tragic America," "Thoreau," and "Home."[3]

Born in Terre Haute of German parents, Dreiser was educated in the public schools of Warsaw, Ind., and in Indiana University. He organized the National Child Rescue campaign in 1907.[4]

3. *The "Genius"* is not a volume in the Cowperwood Trilogy; "Home" is a short poem in Dreiser's poetry collection *Moods, Philosophical and Emotional (Cadenced and Declaimed)* (1935).

4. While the editor of the *Delineator*, Dreiser in 1907 organized a campaign to place orphaned children in foster homes. The campaign attracted national attention and continued throughout his editorship.

Theodore Dreiser Talks to a Friend

BY ESTHER MCCOY

*

People's World (San Francisco), 3 January 1946, p. 1.

Esther McCoy (1904–89) worked for Dreiser as a secretary and researcher on several occasions both in New York and Los Angeles after their initial association in 1927. In the early 1940s she married Berkeley Tobey, a Hollywood screenwriter who shared her communist sympathies, and the Tobeys and Dreisers often saw each other during Dreiser's final Los Angeles years. Since Dreiser had died on 28 December 1945, McCoy's recollection of her various discussions with Dreiser after he joined the Communist Party in July 1945 was no doubt written for the *People's World*, the West Coast organ of the Communist Party, in response to his death.

Los Angeles, Jan. 2.—Just after Theodore Dreiser joined the Communist Party he was showing me a magazine that he edited in 1894.

It was a trade magazine got out by a music publisher, and you might have supposed that the promising young editor would have written an editorial slanted toward the people who would read it. No. He wrote on the flagrant inequities in Russia and predicted the early overthrow of the Czars.[1]

"But," he said in explanation, "you can't get the kind of education I had without developing. I shined stoves and drove a laundry wagon and collected for a time-payment house. I saw a lot then, and when I began to work for newspapers I got a first-hand view of the way capitalists treated the people."

This work was in the Chicago of Multimillionaire Yerkes, the McCormick strike and Haymarket riots—a Chicago overripe with terrorism and corruption, with violent contrasts between wealth and squalor.[2]

1. Although Dreiser edited the cited magazine, *Ev'ry Month*, from October 1895 to August 1897, no "editorial" of this description has been found in the magazine for this period. Dreiser, however, may be referring to the caption of a photograph of Czar Nicholas II that appeared in the magazine's December 1896 issue. The caption describes the czar as "a menace to civilization" and the product of an "iniquitous inheritance system."

2. Dreiser held a number of odd jobs in Chicago from the summer of 1887 to the summer

He went often to interview Yerkes on his plans for Chicago, and later he wrote a trilogy based on his life—"The Financier," "The Titan," and the recently completed third volume, "The Stoic." He found in Yerkes what he later found in Woolworth, an insatiable hunger for money and power.[3]

"And when they got it they didn't know what to do with it," he said.

"I always asked millionaires when I interviewed them—and I've interviewed nearly all the big ones—why they didn't hand back more to the people who worked for them in wages and benefits, since they couldn't use beyond a certain amount anyway. Not one of them had the imagination to see it."

From Chicago to St. Louis to Pittsburgh he covered strikes—streetcar, steel, many others—and he began to see that Chicago was no different from other cities in its brutalities and denial of human rights.[4] And finally when he got to New York and saw the last word in contrast between idleness and drudgery he was ready to say something.

"I was glad when I was fired from The World.[5] There was a fight in one of the bars of the big hotels between two society 'names.' The city editor told me not to come back if I didn't get it."

Dreiser didn't want to get the story. Because he knew there was another story back of it that he couldn't write.

He had a sixth sense—built-in—that got him to the roots of things.

It was the thing that sent Dreiser off on endless missions.

He would get a telephone call at night asking him to come to some town where there was a strike. Once there was a steel strike where a striker was killed. The body was hidden, because the steel company thought that a funeral at the time would focus attention on the injustices against which the workers were striking. The strike committee called Dreiser to come up and help them find the body of their dead comrade. He came.

---

of 1889 and then again from the summer of 1890 to mid-1892, when he became a reporter for the *Chicago Globe*. There was a violent strike at the McCormick Harvesting Machine Company plant in the spring of 1886; the Haymarket Riot, in which several policemen were killed by a bombing at an anarchist protest meeting and during the subsequent melee, occurred on 4 May 1886. Charles T. Yerkes (1837–1905) arrived in Chicago in 1881 and soon began acquiring streetcar and gas franchises, often through the corruption of public officials.

3. Dreiser may have interviewed Yerkes while he was a reporter for the *Globe*, between June and November 1892, but no published interviews have been identified. Frank W. Woolworth (see also p. 22, n. 6) created a large fortune by aggressively popularizing the "five-and-ten-cent store" throughout the country.

4. Dreiser refers to the period between October 1892 and November 1894, when he was a reporter in St. Louis, Toledo, and Pittsburgh. His only extant strike reporting of this period is that of a Toledo streetcar strike in late March 1894, an event on which he drew for his account of Hurstwood's participation in a Brooklyn car strike in *Sister Carrie*.

5. This occurred in February or March 1895.

He walked into the offices of the local newspaper. They took his hand and said, "Mr. Dreiser, this is an honor," but when they heard what he had come for they said, "You've worked on a newspaper, Mr. Dreiser. You know how it goes."

Dreiser hammered away at them until they actually wrote something about the missing body.

Then he went to the local ministers and said, "This is your business, isn't it? The man is dead. The authorities won't give up the body to the widow." And he hammered at them until they began to see that the widow's rights were their concern.[6]

Down to Harlan County

When he went down to Harlan County in 1931 it was the same thing. He went up to the mine owners and asked them questions. There was a hearing and he hammered away at the mine owners.[7]

Little papers all over the country talked about Dreiser being there and asked editorially: "What business is it of his?"

But it was his business.

In 1932 Mooney was his business. And the Red squad in Los Angeles was his business.[8] He was always asking officials, "By what right do you do this?"

Spain was his business. He went to Spain and watched the Loyalist wounded being loaded into open coal cars to be shipped into France. And later in Paris at a meeting when it became obvious that he was going to speak honestly about the rape of Spain, an attempt was made to sidetrack him. They pushed his place further back on the program until the meeting began to break up. He got up and walked to the front of the platform and said "Wait! I've got something to say about Spain," and they came back and waited.[9]

He said the only thing that day that was said about what was really happening in Spain, and the papers printed it.

There were always people who didn't want him to talk, because he was too forthright. But when he wanted to talk he talked. He went back home and went to Roosevelt and talked to him about Spain. He told him about

6. This incident has not been identified.

7. For Dreiser and Harlan, see p. 245, headnote.

8. For Dreiser and Tom Mooney, see p. 212, n. 8; for Dreiser and the Los Angeles Red Squad, see p. 264, n. 4.

9. Helen Dreiser also relates this incident about Dreiser's July 1938 speech at the Paris meeting of the International Association of Writers for the Defense of Culture; see her memoir *My Life with Dreiser* (Cleveland: World, 1951), 260.

the sickness among the people, and the lack of soap. "I can get soap for you," Roosevelt said. "First get a committee."[10]

Dreiser spent weeks trying to get a committee to save Spain. He went up to doors of the great and came away empty handed. They didn't want to fight fascism. They didn't want to fight anything. They wanted their profits.

"Why did you join the Communist Party?" I asked.

"I've always been a Communist. Joining was a mere formality," he said.[11] "What I saw in the Soviet Union in 1928 was enough to convince me that the only answer is a people's government. I've never wavered in my belief in the Soviet Union. The way they fought the Germans was only as a great united people could fight. I'm glad to identify myself with that spirit."

10. Dreiser visited Barcelona in August 1938 after giving his speech in Paris. On his return to the United States, he met with Roosevelt on 7 September to plea for lifting the American embargo on trade with Spain so that food and supplies could be sent to the Loyalists. Roosevelt suggested the formation of a committee independent of the government for that purpose, but Dreiser's efforts to form a Spanish relief committee were largely unsuccessful.

11. In fact, Dreiser was turned down for membership in the party in early 1932 by its then head, Earl Browder, who considered Dreiser's beliefs to be unreliable. It was only in mid-1945 that he again applied for membership and was accepted.

HISTORICAL COMMENTARY

Dreiser took a dim view of interviews during the last decade and a half of his career, when he often seized on the forum offered by an interview to express, with increasing vehemence, his contempt for such institutions and groups as the Catholic Church, the courts, the American political system, and almost every other facet of American civil and economic life. These sensationalistic attacks by a (and perhaps *the*) major American writer of the period were of course newsworthy, but to almost all but left-wing journals they were also troublesome in their inflammatory outspokenness, and Dreiser claimed that the interviews as published modified or completely suppressed his views. "All newspaper interviews are stupid" (218),* he helpfully announced to a *New York Herald Tribune* reporter in July 1930 at the onset of their interview. "For years I have not seen one that is worth anything. I will bet you $10 that you cannot get into your paper the things I am going to say." In August 1936 he told a French reporter who was interviewing him for *Les Nouvelles Littéraires*, "I've given a multitude of interviews to the *New York Times,* to the *Herald Tribune,* to other newspapers; every time I happened to say anything significant, it was glossed over" (290). There is apparently considerable truth to Dreiser's perception that his interviews of this period were subjected to censorship. For example, in December 1933 the reporter Allan Chase interviewed Dreiser for the Central Press newspaper syndicate, but as Chase informed Dreiser, the interview never appeared because his editors had found some of Dreiser's remarks "unacceptable."[1]

That Dreiser's interviews from this time were occasionally censored does not diminish their importance in documenting one of the most significant careers in American literary history. Indeed, the censorship—both its causes and nature—is itself a valuable commentary on the social climate of the moment. Moreover, despite his late complaint about the suppression of his beliefs, Dreiser welcomed and often brilliantly used the interview as a form of self-expression and self-advancement throughout his career. His over 180 interviews during a more than forty-year period fully reveal his experience, ideas, and concerns from the turn of the century to the close of World War II and thus serve as an invaluable repository of information about both Dreiser himself and many dimensions of his era. Bruce Crawford, an admirer

*References to interviews are to the page numbers in this volume.
1. See the headnote (268) to Chase's interview in this volume.

and left-wing colleague of Dreiser, interviewed him in November 1935 and commented: "Yes, he is a dinosaur of his period, or a literary mastodon— it's so easy to apply terms of vastness to him—whose bones will be something for coming generations to marvel at. Indeed, future historians, when they dig into the debris of American civilization of the early twentieth century, doubtless will unearth great hunks of Dreiser" (286). To briefly pursue Crawford's somewhat lugubrious metaphor, the "great hunks of Dreiser" that his interviews constitute do indeed offer rich insight into the nature of his civilization.

* * *

Although the interview appears occasionally in early eighteenth-century journalism, its full possibilities were not exploited until the 1830s, when James Gordon Bennett, the editor of the *New York Herald,* popularized it as a form of sensationalistic newspaper reporting involving celebrity criminals. By the 1870s, however, it was fully established both in England and America as an instrument of popular journalism for reporting the ideas and activities of prominent individuals of all kinds; by the early twentieth century it had become a staple of the literary sections commonly found in the large Saturday or Sunday editions.

The interview is an extremely flexible literary form. It can be narrowly focused (and thus often brief), with little sense of its material setting—that is, of a time and place or the physical presence and appearance of interviewer and interviewee. It can also, however, take on some of the character of a one-act play. The interviewer sets the scene carefully and then engages the interviewee in a lengthy dialogue in which the transmitted information about the interviewee's career, enthusiasms, and current projects constitutes both a concise review and an interpretation of his or her life and work.

Dreiser's interviews partake of this flexibility, though they also have a distinctive quality derived from the distinctive character of his life and interests. Of course, his current preoccupations sometimes controlled the direction of the interview, whatever the interviewer's initial intent. In addition, interviews conducted in relation to a specific event in Dreiser's life—his travels, for example, or his participation in an act of social protest—are usually confined entirely to that event. Nonetheless, when a sympathetic individual interviewed Dreiser at length, the published result often took a typical shape. After noting the circumstances of the setting of the interview, the interviewer will ask a question that leads Dreiser into an account of his life and work in which he stresses his early hardships in Indiana and Chicago, tells of his years as a reporter and his efforts to become a writer (almost always including the *Sister Carrie* suppression story), and closes with a statement of his determination to maintain his career in the direction he wishes, whatever the consequences. Such almost ritualistic surveys (which nevertheless often contain surprisingly fresh details not available elsewhere)[2] serve the important purpose of establishing Dreiser's authenticity: he has come out of the trenches, so to speak, and thus his beliefs, as expressed in his works and in the interview at hand, are those of someone who has experienced the difficulties of American life—both as an individual in general and as a writer in particular—and can write and speak about them with insight and authority.

The heart of the interview, in which Dreiser expounds on an issue of the moment, follows the opening biographical account. Early in his career this will usually be a forthcoming book; later, it will frequently be a current political or social event. Often, however, the interview will have a free-flowing associational center and range from the nature of a recent book to Dreiser's likes and dislikes and then to such themes as the tragic nature of life, the force of the sex drive, or a specific issue related to one of these interests.

Of course, an interview is written by the interviewer and inevitably reflects his or her attitudes, knowledge, and capability. Few of those interviewing Dreiser are today commonly known, but some had considerable status as authors or journalists in their own time. Montrose J. Moses, for example, was a critic and scholar of the American drama, and Robert van Gelder wrote regularly on books for the *New York Times*. Others, such as Albert Mordell, Burton Rascoe, Bruce Crawford, and Esther McCoy, were well-known literary or political radicals. The great majority of those interviewing Dreiser, however, especially for newspapers outside large metropolitan areas, were garden-variety working journalists, many of whom even lacked a byline. During Dreiser's early career most journalists rendered his beliefs with evident sympathy. He was then not a literary lion but a struggling writer seeking the freedom to speak truthfully in his works, and most reporters no doubt found it difficult not to identify with him to some degree. In his later career, however, when he had become rich and famous with the great success of *An American Tragedy,* and especially after 1930, when he openly espoused far-left causes, the tone stiffens and indeed sometimes becomes derisive. His beliefs are those of the "Sage of Manhattan" (223) and "St. Theodore" (224), an interviewer noted, and he is portrayed as declaiming against American injustice from an expensive hotel room with a glass of scotch in his hand (260).

---

2. For example, see Dreiser's accounts of losing his Catholic faith (146) and his admiration for the work of Havelock Ellis, an English scholar who wrote on sexual subjects (117).

Although Dreiser welcomed interviews during his early career, he became wary later—except when he had a specific political belief or cause to promulgate—and developed a strategy to avoid them. Bessie K. Roberts, who interviewed him in February 1930, noted, "It is not easy to gain access to the writer. He feels that he cannot afford to waste his time on futile interviews. They must look promising. They are arranged through his publisher, Horace Liveright, to whom one must submit questions. If the questions strike his fancy the interview is granted" (190). Dreiser apparently employed another basis for accepting an interview, one that functioned throughout his career: the reporter's gender. In a period when relatively few journalists were female, twenty-seven of Dreiser's interviews were by women. Several of these are among his best—those by Jean West Maury in 1927 and Vivian Richardson in 1930, for example—as a capable journalist turned Dreiser's personal engagement in the moment into an opportunity for an especially lengthy and self-revelatory interview. On other occasions, however, Dreiser's aggressive interest in a woman reporter made the occasion tense and edgy. Rose Feld, who interviewed him for the *New York Times Book Review* in 1923, recalled the event many years later for Dreiser's biographer W. A. Swanberg: "He asked me very personal questions. . . . There was an air of tension about him. I could see that if I gave him the slightest encouragement the situation could grow embarrassing. I adopted an attitude of severest reserve."[3]

The sites of Dreiser interviews correspond to his places of abode and his travels. He is interviewed in his sparse Greenwich Village flats of the late 1910s and early 1920s, in his Fifty-seventh Street luxury apartment and on his country estate during the late 1920s and early 1930s, and in hotel rooms on his journeys to the Far West, to the coal mining area of Kentucky, and to Europe. On one notable occasion Isaac Goldberg interviewed him during a cold automobile ride through Brooklyn in an open car; on another, a pair of persistent Port Huron, Michigan, reporters trapped him on a street after he had eluded them in his hotel. In their descriptions of interview sites, the interviews from the early 1930s often introduce the disparity between his plush and beautifully decorated Fifty-seventh Street apartment and his radical views on the unequal apportionment of wealth in America. Most reporters permitted the disparity to speak for itself, although a few could not help an editorial comment, as when an interviewer in July 1930 remarked that Dreiser "scolds as any Isaiah, although, the Lord knows, he himself is well-heeled with a millionaire's town place, a broad farm in the Croton neighborhood, motor cars and bonds in the safe deposit box" (224).

3. See the headnote (88) to Feld's interview. Dreiser appears to have sought—or conducted—affairs with Berenice Skidelsky (who interviewed him in 1918 and 1920) and Sulamith Ish-Kishor (who interviewed him in 1929).

Another troublesome aspect for some reporters was the frequent presence of Helen Richardson. She and Dreiser had met in 1919 and lived together sporadically thereafter, although they did not marry until 1944. Helen
is therefore sometimes called "Mrs. Dreiser" in interviews, even though the
"real" Mrs. Dreiser—Dreiser's first wife, Sara, whom he never divorced—
lived until 1942. And occasionally there is a "Mrs. Dreiser" who is neither
Helen nor Sara.

Of course, Dreiser himself was the principal focus of interviewers. They
often noted his height, stoop, and large or "leonine" head, but undoubtedly
the characteristic that most caught their attention was his lifelong habit of
constantly folding and unfolding a linen handkerchief. (In later years he
occasionally substituted paper handkerchiefs.) Some attributed this habit
to nervousness; others saw it as an aid to thinking. In addition, interviewers often commented on the seeming disparity between Dreiser's calm de-
meanor and "level, impersonal tone" on the one hand and his "bitter" words
on the other (236). The interviewer Raymond Dannenbaum posited a relationship between Dreiser's handkerchief manipulation and his voice when
he commented: "I noticed that although he spoke vehemently but quietly,
and seemed to possess great repose, nevertheless his mind and body were
taut. The tension expressed itself when he took out a fresh white handkerchief, relieved it of its iron folds, and meticulously folded it into long tucks,
of which eventually he devised an accordionlike structure" (209). Whatever the degree of nervous tension that Dreiser brought to an interview, he
was usually courteous during the event itself and on occasion even attempted
a humorous remark. Exceptions to his willingness to play along with the interview convention of a polite conversation occurred principally in his later
years, especially when an interview was conducted by a group of reporters
and he was expressing beliefs that many in the group found unacceptable.
On such occasions, most clearly so in Toronto in 1942, he appears to have
been goaded by the tone of the questions (as well as, perhaps, by alcohol)
into gross overstatements of his views.

Two recurrent motifs in Dreiser's interviews were his homage to his literary mentors Balzac, Hardy, and Dostoyevsky, which he expressed in early
interviews, and his almost inevitable retelling of the suppression of *Sister
Carrie* in 1900 by its publisher, Doubleday, Page and Company. Both served
important roles in Dreiser's fashioning of his public image and thus demanded emphasis through repetition. Often attacked in the years before *An
American Tragedy* for the sexual sensationalism of his fiction, Dreiser sought
to place himself in the tradition of nineteenth-century European tragic realism rather than that of Zolaesque naturalism.

Dreiser never tired of telling his somewhat embroidered version of the

Sister Carrie suppression story. It is the subject of his first recorded interview, in January 1902,[4] and he tells it yet again, after many intervening recountings, during his last important interview on literary subjects, in March 1941. The story played an obvious role in Dreiser's metastory, that is, his overarching vision of himself as a writer who had fought a lifelong and occasionally losing battle against the puritanism and duplicity of the American publishing scene in an effort to express a truthful fiction. As he told Otis Notman of the *New York Times* in June 1907, in an interview held in conjunction with the republication of *Sister Carrie*, "I have had my share of the difficulties and discouragements that fall to the lot of most men. . . . I look into my own life and I realize that each human life is a similar tragedy" (5–6).

Dreiser had been deeply hurt by the suppression of *Sister Carrie*, but repeatedly retelling the story of Doubleday's perfidy no doubt helped relieve some of this pain. As he remarked to Robert van Gelder in 1941, many of those engaged in the suppression later admitted that they had been wrong in their actions. And as *Sister Carrie* rose to the stature of an American literary classic, the story became at once a celebration of its author and a condemnation of his literary and social world, two themes that Dreiser (and perhaps most authors in a similar situation) found hard to resist expressing through the retellings.

* * *

Dreiser's interviews are an invaluable source of information about his life, work, and times. On the most obvious level, they record, with an immediacy of reaction often not available elsewhere, his response to many of the significant events of early twentieth-century American life, especially if the interviews either preceded or followed his participation in these events. His two-month trip to Russia in late 1927 and early 1928, for example, reflects the fascination with which many American leftists of the period viewed communism, his own initial mix of skepticism toward and endorsement of its Russian version, and his swift recognition of the use he could make of Soviet life to flay American society for its inadequacies. Many of Dreiser's interviews from the 1930s occurred before, during, and after his frequent journeys across the country during this period of nationwide hardship and poverty. Local reporters interviewing a literary lion usually wanted to talk about lit-

4. Richard Lingeman, in his *Theodore Dreiser: At the Gates of the City (1871–1907)* (New York: Putnam, 1986), 214, 439, identifies as an interview a brief press release, distributed on 7 August 1898 by the McClure Syndicate, in which a forthcoming book of poems by Dreiser is discussed. However, the clipping of the release among the Dreiser papers in the Lilly Library, Indiana University, reveals that though it may be based on an interview with Dreiser, he is never quoted directly. The interview of 26 January 1902 therefore appears to be Dreiser's first extant interview.

erature, but Dreiser almost always turned the interview into a vehicle for his bitter condemnation of the American political and economic scene. In early November 1931 Dreiser received national attention, and was frequently interviewed, when he led a group of left-wing writers who journeyed to Harlan, Kentucky ("Bloody Harlan," as it was already called), to investigate the violent suppression of efforts to organize the area's coal workers. Dreiser's prominence and the committee's dramatic and sometimes comic experiences in Harlan (Dreiser was charged with adultery and produced an unlikely alibi)[5] heralded the social-activist roles that writers were to play throughout the decade. Dreiser's last journey to receive major news reports and interviews was his ill-fated September 1942 trip to Toronto to give a lecture. In the midst of the war, with Canada a staunch ally of England, an interviewer baited Dreiser into expressing his contempt for the English.

Dreiser's interviews also reflect many of his permanent interests in ways that add considerably to our understanding of their role in his thought. The Jews constituted one such subject. Four interviews, all in Jewish journals, reflect both Dreiser's interest in the "Jewish problem" and the interest of the Jewish community in Dreiser.[6] *The Hand of the Potter,* his play dealing sympathetically with East Side Jewish life, had been published in 1919. In September 1933, however, the *American Spectator* published the proceedings of a much noted "Editorial Conference" on the Jews in which Dreiser, with Hitler newly seated as Germany's chancellor, charged Jews with excessive sharpness in their commercial and professional dealings. Nonetheless, until the latter event the Jewish press sought out Dreiser. As a writer with immigrant roots whose subject was often the urban working class, he was viewed as someone who could identify with the Jewish experience in America.

Indeed, when speaking with Jewish reporters Dreiser for the most part expressed admiration for the Jews' love of art, their industriousness, and their overall contribution to the American scene. Present as well, however, is his occasional participation in the conventional stereotypes of the Jew: "natural-born traders" (172), Jews are often clannish, over-competitive, and over-sensitive to criticism. By the early 1930s, as is clear from Dreiser's use of similar stereotypes elsewhere in his interviews,[7] his difficulties with Jewish-owned film studios and publishing firms during the late 1920s and early 1930s had caused him to harden prejudices perhaps unconsciously held into the explicit and firm positions expressed in the *American Spectator* article.[8]

---

5. See pp. 253–55.

6. The four interviews can be found on pp. 69–70, 95–97, 171–75, and 208–14.

7. See Dreiser's comments during the 1930s on "pants pressers" (235) and "some fellows from Bessarabia and Galicia" (244).

8. In fact, Dreiser's reputation as an anti-Semite stemmed less from the *American Spectator* article than from the more extreme positions he later expressed in letters to Hutchins

Dreiser's interviews also reveal his active interest not only in contemporary fiction and philosophy but in the plays, films, art, and music of his time. An active theatergoer all his life following his stint as a drama critic for the *St. Louis Globe-Democrat* in 1893, Dreiser comments frequently on the plays that interest him and, less frequently but often pointedly, on current music and art. Of particular interest are his comments on films and the film industry from the early 1920s (when he lived in Los Angeles for several years) until his death, a period in which movies came to dominate American popular art. Dreiser initially felt only contempt for movies and everything connected with them, including Los Angeles itself, a contempt confirmed and strengthened by his quarrel with Paramount in 1931 over its film of *An American Tragedy*. By the mid-1930s, however, he was willing to accept the movies both as a major force in popular culture and as a significant art form; indeed, he increasingly sought to have his own work appear in film form.

* * *

Throughout all his interviews Dreiser often recounted his life history, emphasizing his struggles to gain acceptance and success. In addition, he was always eager to discuss a recent or forthcoming publication. Some of his most informative comments on the sources and themes of such works as *Jennie Gerhardt*, *The Financier*, and *An American Tragedy* occur in interviews he gave around the time they appeared in print. And finally, because Dreiser seldom viewed an interview as merely a friendly chat about trivial matters, his interviews represent trenchantly and in detail what was on his mind at the time.

During his early career, from shortly after *Sister Carrie* came out until roughly the mid-1910s, Dreiser's interviews provide rich insights into both his philosophic beliefs and the fictional aesthetic he believed could best express them. In his first recorded interview, in January 1902, Dreiser stated that he wished to write about "every phase of life from a philosophical standpoint" (4). As he explained in later interviews from this period, he wrote about individuals' tragic struggles to overcome the forces arrayed against them, by which he meant such conditions as the vast differences in innate capability, the powerful role of wealth and class in affecting opportunity, and the ineffable play of chance in determining the outcome of an event.[9] To Dreiser, this vibrant center of life—the individual's often fruitless struggle for survival or success—was "intensely interesting" (6). As he explained in November 1911 in one of his most significant interviews of the period, "Now Comes

Hapgood. Hapgood questioned Dreiser about his attitude toward the Jews after he had read the article and then published this correspondence as "Is Dreiser Anti-Semitic?" *Nation* 140 (17 Apr. 1935): 436–38.

9. See in particular the interviews of 15 June 1907 (5–6), 12 November 1911 (19–23), and 7 December 1913 (41–44).

Author Theodore Dreiser . . . ," Jennie Gerhardt's tragic life does not reflect a pessimistic philosophy: "I don't feel any the less happy about life on account of it. Life interests me intensely for that very reason. It is dramatic. It is more thrilling than the most gorgeous spectacle that man ever planned" (11).

Dreiser viewed human sexuality as inseparable from both the tragedy and the beauty of the spectacle of life. His initial interviews show him defending his depiction of the power of desire in human affairs, but he soon moved, in an interview of 15 November 1911, to the baldly stated claim that "the keynote in a man's or a woman's life is to be found in sex relations" (16). He went on to state that "writing a realistic novel without bringing in sex relations is like trying to build a serviceable house without doors or windows" (16), a comment that reveals the link between his beliefs and a realistic or naturalistic form of expression. According to Dreiser, the proper subject matter and theme of the American novel in the early twentieth century consisted above all in a depiction of humans as sexual beings living often desperate lives within a great city in an increasingly industrialized society. Dreiser openly contrasted fiction of this kind with that of the foremost realist of the time, William Dean Howells. Howells's novels, he argued, are "still under the handicap of American prudery" (16) and do not depict the "modern conditions" of our "big financial combinations" and "tremendous industrial developments" (16). In these and similar remarks in his interviews from 1911 to 1915, Dreiser not only marked the decline of the Howellsian aesthetic that had dominated discussions of American realism for three decades but also laid the groundwork both for twentieth-century American literary naturalism in general and, more specifically, for his own centrality in the movement.

The New York Society for the Suppression of Vice banned *The "Genius"* in 1916, an event that, as the interviews show, spurred Dreiser's nearly decade-long preoccupation with the issue of artistic freedom. In many of his interviews dealing with censorship, he went on to attack the underlying aspects of American culture that permitted it to occur. With respect to this issue Dreiser no doubt was influenced by H. L. Mencken, his close friend and ally in the period's culture wars. Like Mencken, he identified as "puritanism" those strains in American society that, because of a fear of human nature, wished to suppress free expression in life and art. The country, Dreiser stated as early as 1914, was close to living in "actual barbarism" insofar as most Americans discarded "the opinions of those at the highest part of the intellectual scale for the prejudices and stupidity of the multitude" (46).[10]

---

10. Dreiser despised both American mass taste and puritanism, believing the former often to be responsible for outbreaks of the latter. In an interview of May 1929 he attacked "the people who put on sordid, cheap shows, and who publish trashy magazines, books and papers, and the ignorant ones who patronize the obscene shows and buy the trashy 'art' magazines" (183). They

It should be clear, however, that although Dreiser often emphasized the importance of sexual themes in realistic novels during the period when he was leading the revolt against a Howellsian reticence in this area, his later interviews reveal a position roughly similar to Howells's call for the principle of proportion in the depiction of sex in fiction. In December 1923, for example, he told an interviewer, "You can't write a novel of realism and let sex out of the picture even as you can't write a novel full of sex and call it realism" (92). He expanded on this theme later in the same interview: "Many of the younger writers disgusted with this sniveling hypocrisy have swung to the other extreme and do nothing but talk sex from cover to cover. I don't know which is worse. Neither is the truth. Neither is giving the subject its real value in life" (93).

As the 1910s shaded into the 1920s, Dreiser's interviews also begin to reflect his shift toward radical political and economic positions. The dismay caused by the collapse of war idealism during the Versailles Treaty negotiations, the vast fortunes accumulated during and after the war, and the apparent success of the Bolshevik Revolution—these and other disturbing events of the period influenced Dreiser and many other writers to focus increasingly on specific shortcomings of the American capitalist system. Speaking to an interviewer in June 1919, in a statement whose strident absolutist tone anticipates many more to come, Dreiser insisted that the "ordinary man is forced to think and act as the moneyed class of the nation see fit" (64).

For several years after the success of *An American Tragedy*, Dreiser was frequently interviewed on the sources and themes of the novel. He seized on these opportunities to attack the destructive illusion that the United States is a nation of social and political equality. With the onset of the Depression, however, Dreiser shifted his focus; whereas earlier he had been willing to talk about his books in social terms, he was now unwilling to talk about anything except the economic disaster area that America had become. "I am glad this is not about books," he told an interviewer in May 1930. "I am weary of talking books" (198). What he wished to talk about instead was either a current instance of social injustice—the imprisonment of the labor leader Tom Mooney, for example, or the condition of the Harlan miners—or the most recent examples of the outrages perpetuated on the American people by trusts and corporations, which controlled government through their great wealth. In the face of this power, he insisted again and again, the people were being herded into poverty and intellectual slavery, with dissent severely punished. Their only recourse was to revolt.

"are the ones," he claimed, "who bring about censorship" (183) by offending the puritans in American culture, who then attempt to suppress both meretricious and high art.

Not surprisingly, given his often-expressed radical beliefs, Dreiser was repeatedly asked, especially after his trip to the Soviet Union in late 1927 and continuing until his death, whether he was a communist. (He often volunteered this information even when not asked.) He usually answered that he supported communist tactics and beliefs but did not think that the Soviet version of communism (by which he meant principally the absolute authority of the state) would work in America. Nevertheless, on occasion he did flatly ally himself with communism, with little qualification. In August 1934 he told an interviewer that he was "a convinced communist" who believed in "a complete transfer of power and ownership from the capitalists to the workingmen" (280).

During the early 1930s such sentiments were of course common among the American left in response to the seemingly worldwide collapse of capitalist economies. By the late 1930s and early 1940s, however, Dreiser's support of the Communist Party's position in international matters caused him to be increasingly isolated from the great number of radical writers and artists who had left the party in reaction to the Stalinist purge trials, the Nazi-Soviet Pact, and the Soviet invasion of Finland. Thus, during the period between the Nazi-Soviet Pact of August 1939 and the German invasion of Russia in June 1941, when almost all Americans had come to recognize the danger that Nazi Germany posed to the world, Dreiser vehemently endorsed the party line that "imperialistic" France and England (302) were a greater threat to the Soviet Union than was Germany. Combined with his long-standing dislike of the English, this conviction produced bizarre comments; for example, in an interview of February 1941, he rhetorically inquired, "Does anyone really think there is less Hitlerism in the British Empire than in Nazi Germany?" (304). It is little wonder that reporters interviewing Dreiser following America's entrance into the war generally confined the conversation to noncontroversial subjects.

From the publication of *An American Tragedy* in 1925 to his death, Dreiser was heavily engaged in constructing a philosophical system. During much of the 1930s, when not speaking or writing on social topics, he worked on a book of speculative philosophy dealing with the nature of all life. Given the occasion—a return from a stay at a biological research station, for example, or one of his numerous birthday interviews of the decade—Dreiser frequently introduced this concern into interviews. Because of the needs of journalism, the interviews often provide accounts of his philosophical ideas more tersely and piquantly stated than are those in his published writings on the subject. "I believe that life is a mechanical phenomenon, that men are mechanical beings," he told an interviewer in August 1936. He continued: "I don't think of myself as an individual, not more than anyone else.

This has always amused me: how did men manage to set themselves up as individuals? I am part of a flock of birds. No flock, no birds" (291). Or, as he told another interviewer in February 1938, after recounting some of the inequities most men face: "If there is a criminal in all this, it is nature. Life is the crook, if there is one. For life is the author of every drama, tragedy, dream or eulogy that has ever appeared. There is no other author; we are fountain pens in some big hand" (294).

In several of the interviews in which Dreiser announced that humans are "the plaything[s] of blind and implacable fates" (132), he also displayed a faith in progress by discussing the efforts that he and others were making to improve contemporary social conditions. Dreiser's ability to express both attitudes in the same interview—as he did with a French interviewer in August 1936—indicates that he did not find them incompatible. Indeed, he never had. As his interviews from 1911 onward reveal, he never perceived an incongruity in responding positively to the need for social change while simultaneously accepting the premise that the individual is powerless in the face of the great natural and social forces governing all existence. What differed as time passed was his more pronounced views in both areas—the final evolution of his beliefs into communism and mechanism—and therefore the more obvious evidence of contradiction. On strictly philosophical grounds, there is no easy way of reconciling the contradiction. On the more human level of a specific artist searching for truth of different kinds, however, there is perhaps not a contradiction but rather a duality of perspective. From the beginning to the end of his career, as his interviews illustrate, Dreiser was deeply sympathetic to the human condition as he found it and hoped to play a role in alleviating its worst inequities, and he was also drawn to a speculative belief in the mechanistic character of all existence. Of course, the two great "isms" of Dreiser's half-century on the American scene—Marxism and Freudianism—also posit a human condition controlled by deterministic social and physical forces while permitting individuals to play roles in improving the welfare of themselves and others. Dreiser's expression of an analogous duality in his interviews thus brings his basic social position close to a major characteristic of the thought of his time.

TEXTUAL COMMENTARY

Although the principal Dreiser bibliography—*Theodore Dreiser: A Primary Bibliography and Reference Guide* (1991)—groups his interviews and speeches under one heading, we have decided to limit this volume to his interviews. By *interview* we mean an occasion during which Dreiser and an interviewer exchanged questions, answers, and commentary, with the published version of the occasion representing this exchange. Reports of speeches and lectures differ significantly from interviews, for a report usually reflects a written document (the speech or lecture) and also lacks the lively give and take of ideas and opinions that marks an interview.

As the bibliography indicates, Dreiser gave some 165 fully identified interviews in the course of his career. (He may have given considerably more; newspapers are typically not indexed, making an exact count difficult, and if Dreiser himself did not preserve an interview published in a relatively obscure publication, it may well be lost.) We have selected 74 of these for publication. Many of those not chosen are either extremely brief—a few hundred words at most—or deal with the same occasion or issue present in interviews we include. Others are superficial, especially those during the last twenty years of Dreiser's life, when he had reached celebrity status. Given the relative rarity of Dreiser interviews before the early 1910s, we have included almost all those of any substance from this period. Although a few of these early interviews have been republished elsewhere, we thought it best to include them in order to make this volume a single repository of those Dreiser interviews worth preserving.

Dreiser's literary estate at the University of Pennsylvania Library—the Theodore Dreiser Papers—contains a large number of his interviews in clipping form, which were invaluable in identifying his interviews. We have not relied on them for either publication data or textual content, however, because some have incomplete or marred texts and many contain erroneous or incomplete citations. Unless otherwise noted, all interviews reproduced in this volume or included in the bibliography derive not from clippings but from the text of their original periodical publication.

* * *

Interviews are written by the interviewer rather than by the interviewee. In addition, the bulk of Dreiser's interviews appeared in newspapers, publications that, with few exceptions, are not known for exacting standards of textual correctness. As a result, editors of interviews must use editorial conventions somewhat different from those used to prepare other editions of an author's work, since there seems to be little value in preserving inconsistencies and errors that are not the author's. In accord with this principle, we have normalized and corrected the texts of the interviews as follows:

— Capitalization in titles, subtitles, and subheads has been regularized; periods in titles, subtitles, and subheads are omitted.
— When known, the name of the interview's author follows the title, introduced with *by*.
— Any headnote written by the interviewer or a copy editor is omitted unless it adds to the understanding of the interview. If so, we have incorporated it into our headnote.
— Typographical errors are silently corrected except where an error is suspected but is not proved, in which case a correction is cited in a note.
— Grammatical errors are preserved without comment unless the meaning is obscure, in which case we suggest a meaning in a note.
— Major errors in punctuation, such as omitted periods and question and quotation marks, are corrected without the use of brackets or notes; except when painfully obtrusive, however, merely idiosyncratic punctuation has not been normalized.
— In the few instances where the meaning is unclear because of an apparently missing word or phase, we supply the missing wording in brackets in the text.
— Errors in the titles of commonly known works and in the names of commonly known authors are silently corrected, except that accepted variations in spelling are preserved (e.g., *Tolstoi* for *Tolstoy*). Errors in the names of less commonly known authors and works are preserved in the text and corrected in the notes.
— Dreiser's novel *The "Genius"* is almost uniformly given in his interviews as *The Genius;* this error is preserved in the text without comment in the notes.
— Quotation marks for book titles (an almost universal newspaper practice) are maintained, but in such instances single quotation marks are normalized to double ones. Other punctuation used with quotation marks is normalized to standard American usage.
— End-of-sentence ellipses are normalized to four.
— Hyphen usage is not normalized.

* * *

We have provided two forms of annotation, headnotes and footnotes. When deemed necessary for understanding the biographical and social context of an interview, a headnote supplying this information is provided. (Headnotes are distinguished from the interview text by rules above and below, as well as by smaller type and narrower margins.) Available information about the interviewer and about the appearance of the interview in other contemporary journals and newspapers is also supplied in the headnote. In the case of syndicated interviews, which often appeared with varying titles and contents, only the names of the newspapers and the dates are cited for the other versions.

The footnotes seek to identify specific people, events, works, allusions, and quotations when these are not, in the editors' belief, part of common knowledge. For example, Nathaniel Hawthorne and President Woodrow Wilson would not be identified, although a specific minor work by Hawthorne or a Wilson policy would be identified or explained. To avoid constant repetition, cross-references direct the reader to earlier headnotes or footnotes annotating the same figure or event. When we have been unable to identify a reference, we indicate this in a footnote. When a full name appears in the text, only the last name is used in the notes.

BIBLIOGRAPHY

The bibliography is divided into four sections. The first lists fully identified interviews, including those not reprinted in this volume. The second section lists interviews that exist in full or fragmentary clipping form but whose complete circumstances of publication have not been identified. Almost all the items in this list derive from clippings in the Theodore Dreiser Papers at the University of Pennsylvania Library. The third lists interviews that the Dreiser Papers collection contains in manuscript form but for which the editors could find no published form. The last identifies those items listed in part F, "Interviews and Speeches," of Donald Pizer, Richard W. Dowell, and Frederic E. Rusch, *Theodore Dreiser: A Primary Bibliography and Reference Guide,* 2d ed. (Boston: G. K. Hall, 1991), that are reports of speeches or lectures by Dreiser. Part F does not distinguish between interviews and reports of speeches or lectures; this bibliography remedies that omission. The entries are arranged chronologically in each section.

FULLY IDENTIFIED INTERVIEWS

Interviews reprinted in this edition are noted with an initial asterisk. Later reprintings of an interview are noted immediately following the interview. The following abbreviations are used:

Uncollected Prose Donald Pizer, ed. *Theodore Dreiser: A Selection of Uncollected Prose.* Detroit: Wayne State University Press, 1977.
Sister Carrie Theodore Dreiser, *Sister Carrie.* Ed. Donald Pizer. 2d ed. New York: W. W. Norton, 1991.

1902

*"Author of 'Sister Carrie' Formerly Was a St. Louisan." *St. Louis Post-Dispatch,* 26 January, p. 4. Repr. in *Uncollected Prose.*

1907

*Otis Notman. "Talks with Four Novelists: Mr. Dreiser." *New York Times Saturday Review of Books,* 15 June, p. 393. Repr. in *Uncollected Prose; Sister Carrie.*
*"'Sister Carrie' Theodore Dreiser." *New York Herald,* 7 July, Literary and Art Section, p. 2. Repr. in *Sister Carrie.*

1908

"President Orphans' Friend." *Washington Evening Star*, 10 October, p. 9.
"President Told of Babies." *Washington Herald*, 11 October, p. 10.

1911

*[Almer C. Sanborn]. "Now Comes Author Theodore Dreiser Who Tells of 100,000 Jennie Gerhardts." *Cleveland Leader*, 12 November, Cosmopolitan Section, p. 5. Appeared in *New York Morning Telegraph*, *Buffalo Evening News*, and *Pittsburg Leader* on the same day. Repr. in *Uncollected Prose* (excerpts).
*"Theodore Dreiser." *New York Evening Post*, 15 November, pp. 6–7. *New York Daily People*, 20 November, p. 3 (as "Realistic Novelists").
*"Novels to Reflect Real Life." *New York Sun*, 21 November, p. 9. *Denver Times*, 23 November, p. 20 (as "A Realist of American Fiction"). Repr. in *Uncollected Prose*.

1912

*Montrose J. Moses. "Theodore Dreiser." *New York Times Review of Books*, 23 June, pp. 377–78.
*"Theodore Dreiser on the Novel." *New York Evening Sun*, 28 September, p. 7. *Terre Haute Star*, 27 October, p. 6 (as "Theodore Dreiser Warns Prolific Novelists . . .").
*"Theodore Dreiser Now Turns to High Finance." *New York Sun*, 19 October, pt. 2, p. 3. Repr. in *Uncollected Prose*.

1913

"Calls American Mothers Unfit." *Chicago Examiner*, 13 January, p. 8.
*"Dreiser on Need of Liberty in Writing." *New York Sun*, 29 November, Literary Section, p. 4.
"An Author 'Personally Conducted.'" *New York Times Review of Books*, 30 November, p. 696.
*Albert Mordell. "Theo. Dreiser—Radical." *Philadelphia Record*, 7 December, pt. 3, p. 8.

1914

"Dreiser Plays Role of Van Winkle Here." *Chicago Daily News*, 17 March, p. 3.
"City Censored to Death, Says Author. Theo. Dreiser Cries City Is Backsliding." *Chicago Daily Journal*, 18 March, p. 1.
"Civic Torpidity Retards City, Says Dreiser." *Chicago Daily Journal*, 20 March, sect. 2, p. 1.
*"Author Criticises Orthodox Editors." *Philadelphia Public Ledger*, 26 April, p. 7.
*Marguerite M. Marshall. "Business Overlords of America Greatest, Most Powerful Men since Days of Old Rome." *New York Evening World*, 18 June, p. 3. *Rochester Union and Advertiser*, 10 July, p. 2 (as "Business and Morality Are to Be Separate").

1915

Bennett McDonald. "Genius Is a Merciless Obsession, Says Dreiser." *New York Tribune*, 5 December, pt. 5, p. 3.

1916

*"No More Free Ads for Racy Novels." *New York Tribune,* 20 August, pp. 1, 3.
"Vice Society Assails Book." *New York Times,* 21 August, p. 20.
"Sees Literary Reign of Terror." *New York Tribune,* 9 September, p. 9.

1917

R[alph] F. H[olmes]. "Musing with the Muses." *Detroit Journal,* 1 December, p. 4.
R[alph] F. H[olmes]. "Musing with the Muses." *Detroit Journal,* 5 December, p. 4.

1918

Karl L. Kitchen. "To Batter Down Gates of Fame." *Cleveland Plain Dealer,* 24 January, p. 8.
David Karsner. "Theodore Dreiser." *New York Call,* 3 March, Call Magazine, pp. 20, 16.
*Berenice C. Skidelsky. "Theodore Dreiser Deplores Suppression of His Novel, 'The Genius,' by Vice Agent." *Brooklyn Daily Eagle,* 26 May, [sect. 3,] pp. 2, 5.
Frank Harris. "Theodore Dreiser." *Pearson's Magazine* 39 (Oct.): 346–51. Repr. in Frank Harris, *Contemporary Portraits: Second Series* (New York: Frank Harris, 1919), 81–106.

1919

*"Dreiser Favors Federal Control; Hits Financiers." *Huntington Press* (Ind.), 18 June, p. 1.
*"Noted Novelist Visits in City." *Indianapolis Star,* 27 June, p. 5.
"Labor Union of Authors? They Need Protection, Says Theodore Dreiser." *Brooklyn Daily Eagle,* 11 October, p. 9.

1920

*Berenice C. Skidelsky. "America and Her Jews." *Jewish Advocate* (Boston), 5 February, p. 7. *New York Jewish News,* 12 February (as "'As Yeast Added to the Nation's Making . . .'").

1921

Edward H. Smith. "Dreiser—After Twenty Years." *Bookman* 53 (March): 27–39.

1922

*Edith M. Ryan. "Cruel Words, Theodore Dreiser!" *Los Angeles Sunday Times,* 17 September, pt. 3, pp. 13, 15.
*Burton Rascoe. "A Bookman's Day Book." *New York Tribune,* 24 December, sect. 6, p. 22. Repr. in Burton Rascoe, *A Bookman's Daybook,* ed. C. Hartley Grattan (New York: Liveright, 1929), 53–56.

1923

*Elisabeth Smith. "Literary Censorship Bunk and Hokum, Says Theodore Dreiser." *New York Evening Telegram,* 4 March, p. 5. *New York Evening Mail,* 10 March, p. 3 (as "Fears

'Snooper' Government if Censors Get in Saddle"); *Independent* 110 (17 Mar.): 191 (as "The Question of Literary Censorship").

[Harold Stark]. "Young Boswell Interviews Theodore Dreiser." *New York Tribune*, 7 April, p. 11. Repr. in Young Boswell [Harold Stark], *People You Know* (New York: Boni and Liveright, 1924), 68–70.

G. D. Eaton. "A Talk with Theodore Dreiser in His New York Studio." *Detroit Free Press*, 10 June, Magazine Section, p. 4.

*Rose C. Feld. "Mr. Dreiser Passes Judgment on American Literature." *New York Times Book Review*, 23 December, p. 7.

1924

*J. J. [Jean Jaffe]. "Dreiser Wants to Know More about Us." *The Day* (New York), 13 April, n.p.

Diana Rice. "Terrible Typewriter in Parnassus." *New York Times Magazine*, 27 April, pp. 11, 14.

Quiz. "Fixing the Fate of American Letters: Literary Lunch." *New York Post Literary Review*, 2 August, pp. 936–37.

1925

*"Clean Book Bill Slays Freedom, Insists Dreiser." *New York Herald Tribune*, 27 January, p. 4.

*Susan F. Hunter. "See America, Says Dreiser." *New York World*, 5 April, sect. 3, pp. 1, 9.

*Walter Tittle. "Glimpses of Interesting Americans: Theodore Dreiser." *Century* 110 (Aug.): 441–47.

*Isaac Goldberg. "A Visit with Theodore Dreiser." *Haldeman-Julius Monthly* 5 (Oct.): 448–52.

*Flora Merrill. "Master of Creative Art Discusses Modern Problems." *Success* 9 (Nov.): 21, 109.

"Dreiser Interviews Pantano in Death House; Doomed Man Avows Faith in a Hereafter." *New York World*, 30 November, pp. 1, 14.

1926

Dudley Nichols. "An American Comedy—The Long Delayed Golden Shower Falls on Dreiser." *New York World*, 11 April, Metropolitan Section, pp. 1, 12.

*"Theodore Dreiser in Berlin Arranging Novel's Translation." *Chicago Tribune and Daily News* (Berlin edition), 14 August, p. 1.

*Victor Llona. "Un Grand Ecrivain Americain est à Paris" (A great American writer is in Paris). *Les Nouvelles Littéraires*, 25 September, pp. 1–2.

"Theodore Dreiser Mourns Passing of Paris of Du Maurier's Day." *Chicago Tribune and Daily News* (Paris edition), 29 September, pp. 1, 3.

*"'England Gone America Mad,' Dreiser Says on Return Here." *New York Herald Tribune*, 23 October, p. 7.

*Phil D. Stong. "Dreiser Says Jury Systems Fail in 'Knife Edge' Criminal Cases." *Denver Post*, 28 November, p. 24. Appeared in *New Haven Register* on the same date.

1927

Laura Mount. "Theodore Dreiser Defends Heavy Baumes Law Penalty." *New York Evening Post,* 11 January, p. 9.

*Jean W. Maury. "A Neighborly Call on Theodore Dreiser." *Boston Evening Transcript,* 29 January, Book Section, p. 1. Incomplete version in *Literary Digest International Book Review* 4 (Mar. 1926): 223–24 (as "In the Workshop of an American Realist").

"Censor Coming to Stop Sex Wave, Says Dreiser." *New Orleans Morning Tribune,* 3 February, p. 1. Syndicated by United News. Appeared in *San Francisco News* on 4 February and *New York World* on 9 February.

*Philip E. Wood. "An Interview with Theodore Dreiser in Which He Discusses Errant Youth." *Philadelphia Public Ledger,* 3 July, Magazine Section, p. 7

Alexander Harvey. "New York Vicious? 'No, Just Dull,' Says Dreiser." *New York World,* 16 October, Metropolitan Section, pp. 1, 14.

"Dreiser Sails Tonight for Red Celebration." *New York Times,* 19 October, p. 3.

"Theodore Dreiser Sails for Russia." *New York Evening Post,* 20 October, p. 5.

*"Theodore Dreiser Here on Way to Study Results of Sovietism." *New York Herald Tribune* (Paris edition), 27 October, pp. 1, 10.

Bruce Gould. "A New Dreiser Would Meet Same Fight, Says Dreiser." *New York Evening Post,* 29 October, p. 4

1928

"No Bread Line, Says Dreiser, Back." *New York Evening Post,* 21 February, p. 2.

*"Dreiser back from Russia; Praises Soviet." *New York Herald Tribune,* 22 February, p. 6.

*"Dreiser Home, Sees Soviet Aims Gaining." *New York Times,* 22 February, p. 9.

Thomas Burke. "Talks with Theodore Dreiser." *T.P.'s Weekly,* 9 June, p. 203.

H. L. B. Bercovici. "Newspaper Soulless, Dreiser Says." *American Press* 47 (Oct.): 3.

1929

*Sulamith Ish-Kishor. "Dreiser Looks at the Russian Jews." *The Day* (New York), 10 February, [p. 1].

*R. H. Wollstein. "You Know Mr. Dreiser: The American Tragedian Turns His Freudian Eyes on Music." *Musical America* 49 (25 Feb.): 36–37, 55–56.

*Carol Bird. "Theodore Dreiser Speaks." *Writer's Monthly* 33 (May): 392–98.

1930

Forrest Davis. "'1980': Theodore Dreiser Foresees a Ban on Babies." *New York Telegram,* 24 January, p. 7.

*Bessie K. Roberts. "Theodore Dreiser Gives His Views on Many Things." *Fort Wayne News Sentinel* (Ind.), 19 February, pp. 1, 3.

Gilbert Cosulich. "Next 25 Years Will Find Folks Happier, Famous Author Says." *Tucson Daily Citizen,* 6 April, pp. 1, 4.

"Sock, Sock, Sock, Theodore Dreiser in Town . . ." *New Mexico State Tribune* (Albuquerque), 19 April, pp. 1, 3.

Gilbert Cosulich. "Theodore Dreiser Asserts Religion Is Total Loss and Its Dogmas Worn Out." *Tucson Daily Citizen,* 30 April, p. 7.

"Dreiser Ired at Censoring by Humanists." *Dallas Morning News*, 6 May, pp. 1, 16.

Bob Willson et al. "Dreiser Warns against College-Going Disease." *Semi-Weekly Campus* (Southern Methodist University), 10 May, pp. 1–2.

*Vivian Richardson. "Dreiser Talks about Women and Russia." *Dallas Morning News*, 18 May, Feature Section, p. 2.

Milly Bennett. "Dreiser Goes to See Mooney in Quentin." *San Francisco Daily News*, 30 May, n.p.

"Author Laughs at Democracy of Americans." *San Francisco Chronicle*, 31 May, p. 3.

*Raymond Dannenbaum. "Theodore Dreiser Discounts Intermarriage." *Jewish Journal* (San Francisco) 3 (4 June): 3, 16.

*David W. Hazen. "Dreiser Asserts His Books Never Will Sell for $1.50." *Portland Morning Oregonian*, 13 June, p. 9.

*James Flexner. "Dreiser Brings Pessimism Back from U.S. Tour." *New York Herald Tribune*, 8 July, p. 14.

*Forrest Davis. "Dreiser Now Rediscovers America." *New York Telegram*, 9 July, p. 9.

*Karl Sebestyén. "Theodore Dreiser at Home." *Living Age* 339 (Dec.): 375–78.

1931

"Slapping Lewis Proves Nothing, Dreiser Admits." *New York Herald Tribune*, 22 March, p. 3.

"Lewis Calls Witness to Challenge Dreiser." *New York Times*, 25 March, p. 27.

"Dreiser Threatens Suit." *New York Times*, 9 April, p. 28.

"Dreiser Scorns Movies." *New York Times*, 11 April, p. 17.

*"'Hooeyland' Says Dreiser, back from Film Capital." *New York American*, 12 April, p. 22-L.

*Elenore Kellogg. "Dreiser Wants Courts to Save 'Tragedy' Film." *New York Herald Tribune*, 12 April, p. 4. Incomplete version in *Literary Digest* 109 (2 May): 21 (as "Dreiser on the Sins of Hollywood").

*"Dreiser, 60, Glad He's Rich, but Doubts He's Happier." *New York World-Telegram*, 27 August, p. 3.

*Elenore Kellogg. "Dreiser Carries His Pessimism Lightly at Sixty." *New York Herald Tribune*, 28 August, p. 11.

Alexandra Kropotkin. "To the Ladies." *Liberty* 8 (26 Sept.): 63–64.

*"Writers Are to Test Harlan 'Free Speech' for Miners on Nov. 8." *Knoxville News-Sentinel*, 3 November, p. 3.

"Dreiser and Group in Mine War Area." *New York Times*, 6 November, p. 9.

*Edward B. Smith. "Dreiser Demands Witnesses' Safety." *Knoxville News-Sentinel*, 6 November, pp. 1, 12.

*"Dreiser Speaks His Mind Here." *New York Sun*, 12 November, p. 9.

"Dreiser Here Says Miners Will Rebel." *New York Times*, 13 November, p. 18.

"Dreiser Ready to Come Back if Necessary." *Knoxville News-Sentinel*, 13 November, p. 24.

*Dexter H. Teed. "Dreiser Case May Be Fight to Finish . . ." *Knoxville News-Sentinel*, 23 November, p. 2. Syndicated by NEA Syndicate and appeared in *Kentucky Post* on 22 November.

1932

"Dreiser Promises Vote to Communist Ticket." *New York Herald Tribune*, 5 July, p. 4.

"Dreiser at 61 Still Lost in Riot of Words." *New York Herald Tribune*, 26 August, p. 11.

"Dreiser Here, Sees Hope for Tom Mooney." *San Francisco Call-Bulletin*, 5 November, p. 3.

Edward McQuade. "Indignant Dreiser Sees Victory for Masses Ahead." *San Francisco News*, 5 November, p. 2.

*Zilfa Estcourt. "Dreiser Holds Mooney Bomb Sympathy Act." *San Francisco Chronicle*, 6 November, p. 4.

Don Ryan. "Parade Ground." *Los Angeles Daily News*, 12 November, p. 17.

*George Britt. "Dreiser Overlooks His Former Experiences with Hollywood . . ." *New York World-Telegram*, 15 December, p. 15.

1933

"News of Books." *New York Times*, 2 March, p. 15.

*"Dreiser Says NRA Is Training Public." *New York Times*, 28 August, p. 19.

"Dreiser in Court Action." *New York Times*, 11 November, p. 12.

1934

Jeanette Smits. "'Tragedy' Case Fails to Stir Dreiser." *New York Evening Journal*, 8 August, p. 4.

Bonita Witt. "Theodore Dreiser Isn't Surprised over Parallel between His Novel and Real-Life Drama in News." *Passaic Herald-News* (N.J.), 15 August, p. 2.

*Henry Paynter. "Dreiser, at 63, Believes His Best Book Is to Come." *New York Post*, 27 August, p. 12.

*Earl Sparling. "Dreiser to Commit Suicide if Bored, He Insists at 63." *New York World-Telegram*, 27 August, pp. 1, 8.

"No 'Sitting in Shade' for Dreiser, at 63." *New York Times*, 28 August, p. 19.

1935

David W. Hazen. "Dreiser Laughs at Nursing Case." *Portland Sunday Oregonian*, 30 June, pp. 1, 3.

"Rake Calls to Dreiser." *Los Angeles Times*, 29 July, pt. 2, p. 1.

"Dreiser Looks Back from 64." *Los Angeles Examiner*, 27 August 1935, sect. 2, p. 1.

"Dreiser at 64 Today, Deplores World Thrills." *Los Angeles Times*, 8 September, Rotogravure Section.

*Bruce Crawford. "A Day with Theodore Dreiser." *Real America* 6 (Nov.): 49, 68–69. Repr. in *Bluefield Sunset News* (W.V.), 18 April 1938, pp. 1, 10 (as "Ere the Sun Sets").

Charles Carson. "Dreiser, 'Reporter of Life,' Comes Back to Toledo." *Toledo News-Bee*, 16 November, p. 2.

1936

Selig Greenberg. "Dreiser Finds Journalism Has Improved Literature." *Providence Evening Bulletin*, 24 April, pp. 1, 4.

*Vladimir Pozner. "Le Cinéma Tuera-t-il le Roman?" (Will the movies kill the novel?) *Les Nouvelles Littéraires*, 29 August, p. 6.

"Dreiser, at 65, May Quit Reds for Roosevelt." *New York Herald Tribune*, 22 August, p. 9.

"Dreiser, at 65, Hails Roosevelt on Peace." *New York Times*, 30 August, sect. 2, p. 2.

"Dreiser Explains Views." *New York Times*, 3 September, p. 19.

1937

"Sad Dreiser Grows Gay in Scientific 'Monastery.'" *New York Herald Tribune*, 25 August, p. 13.

1938

*May Cameron. "Author! Author! Theodore Dreiser, Cheerful at Sixty-six . . ." *New York Post*, 5 February, p. 7.

Cosulich, Gilbert. "Mr. Dreiser Looks at Probation." *Probation* 16 (Apr.): 54, 64.

*Lon Tinkle. "Theodore Dreiser Discusses Dallas and His Next Novel." *Dallas Morning News*, 14 August, sect. 2, p. 8.

"Says Roosevelt Uses Karl Marx's Ideas." *New York Times*, 22 August, p. 3.

"Dreiser, Now 67, Is Critic of Critics." *New York Times*, 27 August, p. 16.

John Neissen. "What Dreiser Seeks in a Test Tube." *New York Journal-American*, 25 September, p. 10.

Lorna D. Smith. "Author Dreiser Stresses Need for Greater Political Understanding among Youth." *People's World*, 28 December, p. 5.

1939

Neil Hitt. "Theodore Dreiser: Author and Destiny Reach a Compromise." *San Francisco Chronicle*, 10 February, p. 7.

Radio Interview during San Francisco Exposition, recorded in San Francisco, 13 February 1939. Repr. in *American Literary Realism* 11 (Autumn 1978): 284–94 (as "Dreiser on Society and Literature: The San Francisco Exposition Interview").

*"Flirting Powers Held in Danger." *Portland Oregonian*, 16 February, p. 1.

*"Dreiser Here to Talk, Asks U.S. to Awake." *Salt Lake City Deseret News*, 20 February, p. 1.

"Noted Author Predicts Another War." *Salt Lake Tribune*, 20 February, p. 16.

Clarence Williams. "'Awake, Get Ready for War,' Dreiser Admonishes U.S." *Salt Lake Telegram*, 20 February, p. 11.

Arthur Millier. "American Literature's 'Gloomy Gus.'" *Los Angeles Times*, 12 March, Magazine Section, pp. 5, 8.

Max Brunstein. "Hour with Dreiser." *Huntington Park Signal* (Calif.), 18 October, pp. 1–2.

1940

"Theodore Dreiser Derides Discussion about Activities of Fifth Column." *Portland Oregonian*, 21 June, p. 7.

W. H. Shippen Jr. "Dreiser Says England Seeks to Drag U.S. in European War." *Washington Evening Star*, 10 November, p. A-3.

1941

*Edward Robbin. "Radio Interview with Theodore Dreiser" 1 Feb. 1941, 5 pp. Published in *People's World*, 6 March, p. 5 (as "Theodore Dreiser Airs His Views").

*Robert van Gelder. "An Interview with Theodore Dreiser." *New York Times Book Review*, 16 March, pp. 2, 16. Repr. in Robert van Gelder, *Writers and Writing* (New York: Scribner's, 1946), 164–68.

"Dreiser Asks End of Aid to British." *Indianapolis News*, 21 November, p. 5.

Arthur P. Tiernan. "Not a Communist, Dreiser Declares; Answers Chaillaux." *Indianapolis Star*, 21 November, pp. 1, 16.

"Dreiser Lauds Soviet System." *Indianapolis Times*, 21 November, p. 5.

1942

"Theodore Drieser [*sic*] Visits I.U. Class Here . . ." *Indianapolis Star*, 6 March, p. 4.

Frederick C. Othman. "Filmland Just Has Him Down." *Boston Post*, 15 May, n.p. United Press syndication.

Philip K. Scheuer. "Theodore Dreiser Goes All-Out for New Pictures." *Los Angeles Times*, 25 May, pt. 2, p. 14.

*"Abuse for Britain Dreiser's Contribution to Anglo-U.S. Amity." *Toronto Evening Telegram*, 21 September, p. 2.

*George McIntyre. "PM Interviews Dreiser to Learn What He Said in *That* Interview." *PM* (New York), 22 September, p. 13.

*"Second American Tragedy. Novelist Dreiser Dodges Interview . . ." *Port Huron Times Herald* (Mich.), 24 September, pp. 1–2.

"Dreiser Gibes at Canada." *New York Times*, 25 September, p. 6.

1944

Earl Wilson. "I Take in Some Saloons with Theodore Dreiser (Salted)." *New York Post*, 18 May, p. 31. *Philadelphia Record*, 22 May 1944, p. 22 (as "Dreiser Sips His Drink as He Blasts the Rich").

Dorothy Norman. "The Eternally Youthful Theodore Dreiser." *New York Post*, 10 July, Magazine and Comic Section, p. 1.

1946

*Esther McCoy. "Theodore Dreiser Talks to a Friend." *People's World*, 3 January, p. 1.

NOT FULLY IDENTIFIED INTERVIEWS

The annotation "Not Found" below means that the journal has been searched for the period of publication cited on the clipping but the item has not been found. (Some clippings may be erroneously marked; others may be from an edition of the newspaper that has not been preserved on film.) The annotation "Unavailable" means that we could not find the serial publication on microfilm. Note that few if any of the interviews in this section are of any substance.

"Hope Is in American Women." *Louisville Times*, 22(?) December 1908. Not found.

Baldwin Macy. "New York Letter." *Chicago Evening Post Friday Literary Review*, 24 November 1911, p. 6. Not found.

Interview in *Tuz* (Budapest), 1 March 1923. In Hungarian. Unavailable.

Harry Salpeter. "Dreiser Reports on Life." (October?) 1926. Publication not identified.

Junius B. Wood. "Theodore Dreiser Reveals His Views on Russia in Interview." *Huntington Advertiser* (W.Va.), 12 February 1928. Unavailable.

Helen Worden. "How Would You Spend $10,000,000 to Aid Mankind?" *New York World*, 3 May 1929, p. 23. Not found.

"Theo. Dreiser Thinks People Over-Regulated." *Albuquerque Journal*, 19 April 1930, p. 7. Not found.

"Dreiser Says Religion Total Loss in America." *El Paso Evening Post*, 26 April 1930, pp. 1, 8. Unavailable.

"A Sneer for Hollywood." *Kansas City Times*, 10 April 1931, p. 1. Unavailable.

Cedric Worth. "Angry Mr. Dreiser Speaks His Mind." *New York Evening Post*, 12 November 1931. Not found.

"Labor's Plight Is U.S. Tragedy, Dreiser Finds." 8 July 1933. Publication not identified.

"Dreiser, at 63, Clings to Hope of Better World." *New York Herald Tribune*, 28 August 1934. Not found (see p. 278, headnote). Published in this volume.

Alan D. Goodman. "Theodore Dreiser—An Interview." *The Progress* (Nov. 1935?), pp. 7–9. Publication not identified.

Richard Purdy. "A Visit with Dreiser." *Fayette Review* (Ohio), 7 November 1935. Unavailable.

May Cameron. "Play Critics Wrong Again, Groans Theodore Dreiser." *New York Post*, 25 March 1936. Not found.

Charles B. Driscoll. "New York Day by Day." Syndicated, 13 July 1938. Publication not identified.

"Hughes Defends Scenarists against Views of Dreiser." *Los Angeles Times*, 15 December 1938, pt. 2, p. 7. Not found.

"Life Is Good, Dreiser Finds." 9 February 1939. Publication (from Oakland?) not identified.

Bill Gray. "Dams to Be Used for War Goals, Protests Dreiser." *Portland Morning Oregonian*, 16 February 1939. Not found.

Louella O. Parsons. "'Film Plays Need No Stage Tryouts First'—Theodore Dreiser." 17 May 1942. Publication not identified.

W. E. Oliver. "Theodore Dreiser Is Not Mad at Hollywood." *Los Angeles Herald*, 20 May 1942. Not found.

INTERVIEWS EXTANT IN MANUSCRIPT FORM ONLY

Harris, Reed. "Theodore Dreiser Interviewed on the Subject of Charles Fort." Thirty-five typescript pages. Late 1920s–early 1930s (internal evidence).

Chase, Allan. "Interview by Allan Chase for Central Press." Four typescript pages. December 1933. Published in this volume.

Elizabeth Kearney. "Theodore Dreiser: An Interview." Eight typescript pages. Early 1940 (internal evidence).

"Questions Asked of Theodore Dreiser by The Asahi Shimbun—Leading Newspaper in the Far East." Three typescript pages. June 1941.

ITEMS OTHER THAN INTERVIEWS IN
PART F OF THE DREISER BIBLIOGRAPHY

"The Londoner and His 'Rather Dreary Situation.'" *London Evening Standard and St. James's Gazette*, 6 September 1913. Reprint of portion of Dreiser's article on London in the *Century* of September 1913.

"Kentucky Editor Questions Dreiser." *New York Times*, 7 November 1931, p. 19. News report.

Edward B. Smith. "'Law' in Capitalists' Hands in Labor War, Says Dreiser." *Knoxville News-Sentinel*, 9 November 1931, p. 11. First-person report by Dreiser, "as told to Edward B. Smith."

"Public Blinded, Avers Dreiser." *Knoxville News-Sentinel*, 12 November 1931, pp. 1, 18. Reprints statement by Dreiser.

Alva Johnston. "Theodore Dreiser, Explaining His Political and Economic Views . . ." *New York Herald Tribune*, 22 November 1931, sect. 8, p. 2. Consists entirely of one long statement by Dreiser.

"Dreiser Plea for Mooney." *San Francisco Call Bulletin*, 7 November 1932, p. 2. Report of a speech.

"Dreiser Debunks 'Good and Evil' Code; Sees Churches 'Failing Miserably.'" *Toledo News-Bee*, 16 November 1935, pp. 1–2. Report of a lecture.

"Dreiser Sees Lone Writer Doomed by Movie and Radio Specialists." *New York World-Telegram*, 24 February 1937, p. 4. Report of a speech.

"Americans Favor U.S. Action to End Bombing, Dreiser Says." *International Herald Tribune* (Paris), 24 July 1938, p. 8. Report of a speech.

"Loyalists Called Not Anti-Religious." *New York Times*, 16 September 1938, p. 10. Report of a speech.

Zilfa Estcourt. "Right off the Chest." *San Francisco Chronicle*, 15 February 1939, p. 13. Report of a lecture.

"Dreiser Scores Sham Democracy." *Salt Lake Telegram*, 21 February 1939, p. 9. Report of a lecture.

"Dreiser Views Challenge to Democracy." *Salt Lake Tribune*, 21 February 1939, p. 22. Report of a lecture.

"Theodore Dreiser Warns of Anglo-French Duplicity." *Salt Lake City Deseret News*, 21 February 1939, p. 3. Report of a lecture.

John D. Barry. "Ways of the World." *San Francisco News*, 21 February 1939, p. 14. Report of a lecture.

"Theodore Dreiser: Gentleman for Lousy Reasons." *Hollywood Tribune*, 17 July 1939. Report of a lecture.

Lorna D. Smith. "Theodore Dreiser's Plan to Enlighten U.S. Workers." *People's World*, 7 November 1939, p. 5. Report of a speech.

Charles E. Blake. "Mr. Dreiser's Says Earful to Clubwomen." *Los Angeles Evening Herald*, 22 November 1939, pp, 2, 8. Report of a lecture.

Jack Young. "3000 Jam Biggest L.A. Peace Rally." *People's World*, 15 January 1941, p. 3. Report of a speech.

Mike Quin [Paul W. Ryan]. "Double Check." *People's World*, 29 January 1941, p. 5. Report of a speech.

"Dreiser Stresses Need to Spread Truth of U.S.S.R." *Sunday Worker* (New York), 2 March 1941, p. 3. Report of a speech.

"Dreiser Tells Friends Here of Speech Intended for Audience in Toronto." *Indianapolis Star*, 4 October 1942, p. 39. Report of a communication by Dreiser.

INDEX

FREDERIC E. RUSCH, professor emeritus of English at Indiana State University, is a cofounder of the International Theodore Dreiser Society and former editor of *Dreiser Studies*. Among his books are *The Collected Plays of Theodore Dreiser* (2000), coedited with Keith Newlin, and—with Donald Pizer and Richard Dowell—*Theodore Dreiser: A Primary Bibliography and Reference Guide* (1991).

DONALD PIZER, Pierce Butler Professor of English emeritus at Tulane University, has published widely on late nineteenth- and early twentieth-century American literature. Among his books are *The Novels of Theodore Dreiser: A Critical Study* (1976), *Theodore Dreiser: A Selection of Uncollected Prose* (1977), and—with Richard Dowell and Frederic E. Rusch—*Theodore Dreiser: A Primary Bibliography and Reference Guide* (1991). He is a Guggenheim Fellow and has also received senior research fellowships from the National Endowment for the Humanities and the American Council of Learned Societies.

The University of Illinois Press
is a founding member of the
Association of American University Presses.

———————————————————————

Composed in 10.5/13 Goudy
with Goudy display
by Jim Proefrock
at the University of Illinois Press
Manufactured by Edwards Brothers, Inc.

University of Illinois Press
1325 South Oak Street   Champaign, IL 61820-6903
www.press.uillinois.edu